BLUES GUITAR

THE MEN WHO MADE THE MUSIC

From the Pages of Guitar Player Magazine

EDITED BY JAS OBRECHT

EXPANDED & UPDATED SECOND EDITION

GPI BOOKS
An Imprint of
mf Miller Freeman Books
San Francisco

To Jim O'Neal and Gayle Dean Wardlow,
for their mighty contributions to our understanding of the blues

Published by Miller Freeman Books,
600 Harrison Street, San Francisco, CA 94107
Publishers of GPI Books and *Guitar Player* magazine
A member of the United Newspapers Group

© 1993 by Miller Freeman, Inc.

The "Robert Johnson," "Johnny Shines," "John Hammond," "Muddy Waters,"
and the latter part of the "John Lee Hooker" chapters
are exclusive, copyrighted excerpts from
Jas Obrecht's book-in-progress *Early Blues*,
© Jas Obrecht 1993. Used by author's permission.

Distributed to the book trade in the U.S. and Canada by
Publishers Group West, P.O. Box 8843, Emeryville, CA 94662

Distributed to the music trade in the U.S. and Canada by
Hal Leonard Publishing, P.O. Box 13819, Milwaukee, WI 53213

Library of Congress Cataloging-in-Publication Data

Blues guitar : the men who made the music : from the pages of Guitar player magazine /
edited by Jas Obrecht. – Expanded & updated 2nd ed.
    p.   cm.
  Includes index.
  ISBN 0-87930-292-5 (pbk.)
   1. Blues musicians–United States–Biography. 2. Guitarists–United States–
Biography. I. Obrecht, Jas. II. Guitar player.
ML399.B53 1993
787.87'1643'0922–dc20
[B]   93-6393
                                                  CIP
                                                    MN

ISBN 0-87930-292-5

Designed by Chris Ledgerwood
Proofreader: Tom Hassett
Cover photo: B.B. King, by Luciano Viti/Retna Ltd.
Photo of Ishman Bracey, page 7: courtesy Gayle Dean Wardlow collection
Photos of Rev. Gary Davis, pages 43 and 44: © Stefan Grossman

Printed in the United States of America
93 94 95 96 97   5 4 3 2 1

CONTENTS

INTRODUCTION

NINETY YEARS HAVE PASSED since W.C. Handy was awakened in the Tutwiler, Mississippi, train station by the strange sounds of a ragged black guitarist. "As he played, he pressed a knife on the strings of the guitar in a manner popularized by the Hawaiian guitarists who used steel bars," Handy wrote in his autobiography, *Father Of The Blues*. "The effect was unforgettable. His song, too, struck me instantly: 'Goin' where the Southern cross the Dog.' The singer repeated the line three times, accompanying himself on the guitar with the weirdest music I had ever heard." This description of a slide guitarist is one of the earliest known references to blues music. Ever since then, blues guitarists have been pressing slides and fingers to strings, attempting to create the unforgettable. This book profiles some of the best.

While blues music as we recognize it probably began around the turn of the century, the recording of solo blues guitarists didn't commence until November 2, 1923, when Sylvester Weaver of Louisville, Kentucky, recorded "Guitar Blues" in New York City. A simple instrumental with slide melodies and sparse chords, the song easily conjures images of Handy's unknown guitarist. Mr. Weaver was also the first guitarist to back a blues singer on record, a feat he'd accomplished a week earlier with Sara Martin. OKeh Records called him "The Man with the Talking Guitar" and claimed "he certainly plays 'em strong on his big mean, blue guitar." By January 1924, Bessie Smith and Clara Smith had recorded with studio guitarists.

The recording of rural male blues singers began a few months later in Atlanta, when an OKeh field unit headed by Ralph Peer waxed two sides by Ed Andrews, a rough-hewn vocalist with a wide-shaking vibrato similar to Johnny

The first star of blues guitar, the great Blind Lemon Jefferson.

Shines'. Andrews accompanied himself with utilitarian pick-and-strum guitar while stringing together back-country verses such as:

"My mama told me when I was a chile,
My mama told me when I was a chile,
'Running around and women gets you after while'"

The 78's flip side was virtually the same song, and Andrews never recorded again. A few other long-forgotten blues guitarists made records during 1924. Johnny Watson, a former minstrel performer who billed himself as Daddy Stovepipe, cast deep, plaintive vocals and winsome harmonica fills above roots-simple guitar, as did Cincinnati's Sam Jones, an old street singer who called himself Stovepipe No. 1.

The first bona fide blues guitar heroes emerged in 1926. Launching his recording career with a gospel 78, Blind Lemon Jefferson went on to become the most famous bluesman of the Roaring Twenties. A man well-acquainted with booze, gambling, and heavy-hipped mamas, Jefferson lived the roll-and-tumble themes that dominate his songs. His lyrics create a unique body of poetry–humorous and harrowing, jivey and risqué, a stunning view of society from the perspective of someone at the bottom. He was a *serious* showman, balancing a driving, unpredictable guitar style with a wailing, two-octave voice that could boom over the din of flatbeds and flivvers. His guitar became a second voice that complemented rather than repeated his lyrics, and he often launched into elaborate solos. Blind Lemon's 78s shattered racial barriers, becoming popular from coast to coast and influencing a generation of

The unrivaled master of ragtime blues. Some of Blind Blake's 78s cast him as a jivey hipster; others walked the long lonely road to the gallows.

blues starvation box or comp and fill like a piano. His crisp rhythms revealed a vast chord vocabulary, and he had a fabulous way of ending songs with elegant chord climbs. His one-of-a-kind finger vibrato could approximate the sounds of a zither, mandolin, or bottleneck guitar. Significant portions of the guitar vocabulary he introduced have survived intact into the modern era. Lonnie Johnson was surely the Jimi Hendrix of his generation–"one of the transcendental people who influenced *everybody*," as Ry Cooder describes.

Other transcendental musicians populated the burgeoning prewar blues scenes. From southwest Louisiana came Huddie Ledbetter, better known as Lead Belly, King of the 12-String Guitar Players of the World. Lead Belly's voice was field-holler powerful, his 12-string guitar playing forceful and nimble. He created muscular bass lines and had a brilliant feel for time, easily jumping tempos to heighten a song's drama. Like his acquaintance Blind Lemon, he excelled at speedy single-string breaks. Lead Belly's repertoire was estimated at 500 songs, and he recorded everything from cattle calls, slave songs, and spirituals to square dances, children's music, protest songs, monologues, and Tin Pan Alley. "But when does your guitar talk the best?" his friend Woody Guthrie asked him. "Well," Lead Belly drawled, "my guitar talk the best when I'm playin' and singin' blues."

Beaumont, Texas, was the fearsome stage for Blind Willie Johnson, a street-corner evangelist with a fierce growl of a voice. Blind Willie was gifted with an exquisite sense of melody, timing, and tone, using a pocketknife or ring slider to duplicate his vocal inflections or to produce an unforgettable phrase from a single strike of a string. Void of frivolity or uncertainty, his spiritual 78s are intensely moving, and he's certainly among the greatest of the slide guitarists.

Atlanta's thriving first-generation blues community was headed by Peg Leg Howell, Buddy Moss, Curley Weaver, and 12-string masters Barbecue Bob, his brother Charley Lincoln, and Blind Willie McTell. A Depression-era recording star, McTell was a shrewd, intelligent man with a phenomenal repertoire of mellow blues, hillbilly music, spirituals, quick-fingered rags, minstrel tunes, and even semi-pornographic ditties. He played with a light touch on a big-bodied Stella 12-string, specializing in shifting rhythms and reso-

musicians.

The high sales of Jefferson's 78s sent record scouts scrambling to sign blues artists. In the fall of 1926 Paramount recorded Blind Blake, a swinging, sophisticated guitarist whose warm, relaxed voice was a far cry from harsh country blues. Some of Blake's 78s cast him as a jumpin' jazzman or jivey hipster; others walked the long lonely road to the gallows. The man with the "famous piano-sounding guitar" is still regarded as the unrivaled master of ragtime-blues fingerpicking.

Lonnie Johnson, who launched his recording career in late '25, could well be the most influential of all blues guitarists. His uncanny dexterity and sophisticated harmony enabled him to transcend stylistic barriers to record classic jazz with Louis Armstrong and Duke Ellington, groundbreaking guitar duets with Eddie Lang, and blues, ballads, and plenty of pop under his own name. The 5'10" bluesman was gifted with strong hands and a wonderfully fertile imagination. He could make his guitar thump like a country nant melodies that were as distinctive as his clear, somewhat nasal voice. His best-known song was "Statesboro Blues," a 1928 fingerpicking showpiece named after his Georgia hometown. A great improviser, McTell sometimes composed with great deliberation, while other tunes reflect a stream-of-consciousness approach bordering on poetry. Meanwhile, Blind Boy Fuller was very influential in the Southeast tobacco belt, where guitarists such as Blind Gary Davis, William Moore, and Willie Walker blended ragtime and blues.

Memphis, the gateway to the Mississippi Delta, Arkansas, and the North, was another thriving blues mecca. On Beale Street, thumping back-country guitar stomps could commingle with white hillbilly music, drum-and-fife influences, polished jazz, and the famous jug bands led by Gus Cannon and Will Shade. Frank Stokes, Jim Jackson, Furry Lewis, and Robert Wilkins were Memphis regulars, while men such as Hambone Willie Newbern and Sleepy John Estes, who played country balls and picnics around Brownsville, came there to record, as did many fine and ferocious Delta-bred guitarists.

Down in Mississippi, Charley Patton, Son House, Willie Brown, Tommy Johnson, Skip James, Ishman Bracey, Garfield Akers, Bo Carter and the Mississippi Sheiks, Bukka White, and others were rocking house parties, fish fries, and juke joints with their powerful, mantra-like blues, just as Robert Johnson, Johnny Shines, Tommy McClennan, and Muddy Waters would in the years to come. (The juke tradition still flourishes today with musicians such as Junior Kimbrough and R.L. Burnside in Holly Springs and Big Jack Johnson in Clarksdale.) Country blues influences even echoed in the 78s of white guitarists such as Frank Hutchinson, Riley Puckett, Darby & Tarlton, and Jimmie Rodgers, all of whom learned from rural black musicians.

In the vanguard of a smoother, more urban-sounding trend was Indianapolis' Leroy Carr, a dominating force in blues piano, and his partner Francis "Scrapper" Blackwell, a criminally underrated guitarist if ever there were one. Chicago's urbane, uptown sound was dominated by pianists Big Maceo and Memphis Slim and guitarists Big Bill Broonzy, Lonnie Johnson, Memphis Minnie, and Tampa Red. A very fertile field for study, the prewar era produced many other fine,

often-overlooked guitarists–Kokomo Arnold, John Hurt, Buddy Boy Hawkins, and Casey Bill Weldon among them.

Our Country Roots section pays homage to the prewar blues pioneers. Here you'll encounter the mysterious Robert Johnson, as well as Johnny Shines and Robert Lockwood, Jr., who reflect on their adventures with Robert and subsequent lives in the blues. Skip James and Rev. Gary Davis recorded before Johnson and outlived him to become leading voices of the 1960s blues revival. Mance Lipscomb and Mississippi Fred McDowell soon joined them centerstage, while John Hammond and John Cephas help keep old-time blues alive today.

The Prime Movers section concentrates on electrifying postwar performers such as Muddy Waters, John Lee Hooker, Guitar Slim, Albert Collins, and the three Kings. You'll also meet a host of Chicago's finest–Elmore and Homesick James, Jimmy Rogers, Buddy Guy, Otis Rush, and J.B. Hutto among them–as well as Gatemouth Brown, Howlin' Wolf

The essence of taste and elegance, Lonnie Johnson could well be the most influential of all blues guitarists.

A shrewd, intelligent man, Atlanta's Blind Willie McTell had a phenomenal repertoire of blues, hillbilly music, spirituals, quick-fingered rags, and minstrel tunes.

The chapters on Elmore and Homesick James, Gatemouth Brown, Little Milton, Robert Lockwood, Jr., John Hammond, and Johnny Winter are new to this edition. Many of the others have been overhauled since the 1990 edition of *Blues Guitar*. New conversations expand the Otis Rush, B.B. King, John Lee Hooker, Albert Collins, and Buddy Guy coverage. I've also added a blues records listening party with Mr. Hooker and the first interview B.B. and John Lee have ever done together. Recently discovered details about his childhood, friendships, travels, and murder add flesh to Robert Johnson. The expanded Muddy Waters biography includes fresh insights from musicians who knew him, as well as healthy portions of the historic Waters interviews with Jim O'Neal and Amy van Singel. Rich with details on the lives of itinerant bluesmen during the Robert Johnson era, Johnny Shines' entire 1989 interview replaces the previous edition's edited version. All discographies have been updated.

Interviewing has taught me that the language of men such as John Lee Hooker and Muddy Waters is as deep and rhythmic as their playing. Wherever possible, artists' words are preserved exactly as spoken.

Many people helped revise *Blues Guitar*. My heartfelt thanks go to Mary Katherine Aldin, Larry Cohn, Ry Cooder, Bill Ferris, Dan Forte, Billy Gibbons, Stefan Grossman, Buddy Guy, John Hammond, Tom Hassett, John Lee Hooker, Homesick James, Matt Kelsey, B.B. King, Steve LaVere, Chris Ledgerwood, Peter Lee, David Leishman, Jim O'Neal, Johnny Parth, Keith Richards, Otis Rush, Frank Scott, Gayle Dean Wardlow, Johnny Winter, and the staffs of *Living Blues*, *Guitar Player*, Down Home Music, Roots & Rhythm, and the University of Mississippi's Blues Archive for their generous contributions. And thank you to Michelle La Place for smiling through my endless hours lost in blues.

'Nuff said. Let's get to it.

Jas Obrecht
August 1993

sideman Hubert Sumlin, Jimmy Reed, Little Milton, Mike Bloomfield, and Johnny Winter.

This is not a definitive history of blues guitar; no book without fat chapters on Lonnie Johnson, Blind Lemon Jefferson, Blind Blake, Blind Willie Johnson, Lead Belly, Charley Patton, Son House and Willie Brown, Tampa Red, T-Bone Walker, Lightnin' Hopkins, Earl Hooker, and many, many others could pretend to be. Instead, it's a collection of the best blues articles published in *Guitar Player* magazine between 1974 and '93. The focus is on players who've spent most or all of their careers as bluesmen (thus no fat chapters on Eric Clapton, Stevie Ray Vaughan, and dozens of other deserving practitioners).

COUNTRY ROOTS

Robert Johnson

September 1990

BY JAS OBRECHT

"ROBERT JOHNSON IS THE GREATEST folk-blues guitar player that ever lived," declares Eric Clapton. "He's the greatest singer, the greatest writer." Robert Johnson mastered the Delta style as none had before, learning firsthand from men such as Willie Brown and Son House, and then expanded his music with outside influences from 78s by Lonnie Johnson, Kokomo Arnold, Leroy Carr, and many others. A slide guitarist without parallel, Johnson cast strikingly original lyrics with Shakespearean skill. He was truly standing at a musical crossroads when he made his 29 recordings, simultaneously looking back to old-time Delta blues while foretelling the future of electric blues, R&B, and rock and roll.

Robert's spectacular talent, shrouded background, and unsolved murder gave rise to wild speculations: He was a fierce, driven man, it was whispered, who walked side by side with the devil and swapped his soul at a lonely cross-roads for ungodly talent. Slowed by stones in his passway, betrayed by evil-hearted women, dogged by hell hounds, he drifted shadow-like, never staying long in one place. When his number was up, many believed, he went out on his hands and knees, barking and snapping like a dog.

Fueling the mystery was the fact that no photograph of Robert Johnson was published until 1986. Today, thanks to the research of dedicated scholars such as Steve LaVere, Gayle Dean Wardlow, Jim O'Neal, and Robert Palmer, a new sense of the historical Robert Johnson has emerged.

His grandparents were born into slavery. His mother, Julia Ann Majors, had married Charles Dodds, Jr., in Hazel-hurst, Mississippi, during 1889 and bore him seven daughters and two sons, as well as a set of twins that died at birth. A respected farm owner and maker of wicker furniture, Dodds had another pair of sons by his mistress Serena. Around 1907, a vendetta with a prominent white family caused Dodds to flee to Memphis with a lynch mob at his heels. He assumed the last name of Spencer and sent for his mistress and her sons, as well as several of Julia's children. Uprooted from her farm, Julia stayed in Hazelhurst and became lovers with Noah Johnson.

On May 8, 1911, Robert Leroy Johnson was born out of wedlock in Hazelhurst. Soon afterwards, Julia signed a contract with a Delta labor supplier, and Robert spent his infancy in hardscrabble migrant labor camps. When he was about two, Julia broke her labor agreement and fled from an Arkansas plantation in the middle of the night with a deputy in pursuit. She bundled Robert and his half-sister Carrie off

to Memphis, where they joined the family of her ex-husband and assumed the last name of Spencer. For a brief while, Julia also lived in Handwerker Hill with the extended family. During his 1942 visit to the Delta, Alan Lomax encountered a woman who claimed to be Johnson's mother and told him that "Little Robert" was a puny baby and church-loving child who never gave her trouble until he began associating with musicians and started playing "the devil's instruments."

Robert, who'd become increasingly strong-minded and disobedient while living in Memphis, was returned to his mother's care in 1918. By then she was married to a hard-working fieldhand named Willie "Dusty" Willis and living at Commerce, a sharecroppers' settlement on Richard Leatherman's plantation near Robinsonville, some 40 miles south of Memphis. Their shack was near the levee, and Robert loved to fish the Mississippi with his boyhood pal Wink Clark, whose mother did church work with Julia. Robert learned the basics of reading and writing at the Indian Creek School; record books from 1924 and '27 confirm that Robert Spencer attended classes during those years. Robert suffered from poor vision–a lifelong problem–and while Carrie bought him glasses, he seldom wore them.

Johnson's relationship with his stepfather was fraught with friction; neighbors recalled seeing Willis beat the boy for refusing to work the cotton fields. On occasion Robert ran off for a week or two to stay with some of his many relatives scattered around Mississippi. He went by the last name of Spencer until his teens, when his mother told him about Noah Johnson. Depending upon the community he was visiting, he used other names as well: Robert Dodds, Robert Moore, Robert Saxton, or Sax. When he lived around Hazelhurst during the early '30s, he was known as R.L. Johnson. In several songs, Johnson referred to himself as Bob.

Like many Delta performers, Robert's first instruments were the Jew's harp and harmonica. Son's wife, Evie House, remembered his displays of harmonica prowess during recesses at a one-room Methodist church near the R.S. Cox plantation. In the 1992 film *The Search For Robert Johnson*, Wink Clark described Robert playing a three-string diddley bow that he fashioned by driving nails into a wall, attaching strands of wire to the nails, and using bottles as bridges and a slider: "He'd put him a bottle under the wires at the bottom and top, push 'em up tight, and it was just like tunin' a guitar. He could play what he was singin', but I never could get no sense out of it." Around 1927, Robert acquired a bona fide guitar. One of the first tunes he worked out was Leroy Carr's 1928 hit, "How Long–How Long Blues." He built himself a harmonica rack out of baling wire and string.

Willie Brown, a much-admired guitarist living in Robinsonville, showed Robert some chords and demonstrated his clean, aggressive picking and violent, string-snapping bass patterns. It's likely Brown coached Johnson in open-*G* tuning and taught him "The Jinx Blues," which Son House later recorded. Neighbors remembered seeing Willie backing Robert at a juke north of town. Years later Robert celebrated his friendship with Willie in "Cross Road Blues":

"You can run, you can run, tell my friend-boy Willie Brown,
You can run, tell my friend-boy Willie Brown,
Lord, that I'm standin' at the crossroad, babe,
I believe I'm sinking down"

> *For many plantation hands, blues was "devil's music" and strictly taboo.*

A well-known center for homemade corn liquor, Robinsonville had a very active musical scene, and Johnson began making the rounds of house parties and picnics at nearby settlements, playing for drinks and tips. Wink Clark recalled that Johnson "couldn't play unlessin' he had a pint of that stuff in him." Sometimes Robert hopped freight trains or hitched rides to other parts of the Delta, living off the pocket change he made by playing.

In February 1929, Johnson married 15-year-old Virginia Travis in Penton, Mississippi, and moved in with his half-sister and brother-in-law, Bessie and preacher Granville Hines, on the Klein plantation just east of Robinsonville. Bessie encouraged Robert to give up blues–"the devil's music," she called it–and for a while Robert settled down and worked the fields. When Virginia became pregnant and rejoined her family, he resumed his ramblings. Fourteen months after his wedding, Robert Johnson returned home to find that his wife and baby had died during childbirth. Many in the community turned on him, believing his waywardness had caused the deaths. "Among the old people," explains Gayle Dean Wardlow, "there was a superstition where the blues were considered the devil's trademark. If you played or associated with the blues, then you were part of the devil's workshop, and you were considered to be going to hell."

Robert found his greatest musical inspiration when Son House settled in Robinsonville around June 1930. A failed preacher who'd recently served hard time for manslaughter, Son had done a session for Paramount in Grafton, Wisconsin, just a week or two before arriving in Robinsonville, and he proudly showed off the $40 he'd earned. His voice a window-rattling holler, House had recorded a stack of solo sides, including his monumental two-parters "Preachin' The Blues" and "My Black Mama," which contain verses and guitar figures that would reappear in Robert's repertoire. At the same Grafton session, Willie Brown recorded "M&O Blues" and "Future Blues," playing with fierceness and precision, his voice field-holler tough. Charley Patton, Paramount's biggest star, wrapped up the historic session with four tracks, at least three of which featured Willie Brown on second guitar. (Son House always insisted that Willie Brown was the best guitarist of the three–"way better, twice better than Charley.") With its powerful bass thumps and clipped, note-perfect bottleneck, Son's style had an enormous impact on Robert, as it would on Muddy Waters.

Rory Block, a superb guitarist who specializes in close covers of deep Delta blues, feels that House is the musician Robert most resembles: "He fell in love with Son's playing, put his own stamp on it, and went beyond what Son was doing. He probably got his command of the popular open-G tuning from Son House and Willie Brown. Willie Brown had a great snapping bass-string style and was putting percussion and unbelievable rhythm to that tuning. He was also very clean and precision-oriented.

Charley Patton, the most famous progenitor of the Delta guitar style.

Charley Patton did all that pounding and strumming, and he was snapping the bass strings too. But where Patton was using open G in a really smooth way, Johnson took it away from the flowing sound into this dimension of sophisticated rhythms and percussion. Son House was definitely from the same school, but nobody got it as incredibly sophisticated as Johnson. Robert's slide style was spectacular too, especially with its separation of individual notes. Robert Johnson learned to combine it all into one style–the strumming, the slide, the percussion, the snapping, everything. He's it. He's the king."

Son settled just north of Robinsonville at the tiny Lake Cormorant railstop, where he became neighbors and regular playing partners with Willie Brown. Charley Patton and his wife Bertha Lee tried living there too, but departed after a couple of months. Many times, House recalled, the trio would throw their guitars over their shoulders and walk four or five miles to a gig. They'd line three chairs up and drink and play together, taking turns singing verses. Johnson attended these shows, during which the musicians would occasionally down too much moonshine and growl, "Beat it, kid–you'll get stepped on!" House told Lomax that young Robert was "just as proud as a peafowl and terribly nervy."

Robert picked up experience playing with Son's brother Frank House, appeared at barrelhouses with pianist Punk Taylor from nearby Lost Lake, and worked around Hughes, Arkansas, with a second guitarist named Wash Hemp. By then Robert had what was surely one of the loudest guitars around–a wood-bodied Stella with a metal resonator. It suited his style, which was soon to expand beyond his mentors'. "When Saxton'd be playin'," Willie Moore told Gayle Dean Wardlow, "he want to play lead all the time." Around this same time, Wardlow reports, "Willie Moore was arrested with Robert Johnson on the streets of Robinsonville, and they got put in the city jail for two or three hours. The reason was because they were singing about the local sheriff! Robert had been playing lead, while Willie played second guitar on the bass strings."

A former playing partner of Charley Patton and Willie Brown, Willie Moore chanced upon Johnson in front of a Robinsonville grocery store around 1930 and joined him in an impromptu jam. Decades later, Moore described Johnson's repertoire to Gayle Dean Wardlow and Stephen Calt for an account published in *78 Quarterly*: "He sing about: 'Captain George, Did Your Money Come.' Next thing he played about: 'Make Me Down,' but he never did say '*Make* me down a pallet,' he say: '*Flung* me down a pallet on your floor, an' make it so your man won't never know.'" Johnson then launched into "Black Gal, Whyn'cha Comb Your Head," "You Can Mistreat Me Here But You Can't When I Go Home," "President McKinley" (a slide song derived from "Frankie And Johnny"), "East St. Louis Blues," and a bottleneck "Casey Jones" renamed "A Thousand And Five On The Road Again." From this account, Wardlow speculates, "it would appear that the only one of Johnson's recordings that might have been typified by his early repertoire was 'Last Fair Deal Gone Down,' a 16-bar 'rag' ditty Henry Thomas had recorded as 'Red River Blues.'"

Not long after his encounter with Willie Moore, Robert headed south to his birthplace in search of his father. The Great Depression was wreaking havoc throughout Mississippi, but many laborers in Hazelhurst had cash to spend, thanks to the nearby WPA highway project. Robert played Copiah County's rough-and-tumble jukes, sometimes in the company of an older musician named Ike Zinnerman. Born in Grady, Alabama, Ike was a skilled blues guitarist who claimed to have learned to play while sitting atop tombstones in a graveyard at midnight. Carefully rehearsing and refining what Ike had shown him, Robert jotted song ideas in a small book. Before hitting the jukes on Saturday night, he'd spend the afternoon performing on the courthouse steps.

During a visit to a lumber camp at Martinsville, a few miles south of Hazelhurst, Robert met 30-year-old Calleta "Callie" Craft, who was twice married and had three young children. The kindhearted Callie fussed over Robert, going to his performances, serving him breakfast in bed, or allowing him to stay out all night with Ike. They shared a love of

Robert's life on the road was littered with heartbreak women, empty whiskey bottles, Jim Crow laws, and scrapes with cops and railroad bulls.

dancing, and Robert was apparently an agile tap dancer. The couple obtained a marriage license from the Copiah County clerk on May 4, 1931, and were secretly wed. At the same time, Virgie Jane Smith, an 18-year-old housekeeper, may have been carrying Robert's child. On December 16, 1931, Virgie gave birth to an illegitimate son named Claud Johnson. The birth certificate lists "R.L. Johnson" as the father. Although Claud believes his dad's name was Robert Lee Johnson, he's certain it was none other than the famous bluesman. "I seen him when I was near seven years old, and I remember him right now, just like it happened," he claimed in 1991. "I never seen him again. But he played guitar and singed." Around 1932 Robert and Callie packed up her kids and moved to Clarksdale, where Callie evidently suffered a breakdown. Robert deserted the family, and Callie passed away a few years later without ever seeing him again.

On his return to Robinsonville, Wardlow reports, Johnson was performing "Kind Hearted Woman Blues," "32-20 Blues," "Ramblin' On My Mind," "Cross Road Blues," and "Come On In My Kitchen," which is melodically similar to the Mississippi Sheiks' popular "Sitting On Top Of The World." According to Alan Lomax, he sometimes wore a broad belt stuffed full of harmonicas. During the Hazelhurst sojourn, Robert had transformed himself into the Delta's most progressive bluesman. Robert Palmer describes in *Deep Blues*: "He made the instrument sound uncannily like a full band, furnishing a heavy beat with his feet, chording innovative shuffle rhythms, and picking out a high, treble-string lead with his slider, all at the same time. Fellow guitarists would watch him with unabashed, open-mouthed wonder. They were watching the Delta's first modern bluesman at work, and the experience must have induced more than a few cases of future shock." Johnson's extraordinary musical metamorphosis caused witnesses to wonder whether he'd sold his soul to Satan at a fork in the road in exchange for his talent. It was an old superstition, and Robert promoted the notion in his lyrics and conversations with girlfriends.

We'll never fully understand the extent of Ike Zinnerman's coaching, since he was never recorded. There's a strong probability that much of Johnson's extraordinary growth was due to his ability to copy music from records. Lonnie Johnson's brilliant single-string solos no doubt inspired him to expand his dexterity and harmonic awareness. Robert patterned "Malted Milk" and "Drunken Heart-

The field-holler vocals of Ishman Bracey influenced Robert Johnson's singing, although it's uncertain whether the musicians knew each other.

Broom." Johnny Temple, who learned the *E* minor tuning from Skip James, showed Robert the pattern for James' "Devil Got My Woman," which Robert transformed into "Hell Hound On My Trail." Skip's "22-20 Blues" was recast as "32-20 Blues," the frantic quality of which, notes David Evans, "seems to foreshadow the ascendancy of jive and bebop music in the late 1930s and the 1940s." Utilizing Ishman Bracey's rapid vibrato and field-holler phrasing, Peetie Wheatstraw's studied laziness, and the falsetto jumps and yodels of Tommy Johnson and Skip James, Johnson developed an emotional vocal range extending from growls and howls to sly innuendos, passionate come-ons, and desperate pleas.

Johnson, it seems, was gifted with one of the best musical ears in the Delta. "Robert only had to hear something once–not twice, *once*," insisted Johnny Shines, who began his celebrated rambles with Johnson in 1935. "Whatsoever you did on a horn or on a piano, he figured he could do on a guitar, and he did it. And he didn't look for it, either. I never seen him practice. I never seen him look for nothin'. He'd just sit down, tune a guitar, whatsoever you wanted him to play, he'd play it. Robert heard something on the radio he liked, he never stopped talking with you. Tonight or tomorrow, he'd pick up his guitar and play the song, note-for-note, chord-for-chord, word-for-word. He was way before his time. I know many chords he never heard of, because he couldn't read music, but he could just pick up a guitar and make them. He was a genius."

After playing Robinsonville's jukes and street corners for a month or two, Robert moved to Helena, where Sonny Boy Williamson II, Robert Nighthawk, David "Honeyboy" Edwards, Houston Stackhouse, Howlin' Wolf, Johnny Shines, and Memphis Slim were members of a thriving blues community. While Helena and West Helena would serve as Robert's home base for the rest of his life, "I've got ramblin', I've got ramblin' on my mind" could well be his most autobiographical lyric. Driven by wanderlust, he spent his last

ed Man" on Lonnie's tunes, and while living in Hazelhurst claimed that his middle initial "L" stood for Lonnie. He drew from pianists too. Leroy Carr's lush chording and rolling rhythms and Roosevelt Sykes' rumbling bass may have been sources for his boogie bass lines. Johnson reworked Carr's "When The Sun Goes Down" as "Love In Vain Blues."

Robert undoubtedly heard Kokomo Arnold 78s, recasting Arnold's 1934 hit "Old Original Kokomo Blues" (along with its predecessor, Scrapper Blackwell's 1929 "Kokomo Blues") as "Sweet Home Chicago." He mined the 78's flip side for a line for "Milcow's Calf Blues," which also borrowed from Son House's "My Black Mama." Arnold's "Sagefield Woman Blues" provided the title verse of "I Believe I'll Dust My five years drifting from town to town, woman to woman, seldom staying long enough to make deep friendships. While his records probably netted him a few hundred dollars–good money during the Depression–most of the time he lived hand-to-mouth, playing for tips at plantations, levee camps, railroad stations, house parties, and street corners.

After orbiting Clarksdale, Friars Point, Rosedale, Lula, Moorhead, Itta Bena, Drew, Tunica, and other Delta towns, Robert ventured to St. Louis and Memphis. Johnny Temple, who picked up his "Lead Pencil Blues" boogie-bass lick from Johnson, was interviewed by Gayle Dean Wardlow in 1967 and '68. Wardlow reveals: "Temple told me that R.L. was living in Hattiesburg, Mississippi, around 1932. He said that R.L.–and that's the name he knew Johnson by–would hop a freight train from Hattiesburg to Jackson on Friday afternoons, and then he and Temple would play together in Jackson on Friday nights. On Saturdays, he told me, R.L. would ride the freight to Sunflower County to play up there. Then he'd ride back home."

Robert's life on the road was littered with heartbreak women, empty whiskey bottles, Jim Crow laws, and scrapes with cops and railroad bulls. As Shines describes it, after riding the rails or hitchhiking to a town, they'd head straight for the black neighborhood and play "as long as there's nickels and dimes afloat. When they quit, then we'd just walk on." For stays of more than a few days, they found it advisable to take on a menial job.

What sort of traveling companion was Robert Johnson? Shines remembers him as a talkative, peaceable man who "wouldn't carry a gun huntin'"–until intoxicated: "He started drinking, he'd do any goddanged thing. Wasn't nothin' too good for him to do." While performing, Robert would often single out a woman in the audience and sing directly to her, regardless of whether she was alone or with her mate–a practice that occasionally caused trouble and probably played a role in his murder. For an extended stay in a town, Johnson sometimes sought out the homeliest woman he could find, figuring she'd be unattached, generous with food and lodgings, and grateful for his attentions.

While Shines and Johnson shared freight cars, meals, and boarding houses, they did not play together. Shines worked one side of the street, while Johnson worked the other: "He'd draw his gang; I'd draw mine." On occasion Robert did perform with a backup guitarist, though: Johnny's cousin Calvin Frazier. Born in Osceola, Arkansas, Frazier, like Shines, was a few years younger than Robert. During 1922 and '23 Johnny had lived with the Fraziers in Memphis, and he recalled the sanctified family celebrating God with "music and dancing into the night." Calvin met Robert Johnson on a Helena street corner, and they became close

enough friends that Johnson invited him to attend one of his recording sessions, although Calvin was injured and unable to go. Calvin Frazier's October 1938 duets with Sampson Pittman, recorded in Detroit by Alan Lomax for the Library of Congress, used Johnson-style chord voicings and melodies. Sections of "I'm In The Highway, Man" and "She's A Double Crossing Woman" mirrored Robert's "Kind Hearted Woman Blues," while "Lilly Mae" paralleled "Honeymoon Blues." After recording "Welfare Blues," Frazier told Lomax that he'd written the song in Detroit on December 22, 1936, although a month before that date Johnson had recorded the melody as "Sweet Home Chicago."

"Listening to Calvin Frazier, I can tell Robert wasn't alone," observes Keith Richards. "This cut 'I'm In The Highway, Man' also reminds me a bit of Blind Blake. Robert was hanging out with some guys! Same inflection, with the double-voice chat going on underneath. So that's where Robert Johnson was for six months–with Calvin, eh? [*Laughs.*] Now we know. It's so similar. Who took from who? And where did both of them get it from? The style is incredibly similar. But it's interesting because when you listen to Blind Blake, you can almost hear the crossovers going on.

"Calvin's playing is not as precise as Robert, but he had the basic idea. It's so close. Robert must have hung with the guy. He just put more sting in it because he was more manic. I mean, that's why he died so young. The man was asking for trouble and didn't mind saying so. In all of his records, the man's asking for trouble all the way down the line. All his deals with the hellhounds and the bitches–one of them will get you. It's an interesting connection."

During their rambles, Johnson owned a Kalamazoo archtop, while Johnny Shines played a Regal. Neither owned a case, so they slung their guitars across their backs. "We used regular tuning, most time," Shines observed, "but we'd tune them in open G or open A for bottleneck. Open D, E. Open A was called Vastopol." (A guitar in open G is tuned D G D G B D, low to high; open A is the same pattern a whole-step higher. Open D is D A D F# A D, and open E follows the same configuration two frets higher.) Aural evidence suggests that Robert sometimes used an unwound third string.

Johnson fashioned his own slides by breaking long-necked bottles and trimming them to size with a pair of pliers. "He used the slide on his little finger; it wasn't long enough to fret across the whole neck," Johnny remembers. "For certain tunes he liked using a knife. As far as picking, he'd play with a thumbpick, fingerpick, straight pick, and sometimes he'd ride bareback. He'd play with his thumb and first finger mostly, though he'd sometimes use his thumb and two fingers." In the famous studio portrait on the cover of *The Complete Recordings*, Robert plays a maple-body

GAYLE DEAN WARDLOW COLLECTION

H.C. Speir's store, 1929, with H.C. smiling at right. Robert Johnson cut his "Kind Hearted Woman Blues" demo upstairs.

Gibson L-0 with a 12-fret neck. In the so-called "dime store" photo, he holds a 14-fret-neck model, possibly a modified Gibson L-00 or more likely the cheaper Kalamazoo version made by Gibson in the mid '30s.

With his disfigured left eye and scarred cheek, Johnson was sometimes described as a seedy, low-life character, but this image is strikingly contradicted by the 1935 Memphis studio portrait: Smiling broadly, Robert wears a plastic thumbpick while fretting his round-hole acoustic. With his perfect three-piece pinstripe suit, high-gloss wingtips, and jaunty fedora, he exudes the essence of 1930s cool; in this getup, one senses, he could easily be whisked into a swank Harlem bijou. Shines says his language matched his image: "He talked really hip. Like, 'Yeah, man,' you know, or 'Look, daddy so-and-so' and 'Look, baby so-and-so'–like that."

Honeyboy Edwards recalls that Robert wore a hat most of the time, "broke down over that bad eye." For several months Johnson courted Honeyboy's cousin, Willie Mae Powell, who has fond memories of Robert playing "Stones In My Passway" and "I'm A Steady Rollin' Man" on her back porch. Willie Mae thought that Robert's smaller left eye was a birthmark, and she remembered him "as very handsome–

the cutest little brown thing you ever seen in your life." (Unbeknownst to Willie Mae for more than a half-century, Robert had called out her name in "Love In Vain Blues.")

Another of Johnson's lovers was Stella Lockwood, the mother of Robert Lockwood, Jr., who was in his late teens when Robert Johnson first started coming around his house in Helena. He has fond memories of Johnson helping him hammer together a homemade guitar with the body fashioned from an old phonograph. "Robert Johnson was one of the nicest people I ever met," he told Peter Lee. "He was very sharp, patient, and I figured he was just right, 'cause he showed me something that didn't leave. He taught me, period. My first thing I was playing was 'Sweet Home Chicago.' Yeah, that's the first thing Robert taught me. He started recording, and I had them records around there to play."

Robert Johnson's first recording sessions were arranged by H.C. Speir, who owned a music store at 111 N. Farrish in Jackson, Mississippi. Years before, Speir had proved his uncanny talent for recognizing blues talent, arranging sessions for many of the Delta's finest musicians–Charley Patton, Son House, Willie Brown, Tommy Johnson, and the Mississippi Sheiks among them. On occasion he cut demo

THE ZINTGRAFF STUDIO COLLECTION / THE INSTITUTE OF TEXAN CULTURES

The Gunter Hotel in the late '30s. When Johnson recorded here, he probably used the "colored" entrance around the back.

acetates on the recording machine upstairs from his shop; Tommy Johnson and Ishman Bracey both recorded there in 1928. "Mr. Speir just loved old blues and fiddle music," reports Gayle Dean Wardlow, "and he started scouting to earn extra money. The way it worked was a guy would come in, and he'd listen to him, and then he'd go back out the door. As far as I know, his store was not a hangout for musicians. They'd come by and audition, but as far as sitting around playing goes, no.

"Robert Johnson auditioned in 1936 with 'Kind Hearted Woman Blues.' Mr. Speir had recorded in Hattiesburg in July of '36–Blind Roosevelt Graves, people from south Mississippi–so Johnson missed that session by three or four months. The record company, ARC, hadn't paid Speir for that session. He was angry about it, but he must have thought Johnson had talent, so he sent his name to Ernie Oertle, ARC's sales rep for Louisiana and Mississippi. He trusted Oertle. When I interviewed him, Speir remembered Johnson playing 'Kind Hearted Woman,' but other than that, he thought he was just

another musician. Remember, he'd heard a lot of great guitar players; he listened to guitar all the time." Steve LaVere believes that Johnson too may have recorded at Speir's: "Robert cut a sample record and gave it to his sister. His sister told me that she had a disk of that nature until it wore out and she threw it away."

Ernie Oertle sought out Johnson, heard him play, and offered to take him to San Antonio to record. Robert was elated, going over to Georgia Street to share the good news with his sister Carrie. The men traveled to Texas by automobile. On Monday, November 23, 1936, Oertle brought Robert Johnson to the Gunter Hotel for his first recording session. (Lawrence Brown, a researcher in San Antonio, questions the location: "The notion of Johnson recording in a makeshift studio in a hotel room is a myth. Those sessions were held at the KONO radio station facilities at the Blue Bonnet Hotel, which was very near the Gunter. Vocalion cut records on the second floor there." But according to information provided by Don Law, ARC's Regional Branch Manager who oversaw the session, the location was the Gunter.)

ARC's recording crew had already been on location for several days, and an item appearing in that afternoon's *The San Antonio Light* suggests that the sessions were hectic: "Brunswick [ARC's sister company] recording crew here figures it set a record when it got under the wire with 105 recordings made in the first three days of its San Antonio set-up." LaVere's research through the file cards at CBS, though, indicates that Johnson was the only one who recorded on the 23rd, cutting eight masters. On the day before, six masters were cut by W. Lee O'Daniel And His Hillbilly Boys.

Robert began with two takes of his best-rehearsed number, "Kind Hearted Woman Blues." Each performance was a gem, with deliberately paced, perfect guitar playing and falsettos cooler than Little Richard's. He followed with a pair of songs destined to become postwar standards: "I Believe I'll Dust My Broom" and "Sweet Home Chicago." By day's end, Johnson had completed two masters each of "Ramblin' On My Mind," "Phonograph Blues," "Come On In My Kitchen," and "When You Got A Good Friend." The session also produced the single surviving take of "Terraplane Blues," a sexy automobile blues that became Johnson's biggest-selling record. ("Robert didn't have one," Shines remembered, "but that was a hell of a car at that time–fast!") Johnson's lyrics gave layers of meaning:

> *"I'm 'on' get deep down in this connection, keep on tan-*
> *glin' with your wires,*
> *I'm 'on' get deep down in this connection, whoo ah, keep*
> *on tanglin' with these wires,*
> *And when I mash down on your little starter, then your*
> *spark plug will give me fire"*

What happened after the session? That night in San Antonio Paul Muni was reading *The Story Of Louis Pasteur* at the Lux Radio Theatre, but according to the liner notes for the first Robert Johnson album, 1961's *King Of The Delta Blues Singers*, Robert had another sort of entertainment in mind: "A country boy in a moderately big town, Johnson found trouble within hours after he arrived. Don Law considered himself responsible for Johnson, found him a room in a boarding house [on North Cherry St., in San Antonio's black section], and told him to get some sleep so he would be ready to begin recording at 10:00 the following morning. Law then joined his wife and some friends for dinner at the Gunter Hotel. He had scarcely begun dinner when he was summoned to the phone. A policeman was calling from the city jail. Johnson had been picked up on a vagrancy charge. Law rushed down to the jail, found Johnson beaten up, his guitar smashed; the cops had not only picked him up but

had worked him over. With some difficulty, Law managed to get Johnson freed in his custody, whisked him back to the boarding house, gave him 45¢ for breakfast, and told him to stay in the house and not to go out for the rest of the evening. Law returned to the hotel, only to be called to the phone again. This time it was Johnson. Fearing the worst, Law asked, 'What's the matter now?' Johnson replied, 'I'm lonesome.' Puzzled, Law said, 'You're lonesome? What do you mean, you're lonesome?' Johnson replied, 'I'm lonesome and there's a lady here. She wants 50¢ and I lacks a nickel.'" The vagrancy story can't be confirmed, since the San Antonio police records were destroyed by fire long ago.

Three days passed before Johnson recorded again. In the interim, masters were cut by a pair of guitar-playing Mexican sisters, the Hermanas Barraza, and by a fine white gospel group known as the Chuck Wagon Gang. On November 26, the Chuck Wagon Gang preceded Johnson with six masters, and then Robert cut one master of "32-20 Blues" while Mexican musicians Andres Berlanga and Francisco Montalvo awaited their turn. On the 27th, Johnson went first, followed by the Hermanas Barraza and pianist Daniel Palomo. This final session on Friday produced some of Robert's wildest and most memorable sides. Starting out with the hokumy "They're Red Hot" and "Dead Shrimp Blues," Johnson then bared his soul in two takes of "Cross Road Blues." He began with a mighty slide, followed by a patented turnaround. His voice charged with otherworldly passion, he sang:

> *"I went to the cross road, fell down on my knees,*
> *I went to the cross road, fell down on my knees,*
> *Asked the Lord above, 'Have mercy, save poor Bob if*
> *you please'*

> *"Mmm, standing at the cross road, I tried to flag a ride,*
> *Standing at the cross road, I tried to flag a ride,*
> *Didn't nobody seem to know me, everybody pass me by"*

This was the stuff legends are made of. Johnson's next selection was "Walking Blues," a sophisticated 12-bar composition that's become a Delta staple. With its frantic *drive*, Robert's next song, "Last Fair Deal Gone Down," is a direct ancestor of rock and roll. He cut "Preachin' Blues (Up Jumped The Devil)," and wound things up with "If I Had Possession Over Judgment Day," a hypercharged arrangement with stratospheric slide that used Hambone Willie Newbern's familiar "Roll And Tumble Blues" as its basis. For songs in the key of B, such as "Walkin' Blues" and "Cross Road Blues," Robert's guitar was either tuned in open A and capoed at the second fret, or tuned in open G and capoed at the fourth.

(Some of Patton's best sides were also played in open G, capoed at the fourth.) "Preachin' Blues (Up Jumped The Devil)" was probably recorded without a capo in open E.

Don Law, the A&R man in charge of Johnson's session, was asked to recall the event a quarter-century later for *King Of The Delta Blues Singers*. Law remembered Robert as "slender, handsome, of medium height, with beautiful hands and a remarkable ability to project while he was singing or playing guitar." Law added this curious description: "Embarrassed and suffering from a bad case of stage fright, Johnson turned his face to the wall, his back to the Mexican musicians. Eventually he calmed down sufficiently to play, but he never faced his audience." Ry Cooder, for one, challenges this account: "Listen to Johnson's singing and his forceful personality. This is a guy who was afraid of the audience? Hell, no! This is a 'chew them up and spit them out' kind of a guy. I'll tell you what he was doing. I think he was sitting in the corner to achieve a certain sound that he liked.

"Find yourself a plaster corner without wallpaper or curtains sometime—all those hotel rooms were plaster. Go and sit facing the corner with your guitar tight up against the corner, play, and see what it sounds like. What you get is something called 'corner loading.' It's an acoustic principle that eliminates most of the top end and most of the bottom end and amplifies the middle, the same thing that a metal guitar or an electric guitar does. The midrange is where that metallic, kind of piercing sound is. Robert Johnson sounds funny, let's face it. He doesn't sound like anybody playing an acoustic wood guitar, but it's not a metal guitar. If you stick your face up into that corner and listen, you'll hear that sound. It ties the notes together and compresses the sound too. And his sound is very compressed.

"I'm sure he would have liked somebody to say, 'Robert, I'm going to boost the midrange'—because it's a dry sound, the acoustic guitar, finally. It's a boring sound for Robert. He wants to hear *wang!* He wants to hear the electric; he wants to hear that boosted midrange. I bet if you could have done that with equalizing and headphones in the modern era, he'd have been very glad. I'll bet you if you'd have given him a Marshall amp to play through, he would have been *extremely* glad. But sitting in the corner, he could achieve something like that."

"He was after a sound," agrees Keith Richards. "He was playing with rooms, which we all still do. I think that he was very, very aware of sound and a room and where the sound

of his guitar would bounce off the corner. He was into ambience."

Steve LaVere agrees that Johnson may have faced the wall for sonic reasons, but adds: "More than anything, Johnson was very protective of his playing because he was doing things on the guitar that nobody else was doing at the time. Rather than take a chance even with the Mexican musicians—especially musicians who were about to make records—he wasn't going to share what he knew."

Pete Welding's liner notes for *King Of The Delta Blues Singers, Vol. 2* portray Johnson as a tireless perfectionist who carefully worked out arrangements: "Those musicians who knew and worked with him—Johnny Shines, Henry Townsend, and David Edwards, among others—have commented on this aspect of his music, remarking that once Johnson had developed a song to his satisfaction, he performed it exactly the same way every time he did it thereafter. This is supported by a comparison of the several takes of some of his recordings; in most cases where alternate versions of his songs exist, they are almost identical, even down to the smallest subtleties of accompaniment, to the originally issued takes. The few exceptions to this ('Ramblin' On My Mind' being the most notable) are probably the result of Johnson's not yet having brought the songs to the ultimate shape he desired. In these cases, the second take is usually much stronger, more tightly focused. That this attention to detail paid off handsomely is self-evident: Listen to the performances, and you'll hear some of the most forcefully impassioned and starkly beautiful blues ever recorded."

The following summer Robert Johnson made his final 13 recordings at ARC's Dallas branch. "This took place in an office building, a distribution point for Brunswick Records," describes Steve LaVere. "Robert recorded on the third floor, which had an open area, like a warehouse storage area for records. They just set up some baffles and did the recording." He cut three disks on Saturday, June 19th—one master each of "Stones In My Passway," "I'm A Steady Rollin' Man," and "From Four Until Late," a show-bizzy tune that somehow seems better suited for someone like Blind Willie McTell. Robert returned on Sunday for his final, most productive session. With only Law and an engineer present, he began with "Hell Hound On My Trail," described by Palmer as "pure, icy cold paranoia." His voice a wounded cry, Johnson infused the lyrics with what may be the most apocalyptic vision in all blues:

Each performance was a gem, with deliberately paced, perfect guitar playing and falsettos cooler than Little Richard's.

"I got to keep movin',
I've got to keep movin',
Blues fallin' down like hail,
Blues fallin' down like hail,
Mmm, blues fallin' down like hail,
Blues fallin' down like hail.
And the day keeps on worryin' me,
It's a hell hound on my trail,
Hell hound on my trail,
Hell hound on my trail"

While only one take of this monumental track survives, LaVere speculates that others were probably cut: "ARC's standard practice at that time was to record enough to get two acceptable masters. See, in San Antonio the masters were made on wax, so any alternates that might have been recorded were scraped clean and destroyed on the spot. The Dallas recordings were made on the first batch of the advanced new process of acetate recording. When they cut into acetate, any masters that were not acceptable or damaged were returned to the plant for replating. Aluminum discs were rather rare at that time, so they would strip the acetate off the disk and replate it. The only song he may not have done a second take of was 'Honeymoon Blues.'"

Robert then retuned his guitar from open E minor to standard for two masters of "Little Queen Of Spades" and one of "Malted Milk." His voice took on a very soulful quality in "Drunken Hearted Man," convincingly delivering its message of repentance. His next selection, "Me And The Devil Blues" echoed the harrowing theme that inaugurated the session:

"Early this morning, when you knocked upon my door,
Early this morning, whoo, you knocked upon my door,
And I said, 'Hello, Satan, I believe it's time to go'

"Me and the devil was walkin' side by side,
Me and the devil, whoo, was walkin' side by side,
I'm goin' to beat my woman until I get satisfied"

"Hell Hound On My Trail" and "Me And The Devil Blues" did much to promote tales of Johnson's pact with the devil. It's a tribute to his terrifying genius that neither song has been adequately covered. ("In these songs," says Rory Block, "the intensity of Robert Johnson's life came straight through his music. You don't just hear technique; you hear this *lonesome* man, this incredibly soulful, confused, powerful person. His soul is just beaming through the music. That mysterious presence is what makes his music so magnificent.") Johnson spent the rest of the session recording "Stop

Breakin' Down Blues," "Traveling Riverside Blues," "Honeymoon Blues," "Love In Vain Blues," and "Milkcow's Calf Blues." Once again, the takes were very close: "Johnson was a very studied musician," LaVere says. "Comparing alternate takes, you might find an additional verse or the omission of a verse, but in some cases–and this includes most of the Dallas session–most of the duplicate versions are nearly identical."

When he stepped back out onto the streets of Dallas on June 20, 1937, Robert Johnson had less than 14 months to live. Shines says that they met up in Red Water, Texas, not long afterwards, and headed south to cotton country when cold weather set in. Shines went on to Hughes, Arkansas, to visit family, while Johnson spent some time with Robert Lockwood's mother in Helena, and then made several stops in the Delta. He came back for Shines, and they set out for St. Louis and Memphis. "St. Louis was a profitable town," Johnny explains, "and Memphis was always good. You never got to be too well known in Memphis. I'd go down to Handy's Park, play with the guys down there. Now, a guy over here have a big crowd, and we'd strike up over there and probably pull half his crowd or all of his crowd. If you pull all of his crowd, that's what we called 'headcuttin',' you know–we just cut his head! Yeah."

With his uncanny ability to mimic practically any music he heard, Robert was no doubt one of the baddest headhunters of all. As Shines described in *Frets* magazine, Johnson was a master of the musical change-up pitch: "He could play anything–in the style of Lonnie Johnson, Blind Blake, Blind Boy Fuller, Blind Willie McTell, all those guys. And the country singer Jimmie Rodgers–me and Robert used to play a hell of a lot of his tunes, man. Robert was good at ragtime, pop tunes, waltz numbers, polkas. A whole lot of them things nobody else played with a slide, he played them with a slide. It was just natural to him." "Yes, Sir, That's My Baby," "My Blue Heaven," and "Tumbling Tumbleweeds" were among Robert's favorite pop tunes.

During a four-month journey, LaVere indicates, Johnny Shines, Calvin Frazier, Sampson Pittman, and Robert Johnson left Helena and made "a straightforward shot to St. Louis, up through Decatur, Illinois, where they played a square dance for white people, and then they went on to Chicago, Detroit (where Calvin and Sampson remained), New York, and then back home. When they got back South, Johnson said he was going to Mississippi, and Shines said, 'That's where he got rid of me.' Shortly thereafter, Johnson died."

While visiting Detroit, the men crossed over into Windsor, Ontario, to play a radio show: "It was called *The Elder Moten Hour*," Shines explained. "He was a preacher, and he broadcasted out of Canada. Lots of people could pick him up back over there in Detroit and all over Canada. He was a sanctified preacher, and he wanted a lot of music with his outfit, you know. He had a pretty good-sized choir. Robert, Calvin, and myself, we go over there and play for him. Calvin Frazier was my first cousin. We was playing gospel music. Regular old gospel songs, like 'Ship Of Zion,' 'Stand By Me,' 'When The Saints Go Marchin' In,' 'Just Over In Glory Land,' songs like that."

Robert Johnson lived long enough to hear his 78s, which were issued on the Vocalion label and ARC subsidiaries such as Oriole, Perfect, and Romeo. By 1938, even the Sears, Roebuck company carried Johnson 78s in its Conqueror line–"I Believe I'll Dust My Broom" backed with "Dead Shrimp Blues" was the first. Near the end, Robert was said to have visited some of his illegitimate children, giving each of them one of his 78s. It's also been rumored that he acquired an electric guitar in 1938 and was seen leading a small band in a Belzoni juke, the drummer having painted "Robert Johnson" across his bass drum.

"If Robert Johnson had lived into the era of electric guitar," speculates Keith Richards, "he'd have killed us all! If Johnson had just been a little nicer to his chicks, knew how to play the ladies a little better, then he might have been there instead of Muddy. I have the feeling he would have gone into a band thing. I've heard rumors that he did have a band before he died. I don't know if that's wishful thinking, but at the same time I don't discount it. With what he had together, this man was heading for a band–an orchestra, in actual fact. When you listen to him, the cat's got Bach going on down low and Mozart going up high. The cat was counterpointing and using incredible shit. If he hadn't have died, the next natural progression would have been to put a band together with Calvin. But then the war would have got in the way. Very few people recorded from '41 to '46."

Mystery shrouds the death of Robert Johnson on August 16, 1938. According to Honeyboy Edwards, who was there the night Johnson's last fair deal went down, Robert was poisoned while appearing at a variety store/jukehouse at the Three Forks located just outside of Greenwood where Highway 49E joins 82. When Honeyboy arrived on the back of a flatbed at about 11:00 P.M., Johnson was already slumped in a corner. People started calling out the names of Johnson's tunes, trying to get him to play. Robert attempted to play,

but was too sick to go on. He lay down for a while, and was transported back to where he was staying in the Baptist Town section of Greenwood.

"They brought him back 'bout 3:00 to Greenwood, to his room," Edwards told *Living Blues*. "And Sunday he was so sick he didn't know nothing, hardly nothing. And he was sick Monday. He was crawling around, just crawling and crawling around the floor. Hollering and going on. He died Tuesday night, Tuesday evening. I wasn't there but I come in that evening, late. They had him sitting out–he'd been moaning, screaming, crawling around yelling. Moaning and groaning and hurting. And when I got there he just laying there." Edwards believes that a woman handed Johnson some poisoned moonshine prepared by the juke's operator, who'd found out Johnson had been sleeping with his wife or girlfriend. He thought the deliverer of the poison was an unsuspecting accomplice.

Queen Elizabeth "Bet" Thomas, Johnson's girlfriend at the time of his murder, claims in *The Search For Robert Johnson* that Johnson had recently beat her up: "He bust my head right up! Boy, if I'd had a shotgun, I'd have shot him just like I was shootin' a durn rabbit! Oh, yeah. I'd of killed him dead as a micah! Don't hit me in my head, like I'm a durn hog!" Miller Carter, whose shack overlooks Payne Chapel, lived with Bet Thomas during the early 1940s. Carter insists that Bet Thomas' father killed Johnson. "Her daddy killed him," he told me in 1990. "His name was Jonas Thomas, and I'm sure he did it." He's uncertain of the method–offering shooting as a possibility–but is sure of the motive. Johnson, he says, had slapped around Bet just a few days before his appearance at the Three Forks juke, and Jonas Thomas simply evened the score.

Shines and Frazier, who weren't there, echoed Edwards' take: "Before he died," Johnny added, "Robert was crawling along the ground on all fours, barking and snapping like a mad beast." Chances are, Johnson lingered between life and death for a few days: "He was playing on a Saturday night, and his date of death, August 16th, is a Tuesday," explains Wardlow. "When you're poisoned, you bleed internally, so that story about him barking was probably a description of him gagging or vomiting. He obviously died of internal bleeding."

The death certificate filed with the State of Mississippi

two days after the murder indicates that his body was taken by his family to Greenwood's Zion Church for burial. The certificate states that Robert L. Johnson was 26 years old and had been a musician for 10 years. In place of the cause of death is a handwritten "No doctor," which leads Honeyboy Edwards to insist that Johnson "died for attention."

According to Queen Elizabeth, who claims to have attended the funeral, Johnson was buried in the Payne Chapel graveyard near Quito, two miles north of Zion on Highway 7. No one's certain of the exact location of Johnson's grave, but if the Payne site is accurate, the grave diggers heeded his request in "Me And The Devil Blues":

"You may bury my body down by the highway side,
(Baby, I don't care where you bury my body when I'm
dead and gone),
You may bury my body, whoo, down by the highway
side,
So my old evil spirit can get a Greyhound bus and ride"

Johnson's family came to Greenwood for his burial and brought his guitar back to Carrie's house in Memphis. She lent the guitar to Robert's half-brother, Charles Spencer, who never brought it back. Ironically, Johnson's death occurred at a time when, unbeknownst to him, his career could have taken off. Columbia's top talent scout, John Hammond was convinced that Robert Johnson was "the greatest primitive blues player of all time" and was anxious to book him for his 1938 presentation of American Negro music, the Spirituals To Swing Concert at Carnegie Hall. Had things gone as planned, Johnson would have been presented on the same stage with Count Basie and boogie-woogie piano greats Meade Lux Lewis, Albert Ammons, and Pete Johnson. Who knows–in the following weeks, he may have been entertained and lionized by the same intellectuals who had swarmed around Leadbelly a few years earlier. But by then Johnson had been dead four months.

Hammond's program notes eulogized: "Robert Johnson was going to be the big surprise of the evening. I knew him only from his blues records and from the tall, exciting tales the recording engineers and supervisors used to bring about him from the improvised studios in Dallas and San Antonio. I don't believe that Johnson ever worked as a professional musician anywhere, and it still knocks me over when I think of how lucky it is that a talent like his ever found its way to phonograph records. At the concert we will have to be content with playing two of his records…" Hammond selected "Walkin' Blues" and "Preachin' Blues," and Big Bill Broonzy appeared onstage in Robert's place.

Robert Johnson made an immediate impact on other musicians, especially young Muddy Waters. "I was influenced by Son House and Robert Johnson," Waters explained. "Robert's records were out in 1937, like 'Terraplane Blues' and 'Walking Blues.' I never followed him around to hear him or anything like that, but Son House I did follow around and listen to. And I do believe that the way Robert played, you could hear some of Son House in him. Robert was putting in more notes. It was about three notes to one. Robert was one of the greatest of the slide players."

Muddy, Elmore James, Johnny Shines, Robert Lockwood, and scores of others electrified Robert's music in the '40s and '50s, making it a cornerstone of modern blues. The release of *King Of The Delta Blues Singers* in 1961 and *King Of The Delta Blues Singers, Vol. 2* in 1970 carried his music to a new generation. Eric Clapton, Taj Mahal, Johnny Winter, and the Rolling Stones helped transform Johnson's music into rock and roll, while artists such as John Hammond and Rory Block launched their careers with eerie acoustic covers of Johnson songs.

Robert Johnson's influence still reverberates through popular music. It's there in lyrics, cool turnarounds, boogie bass lines, and most important of all–*attitude*. "I know he played rock and roll," Shines insists. "It was the same beat, but it just wasn't called rock and roll. That's all." When one returns to the source–Columbia's *The Complete Recordings*–the emotion-charged voice, troubled lyrics, and superb guitar playing remain as fresh and potent as any music yet recorded.

The author thanks Rory Block, Miller Carter, Ry Cooder, Stefan Grossman, John Hammond, Steve LaVere, Peter Lee, Robert Lockwood, Jr., Jim O'Neal, Robert Palmer, Keith Richards, Gayle Dean Wardlow, and the late Johnny Shines for their contributions to this article. Quotations from the lyrics of Robert Johnson's songs © King Of Spades Music. Used by permission; all rights reserved.

Johnny Shines

April 1989

BY JAS OBRECHT

JOHNNY SHINES AND ROBERT JOHNSON hoboed together through Depression-era America. They hopped freights, played on street corners, shared rooms and whiskey, and made it as far north as Canada. Johnson, the Mississippi Delta's most celebrated blues performer, was murdered more than a half-century ago, and yet his spirit still haunts the music of Johnny Shines. It's there in the turnarounds, the mournful bottleneck slides, impassioned lyrics, and falsetto moans. At clubs, concerts, house parties, or high schools, Johnny Shines is just as likely to play Robert's "Crossroads Blues," "Terraplane Blues," and "Sweet Home Chicago" as he is his own "Evil-Hearted Woman Blues," "A Little Tenderness," and "Evening Sun."

Raised in Tennessee and Arkansas, Shines took up guitar in 1932, and within three years began rambling with Johnson. He moved to Chicago in 1941, amplified his guitar, and staked Frost's Corner as his home turf. He played Tom's Tavern for many years with pianist Sunnyland Slim, and worked in nearby Robbins with the jazzy Dukes Of Swing. His first recordings, four 1946 sides on *OKeh Chicago Blues*, remained unissued for a quarter-century. In fact, bad luck seemed to dog Johnny's recording career the whole time he lived in Chicago. After two 1950 sides as Shoe Shine Johnny, a pair for Chess in '52, and a handful for J.O.B. with harmonicist Walter Horton in '53, he pawned his guitar and quit music altogether. He wasn't persuaded back into the studios until 1965's *Chicago/The Blues/Today!* During the '70s, Shines became a blues celebrity, touring America and Europe and recording for Biograph, Testament, Flyright, Advent, Rounder, and other labels.

A kind, intelligent man with a subtle wit, Johnny has lived near Tuscaloosa, Alabama, since the late '60s. A stroke may have slowed his fretting hand, but his powerful voice is still remarkably similar to his earliest records, echoing the deep Delta blues of a bygone era. At 73, he was playing California clubs and house parties during the week of this interview, which was held in a Watsonville farmhouse on January 23, 1989. On the table in front of us were three albums—*Hangin' On*, *Mister Blues Is Back To Stay*, and Advent's *Johnny Shines*—as well as a Xerox copy of the Johnny Shines sessions listed in Mike Leadbitter and Neil Slaven's *Blues Records*. Several minutes into the interview, I handed Johnny a framed photograph of Robert Johnson.

Were you born John Shines?
John Shines, that's right. John Ned Lee Shines. I had two

middle names. That was from my uncle and great uncle. Ned was my great uncle, and Lee was my uncle.

Do you consider yourself a Delta bluesman?

That's what I am, a Delta bluesman. And now I'm considered the king of the Delta blues.

A few years ago you were working on an autobiography.

Yeah. I never did anything with it so far. Yes, sir. I been so busy going to school, you know, and doing different things. I go to school every day for upholstery.

Is this a new sideline you want to get into?

Well, yes. That will be my main line. See, I had a stroke back in '80, and this [left] hand here is not very good. It affected my playing very badly. So the biggest playing I do now is slide, because I can't hold a chord down good. The chord is all muted out. So I've taken these trades as therapy as well as a position in life.

Could you play at all right after your stroke?

I've been playing just about as good as I play now, ever since I've had a stroke. Well, I play a little better now than I did before, when I first had it. My stroke happened after I had done _Hangin' On_. When I did that one, why, shit, I was playing like hell.

You mean good or bad?

Good! Now this one here, _Mister Blues Is Back To Stay_, let me see. _Hangin' On_ was my first. See, on this one here [picks up _Mister Blues Is Back To Stay_], I had had the stroke, and I didn't play at all on it.

What are your favorite tracks on those albums?

I think "Soul Power" was pretty powerful. I like the way it was done and the arrangement.

What about on Hangin' On_?_

Well, yeah. "Razzmadazz." "Full Grown Woman" I thought was pretty good. Robert Jr. and I were doing those acoustic, just the two of us.

Do you prefer playing acoustic guitar?

Well, yes. I prefer playing acoustic over electric, but since I've had the stroke, I have to play electric to really be heard, because I mutes the strings out so bad.

That didn't come across when you played electric onstage last night.

A lot of things people don't hear [_laughs_]. A lot of things they hear, but they don't be goin' on.

Are you critical of your own playing?

Very much.

Where can someone hear the best of Johnny Shines' guitar work?

I think they should look this one up [_Hangin' On_]. I like "Razzmadazz," "Big John," "Early In The Morning" and "Lonesome Whistle." Those songs was done acoustically–just Robert and myself–and I was in the peak of my playing

right then.

What do you think of your earlier records? What about the Advent album?

Well, that's a good record. I didn't like it at all, until lately. Because the song that I really did to sell this record was fucked up from the get-go. It was the first song on side two, "My Love Can't Hide." See, the introduction should have been an _Ebm_ when it was the piano, and the guy just claimed he couldn't do it. He just could not do that. Okay, now in the middle of the damn song, when he gets ready to take a solo, here he come with the introduction–what I wanted him to do at first! And that just pissed me off. I damn near hated the record from there.

Let's go back even further. What do you like about your very first sessions in Chicago?

"Delta Pine" and "Ride, Ride Mama." Well, all of them were pretty good, I think [points to Feb. 24, 1946 entry in _Blues Records_]. "Joliet Blues" and "So Glad I Found You" was good. "Ramblin'" was good, "Evening Sun" was good, and "I'm Gonna Call An Angel" was good.

After that, you didn't do any more sessions as a leader until 1965.

I had really retired when I did that, and I am very unhappy with it [_Chicago/The Blues/Today!_], because I didn't intend to ever record again. I'd been whupped around and screwed around, so I just said I wasn't going to record no more. Matter of fact, I quit playing. I took all my stuff, 'bout $3,000 worth of material, and carried it to a pawnshop and got $100 for it. I tore the ticket up and threw it on the floor, because I didn't want the stuff. I just quit, give up.

Then these two fellows from England, they started writing to me, and I got hip to what they was trying to do, so I quit answering their mail. Doorbell rang one morning, my wife went to the door and said, "Here's two men out here. They talk silly, but I don't know what they're saying." I said, "Send them here. I'll know what they're saying." So she sent them in, and it was Frank Scott and another fellow. I can't remember the man's name. Anyway, they came in and I talked with 'em. So they hung around and hung around until finally they got me to say I'd do one more recording session. So I did, and Sam Charters was the one I did it for. I did these songs [_points to the Vanguard entries_]. "Rockin' My Boogie"–I really didn't have that song in mind. That was something I pulled the musicians in and made them do. That's the first time Charlie Musselwhite had ever been in the studio, the first time he'd ever blowed on a recording session. And his leg got rubber; he fell out on the floor, couldn't stand up. That was a session without any rehearsal whatsoever.

What led you to decide to give up music altogether?

I had some pretty shitty deals. I was playing about seven nights a week, but I was turning in three to the union–only paying the tax on three things. They caught up with me because one of my musicians got mad with me and went to the union and told them what was happening. But now in the meantime, my old lady and I had cooked up food and stuff like that, you know, to entice peoples to come down and vote for the president of the union when they was trying to kick him out of the union. And they fined me four hundred and some dollars, and I thought he should have said, "Fine suspended," or anything. You understand what I mean? But he didn't say a damn word. He just sit there and let it go. Then too the union never got me a job in my life. I paid my dues, sit down there goddamned day in and day out, never got a job in my life. Boys just drive in town to get jobs. It overlooked me, so I felt pretty bad towards the union. Then I was trying to play jazz too, and I wasn't doing no good at that. Progressive jazz.

This is when you had a small band for about seven years?

Mm hmm. It was in Chicago, yeah. So I got disgusted. Went in one night and the goddamned plug was in my door–I couldn't get in my door because I hadn't paid my rent. A lot of things happened to me, man, very disgust-

"Big Bill was a hell of a man," Shines insisted. "He and Tampa Red were mountain of men towards musicians." Here's Big Bill Broonzy in 1925, with an elegant Gibson Style-0.

ing. I just got disgusted and just took this shit and said, "Man, I give it up." Carried it to a pawnshop and got me $100 on it. That was about '54.

What was it like when you first got to Chicago in September 1941?

A lot of guys was playing then–Big Bill Broonzy was playing, Arthur Crudup was playing, Tampa Red was playing. Dr. Clayton was singing somewhere, Memphis Slim was singing somewhere. Memphis Minnie and Son Joe was play-

ing somewhere. Everybody was playing, so pretty soon I got started playing. It wasn't bad.

Did you usually work by yourself or with another guitarist?

I played with a piano player. I didn't need no other guitar player.

When you were growing up in Helena, Arkansas, weren't there several two-guitar teams in town?

Oh, yeah. June Clay and Ollie Burks–they was good.

They was good as a team. They was two stepbrothers.

Did you know them when you were young?

Mm hmm. Yeah.

How old were you when you started playing?

I really was 16 when I started playing, but I didn't turn professional until I was about 17.

Did you play anything before that?

I played a little organ as a kid. Gospel music, you know.

Where did you get such a powerful voice?

I don't know.

Is it from singing in places without electricity?

No. I've always had a powerful voice. When I was a little boy like this [*holds hand a few feet above ground*], I used to stand and squeal. You know how children squeal? Just squeal–*heeeee.* And people could hear me for a half a mile. Just like a person whistles, that's the way I squeal, you know. Same sound. I could call my auntie from over here and my uncle from over there.

Did you ever hear people refer to blues as devil's music?

Ah, yes, I did. When I was a kid, a person heard you singing the blues like from here over to that mountain over there [*waves to an outcropping about a half-mile away*], if they heard you singing the blues and recognized your voice, you couldn't go down their house, around their daughters.

Is that why bluesmen traveled around?

No, that wasn't why they was travelin' around. They was travelin' around to make paydays and things like that, where there was cash money being out.

Was most of the work on the street or in clubs and road-houses?

There wasn't many roadhouses at that time. There was little clubs. You see, after Prohibition was broke, whiskey come back. And then you could go into little taverns and play. But you went in on your own; they wasn't hiring you. There was many times when I just went in and sit down, and the guy said, "You play?" "Yeah." "Sit over there and play us a tune." You sit there and play all night, long as people are pitchin' in nickels and dimes. Sit there and make yourself seven or eight dollars, and that was good money in those days. People work for much less than that for a week.

What were the first songs you learned?

"Jim String," "Bumblebee Blues," "Rollin' And Tumblin'." "Jim String"–that was a song about a pimp and his whore. He killed his whore, and that's what the song's all about. "Jim String killed Lulu one Friday night."

Did you learn slide and fingerpicking at the same time?

Well, yes, I did. See, my picking–I don't know whether you notice or not, most people think it's two guitars when I'm picking by myself. Well, that's because I learned to carry my own background by using two fingers and a thumb. I

learned to carry my own background.

By carrying a steady bass beat with your thumb.

Mm hmm.

When you were young, who showed you things on guitar?

My brother was a guitar player. He tried to show me how to play the "Bumblebee Blues," and I learned that from him. "Jim String"–I learned that from him. "Rollin' And Tumblin'"–I learned that from him. But when it come to the heavy stuff, I had to go to somebody else, like Willie B. Burnam or Willie Tango or Eddie Vann, some of those guys. They'd show it to me. Willie Tango was a boy around the Memphis area. He was one of the good ones. Played a lot of the popular numbers and jazz and things like that.

When did people refer to you as Little Wolf?

That was when I first started to playing. Now, you see, I was playing mostly songs that Wolf was singing, and other people. Because I didn't know too many other songs. And when I started, I started on Wolf's guitar.

How did that happen?

Wolf set his guitar down to take a break, and I sit there and watched him that night. I said to myself, "Hell, I can do what Wolf's doin'," so I picked his guitar up and started to frailin' the hell out of it, you know, singin' this song. So Wolf came back and I had the joint jumpin'–everybody was dancin', just like it was when he was playin'. I set the guitar down. Before that, they called me Jim String. After that, they started calling me Little Wolf. All around through the country, they called me Little Wolf. And when I started playing professionally, they still called me Little Wolf. But the Little Wolf died out. It was Johnny Shines, Johnny Shines, Johnny Shines, you know.

What other musicians did you know when you were coming up in Helena?

Well, Houston Stackhouse was about the only somebody until I met Robert Johnson.

You met Robert Johnson a little later, right?

Yeah.

Around '35 or something.

Yes.

Through a piano player?

M&O.

I brought you a gift. [*Shines is handed a framed 5x7 print of the Robert Johnson photo that had just been published for the first time in* Rolling Stone *issue #467.*]

Thank you, thank you, thank you. Thank you, thank you, thank you. [*Stares intently at it for about 20 seconds.*] Yes, sir.

Did you have a copy of that?

No, I didn't. I'm really glad to get this.

Is that the guy?

That's him. That's him. [*Long pause.*] Yes, it's him.

Do you remember that guitar?

No, I don't.

Looks like a Gibson or Kalamazoo.

No, I don't remember. It might be the one that we bought in Steele, Missouri. We bought a flat-top in Steele, Missouri. This is not a archtop, but he really liked that archtop.

Cigarette smoker too.

Mm hmm. Yeah.

Was he a little man?

Yeah, he was slender.

Was he as tall as you?

Just about.

What would he have thought if he could have foreseen how much his music would come to mean to people, that a half-century later he'd be regarded with the same respect as Charlie Parker or John Coltrane?

To me, he was just as great as Charlie Parker. The man did everything they did–whatsoever you did on a horn or on a piano, he figured he could do on a guitar, and he did it. And he didn't look for it, either. I never seen him practice. I never seen him look for nothin'. He'd just sit down, tune a guitar, and play it. Whatever you wanted him to play, he'd play it. I never seen him look for a chord. I know many chords he never heard of, because he couldn't read music, but he could make them.

Could he read or write?

Yeah, he could. But I didn't know this until just a few years ago, because he didn't write anything. I never saw him pick up a newspaper and try to read it.

Did you do much two-guitar music together?

No, he didn't like that.

How would it work?

He'd go one way, and I'd go the other. We'd work in the streets. I'd go over here and start playing, and he'd go over there and start playing. He'd draw his gang; I'd draw mine.

What would you use for a slide?

A bottleneck. You'd find or buy a long-neck bottle and just break it off–get some pliers on there and break it off down where you could use it.

Did you see Robert do that?

Yeah. I did it too.

Did you know Son House?

I learned of Son House later in years. I didn't know him too long before he died.

One of the players you and Robert both admired was

"When I was a kid, a person heard you singing the blues and recognized your voice, you couldn't go down their house, around their daughters."

Lonnie Johnson. Was he one of the top guitar players in those days?

Him? Was he one of the top ones? He was the top. I remember one record of his was strictly jazz, and boy, he was so goddamned fast–whoo! With a straight pick. See, he use a straight pick like another man uses three fingers. I've seen guitar players use three fingers wasn't as fast as him.

Did you use a pick in the early days?

Yeah, I always did use fingerpicks. I used flatpicks a little, though, if I had to. But I always use fingerpicks.

What kind of fingerpicks did they have in the '30s?

Metal ones.

Guitar strings must have been pretty different back then.

You broke up a lot of guitar strings, because at that time I didn't know how to play in all the keys. And I had to use a capo to change keys lots of times, so that was hard on a guitar string–wrapping them down, and tuning with the clamp on, pullin' 'em and backing off of 'em. The guitar strings would rattle and break.

Did you have a store-bought capo?

Make one yourself, or you could buy one. You could take a pencil and string. Put the pencil on the neck, wrap the string around it on the back side, pull it up tight. Just as good as any capo.

When you and Robert Johnson were traveling together, what would you do when you first got to a town?

Just try to find out where the black neighborhood was. Walk up and down the railroad track and just watch to see which side the black kids are on. Whichever side we find the black kids on, that's the side we go, 'cause that was the black side. All the towns was segregated then–whites on one side of the tracks, blacks on the other one.

Did you both have guitars?

Mm hmm. And your clothes that was on you.

What would an average playing day be?

All day, if the money was still hoppin', because we didn't have no particular place to go. As long as there's nickels and dimes afloat. When they quit, then we'd just walk on.

Were there any places where you did especially well?

St. Louis was a profitable town. Memphis was a good town. Memphis was always good. You never got to be too well known in Memphis. I'd go down to Handy's Park, play with the guys down there. Now, a guy over here have a big crowd, and we'd strike up over there and probably pull half his crowd or all of his crowd. If you pull all of his crowd, that's what we called "headcuttin'," you know–we just cut his head! Yeah.

In past interviews, you've mentioned that Robert Johnson played polka music on guitar.

Yeah.

Even today, not many people do that well.

[*Laughs.*] Well, you had to do it. You see, when I come along playing guitar, lots of times you wake up in the morning and you didn't have no money at all. Somebody ask you to play a song, maybe they'd give you a dollar for that song. That meant about four meals off of a dollar, 'cause you could get a meal for a quarter or 30¢. And if you couldn't play that song, you miss that money. So you had to learn to play some of everything you heard. If we passed a place, a white dancing hall, and the big bands was playing in there, whatsoever kind of music they was playing, we used to have to listen to. Hide around outside and listen. So we'd go home, and when we get ready, we'd play those same pieces.

That's why your Dukes Of Swing learned Lionel Hampton tunes.

Mm hmm. "Flying Home." "Hey Ba-Ba-Re-Bop." Things like that that was popular at that time.

So when you were working the streets, you'd only play a blues once in a while.

Lot of popular songs in between. Whatsoever the people seemed like they enjoyed more.

Did you play for whites?

Mm hmm.

Have you ever heard of stages being split, with whites on one side, blacks on the other, and musicians in the middle?

I never played that kind of stage. When we played for a white audience, it was a white audience. Played for a black audience, it was a black audience. When we played for Polish people, we had to play Polish music.

Did you learn to sing any of those songs, or was it always instrumental?

Well, yeah, some of them I learned, like "Beer Barrel Polka," "Too Fat Polka." Several I know, as well as a few Jewish tunes. We had to learn them too. Yeah.

Did you ever carry a gun during your rambling days?

Mm hmm. But not too much, because you subjected to being attacked by the police at any time. If you had a gun on you, why then you went to jail for carryin' a gun, see.

Did Robert carry one?

No, Robert wouldn't carry a gun huntin'.

Was he a peaceable person?

Until he started drinking. He started drinking, he'd do any goddanged thing. Wasn't nothin' too good for him to do.

What did he like to drink?

Why, wasn't nothing but one thing to drink, and that was

that fist-made liquor at that time. Corn liquor. And Ten High when the bonded liquor come in, Ten High and Dixie Dew. Those cheap brands of whiskey. We drank that 'cause that's what we was able to buy. We'd buy a better brand once in a while, such as Old Taylor and Old Grand Dad.

Were you ever much of a drinker?

That's all I would do. Yeah. I had the habit when I went to bed, I had the habit when I woke up, I had the habit when I got up.

Was this when you were younger, or all through your life?

Pretty well all through my life, but younger some.

You talk about hopping freights. Does that mean jumping into an empty boxcar?

Whatsoever. If an empty boxcar was handy, we'd get in it. If it was not, we'd get *on* it.

And then you're stuck riding it until it stops.

Mm hmm, yeah. Or somebody hit you upside the head [*laughs*].

Do you remember that as a good time of your life?

Well, it was some of the best of the times. Yeah, because I had to make my own way through my own skills. I felt more freer then than at any other time. But now, if I got into a town like tonight–on a Monday night–by Thursday I'd have me a job somewhere. Because at that time the police was bad about picking you up for vagrancy. I always had a job to go to. "Where you work at?" "I work at such-and-such a place." "How long you been there?" "Oh, two or three days." He knew when you went there and everything, because if you was a stranger, everybody knew you was a stranger in town. Everybody knew everything you did in those small towns like that. Just tell them you're working at a gas station, car wash, gin, or anything.

Was there ever a time when you supported yourself solely as a musician?

Yes, those was the times. Before Chicago, when I was traveling up and down the road. Those are the times when I was living solely as a musician, with the exception I was getting these small jobs–dishwashing, busing dishes, or something like that. That way I could say I had a job.

Did the guitar seem to be part of your soul back then?

Well, it was. See, these jobs was just some sideline, just something to keep the police off of me. But I was living off the guitar. I'd come in and get off of work in the evening, come and get my guitar and walk down the street, be playing real slow. Somebody go, "Hey! Come over here!" I go, and that's where we pitched the party at. They'd slip me a dollar that night, and I wasn't getting that much for a week's work. I was getting $4.75 or something like that for a week's work.

What were your favorite guitars back then?

Well, I had a little black Regal guitar, and then later on I had a Kalamazoo like Robert had. We both had it. The Kalamazoo was a Gibson with a flaw in it. The Kalamazoo had f-holes in it.

Did you want an archtop because it was louder?

Yeah. Had more body to it.

Did you have a case for it?

No, we didn't have no case.

Just throw it over your back?

Mm hmm.

Did you or Robert spend much time playing guitar when no one else was listening?

No.

You reportedly played "get-backs" during the 1930s. What are those?

Say, for an instant, you live here and you sell corn whiskey. On Saturday night, you're going to have a get-back. You just take the bed and things down, probably throw sand on the floor–that was one way of washing a floor, put sand on the floor. And you put a crap table in the back room, card table somewheres else so you can play cards, and then a dance floor and the musicians in the main room. You'd put a table or a door across something and sell fried fish.

You've also said that some of the places you and Robert played were so tough that they'd only serve in paper cups.

Yeah, I was playing at a place like that down in Memphis. A guy got to fighting with two other guys and one of the guys' wife. That woman cut his guts out. She cut him down. I'm quite sure she killed him. Me and Walter Horton just picked up our stuff and walked out. We saw him get cut, and he fell. Walter and I just walked out, because we knew he was just about dead. She cut his guts out.

There's another story that you and Robert lost some guitars in a fire.

That was West Memphis. Robert and I walked out to get some food or something, and on our way back we looked up and saw this place afire. I said, "Robert, that look like where we live at." He said, "Yeah, it sure do." Sure enough, got there,

Johnny tours Germany, October 1979.

that's what it was. Hunts Hotel–this black fellow had a little place there, nothing but a rooming house. Paper walls and things like that. Rooming houses ain't worth a shit. You could fart in your room and deafen the fellow in the other room [*laughs*].

Was Johnson known as Robert Spencer or Robert Dodds?

Johnson is all I ever knew. He didn't tell me anything about this Spencer and Dodds and all that shit. His stepfather was what he talked about.

Did he like him?

Yes, he did. But now, to be talking about his stepfather, I never knew which one of his stepfathers he was talking about.

Do you know any of his relatives?

Yes, I know one of his sisters.

Were you aware of his records during his lifetime?

Mm hmm. Hear 'em on jukeboxes. He was very proud of having it. In fact, the idea was to get out there–which was a damn good idea, being able to get out there.

I think of Robert Johnson as being one of the first people to play rock and roll.

Well, I know he played rock and roll. It was the same beat, but it just wasn't called rock and roll. That's all.

Did you ever sense that he was going to have a short life?

Who, Robert? No, I never did. It was very hard when I heard he was dead. I just couldn't believe it.

There was sure a lot of mystery around it.

Well, yes, there was. Tell you the truth about it, Honeyboy Edwards was the one who confirmed it with me that he was dead. See, Sonny Boy said Robert died in his arms. Sonny Boy [Williamson II] was such a big liar. Rice Miller, yeah, such a big liar. He speaked lying lies. Still couldn't believe that Robert was dead. I looked any day to walk up on him somewhere as I traveled around. Since I been playing professionally, since I made my comeback, I look any day to walk up on Robert or Robert walk up on me.

Do you ever feel his presence?

Many times. Many times.

Did he have any favorite sayings? Was he a hip-talking guy?

He talked really hip. Of course, we all did because that was the present language at that time. Like, "Yeah, man," you know, or "Look, daddy so-and-so" and "Look, baby so-and-so"–like that. I still use that. I call you baby, honey, and things like that, which I know you're not my baby, you're not a honey, but it's just something that comes out that way. And lots of people look at me like, "Is he funny?" [*Laughs.*]

Tell us about playing The Elder Moten Hour *radio show with Robert Johnson.*

He was a preacher, and he broadcasted out of Canada. Lots of people could pick him up back over there in Detroit and all over Canada. He was a sanctified preacher, and he wanted a lot of music with his outfit, you know. He had a pretty good-sized choir. Robert, Calvin, and myself, we go over there and play for him. Calvin Frazier was my first cousin; he had to leave the United States.

You played blues on a preacher's show?

No! No, no [*laughs*]. No, no, no. I was playing gospel music.

Do you remember what songs?

Yes. Regular old gospel songs, like "Ship Of Zion," "Stand By Me," "When The Saints Go Marchin' In," "Just Over In Glory Land," songs like that.

Did Robert Johnson write "Take A Closer Walk With Me"?

No, no. Robert didn't write that. "Just A Closer Walk With Thee"? No, Robert didn't write that. We met that song on the road.

Do you know the inspiration for any of Robert's songs? What caused him to write them?

No, I really don't. I really don't.

He's got that line, "She's got a Elgin movement from her head down to her toes, break in on a dollar most anywhere she goes."

Well, playing for dances and things like that, you see people dancing, movin' on the floor, you know. You gets inspiration from that.

What about "Terraplane Blues"? Did he have one?

No, but that was a hell of a car at that time. Fast. Supposed to have been a pretty good car, you know. I think that Studebaker was making it first; I don't know. But I know Hudson was the last one made a Terraplane. Terraplane Hudson.

Was it true that Johnson could hear something once or twice and then…

He could hear it once; not twice–once. Just like we're sitting here talking now, the radio be playing. Robert heard something on the radio he liked, he never stopped talking with you. Keep right on talking to you. Tonight or tomorrow or sometime or another, he'd pick up his guitar and play the song, note-for-note, chord-for-chord, word-for-word. He was way before his time, that's all. The man had to go. He was a genius. See, I say he was a genius because chords and things that he'd never heard before, he'd hear it on the radio, and he never tried to look for that chord. He'd just pick up a guitar and make it.

Would you keep your guitars in an open tuning?

Regular tuning, most time.

Even for slide?

No. We'd tune them in open *G* or open *A* for bottleneck. Open *D, E.* Open *A* was called Vastopol.

What advice would you give someone who wants to learn to play slide, especially on acoustic? What are the important things to know?

Learn all the chords along with the slide. Learn the chords which is the accompaniment to the slide. Learn that, and learn how to place the slide. And then he go from there.

Should you should wear the slide on your little finger or ring finger?

Wear it on the finger that you're most comfortable with. I'm most comfortable wearing it on my little finger.

So you can chord with your other fingers?

Mm hmm.

Is it a good idea to lay your other fingers on the strings behind the slide, or do you like the sound without it?

Well, it depends on what you want to do. If you want to heel [damp with the heel of the hand], why then you heel behind the slide. If you don't, why then you just let the slide ring.

When did you get your first electric guitar?

I bought a Kalamazoo in Chicago, another Kalamazoo, and I used a DeArmond pickup on it, which electrified it. That was in '41, '42.

Was Robert Nighthawk already in town?

Well, he came to town. He wasn't already there. He had been there, though. Robert Nighthawk and Honeyboy had been every goddamned where up and down the Mississippi River, north and south.

Is it fair to say that Muddy Waters is the person most responsible for changing the sound of blues in Chicago?

I think Muddy used his style, which was a Mississippi style, of singing. And he changed the style of music, through Willie Dixon. See, a lot of people don't give Willie Dixon no credit for things that happened. Willie Dixon was the man that changed the style of the blues in Chicago. As a songwriter and producer, that man is a genius. Yes, sir. You want a hit song, go to Willie Dixon. Play it like he say play it and sing it like he say sing it–even Willie Dixon can't sing a lick, but just find out what he's talking about and do it–you damn near got a hit.

What were your impressions of Muddy's old bandmate, Leroy Foster?

Leroy Foster was a hell of a guy. Baby Face Leroy, yeah. He was fun, man [*laughs*]. That son of a bitch started lying, he'd get up on one foot and started walking off on one foot, you know, turn his foot that way, and he'd do that for half a block, hopping on one foot! [*Laughs.*] He was lying and carrying on!

What kind of a guy was Tampa Red?

Tampa Red was one of the best guys there ever was. Very good-natured. Kind person. Open-minded.

Sure was close to his wife.

Yes, he was. Those two people was close to each other.

Did you know Big Bill Broonzy?

Oh, yeah. Big Bill was fun. Big Bill was a hell of a man. Very helpful. Tampa Red, same way. Those two guys were

mountain of men towards musicians.

Did you know Memphis Minnie?

Oh, yeah. Yeah, she was good.

Was there something where you two didn't get along?

No, no. We got along. I never had no problem–none whatsoever.

Why didn't you play slide on your early sessions?

I didn't want to. I was pickin' pretty good then.

What's the best band you ever played in?

The best band I ever had was the Dukes Of Swing.

Did you do any Mississippi-style blues with that band?

I did. With them, it could be arranged in that way. Yeah.

Did you have a regular club gig in Chicago, or did you move around?

Well, yes, I played at a regular place. Frost's Corner–I played there. That was on the North Side. I played at Tom's Tavern–Sunnyland and I played there for a heck of a long time. Then I played out in Robbins; that's when I had the Dukes Of Swing. We played out there for about three years. It really was a club. A few people did dance, but most of the people come there to listen and drink, have a good time.

Did you play slide guitar with that band?

Mm hmm.

Did it come as a surprise when white people started to pick up on blues during the '60s?

Well, that's when it become rock and roll. I'm quite sure it was quite a surprise to most of us. Because a lot of us said we wasn't gonna play no rock and roll. Certain men that said they'll never play rock and roll, they're playing rock and roll now.

Do you still perceive a segment of black society that doesn't approve of blues?

Well, yeah, you got a lot of black people that don't go for blues. It's because they think the blues is a degraded kind of music towards black people. Not because they don't like it–they *say* they don't like it, you know. Just like when I was working at Raytheon. A bunch of girls there found out I was in music. "You don't play that Muddy Waters stuff, do ya?" I said, "Yes, I do. Same stuff Muddy Waters is playing–that's what I play." "Ah, I don't like that. I like jazz." "Okay, then, go to with your jazz."

So one night I got off kind of early, and I went by the 708 Club where Muddy was playing at. And all those girls, that's where they was. So when I walked in, they started hiding their face behind the table. So quick as I walked in, Muddy called me, "Come on up here! Come on up here and get this guitar. Come on up here and get this guitar." I went on up

> "*I had the habit when I went to bed, I had the habit when I woke up, I had the habit when I got up.*"

and got to playing good, and the heads popped up, you know. [*Laughs.*] I said, "I'm glad to see a lot of our friends here that I work with out at Raytheon, even though I know they don't like blues, but they here for some reason. I don't know what the reason is." I said, "Muddy, you're a great man. You draw people out here that say they don't like blues."

It must have surprised them to find out who you were.

Yeah, it did. That Monday when I went to work, a lot of people, they stayed way back from me, because they was afraid I was going to say something about, "I saw you Saturday night, I saw you Saturday night!" But I wouldn't do that. I wouldn't say nothing to them. I just went on about my business, doing what I was doing. So finally two or three come over, "Mr. Shines, we think your playing's nice."

Why did you move back to Alabama?

Well, my daughter died and left a bunch of kids, and I had a problem rentin' in Chicago. And we was staying in a kitchenette, and there just wasn't room for them. We had to make some better arrangements, so my wife, she went to Alabama on a vacation. She found this house down there, and she called me back and told me about it. I asked her if she like it, she said yes. I said, well, then get it. So she got it, and I just packed up everything and moved on down there.

Did you raise the children?

Mm hmm. Yes. There was seven of them. And one of my own made eight. Three adults–my wife, my mother, and myself.

Never a dull moment.

No. It was fun, though. That wife and I stayed together about 16, 17 years. I been surrounded by kids all the days of my life.

You had the Stars Of Alabama for a while during the '70s. Was that a blues band?

It was a band, period. Not just a blues band.

Was The Velvet Vampire *film soundtrack recorded in Hollywood?*

Yes, it was. It was recorded in Hollywood.

Was that almost like a soft-core porn flick?

Well, I really don't know what the meaning.

Was it a naked vampire girl movie?

No, no, I wouldn't say naked, but you could tell it was related to being naked and things like that. What it was, this woman she come in, this man is sitting there playing the guitar, you know, and singing the blues. She sits down, and it affects her mind, you know. She begin to think about these things as he's singing about it. Whatsoever he was singing about, that's the way her mind made, you understand what I mean? But she finally recovers herself and walks out, and that's when many other things begin to happen, you know.

Did you just do the title song, or…

That's all.

Did it come out on a record?

No, no. It never did.

During the '70s you recorded for several different labels. Do you like the one you did in England?

I did do one for Blue Horizon. Yes, I like that one. I thought it was a pretty good record. A lot of different companies copied some of the tunes off of it, puttin' them on their label. Now, that's one way of telling whether your record is good or not–if other companies want to put 'em on their label.

Are you getting royalties from any of your records?

Shoot, no.

Have you written any songs lately?

Saturday. I don't remember the title [*laughs*].

What are your best songs, the songs you'd most like to be remembered for?

Well, I really don't know. That's one–"I Don't Know." And "A Little Tenderness"–I'll probably be remembered for that one. "Ain't Nobody's Fault But Mine," which is a gospel song; people think it's a blues. "Evening Sun." Those are the songs the rest of the people learned, most of them.

It's amazing how the blues transcends time and race to speak to so many people on so many levels.

You see, blues don't have no race. Blues don't have no level. The blues is just like death. Everybody is going to have the blues. If they haven't already had 'em, they're gonna have 'em. Because everybody is going to have some bad luck in their life. They are going to be confronted with fortunes unexpected–one way or the other. The blues is only a thought, anyway.

It's not just about hard times, though. It's about seduction, about…

About everything. That's right. You see, whatsoever touches the heart is where the blues come from. Say, for instance, a man might go out here to the racetrack and win $15,000 or $20,000 at the racetrack. Well, he'll have a happy blues, because he's happy from the heart on out, from the inside out. And the man go out there and lose all his money–his wife has told him she gonna quit him if he lose his money again–he got a different blues. [*Laughs.*]

What kind of blues do you have now?

Right now I got the I wanna go home blues [*laughs*]. But I knew that was coming. I knew that was coming before I left home.

Did you do much playing before this tour?

Yeah. I played the Chucker, I played the Getaway. My wife played the Getaway Friday night. The Chucker, the Getaway, and the L&N–I play those three joints in Tuscaloosa.

....standin' at the crossroads.

Johnny Shines

Publicity shot, early '70s: "Whatsoever touches the heart is where the blues come from."

COURTESY STEVE LAVERE, PHOTO ARCHIVES, MIMOSA RECORDS PRODUCTIONS, INC.

Because I thought I'd get more action out of the Alvarez than I was with the Gibson. The Gibson was a very popular guitar–easy to handle and everything–but I thought I'd get more action out of the Alvarez.

What are your plans for the future?

Well, I really wants to get myself together and buy me a nice small farm someplace, preferably a 10-acre farm, where I can put a nice catfish lake on it and a nice trout lake, you know. Let people come and fish, have fun. I like to see people enjoy themselves.

You'll probably always be interested in music.

Oh, yes. I love music. See, I could hear something good in all kinds of music. Makes me no difference what it is–jazz, pop, rock, ballads, gospel, symphony. Don't make no difference. If it isn't the arrangement, it's some kind of beat or something, a rundown or something. A stationary chord or a movable chord. I can always hear something in music that's good to me. Yep, I love all music. I can listen to all music. Some people say, "I can't stand this. I can't stand bluegrass." Heck, I like bluegrass and mountain music.

How many nights a year are you playing?

Oh, about 30 or 40.

After playing for close to 60 years, what are your views on the guitar?

Well, guitar is a wonderful instrument, if you're learning to use it effectively. Now, the acoustic guitar I traded off for the one I got here now, I was just thinking about it. I bought a home and fed 11 people and clothed them, just out of that little round hole there. I went to England with it, come back, and I went to Germany with it, come back. I went to Sweden with it, come back. That means a lots to me, that guitar does. I traded off for this one here, and I'm gonna get it back. That was a Gibson B-25.

Why did you swap that guitar for the Alvarez you're now playing?

Do you ever regret becoming a bluesman?

No, not really.

Was it worth it?

Well, the experience have been worth it, yes. Like the crowd we had Saturday night [in Los Angeles]–I enjoys a crowd like that. I can sing better to them, and I can play better to them. Oh, yeah, they was dancing. Hell of a damn nice crowd–four hundred and some people. So I enjoyed that. I don't really enjoys playing these small clubs where only 50 or 100 people in there, 'cause I feel like when I got a big crowd like that, I know they come to dance. They come because they wanted to hear me. When I got 50 people in the damn club, I don't know whether they was going to come anyway or not, 'cause they may be regular patrons of the place.

What compliment do you appreciate the most after a gig?

Like we played here the other night. One of the greatest compliments was we sold a box of tapes [*laughs*]. Now, that was telling you something, you know. That's better than spoken words, you know–people appreciate your music well enough to buy a whole box of tapes.

Why are Europeans so enamored with the blues?

I'll tell you the truth about it. Those people think that black people are still in bondage over here. Yes, sir, they do. They think we're being told when to go and when to come, how to go and how to come, and everything. They think we're still being whipped at the stake. Even though we are still slaves to the system, but there's another master other than the slaveholder. You're a slave to the system. And even the slaveholder is a slave to his own system, because that's the way the guy was raised.

Talking about the blues, I would like for people to know that the average thing that they listen to really is not the blues. What we call the Delta blues is not blues. It's storytelling. It's something that have happened in somebody's life that they're telling a story about. Say, for an instant, if I walked up to you, and you was fixing to catch a bus and go to work. I tell ya, "My house burned down last night and burnt up three of my children." You say, "Yes, I'll listen to you later. Say, here comes my bus now. I'll see you." You get on your bus and go. But now tonight, when I put music to it, you pay $10 to hear me tell the same story I tried to tell you for free over there at the bus stop. Same story! See?

These what I call blues come out of the story of peoples in slavery time. We're telling the same story now that they was tellin' back there, only it was in a different time. You see, then they went out and walked. Like a song I have, I say, "If a rich man get the blues, he can charter himself a plane and ride. But a poor man get the blues, he walks until he gets satisfied." Same story back then.

When did blues as we know it begin? In the 1890s?

Well, as far as the year is concerned, nobody knows. And they don't know where it come from.

Do you think it started with Charley Patton?

I don't thinks Charley Patton started it. I think the blues was being played before Charley Patton. Because if not, where did Charley Patton get it from? See, Charley Patton could tune a guitar in open tuning; he could play it in straight tuning. And he had to learn that from somebody, because before Charley Patton and lots of others, we only knew cross-tunings, such as open tunings. Because we didn't know how to tune the guitar; we didn't know how to make the chords. G, A, B, D, C, to E, something like that–we didn't know how to make those chords. We only knew how to play with the bottleneck. See, everybody think the bottleneck is something new. The bottleneck was the first guitar playing that the black people did, because he didn't know how to chord a guitar. So he tuned a guitar to open tuning, and he used a slide to make his chords.

Did that come from the Hawaiian music craze or from Africa?

It come from Africa. Matter of fact, all your American music come out of the bowels of slaves. All your American music.

It's amazing that a group of people who were so held down created something that's enriched us all.

Yes, sir. Well, the old saying is, "You can't take what is good and keep it. You've got to share it." And the old saying that "You can't keep a good man down"–the black people have been rising ever since they hit here. Yes, sir.

[*Johnny Shines passed away on April 20, 1992, in Tuscaloosa, Alabama, where he'd lived since 1969.*]

A SELECTED JOHNNY SHINES DISCOGRAPHY

Solo albums: *Johnny Shines And Robert Lockwood: Dust My Broom* (complete J.O.B. sides), Flyright; *Masters Of Modern Blues Volume 1–The Johnny Shines Band* ('66), Testament; *Johnny Shines With Big Walter Horton* ('66/'69) Testament; *Johnny Shines* ('70), Hightone; *Standing At The Crossroads* (solo, '70), Testament; *Sitting On Top Of The World*, Biograph; *Johnny Shines And Co.*, Biograph; *Traditional Delta Blues* (solo acoustic, '72-'74), Biograph; *Mr. Cover Shaker* (with David Bromberg's band, '74), Biograph; *Nobody's Fault But Mine*, Black And Blue; *Johnny Shines*, P-Vine; *Hey Ba-Ba-Re-Bop* (acoustic, '74), Rounder; *Recorded Live* (St. Louis, '74), Wolf; *Too Wet To Plow* ('75), Tomato; *Country Blues* (live with acoustic group, '78), JSP; *Johnny Shines And Friends* (cassette with Bart Pate on guitar, '88), PTP; *Back To The Country* (with Snooky Pryor, '91), Blind Pig.

With Robert Lockwood, Jr. (on Rounder): *Robert Jr. Lockwood & Johnny Shines*; *Hangin' On* ('80); *Mister Blues Is Back To Stay.*

Anthologies: *OKeh Chicago Blues*, Epic; *Chicago Blues: The Beginning*, Testament; *Chicago/The Blues/Today!*, Vanguard; *Drop Down Mama*, Chess; *Atlantic Blues: Guitar*, Atlantic; *Chicago Slickers 1948-1953*, Nighthawk; *Chicago Slickers, Vol. 2* ('53), Nighthawk; *Windy City Blues*, Nighthawk; *The Story Of The Blues*, Columbia; *The Great Blues Men*, Vanguard; *Ann Arbor Blues & Jazz Festival 1972*, Atlantic; *Country Blues Classics, Volume 2*, Blues Classics; *Chicago Blues Anthology*, MCA; *Blues Masters, Volume 2: Postwar Chicago*, Rhino; *Chess Blues* box set; *Rural Blues*, Zeta; *Chicago Blues: A Quarter Century*, P-Vine; *Roots Of Rhythm And Blues: A Tribute To Robert Johnson* ('92), Columbia.

Soundtracks: *The Velvet Vampire* ('71).

On film: *Roots Of American Music* (produced by the University of Washington School of Music, '71); *Good Mornin' Blues* (produced in '78 by Mississippi ETV, available from Yazoo Video); *Mississippi Delta Blues* (Freedom Village concert, produced by the Mississippi Center For Educational Television, '80); *Johnny Shines On And On* (PBS documentary, '89); *The Search For Robert Johnson* (Sony Music Video, '92). Mr. Shines also appeared on PBS' *Lonesome Pine.*

Robert Lockwood, Jr.

July 1991

BY PETER LEE

ONE DAY WHEN ROBERT JOHNSON was taking a break from his roaming, he sat down to make a guitar with his young pupil Robert Lockwood, Jr. What they made wasn't a diddley bow, the one-string instrument many fledgling bluesmen built by stretching a piece of wire between two nails. Johnson and Lockwood were intent on building something more sophisticated. Johnson shaped the wood, and then made the body from a phonograph. Lockwood, who had been happily strumming away on Johnson's Stella, used the guitar for just over a year before it began to tear apart because "we couldn't get the right type of glue."

At that time, Lockwood, now 76, was 13 years old, and Johnson had been teaching him his tunes for nearly two years. The pupil/teacher relationship started when Johnson followed Lockwood's mother home to Helena, Arkansas. Lockwood's parents, Esther and Robert, Sr., had separated in Memphis when he was a small child. (While he has sometimes been referred to as Robert Jr. Lockwood, he prefers the proper order of Robert Lockwood, Jr.)

Robert Lockwood, Jr., already had some musical training when Johnson suddenly appeared on the scene. At about eight or nine years old, he started on organ, surreptitiously playing blues when his fraternal grandfather was away from the house. "I learned the organ first," he says. "I was 'round eight, nine years old. I was just playing at home. I had two cousins who could play, and I learned from them. And I was just playing at home when my grandfather was gone, 'cause I couldn't play when he was there 'cause he was a preacher. I liked the blues and was playing them on organ. We all played them on organ. My grandfather didn't know it. My grandmama wouldn't tell him. Another thing was my uncles on my daddy's side wouldn't tell him. Neither one of them. My grandmama on my mama's side wouldn't tell him nothing."

It's a familiar blues musician's tale–trying to learn secular material in a religious environment. But Robert Johnson's appearance changed Lockwood's course, and changed it radically. "And then Robert Johnson came along," Lockwood continues. "He taught me how to play guitar. He followed my mama home. That's how I first met him. She couldn't get rid of him. He hung around and hung around. He and my mama stayed together, off and on, ten years. My mother's home was his home. That's how I learned to play the guitar. I didn't want to play the guitar; I wanted to play the piano. But I learned how to play that guitar like Robert, and I didn't touch the organ no more."

King Biscuit Time, early 1940s.

© JON SIEVERT

Robert Johnson courted Lockwood's mother and taught him his first song.

Lockwood's stubborn streak of independence had him wanting to play an instrument without any backup. "I never did want help," he recalls. "Robert Johnson didn't need no help." Robert Johnson was more than willing to pass on his skills, something he was not known for with other musicians. In fact, he often tried to hide the chords he was playing from others. With teenaged Lockwood it was different. "He was one of the nicest people I ever met. He was very sharp, patient, and I figured he was just right, 'cause he showed me something that didn't leave. He taught me, period. My first thing I was playing was 'Sweet Home Chicago.' Yeah, that's the first thing Robert taught me. He started recording [in 1936], and I had them records around there to play."

After the first guitar fell apart, the bluesman says, "The next guitar I had was from my auntie Ethel. She bought it for me from Montgomery Ward. It was one of them Gene Autry guitars with the cowboy picture on it. It cost $3.98. I kept that for about four or five years." It was with this instrument that Lockwood started his professional career.

In the early '30s, downhome blues musicians made their living by playing for sharecroppers throughout the small farming communities of the South. They would travel around the plantations, entertaining at small jukes or at informal gatherings near the plantation stores. Traveling around playing the blues was a more lucrative occupation than the back-breaking toil of working the cotton fields. Lockwood joined the ranks of these bluesmen at an early age–he was only 15. But this was nothing unusual for the Deep South. Most children worked the fields, as their parents did. Those too young for hard labor were relegated to carrying water buckets back and forth among the thirsty workers. "I was playing by myself, like Robert," Lockwood explains. "I was going out in the country in the fall of the year, and I was playing till the people got through gathering their crop. We done made as much money as they done made all year."

Johnson, though, had prepared his pupil for life as an itinerant bluesman. "I played three gigs with Robert," Lockwood says. "I played what you call a hayride. A hayride is like you go camping and stuff like that. And I played a couple of joints in Mississippi–Saturday night things."

When the cotton crop had been gathered, musicians would work the Delta villages, the busy Mississippi River towns, and the Beale Street section of Memphis. They played for house parties, gatherings where people would drink and gamble on weekends. "They'd be shooting a little dice, drinking a little liquor, and dancing," recalls the bluesman. "There wasn't no big nightclubs or something like you have now. Well, they had some little gambling joints at that time that you couldn't call house parties 'cause people was gambling in them and there wasn't no sleeping. They had gambling tables and poker tables and stuff like that. Most of these places were wide open. It was legal. People would go to the gambling house just like you go work in the sawmills. There's a certain time to be there, a certain time to stay there, and a certain time to close up. Right here in Helena. The people who owned the place paid you to play."

When they weren't playing the joints or house parties, musicians would set up on street corners, relying on tips from passersby. Lockwood played the Arkansas towns of Helena and Elaine, and not much later, Friars Point and Clarksdale, in Mississippi. At 15, against the wishes of his mother, he was taken to Mississippi by Johnson's sometimes partner, harmonica player Sonny Boy Williamson II (Aleck Miller). "Sonny Boy was the first somebody that took me away from home," he remembers. "I went to Belzoni with him and went home with him and watched him help gather that crop 'round '31, something like that. My mama didn't want me to go to Mississippi. I don't know how he convinced her."

Nevertheless, Lockwood and Williamson teamed up to travel and play. "Oh, we'd go off to Mississippi or Arkansas, stay a couple of months or something like that, and come back home," the guitarist says. "We played different places, really nothing special. Sonny Boy wanted to gamble. He used to gamble a lot and lose his money. Sometimes he'd win. I showed him a few little things on the guitar, and he'd try to play 'em. He was a good harmonica player. Very good. Then I got separated from him 'cause I moved up north to St. Louis, and from St. Louis to Chicago. I didn't see Sonny Boy for a long time." The partnership lasted two or three years before they parted for the first time.

"They wouldn't record me in St. Louis," Lockwood states. "White folks had it sewed up. Wasn't no recording companies or labels for blacks in St. Louis." But once in Chicago, he made the first of many recordings, both as a sideman and under his own name. He also recorded a number of sides with Doc Clayton, a ukulele player who came to the States as a young child. "Doc Clayton could sing like hell. Very edu-

cated. He was from Africa. He said he was from Cape Town [South Africa], but I don't think he came from there. His people brought him here when he was about six or seven years old. But he was really educated. See, Doc Clayton got $5,000 out of RCA Victor, who Lester Melrose was working for. Then, people were only getting $50 for a whole record. That man [Melrose] just went wild over Clayton's voice. He didn't need no mike." The sessions Lockwood was on, however, were recorded for OKeh and included Blind John Davis on piano and an unknown musician on string bass. Recording and playing Clayton's blues was not unfamiliar to the guitarist, though, because Clayton, Davis, and Lockwood had worked together on the streets of St. Louis before they headed for Chicago.

Robert Lockwood, Jr., then recorded for Bluebird under his own name, accompanied by bass player Alfred Elkins. "I went to Chicago to record for Decca, and Mayo Williams [Decca's A&R man] was in New York," he recalls. "When he [Williams] come back, we had done recorded for RCA Victor, and he was mad. 'Little Boy Blue' and 'Take A Little Walk With Me' was on one, and 'I'm Gonna Train My Baby' and 'Black Spider Blues' was on the other. The records were released in 1941."

But Chicago was more than just a recording trip. Lockwood sat in with a number of musicians who were turning the blues away from its Deep South country feel. "I played with Curtis Jones," he states. "I played Big Bill Broonzy's guitar with the group that Big Bill was playing with. Now, a lot of times Big Bill come down for intermission and tell me to finish the set, and he would just leave."

But the move to Chicago wasn't permanent, and Lockwood soon headed back to the South, teaming up again with Sonny Boy Williamson II. "I seen Sonny Boy again when I come back to Helena," he explains. "I recorded and come back home, and Sonny Boy was on *King Biscuit Time* [a radio show sponsored by Interstate Grocery]. We got back together again." Williamson had just landed the job on the new Helena radio station KFFA, playing solo harp during the live, 15-minute midday show. Lockwood, however, added more than just guitar to the lineup. "When we got on *King Biscuit Time* I had a drummer. Sonny Boy didn't want nobody. After about six or seven months, I hired James 'Peck' Curtis and bought him some drums. I was at *King Biscuit Time* a little better than two years ['41 to '43]."

The three musicians used the show not only to advertise their sponsor, but also to let listeners know where they would be playing during the week. In addition to their own gigs, they traveled Mississippi and Arkansas on a flatbed truck promoting King Biscuit Flour. "We used to go to little cities, play 30 minutes and stuff like that, go to another one, come back home, and then go to work," the bluesman remembers. But he was beginning to feel musically restricted. While on *King Biscuit Time*, Williamson had done most of the singing, and Lockwood, already using an electronic pickup before joining the show, was relegated to playing Sonny Boy's downhome blues material. "I was playing electric guitar just before. They had a DeArmond pickup then. I think me and Charlie Christian were the first people who played the electric guitar. They had the thing advertised in the catalog, and I just bought it. I had the money, you know. I was way ahead of my time, like Robert was." (Eddie Durham's solo on Jimmie Lunceford's "Hittin' The Bottle," 1935, is probably the first recorded example of any form of guitar amplification.)

Christian is often cited as an influence on Lockwood, but this is something he is quick to deny. "I never heard any of his records till he was dead," he offers. "You know he was playing with Benny Goodman. Me and Charlie Christian was playing the same type of licks. In the beginning Charlie Christian was a horn player [trumpet], but he had lung trouble and they told him he couldn't play it. So he laid the horn down, picked up the guitar, and transferred the horn down to the guitar."

Lockwood's earlier determination to be a self-reliant musician was coming to an end. "I know I'm the only one who gave Mr. Moore a notice when I got ready to leave *King Biscuit Time*," the guitarist states. "Everybody else just walked away; I gave him about six weeks' notice. 'Oh, where you going?' he asked. I said, 'I don't know where I'm going, but I'm going away from here.' He told Sonny Boy, 'Oh, he'll be back, he'll be back.' I didn't get a chance to leave the station because I had another program at four o'clock in the evening that paid three times the money what King Biscuit was. I advertised Mother's Best [a competing flour company that sponsored 60 shows across the U.S.] for almost two years."

With his new band, Robert Lockwood, Jr., began to play a wider range of styles, particularly concentrating on jazz. The new setting was to change his style forever, as he started using jazz chords instead of the blues structures he had used with King Biscuit. By this time he also was using a Stella guitar, bought for him by a club owner in Elaine, Arkansas.

"I had a jazz outfit when I left *King Biscuit Time*," Lockwood explains. "I had the Starkey brothers–I had six pieces, sometimes seven. We played a lot of old standard tunes and the blues. I didn't change from blues to jazz, but the band I had was all jazz musicians, so I had to learn what they played plus play what I had been playing too. That was my first experience with bands. I always did like big bands–Fats Waller and all them guys. The people who I like is Count Basie, Duke Ellington, and Louis Jordan. But, really, Count Basie was my idea of playing blues. Robert [Johnson] played ragtime. He would have, if he had been living, been playing jazz just like I'm doing. He would be playing everything just like I'm doing, 'cause he was playing ragtime and them old tunes like 'Mother And Me And The Baby Make Three' ["My Blue Heaven"] and that kind of shit, you know."

Lockwood stayed with Mother's Best and the Starkey brothers until he moved to West Memphis, Arkansas, in 1944. When he arrived in Memphis, a club owner gave him a Gretsch picked up at a pawnshop.

The guitarist soon hooked up with another band. "A bandleader give me his six-piece outfit," he affirms. "They didn't have no records, so they appointed me leader because I did. That person was named Struction, and he played all the rhythm section instruments–guitar, bass, drums, piano. That's when I really got some experience playing jazz and all those standards."

It was in Memphis that he had "a little problem" with Gatemouth Moore, the blues singer who had converted to Christianity on a Chicago stage, and who was now a gospel deejay on WDIA, the same Memphis station B.B. King was working for. Lockwood and Moore, in fact, had their differences over King. "Moore told B.B. to don't pay us no attention, because if we were so great we would have done what B.B. done," he remembers. "B.B. really listened to Gatemouth until he found out I was fixing to cut a'loose. Then he told me to give him two weeks, see would he improve. That two weeks cost me a year. B.B. didn't have no sense of time. I was working with him as a sideman all over Arkansas and Tennessee. He had a horn player, a drummer, me, and him. I tried my best to teach him time, but I think that I . . . it was hard for him to understand. When I got ready to leave, B.B. had a contract with somebody who was going to record him and I told the man that he needed a band. I told the man to put eight pieces with him and he would have to listen to the band. So the man put eight pieces with him, which was part of the Newborn family–little Silas and big Silas [Phineas Newborn Jr. and Sr., who recorded for Bullet as the Tuff Green Band]. That was B.B.'s first real band. It wasn't too long after that that Bill Harvey came in town with 12 pieces, and B.B. ain't looked back."

From Memphis, Lockwood moved again to Chicago, becoming a stalwart of the city's vibrant blues scene, as well as a much-counted-on sideman in the Chess stable. "I done recorded with a lot of people–I can't think of all their names," he admits. Yet you don't need a Chess discography to discern the sides with Lockwood. While many of the Chess guitar sidemen had their own styles, Robert's playing stands out on every cut he appears on. His rhythmic empha-

At the 1991 King Biscuit Blues Festival: "People so damned interested in Robert Johnson, why aren't they interested in me?"

sis and jazz chords are very distinct. "I don't play chords that the ordinary people play. The difference is that I play orchestration stuff, and they just play the blues stuff."

In Chicago he again "teamed up" with Williamson for the harmonica player's second Chess session. (On the first session, Williamson was backed by Muddy Waters and his band.) The two, however, never played together again other than in the studio. To Lockwood, the Chess years were "all fun. We'd usually get $150 a session. Long time ago it was $50. Then it finally went up to $75, then to $100. They started doing albums, then it got to be $150 and sometimes $200, according to how much time it took. Lot of good experiences."

Outside the studio, Robert Lockwood, Jr., played with various Chicago aggregations, but not for any particular band or artist. "I played with Sunnyland Slim, Little Walter, Eddie Boyd, Willie Mabon, and Roosevelt Sykes," he recalls. "And I played at The Zanzibar and the 708 Club. I played at 3220 Cottage Grove with the Aces [guitarist Louis Myers, bassist David Myers, drummer Fred Below], all Chess session players too."

Lockwood also had a considerable influence on a number of Chicago guitarists. "All the guys in Chicago trying to play the blues listened to me–including Jimmy Reed," he states. "They would listen to me because I was the only one who could play the guitar by myself and sound decent." In addition, Robert taught Luther Tucker, who was to become a Chess session artist. Lockwood also had great admiration for John Lee Hooker's cousin Earl. "Earl Hooker was a damned nice guitar player. I had a lot of respect for Hooker. But I was much older than he was. He come from under me."

In addition to the Chess sessions, Robert recorded for a number of other labels: "I played with Cadillac Baby and Eddie Boyd on Cadillac Baby's label [Bea & Baby]. I done 'Dust My Broom' for J.O.B., and I don't know what else. I don't know why Joe Brown didn't want to release that; I done it way before Elmore [James]. I tell you, I been getting the funny end of the stick all of my life. Brown sold it to somebody. Somebody else released it in Europe or somewhere. I asked him, 'How come you didn't release it?' 'I don't know,' he said. Elmore James released that doggone record, and it went straight to the top. Me and Sunnyland [Slim, pianist] did it together. It was real good, but sometimes I say that it just wasn't meant to be." J.O.B., however, did issue two titles with Lockwood and Sunnyland Slim, "Aw Aw Baby" and "Sweet Woman Of Mine."

By the early '60s, after recording for Decca, the blues guitarist moved from Chicago to Cleveland. "I got stuck in Cleveland," he says. "My family, all of us got stuck there. When you buy houses you get stuck. In my career I tried not to have a band of my own; I just wanted to play and let somebody else be the bandleader. Then I didn't have no responsibility. But when I came to Ohio, I got out of the stream and had to find my own band."

Although based in Cleveland, Lockwood continued to record in Chicago, doing an album for Delmark, *Steady Rollin' Man*. He also accompanied Helena native Roosevelt Sykes on a Delmark recording. He did two albums for Trix, *Contrasts* and *Does 12* (featuring his amplified 12-string Guild), as well as a live recording, *Blues Live In Japan*, for Advent. The albums show his musical breadth and span material from Robert Johnson to his own jazz-driven sound. In late 1982 he cut an album for the French Black & Blue label, *Plays Robert & Robert*, on solo 12-string guitar. As the title suggests, the album includes a number of songs recorded by Robert Johnson.

In the early '80s Rounder released two albums by Lockwood and his longtime friend Johnny Shines. The two first met as teenagers in Helena, about the time Shines teamed up with Robert Johnson. Although Shines and Lockwood had the same mentor, they never played together in the old days. Both bluesmen play guitar on *Hangin' On*; but by the time they recorded the second album, *Mister Blues Is Back To Stay*, Shines suffered a stroke and could only sing. Shines partially recovered, and the two guitarists annually joined forces at Helena's King Biscuit Festival.

Lockwood, like a fair number of blues musicians, is weary of record label executives and recording contracts. He and his wife, Annie, recently formed their own company. "I got my own publishing and record company so my material comes back to me," he explains. "People started taking my money. They weren't paying me. You know, you just ain't nice to be a fool all your life. Record for people and they pat me on the back and tell me all them lies. *What's The Score?* is the first album on my label [Lockwood's, 7203 Lawnview Ave., Cleveland, OH 44103]. Six pieces–harmonica, two guitars, bass, drums, and tenor."

Today the bluesman plays a number of guitars. "I've got an ES-335, a Gretsch 6-string, a Guild 12-string, a Gibson 12-string, and a Hofner 12 that was built in Germany," he says. "I started on 12-string a long time ago. A young man called Too Tight Henry, who taught everybody, let me play his guitar, but it wasn't comfortable because he had the strings too high off the neck. That was way before *King Biscuit*. I like the 12-string better. I use the Guild most because my wife bought it. I had it before all the rest of them and I'm more comfortable with it. Right now I'm playing the ES-335."

Although Lockwood, live and on record, still covers Johnson's material, he remains ambivalent about the connection. "I ain't thinking about Robert Johnson," he explains. "He's gone and there isn't a damned thing I can do for him. What I really don't understand is why they're so interested in the way Robert played. They're running around trying to find people who play like him and all that goddamned shit. They so damned interested in Robert Johnson, why aren't they interested in me?"

They, whoever they are, should be. Lockwood's history is almost that of the blues. Yet he brought something more to the blues in both his style and in his playing. And in doing that, he can claim much more than most musicians could ever hope to.

A SELECTED ROBERT LOCKWOOD, JR., DISCOGRAPHY

Solo albums: *Johnny Shines And Robert Lockwood: Dust My Broom* (complete J.O.B. sides), Flyright; *The Baddest New Guitar* (mostly J.O.B., early '60s), P-Vine; *Steady Rollin' Man* (first album as a leader, '70), Delmark; *Blues Live!* (Japan, '74), Vivid; *Contrasts*, Trix; *Does 12*, Trix; *Plays Robert & Robert* (solo in Paris, '82), Black And Blue and Evidence; *What's The Score?*, Lockwood Records.

With Little Walter: *The Best Of Little Walter*, Chess/MCA; *The Best Of Little Walter, Volume Two*, Chess/MCA; *Blues Masters, Volume 6: Blues Originals*, Rhino.

With Sonny Boy Williamson (on Chess): *One Way Out*; *Bummer Road*; *Down And Out Blues*; *The Real Folk Blues*; *More Real Folk Blues*; *The Blues, Vol. 6: '50s Rarities*; *The Chess Years*.

With Johnny Shines (on Rounder): *Robert Jr. Lockwood & Johnny Shines*; *Hangin' On* ('80); *Mister Blues Is Back To Stay*.

Anthologies: *Mississippi Blues* (complete '41 Bluebird sides, two '51 Mercury sides), Wolf; *Lake Michigan Blues, 1934-1941*, Nighthawk; *Windy City Blues, 1935-1953*, Nighthawk; *Chicago Slickers, 1948-1953*, Nighthawk; *Mississippi Country Blues, 1935-'51* ('41-'51), Document; *Blues Is Killin' Me* (backing Baby Face Leroy Foster, '51), Flyright; *Blues Masters, Volume 2: Postwar Chicago*, Rhino; *The Best Of Chicago Blues, Vol. 2* (backing Eddie Boyd, '59), Wolf; *Chess Blues* box set (backing Little Walter and Sonny Boy Williamson); *Chicago Blues: A Quarter Century*, P-Vine; *National Downhome Blues Festival, Vol. 3*, Southland; *Rural Blues*, Zeta; *Back To The Blues*, Zeta; *Roots Of Rhythm And Blues: A Tribute To Robert Johnson* ('92), Columbia.

Soundtracks: *Blues Like Showers Of Rain*; *Mississippi Delta Blues* (Freedom Village concert, produced by the Mississippi Center For Educational Television, '80).

On film: Mr. Lockwood has appeared on PBS' *Lonesome Pine*.

ONE OF THE MOST FASCINATING GUITAR STYLES to come out of the Mississippi Delta was that of Nehemiah "Skip" James. Before 1964 this style was a mystery, and could only be heard on a handful of rare old Paramount 78s. Tunes such as "I'm So Glad," "Devil Got My Woman," and "Hard Time Killin' Floor" were performances that seemed unique, and in many ways far from the blues traditions of the Delta.

In 1964 John Fahey and Bill Barth rediscovered Skip in Mississippi. Skip performed at that year's Newport Folk Festival, and subsequently started touring all over America and Europe. His songs became better known, and bands such as Cream began featuring his numbers, the most popular being "I'm So Glad."

Skip had a definite view of life and music, and was at ease to express these feelings. James' comments that follow were taken from a long discussion that covered many aspects of his music, life, and times. In talking with Skip, I discovered that his playing style was influenced by guitarists in his hometown, Henry Stuckey being foremost on the list. Skip was not only a guitarist, but he also had an impressive piano style that was just as interesting as his guitar sounds. Skip passed away in 1971, but he left several excellent LPs and a legacy of wonderfully expressive and highly individualistic blues playing.

I can sit right here with a guitar in each hand, and I can show you day in and day out. But if you're not musically inclined, you'll never get no further than when you first started. But if you *are* musically inclined, you can just go on. You might hear some song, and that sound will stay within until you get someplace where you can try it yourself. You say, "Yeah, I'm gonna change this thing; play it this-a-way." May not be but one verse of a song, and you can hold it until you get home. That way you can practice on it. You can still add onto it, rearrange it, and change it any way you want, or use his ideas about it. I likes to rearrange songs, if I be interested enough in it to learn some of it. But mostly I sings and plays in my own words and my own composin' and music.

I come in contact with lots of musicians–some older than me, some younger. They have their version of playin' music, and I have mine. It seems like mine is kind of complicated to most people, but I often wondered why. They got ten fingers just like myself. And they got a head just like me. And a vocabulary. And they also got ideas just like me. I can play most some of everything I hear, but still, I don't like to make

Skip James

August 1974

BY STEFAN GROSSMAN

it a practice. I like to play somethin' from *Skip*. Why? So it'll be strange to people, to the rest of musicians.

It's complicated to some of them when you mix the minor with the major–some people don't know minor from major. Most of the people I heard played in common *C*, natural guitar tuning; some few in Spanish [open *G*].

I don't start that way, never did. After my teacher learnt me–the rudiment guy [Stuckey]–then I jumped through that; I wanted it different all the way. Contrary to the rest, so I'd have somethin' they couldn't grasp at. So I just fished around findin' those minor chords. I played minor even before I started playin' pretty good. And minor music is the most difficult music to play of anything.

When I play, sometimes I'll have four different instruments: a piano, and then three different guitars in three different tunings. Of those guitars, one may be tuned in natural, one in Spanish, and one in cross-note [*E* minor]. You can comangle all your music together, if you understand. Your major and minor too.

The best thing I've learned to do is this: Whatever I do, I try to do it right. Decently, and in order, regardless of what it is. And I guess that's why I'm so precautious along the line of musical errors. I can get a guitar, and if it's not substantially in tune, I wouldn't hit the stage with it.

When I play I don't have no assistance. Nothin' to float on, and nothin' to depend on, but Skip. Skip's fingers and his motion and his music and his art. No one to have a lendin' hand out in case I should slip or fall. That's why it plays me so hard, 'cause I have to show up everything for Skip, and to carry it; everything direct and correct, properly and in order. If not, well, there's a failin' on Skip.

Suppose I get onstage with another guitarist or two or more. Then there'd be maybe a badly discord made. They [the audience] wouldn't impersonate [point out] the one individual that did that, they'd say he was "they." *I'd* be involved in it as well as the one that did it. And the first thing you'd see, "You know, Skip made a flunk-out. Made that discord." And so rather than that, I always had the idea that if I made a failure in life, it'd be me on it. So there's why Skip would like to play and act by himself, because if I get out in deep water I don't expect to have two paddles–I'd be pullin' this side and you'd be pullin' that side. And then if I sink, I cannot pull the boat for you and myself, too. I tote nobody else but Skip. That fair? If I don't drift, I'll sink.

When I play I never use a pick, because my nails grow strong; that's why I can touch my strings without hittin' the flesh of my finger. There's lots of people use picks, because they can't finger very well. And they use those picks in frailin' and rappin' [strumming] where they're not active enough in the fingers to pick things enough to keep their music in harmony. Mostly people raps with picks; mighty few you see pick with a pick. Mighty seldom do you see me rap with a pick unless'n' it is to harmonize my major with my other notes. I don't believe in no rappin' and frailin'–never did.

And when I started tryin' to learn, I always did want to pick my music clear, where I could understand it. And you know, if I can understand it, quite naturally the people will.

But I can't tell about my music. I try to satisfy the listeners. When I satisfy them and my manager, I'm perfectly satisfied. I like to hear him be satisfied first. I hate to hear him go, "Skip, the listeners aren't satisfied." But if he says, "I'm satisfied, and the listeners are satisfied," that's quite an encouragement–that'll get you through and goin' on further the next time. Is that right?

> *"I like to play somethin' from Skip. Why? So it'll be strange to people, to the rest of musicians."*

A SELECTED SKIP JAMES DISCOGRAPHY

1931 Paramount sides: *The Complete 1931 Session*, Yazoo; *Skip James: Complete 1931 Recordings In Chronological Order*, Document; *Skip James, 1931*, Matchbox; *Early Blues Recording, 1931* (includes a couple of '60s cuts), Biograph. Various Paramount 78s also appear on *Mississippi Blues 1927-1941*, Yazoo; *Lonesome Road Blues*, Yazoo; *Mississippi Blues 1927-1941*, Yazoo; *The Roots Of Robert Johnson*, Yazoo; *Really! The Country Blues*, Origin Jazz Library; *The Mississippi Blues, 1927-1940*, Origin Jazz Library; *The Mississippi Blues, No. 3*, Origin Jazz Library; *In The Spirit, No. 1*, Origin Jazz Library; *The Greatest In Country Blues, Vol. 2 (1927-1936)*, Story Of Blues; *Roots Of Rock*, Yazoo; *50 Years: Mississippi Blues In Bentonia*, Wolf.

1960s solo albums: *A Tribute To Skip James*, Biograph; *Today!*, Vanguard; *Devil Got My Woman*, Vanguard; *Greatest Of The Delta Blues Singers* (Falls Church, '64), Biograph; *Live At The 2nd Fret*, Document; *Skip James "Live"* (Boston '64, Philadelphia '66), Document.

Anthologies: *Three Shades Of Blue* (three tracks from '64), Biograph; *The Great Bluesmen*, Vanguard; *The Great Bluesmen/Newport*, Vanguard; *Living Legends*, Verve/Folkways; *The Blues At Newport, 1964, Part 2*, Vanguard; *Blues At Newport*, Vanguard; *Delta Blues Heavy Hitters*, Herwin; *Giants Of Country Blues*, Wolf; *American Folk Blues Festival, '67*, L+R.

Rev. Gary Davis

February 1974

BY STEFAN GROSSMAN

REV. GARY DAVIS WAS UNIQUE among blues and rag-time guitarists for many reasons. Whereas most guitarists usually perfected one style or perhaps two, Rev. Davis worked on perfecting a dozen. He combined the alternating bass idea with Blind Blake's syncopation, and then added hundreds of his own ideas and methods.

An outstanding teacher, he was always eager to help his students. Today, looking back on his influence, one is amazed at how many musicians have been affected by this man's music. Black bluesmen such as Blind Boy Fuller and Brownie McGhee learned directly from him. Ry Cooder, David Bromberg, Jerry Garcia, Bob Dylan, and a host of other modern-day guitarists also learned his music first hand, either at his home in the Bronx or while he was touring the country.

Rev. Davis' songs have become part of the mainstream of today's pop culture. "Samson And Delilah," "Candy Man," "Cocaine Blues," and "Death Don't Have No Mercy" have been recorded by a wide variety of artists, including Peter, Paul & Mary, Hot Tuna, and Bob Dylan.

Rev. Gary Davis was born in Larens, South Carolina, on April 30, 1896, and died in New York City on May 5, 1972. He was born blind and started to play the guitar at an early age. Moving throughout the South, he played on street corners, and during the 1930s he settled for several years in Durham, North Carolina, where he taught and played with Blind Boy Fuller. In July 1935, Davis and Fuller traveled to New York to record for the ARC Company. Davis joined Fuller on a couple of cuts, and recorded 15 blues and gospel sides on his own, including "I Saw The Light," "I Am The Light Of The World," and "You Got To Go Down." Settling in New York during the 1940s, Davis recorded for many labels in the ensuing years–Stinson and Folkways in the mid 1950s, and Bluesville, Prestige, Vanguard and Kicking Mule in the '60s, among others. Of all the ragtime-oriented bluesmen, Rev. Davis was perhaps the most widely recorded. With so many styles and techniques, he was truly a master of the guitar.

Could you tell us about your way of playing the guitar?

Well, you see, you've got three hands to play a guitar and only two for a piano. Your forefinger and your thumb–that's the striking hand, and your left hand is your leading hand. Your left hand tells your right hand what strings to touch, what changes to make. That's the greatest help! You see, one hand can't do without the other.

I always thought that your guitar styles tend to imitate the piano.

Well, that's the way I always play the guitar. It's supposed to be played just like you're playing a piano.

Why do you use only two fingers to pick?

Because that's all you need.

Do you think guitar students should use only two fingers also?

That's what I use. I teach them the same as me.

Does using two fingers give you a certain sound?

It is a certain sound. You're going to talk about it, you see. You don't give the rest of your hand time to do nothing if you play with all of your fingers.

Were you using fingerpicks when you started playing the guitar?

Oh, no, I started using them about 25 years ago–or longer.

Were you using fingerpicks when you recorded in 1935?

Yes.

Do you think it's better to use fingerpicks?

It saves your fingers!

When do you think a guitarist should practice?

Well, to love for anything to come to you– you practice early in the morning, at seven o'clock until eight, and then put down your guitar. At eight o'clock in the evening until nine, you practice again. After that you should concentrate.

STEFAN GROSSMAN

"My motto's always been to bring out something somebody else hadn't heard before."

Why so early in the morning?

That's because when music comes to you early in the morning your [re]members are alright. There's nothing to stir you, to disturb you. By eight o'clock everything is going on. At eight o'clock at night everything is once again pretty still. By nine you can call it bedtime–something like that.

What type of guitar do you like?

Any types that's good to play. Don't make any difference what type of guitar, as long as it is a good one. I like a guitar that I can just slip down onto–with a good action. A hard-playing guitar will make your fingers sore. You know something about that, don't you?

Where did you learn how to play?

Well, I was in the South when I learned the guitar. I practically picked it up myself. I made my first guitar out of a tin can. I was a boy about ten years old. I drove me a hole in

each end of the pie pan, run me up a stick through there; that's the way I made it.

Did anybody show you how to play?

No, I learned all by myself. My motto's always been to bring out something somebody else hadn't heard before. I always loved to do things different than anybody else did.

Did you ever put down the guitar?

Well, for three years I didn't have no guitar; that's when I was a boy. There was a time also when I broke my wrist. That was in North Carolina. I was carrying on a revival, and I slipped down. I was going along one night, and there was snow on the ground. When I stepped up on a bank of snow, my foot slipped, and to keep from falling, I was shuffling around. I struck my hand on an iron water-dog. I didn't know it was broken until I went to the doctor the next morning. He told me it was broke. He put me up on a table and put me asleep. When I woke up he had a cast slammed up to my elbow. I lost the use of that hand a long time. I thought I was never going to be able to play no more–but I did! [*Author's note: Rev. Davis' left-hand wrist seemed to have been set out of position–a little to the left of its axis–which enabled him to play many unusual chord positions.*]

Did you ever play 12-string guitar?

First 12-string guitar I run across was in 1920. Never heard tell of one before. I went to the store and asked the man to show it to me, and I found out how it was tuned. I played it just like I played a 6-string guitar.

Were a lot of guitarists playing 12-string back in those days?

Yeah! But them guitars didn't have much of a good action. They were mostly old Stellas.

When is the right time for a guitar player to perform in public?

God never called anybody to preach when he didn't have any words to say. It's no use offering yourself to somebody. If they want you, they'll call you. You can go find a lot of puppies, you understand. They all belong to the same dog. When you lay eyes on those puppies you can tell which one is going to be on top. You can pick that one out. You can see some-thing in that one you don't see in the rest. Don't you go picking yourself out to the people. It's them that pick you out.

Do you find it hard to perform?

Ain't no easy job to sit down and play guitar, nohow! Some of the people that look at it think it's easy, because it looks easy to them.

How do you approach the guitar?

I sit down and study how to take advantage of a guitar, you see.

What advice would you give to guitar students?

You know, you can't give a two-week-old baby peas and cornbread. You've got to give it what it's able to eat. Lot of people come here wanting me to teach them things, but they're not able to stand up to it. I'm subject to mistakes. All of us are. Sometimes you're going East, and you're actually going West. That's the way it happens with all of us sometimes. Mistakes is the best stop in life. You know too much, you understand, then you done made a mistake already. You be too perfect, then the mistake's been already made. But you go try to do a thing and make a mistake to start off with, then that's the best start in life. It gives somebody a chance to correct you.

A SELECTED GARY DAVIS DISCOGRAPHY

Solo albums: *Rev. Blind Gary Davis: Complete Recorded Works In Chronological Order 1935-1949*, Document; *Reverend Gary Davis* (1935 and '40 recordings), Yazoo; *The Singing Reverend* (with Sonny Terry, '50s), Stinson; *American Street Song* ('56 gospel recordings), Riverside; *When I Die I'll Live Again* (two-record reissue of 1960's *Harlem Street Singer* and 1961's *A Little More Faith*), Fantasy; *Pure Religion* ('60), Prestige; *Say No To The Devil* ('61), Original Blues Classics; *Reverend Gary Davis* ('62-'70), Flyright; *Ragtime Guitar* (instrumentals, '62-'70), Heritage; *At The Sign Of The Sun* ('62), Heritage; *Children of Zion* (in concert, '62), Kicking Mule; *Lo' I Be With You Always*, Kicking Mule; *Let Us Get Together*, Kicking Mule; *I Am The True Vine* (recorded at home, '62-'63), Heritage; *Reverend Gary Davis*, Heritage; *Pure Religion & Bad Company*, Smithsonian Folkways; *The Sun Is Going Down*, Folkways; *The Guitar & Banjo Of Rev. Gary Davis* (instrumentals, '64), Prestige; *At Allegheny College* ('64), Document; *At 'Al Matthes', Toronto* (private acetates, '66), Document; *The Reverend Gary Davis At Newport* ('65), Vanguard; *New Blues And Gospel* ('71), Biograph; *Blues & Gospel, Vol. 2* ('71), Biograph; *From Blues To Gospel* ('71), Biograph; *Blues & Ragtime*, Guitar Artistry.

Anthologies: *Preachin' The Gospel: Holy Blues* (1935 Blind Gary Davis side), Columbia; *Blues Rediscoveries*, RBF/Folkways; *The Great Bluesmen*, Vanguard; *The Blues At Newport, 1963*, Vanguard; *The Great Bluesmen/Newport*, Vanguard; *Bluesville Volume 1: Folk Blues*, Ace; *All That Blues*, Ace.

On film: *Blind Gary Davis* (11-minute B&W study by Harold Becker, '64, includes "Death Don't Have No Mercy"); *Reverend Gary Davis* (26-minute film, '67, featuring "Candy Man," "Twelve Gates To The City," and "Stove Pipe Rag"); *Black Roots* ('70). Yazoo Video presents B&W solo footage shot by the Seattle Folklore Society, circa '68, on *Rev. Gary Davis And Sonny Terry*, and footage of the Rev. appears in the Stefan Grossman's Guitar Workshop videos *Fingerpicking Guitar Techniques*, *Country Blues Guitar* (*Part Two* and *Part Three*), and *How To Play Blues Guitar*.

Mance Lipscomb

March 1974

By Jim Crockett

BRITISH HISTORIAN PAUL OLIVER has put it best: "Mance Lipscomb's music is first and foremost entertainment, to be enjoyed with the heart and the body rather than be subjected to academic analysis." Mance was a real original. No influences, no teachers, no books–just the music he heard around him, filtered through a life of hardship and joy. As Paul Oliver also said, he was "one of the last great exponents of the Southern Negro folk song forms, before the blues and the mass media which popularized it swept them aside."

Born in Navasota, Texas, in 1895, Mance wasn't raised on the blues, because the music he heard around him came from the pre-blues era–circus tunes, jigs and reels, church songs, breakdowns, and rags. He learned to play guitar while accompanying his father, a fiddler who was born into slavery. As Mance grew older, the blues became a part of his musical life, but in concert he always interspersed them with religious hymns, children's rhymes, ballads, slow drags, and old-time pop songs such as "Polly Wolly Doodle," "It's A Long Way From Tipperary," and "Alabama Jubilee." His fine fingerpickering style underscored his soft, expressive voice, and he used a pocketknife to play slide.

Mance Lipscomb was 66 years old when he made his first major public performance. Previous to that, he would augment his meager sharecropper earnings (as little as $100 per year) by playing for local parties and church meetings in his hometown. In the summer of 1960, Arhoolie Records' Chris Strachwitz and a friend were driving along Texas' Brazos River "blues country," inquiring about singers in the area. The name Mance Lipscomb came up. The two men searched until they found him cutting grass, the "boss" of a three-man highway maintenance team. In Lipscomb's tiny home, they made a few informal tapes that later became *Texas Sharecropper And Songster*, the Arhoolie label's–and Mance's–first record.

The following year Barry Olivier brought the "songster" (Mance's own term for people who use songs of all types to entertain) to the Berkeley Folk Festival. It was Lipscomb's first concert and his first trip outside Texas. More recordings followed, as did additional bookings at colleges, festivals, and clubs. Having enough material was never a problem, since Lipscomb had a repertoire of nearly 1,000 songs.

We met Mance at the 1973 Monterey Jazz Festival, where we sat outside the arena in the grassy area, shaded from the afternoon sun by giant oaks. Mance had his guitar with him, and as soon as we sat at one of the picnic tables, people

JIM CROCKETT

"The electric guitar is a fraud," insisted Lipscomb, seen here with a Gibson J-200.

began gathering around. Inside the arena, Bo Diddley was knocking out fans with his rough, double-entendre blues. But there on the lawn outside, away from the screaming, dancing crowd, Mance gave one of his best, low-keyed performances for a tiny, smiling, spellbound group of students, musicians, middle-aged jazz fans, and newspaper journalists from around the country. After about a half-hour of friendly anecdotes, startling guitar licks, and delightful songs, Mance apologized to the growing audience, put his Gibson J-200 in the case, and began talking about his life in music. Three years later, Mance Lipscomb passed away at the age of 80, leaving behind a legacy of several wonderful albums. Here are Mance's words, just as he spoke them that sunny afternoon in Monterey.

My daddy was a fiddler, and I heard music all the time. Like, it's in my blood. And blood is your life, right? You can learn music easy if it's in your blood.

My mother used to sing all the time. We'd be working the cotton fields together, and she'd be singing. Then one day when I was about 13, a gambler came by where we were working. He was broke and needed some money. He had a little pine guitar with him, and all the time he and my momma were talking, I was staring at it. It only had about three or four strings on it, but it was beautiful to me. He wanted $1.50 for it, and momma bought it for me.

I couldn't play anything, though. My two older brothers played good guitar for parties around town, but they thought I'd break their guitars, so they wouldn't let me near them. When I got my own, it was really a thrill to pluck it.

I'd give my mother my cotton-picking money, then she'd give me 25¢. I'd head for town, buy some bread and sausage, and have 15¢ left for the carnival or Barnum & Bailey circus. The clowns would do their buckdancing, and people would toss coins. I'd stay as long as I could, watching the circus musicians real close. Then I'd go home and try the songs out on my guitar. I didn't think about singing then; I just wanted to make music on that guitar of mine.

I was learning everything by ear, of course, but by the time I was 15 I could accompany my father in his little shows. I did that for years. During the week I'd try playing by myself a little here and there. I figured how to play double-time by myself. Fingerpicking, too. I use my thumb and two fingers. I use a thumbpick now, but I didn't back then. I never heard of picks until many years later. When I was around 16, I started working what they called "breakdown suppers" for my father. He was getting on by then, and people seemed to like my guitar playing, so I started taking over from him.

I never got to hear many players when I was growing up. We were on a farm so there weren't many others, just myself. Oh, maybe I heard three or four guitar players who came through town, but that was about all. I knew one old man who could play two songs, and I'd sit outside his door listening to him play them over and over.

I learned to tune the guitar on my own. I just tune by chords to the sound I like. The two *E*'s are usually in tune, then I tune the rest to them and just wham away on it. I play in three tunings, mostly: *E*; triple *E*, where I also tune the *D* up to *E*; and one where I tune the *A* up three tones and the *D* up two. I just keep tuning until it sounds right.

Nowadays I use a Gibson J-200 [acoustic guitar outfitted with a soundhole pickup]. Someone gave it to me backstage in Minneapolis. I didn't know Gibson from anyone else at the time. People like a good clear sound, so I don't use it as an electric very often. The electric guitar is a fraud; the sound rings because of the electricity, not because of the player. People can't remember electric songs very well, either, because the music's too fast and too loud.

It's not that I don't like today's music–I like portions of *all* music–but if it's stuff in these later years, I don't understand it. I don't catch up to it.

From the time I was 14 until 1961 I was on my own. Then Chris found me sharecropping. By then I had all that music going around in my head. White folks didn't get to hear me, because I wasn't allowed to play the white dances. That Berkeley Folk Festival was my first white crowd. Man, talk about a scared boy!

I'm playing more today than I ever have. I used to play only one day a week, but now I'm working six or seven months out of the year. The phone keeps ringing for jobs all over the nation. And I don't get tired, either. I can play all night; you can't hurt me. But the thing that's wrong with festivals is that you don't have any time when you're performing. No one can do something in a minute–it takes time. I know 350 songs, but I can only do two or three in a show, so I have to cut out the instrumentals, which I hate to do. I got to have at least 40 minutes.

No one plays like me. Oh, they can play maybe three or four notes of mine. They can start it, but they can't finish it.

A SELECTED MANCE LIPSCOMB DISCOGRAPHY

Solo albums (on Arhoolie): *Texas Sharecropper And Songster* ('60); *Texas Songster Volume 2* ('64); *You'll Never Find Another Man Like Mance* (Berkeley, '64); *Texas Songster Vol. 3* (Berkeley, '66); *Mance Lipscomb Vol. 4* ('64 and '66); *Mance Lipscomb Vol. 5* ('68-'69); *Mance Lipscomb Vol. 6* ('73); *Texas Songster* (22-cut CD of material from *Texas Sharecropper And Songster* and *Texas Songster Vol. 3*, with substantial liner notes).

Anthologies (on Arhoolie, except as indicated): *Blues 'N Trouble*; *Texas Blues Vol. 2*; *Blues Festival: Concert & Dance*; *The Roots Of America's Music*; *The Great Bluesmen*, Vanguard; *Blues Masters, Volume 3: Texas Blues*, Rhino; *Back Against The Wall: The Texas Country Bluesmen*, Collectables.

On film: *A Well-Spent Life* (the best Lipscomb study, this 44-minute profile was filmed in Texas by Les Blank, '71); *The Blues Accordin' To Lightnin' Hopkins* (Blank documentary features scenes of Mance backing Lightnin', '68); *En Remontant Le Mississippi/Out Of The Blacks, Into The Blues* ('71 West German/French film featuring Mance's "All Night Long"); *Roots Of American Music* (produced by the University of Washington School of Music, '71). Yazoo Video presents B&W solo footage shot by the Seattle Folklore Society circa '68 in *Mance Lipscomb/Lightnin' Hopkins*. Lipscomb footage also appears in the Stefan Grossman's Guitar Workshop videos *Bottleneck Blues Guitar*, *How To Play Blues Guitar*, *Fingerpicking Guitar Techniques*, and *Country Blues Guitar, Part Two*.

Mississippi Fred McDowell

November 1977

BY TOM POMPOSELLO

ISSISSIPPI FRED MCDOWELL was one of the most important rural guitarists to come out of the 1960s blues revival. Undiscovered until 1959, Fred was first recorded by Alan Lomax on one of the folklorist's many field trips to the South. McDowell's specialty was bottleneck slide, with an eerie, vocal-like tone. In '69 the blues singer switched from acoustic to electric, which, if anything, only added intensity to that subtle, whining quality. McDowell's playing influenced numerous rock and blues slide guitarists, including Keith Richards and Bonnie Raitt. Bonnie remembers: "He thought it was really funny, meeting this 18-year-old girl playing guitar, but he was flattered at my interest, and he taught me."

Fred would take the time to show his music to anyone who would ask. Unlike so many artists who are reluctant to explain the intricacies of their styles for fear (often with good reason) of being ripped off and receiving no recognition, McDowell's philosophy was, "Well, that might be true; that's just what they may do. But I do know that in their hearts, after I'm dead and buried, they're always gonna remember that I was the one that showed it to them, even if they don't tell nobody else."

McDowell was born somewhere between 1903 and 1906. No one seems certain, because back then if you were black and living on a plantation, no one kept accurate documentation of such things. He was born in Rossville, Tennessee–a fact that always used to bemuse him: "They call me Mississippi Fred, but really my home is in Rossville, Tennessee.

"When I was a boy," he continues, "I think the first blues record I ever heard was Blind Lemon Jefferson singing 'Black Snake Moan.' 'O-oh, ain't got no mama now.' Man! I tell you, I thought that was the prettiest little thing I'd ever heard." He became interested in guitar when he was in his late teens. By this time, music was all around Fred. His uncle Gene Shields was a guitarist and the leader of a trio. He credits Shields with being the first person he saw play in the bottleneck style, using a smoothed beef rib bone on his little finger.

The harmonica player in Gene's trio, Cal Payne, showed Fred "John Henry." Cal's son Raymond, who was about the same age as Fred, recalls, "He was a real good guitar player–regular style, not bottleneck." But Raymond would never show anyone anything. "If you'd walk into the room when Raymond was playing," Fred recalled, "he'd right away put the guitar down so you couldn't see what he was doing. Then he'd make some kind of excuse–'I'm tired now' or 'My fingers hurt.' No one could show me nothing anyway. Everyone

could play 'cept me. All the boys. But I had to learn things my own way. Even if you'd be showing me, I'd have to go off on my own and get it my way. They'd all be playing ball or something, and I'd be practicing on Booster Green's guitar." (An older friend, Eli "Booster" Green taught McDowell his celebrated tune "Write Me A Few Lines." In 1966 the musicians were reunited for a couple of tracks on Arhoolie's *Fred McDowell, Vol. 2*.)

The first song Fred ever learned was Tommy Johnson's "Big Fat Mama (With The Meat Shakin' On Your Bones)." "I learned it on one string," he explained, "then two, note by note. Man, I about worried that first string to death trying to learn that song." This note-by-note method became an intricate part of Fred's later-day technical approach. While McDowell experienced his share of obstacles on guitar, he was always sought after as a vocalist. He would sing along with other guitarists at old-time Saturday night suppers, and then take over on guitar when they got tired.

Tired of plowing fields with a mule, Fred left Rossville when he was about 21. During a trip to Cleveland, Mississippi, in the late 1920s, he heard the legendary Charley Patton perform at a juke joint. He was quite impressed, and consciously adapted several of Patton's tunes to his own style. His "Gravel Road," for instance, was adapted from Patton's "Down The Dirt Road Blues." McDowell lived in Memphis during the 1930s, working as a laborer. He tried to master the guitar, but was hampered by not owning his own instrument. Finally, a white man from Texas named Mr. Taylor (whom Fred remembered quite fondly) presented him with one. This was 1941, and soon afterwards Fred decided to move south to Mississippi and settle down near his sister. While living in Como, Fred McDowell refined the style that would lead to his becoming one of the greatest postwar country bluesmen.

In 1959 folklorist Alan Lomax came to Como and asked if there were any local bluesmen that he should hear. Among the first names given was Fred McDowell's. Lomax found Fred at home that evening and proceeded to record him. Fred played well into the night–from 8:00 P.M. until almost 7:00 A.M., as he recalls it. Before departing, Lomax promised that these recordings would bring McDowell fame and fortune. Well, he was half-right. Despite the fact that the payment was nominal, the recordings were met by much enthusiasm in folk and blues circles. They established the 55-year-old as one of the great "new discoveries" in the blues world. Fred had the opportunity to play and record for a whole new audience.

Arhoolie and Testament issued solo albums, and Fred was a sensation at the 1964 Newport Folk Festival. He toured Europe with the American Folk Blues Festival in 1965 and '69, going over especially well in Germany and Great Britain.

Keith Richards heard Fred's version of the spiritual "You Got To Move" and rearranged it for the Rolling Stones.

In 1969 Fred recorded a solo album for the Transatlantic label, using an *electric* guitar. It seems odd today, but the reaction at the time among purists was mixed. Everyone was used to Chicago blues played electrically, but Delta blues? One critic observed that much of the subtlety, especially in McDowell's fills, was lost, but nothing could have been further from the truth. One listen to "Amazing Grace" performed on the electric instrument, and you were a believer. The instrument proved very appropriate for the spirituals Fred loved to perform, intensifying his shimmering tone and sophisticated vibrato. His blues numbers, particularly the percussive, driving rhythmic patterns of songs such as "Shake 'Em On Down" and "Drop Down Mama," were also greatly enhanced. And the electric instrument undoubtedly made Fred's music more accessible to a new generation of blues enthusiasts. He was well aware of this, and used to caution his admirers: "I do not play no rock and roll, y'all. Just the straight and natch'l *blue*."

Prior to 1968, the majority of McDowell's recordings were performed on his old wood-bodied National or his acoustic Hofner. His first electric was a red, dual-pickup imitation of a Gibson ES-335. He then found a good deal on a mid-'60s Gibson Trini Lopez Standard, which he used until his death. His only modification was to slightly raise the action by installing a small metal shim just above the nut. He used light-gauge Black Diamond Electric Strings, but didn't care much about the brand or the gauge, so long as the set included an unwound *G* string. (Whenever purchasing a new set, he'd always check for that unwound string before laying down his money.) To get the necessary clarity on acoustic, Fred would pick with his bare right-hand thumb and index finger. For electric guitar, he used a standard plastic thumbpick and a plastic fingerpick on his index finger. His style of picking ranged from simple note-to-note to heavily syncopated brush strokes.

Most of McDowell's touring during the late '60s and early '70s was done by Greyhound bus. He hated to fly unless it was absolutely necessary. Consequently, he carried only a small practice amp with him, hoping that when he arrived at a club or festival, he could plug into whatever better equipment was available. Sometimes a well-meaning producer would want to record the bluesman through his own amp, insisting that it would be inaccurate to record a blues artist using someone else's equipment, or a club would close-mike his amp through the PA system. Unless this was done absolutely right, the result was a very muddy sound, which is why many of Fred's recordings leave the listener with a false impression of his tone. Judging from his reaction to good amps, he was after a clean, clear sound with good top end.

The first time Fred tried to play bottleneck guitar, he used a pocketknife to emulate Uncle Gene's style. But it didn't take long for him to realize that in order to get the volume and clarity he wanted, he had to switch to a glass bottleneck. Since his style did not utilize full chords barred with a bottleneck, he chose to use a short slide (about an inch long) made from a Gordon's Gin bottle. First, he scribed the bottle with a sharp object along the lines where he wanted it to break. Then he ran it under hot water in a bathtub, then under cold water while he gently tapped it along the scribed seams. It worked on the first try. (It's funny how a musician can get attached to something like a bottleneck. One evening I saw Fred nervously rummaging through his guitar case, and then breathing a sigh of relief upon finding his treasured Gordon's bottleneck. "Tom, if I'd have lost that," he said, "I might as well turned around and went back home.")

Where he wore his bottleneck depended on his tuning–standard, open *A*, or open *E*. On his earlier acoustic records, he often used the open-*A* tuning, wearing the bottleneck on his little finger. In standard tuning, he'd usually play in the key of *E* and wear the bottleneck on his little finger. For open *E*, Fred wore the bottleneck on his ring finger. He preferred to use his bottleneck more often in the *E* tuning, because it lends itself more toward melodic playing. (It's important to note that Fred's tunings were relative, since he tuned to his voice–rather than a piano or tuner–before performing.)

Most of Fred's playing was based in the tonic. He would often thumb the open bass strings while picking slide melody lines with his fingerpick. In songs such as "You Got To Move," he might depart from that procedure and simply play the melody line on the bass strings alone. His guitar part often echoed his vocal phrasing almost exactly, such as in "Baby, Please Don't Go," where his voice would trail off while his bottleneck finished the vocal line: "When you hear me play, if you listen real close, you'll hear the guitar say the same thing I'm saying, too." He was very flattered one time by a perceptive fan who said, "You know, that's the first time I ever heard a talking guitar."

Fred returned home during the winter of 1971, canceling his tour because of severe stomach pains. Undergoing an operation, he was not to leave his home again. I visited him in Mississippi the following spring, and found him in good spirits as he showed me the time of my life. A few days later, he was back in the hospital. He never complained, but it was obvious he was in great pain. In July 1973 Fred McDowell died from abdominal cancer.

I have never heard anybody play or sing like Mississippi Fred McDowell, and I am convinced that what made Fred great as a musician was what made him great as a man. That "Mississippi mystique" of his, that undefinable something, is the spirit of the real blues.

A SELECTED MISSISSIPPI FRED McDOWELL DISCOGRAPHY

Solo albums: *Shake 'Em On Down, 1959* (first recordings), KC; *Mississippi Fred McDowell* ('62), Heritage; *Fred McDowell* ('62), Flyright; *Fred McDowell* (half are spirituals with Fred's wife Annie, '63-'64), Testament; *Delta Blues* ('64), Arhoolie; *Fred McDowell, Vol. 2*, Arhoolie; *Mississippi Delta Blues* (a CD combining *Delta Blues, Vol. 1* and *2*), Arhoolie; *Keep Your Lamp Trimmed And Burning* ('64-'69), Arhoolie; *Fred McDowell And His Blues Boys* ('65/'69), Arhoolie; *Somebody Keeps Calling Me*, Antilles; *My Home Is In The Delta*, Testament; *Fred McDowell & Johnny Woods*, Rounder; *When I Lay My Burden Down*, Biograph; *This Old World's In A Hell Of A Fix*, Biograph; *I Do Not Play No Rock And Roll*, Capitol; *Mississippi Fred McDowell*, Archive Of Folk; *Long Way From Home*, Milestone; *Levee Camp Blues* (some of the earliest songs Fred learned), Origin Jazz Library; *Mississippi Delta Blues* (Black Lion, '65), Vogue; *Long Way From Home* ('68), O.B.C.; *Standing On The Burying Ground* (live in London, '69), Red Lightnin'; *Shake 'Em On Down* ('71), Tomato; *Amazing Grace* (with the Hunter's Chapel Singers), Testament; *Mississippi Fred McDowell In London*, Sire/Warner Bros.; *Mississippi Fred McDowell In London, Vol. II*, Transatlantic; *Mississippi Fred McDowell Live In New York* ('71), Oblivion; *Mississippi Fred McDowell, 1904-1972*, Just Sunshine. **With others:** *Big Mama Thornton In Europe*, Arhoolie; *Honest Tom Pomposello*, Oblivion.

Anthologies: *Roots Of The Blues* (Alan Lomax field recordings, '59-'60), New World; *Atlantic Blues: Guitar* ('59), Atlantic; *The Great Bluesmen*, Vanguard; *Kings Of Country Blues, Vol. 2*, Arhoolie; *Bad Luck N' Trouble*, Arhoolie; *American Folk Blues Festival, 1965*, L+R; *A Double Dose Of Dynamite* (live in '69), Red Lightnin'; *Blues Masters, Volume 7: Blues Revival*, Rhino; *Mississippi Delta Blues Jam In Memphis, Vol. 1* (three songs with Johnny Woods, '69), Arhoolie; *All That Blues*, Ace; *Genuine Mississippi Blues*, Ace. **On film:** *Newport Festival*; *Blues Maker* (14 minutes of outstanding B&W footage, '69, made by the University of Mississippi); *Fred McDowell* (15 minutes, '69, produced by Seattle Folklore Society); *Roots Of American Music* (produced by University of Washington School Of Music, '71). B&W solo footage appears on Yazoo's *Fred McDowell/Big Joe Williams* video; footage also appears in Stefan Grossman's *Bottleneck Blues Guitar* video.

James "Son" Thomas

April 1990

BY DAN FORTE

JAMES "SON" THOMAS is a folk artist in the truest sense of the term–in more ways than one. Although he looks considerably older, he is 63, and the Delta blues he has been playing for close to 53 of those years has scarcely changed since he first started. He also sculpts: From Mississippi River clay mud, he molds birds, rodents, fish, human heads and skulls, and scenes depicting death, such as his open-casket figures, complete with coat-hanger-wire handles. As a boy, Son earned his other nickname, "Ford," thanks to the clay trucks he made.

Thomas grew up in Yazoo County, and his high, ghost-like singing is reminiscent of another Yazoo blues legend, the late Skip James. Tommy McClennan, from Yazoo City, was among the first bluesmen Son heard on records–songs like "Bottle Up And Go" and "Whiskey Headed Woman"–along with Son House, Tommy Johnson, and Robert Johnson. "I heard their records, but I never did meet them," he points out. "The only guy from way back that I met who probably knowed them was Big Joe Williams. Now he's dead, Muddy Waters is dead–I got to meet him, James Brown, Mrs. Reagan." Mrs. Reagan? "I was in Washington, at the Corcoran Gallery up there in '81, with my art," he explains. "She came by to see my sculptures, and we had a picture made," he says, pointing to a framed 8x10 on his bedroom wall showing Thomas with the former First Lady.

"I play a little country music, but mostly blues," says Son. "That's mostly what I like to play. I learned from my uncle, Joe Cooper, and other people who used to be around the house playing. When I got large enough to go out, I used to go listen to Elmo James and Arthur 'Big Boy' Crudup. They played in clubs around Yazoo. I had to wait till they stopped charging at the door, because I wasn't able to pay 50¢ to go in. Elmo would let me plug in his guitar when he'd take a break. He was real nice. Sonny Boy [Williamson II] would get really mad because Elmo would let me play. That was Rice Miller, not the real Sonny Boy; he and Elmo used to play a lot together. Elmo played an acoustic, but he had a silver pickup in it."

His initial exposure to artists like James and Sonny Boy Williamson was via radio. "I heard them on the radio before I saw them," he clarifies. "They played in Helena, Arkansas. Back in them times on the radio, they had 15 minutes of blues, and you wouldn't hear no more blues. I used to quit out in the field to go and listen to that 15 minutes of blues. Mostly you'd hear country music, and I like some of that, too. But the music they're playing now, this disco, I just don't

© AXEL KÜSTNER

Son Thomas and Eddie Cusie at the 1980 Delta Blues Festival.

like it. I can't get nothing out of it."

Son's first local performances were with his uncle: "I'd make a dollar a night; he wasn't gettin' but about three dollars. It was what you call house parties; they used to call them country jukes. People didn't have a way to travel around long-distance. If you're gonna have something in Memphis, now they can jump in their car and go up there. But people didn't travel as fast then as they can now; they didn't have transportation. There was mighty few blacks that had cars, and they used them for taking people to the doctor and stuff like that. After I quit playing with my uncle, it was mostly by myself. Then I started making three or four dollars. My uncle could have left during the time when Tommy McClennan would go and record, but he wouldn't do it."

The first guitar Son owned was a Gene Autry model he bought from a Sears, Roebuck catalog for $8.50. "I picked cotton to make enough money to get that guitar," he remembers, "and then I played on the post office steps and made my money back. Later on, I played an electric for a while–I forget the name. It had three pickups and six dials, but it got stolen. I have a Martin now, with a pickup in the bridge. I tune it standard, but when I play slide I change to a cross-tuning, about like Spanish [open *G*]. I use a steel slide now, on my little finger. I keep my fingernails cut off when I'm

playing. They make me make mistakes. I play with my bare fingers."

In 1961 Thomas moved to Leland, Mississippi, and continued to play strictly around Mississippi until blues scholar William Ferris discovered him in 1967. "I stayed right in this area because I was doing work, and you had to be where your job was. I worked in funeral homes, furniture stores, yard work. Just something to keep the house goin'. Never made no big money–what I call big money–until I started playing. My first trip overseas was in '81. I went to Norway to play for 30 minutes on a television show. I've been overseas about six times."

Besides recording Thomas, Bill Ferris took pictures of his artwork to Yale, resulting in Son's first exhibit, in 1969. "I've been doing that ever since I was a little bitty boy in school," Son recounts. "My uncle used to try to make mules, so I started trying to make mules and other things. I made a skull once to scare my grandfather. I made this skull and put it on the shelf, and he come in and had to light a match to light the lamp, and I put that skull up where he could see it when he'd light that lamp. He made me take it out of the house. Then I tied a string to his bedsprings–those old coil springs–and ran it through a crack in the wall to my room. When him and my grandmother went to bed, I would lay in my bed in the next room and shake 'em up. He accused my grandmother of shakin' the bed, so she got up out of bed to show him she wasn't shakin' the bed. I really shook it then. He said, 'I know what it is. You're bringing these white folks' clothes in here. Some of 'em are dead, and they're coming back for 'em.' From then on, he always believed there was a ghost in the house; he didn't know it was me."

In addition to his own songs, Son still relies on his original favorites for inspiration. "Some of them are mine, and some I record other people's," he says, "but I play it different, you know. I do some of Elmo's, Arthur 'Big Boy' Crudup, and I like Li'l Son Jackson. He lived in Texas, and I thought I'd go to see him, but he was dead. I saw a film once of Lightnin' Hopkins fishing, catching some white perch out in a boat. I never did meet him, but I loved his records." On electric, Thomas sometimes gives Muddy Waters or even B.B. King a run for their money.

Son reaches for his decal-stickered Martin and slides a metal tube onto his little finger. But instead of playing some Lightnin' Hopkins or Elmore James, some Big Boy Crudup or Li'l Son Jackson, he begins the familiar strains of "Steel Guitar Rag" by Bob Wills & The Texas Playboys. "See, I play a little country music," he smiles, "but I change it up a little bit."

[*Son Thomas suffered a stroke and passed away on June 26, 1993.*]

Working-man blues: Son with his beloved Martin.

A SELECTED SON THOMAS DISCOGRAPHY

Solo albums: *Highway 61 Blues* ('69-'82), Southern Culture; *Son Down On The Delta* ('81), Flying High; *Delta Blues Classics*, Swingmaster (Holland, '81); *Good Morning School Girl* ('86), Black And Blue; *The James "Son" Thomas Album*, L+R; *Living Country Blues*, P-Vine; *Bottomlands* (with Walter Liniger), Rooster Blues.

Anthologies: *Blues Live '82*, L+R; *Mississippi Blues Festival 86*, Black And Blue; *Mississippi Folk Voices*, Southern Culture; *Bothered All The Time*, Southern Culture; *Mississippi Delta Blues*, L+R; *Mississippi Moan*, L+R; *National Downhome Blues Festival, Vol. 4*, Southland.

On film: *Mississippi Delta Blues* ('69); *James "Son Ford" Thomas: Delta Blues Singer* ('70); *I Ain't Lying* (folk tales, '75); *Made In Mississippi* (folk art, '75); *Give My Poor Heart Ease* ('76). All of the preceding films were made by William Ferris and are available through the Center for the Study of Southern Culture in University, Mississippi. In addition, Son performs two songs in 1977's *Got Something To Tell You: Sounds Of The Delta Blues*.

R.L. Burnside

April 1990

BY DAN FORTE

E'S THE DIRECT LINK from Robert Johnson to Mississippi Fred McDowell, for that style of slide," says bluesman Joe Louis Walker of R.L. Burnside. But Burnside is not merely a bottleneck specialist; playing solo, his acoustic country blues encompasses the styles of Li'l Son Jackson, Bukka White, Big Bill Broonzy, Muddy Waters, Son House, Lightnin' Hopkins, John Lee Hooker, and many others.

"With a band, he don't sound like himself now," Burnside says of Hooker. "He sounds a whole lot better by himself–that's the way I look at it." R.L. also plays with a band, however, which includes his sons Duane, Daniel, and Joseph, on guitar, bass, and drums, and extends his blues repertoire to B.B. and Albert King, Little Milton, and Bobby Blue Bland. The family band members are just three of the 63-year-old's 12 children, who range in age from 13 to 39.

Four generations of Burnsides, including R.L.'s 82-year-old mother, live in a four-room wooden house near Holly Springs, Mississippi. "I was born five or six miles outside of Oxford," R.L. details, "and I grew up in Coldwater, 10 or 12 miles from Holly Springs, down on 55. We moved from Oxford to Coldwater when I was 7, and I was around there until I was 18." He then moved to Chicago for three years, and after brief stays back in Mississippi, Memphis, and Chicago again, he settled in Holly Springs.

When he was younger, he explains, the centers of blues activity in Mississippi were towns like Clarksdale, Crenshaw, and Holly Springs. "Coldwater was a dry county. Stonewall Mays, he's 80-something now, still plays blues there–and was playing blues before I could play. So he played juke joints up around here."

R.L.'s father played guitar, but, in Burnside's words, "he never was good with it. I guess I just learned from sitting down and watching Fred [McDowell] and then Muddy, when I got to Chicago. He married my cousin, so I used to go to his house back when he was just playing at the Zanzibar every Friday night for whatever they took in at the door. I'd try to play like him, but it wouldn't sound right. My second wife, the one I got now, said, 'Why don't you put that thing down?' I'd fool with it when she wasn't around. Finally, I got pretty good. So one night, maybe a year later, there was this house party, a country supper. They were shootin' craps, drinking whiskey, gambling. Son Hibler was playing, but he got tired and took a rest–laid his guitar down. I asked if I could play his guitar; my old lady said, 'You gonna make a fool out of yourself in front of all these people?' I started to play 'Boo-

– 58 –

gie Chillun' and 'Hobo Blues' from John Lee Hooker. Man, people came out going, 'Who's that guy with the guitar?'"

In addition to hearing Joe Hill Louis, Robert Nighthawk, and Sonny Boy Williamson over the radio from Helena, Arkansas, Burnside listened to records by Tommy McClennan, Washboard Sam, Li'l Son Jackson, and Big Bill Broonzy. "I liked Robert Johnson's type of music, too," he adds. "I played with Robert Junior Lockwood, his stepson, in Montreal, Canada, in '71. I always liked Lightnin' Hopkins and Muddy Waters and Li'l Son Jackson's playing, and Elmo James. Man, I loved his type of music. Never got to meet him, but I play stuff behind his songs. When I lived in Chicago in the '50s, I saw Little Walter and

Holly Springs blues: R.L. with his son-in-law and grandson, July 1993.

Big Walter Horton, Chuck Berry, and Sonny Boy Williamson was playing then. Maxwell Street Jimmy [Davis] was there, John Lee Granderson, Robert Nighthawk. I used to live one street over from Maxwell Street. But I couldn't play guitar then. Since then, of course, I've played in Chicago 30 or 40 times."

Burnside's mentor, Fred McDowell, was from Como, Mississippi, and R.L. points out, "I knew him all my life. When I was too little to even play, I knew him. He was 10 or 12 years older than me. I sort of watched him and caught on to what he was doing. I like a lot of things he was doing. I like those old-time blues.

"In that time, when Fred was playing, it was just one guy. Fred McDowell, Dennis Gardner, or a guy called Son Hibler. Just one guy playing, and maybe a harmonica player, like Johnny Woods. Me and him and Fred all played together, and Ranie Burnette. I'm younger than all of them guys, by eight or ten years. See, at that time, when I was 17 and just started to running around, there wasn't no such thing as big clubs. You'd go to some house party. People would dance and carry on—just Fred playing his guitar. Man, I saw the floor break in!"

Playing solo guitar for dancers probably accounts for the strong rhythmic feel in Burnside's music. "That's right," he agrees. "That's where I got that from." In songs like "Skinny Woman" and "Poor Black Mattie," his approach is close to McDowell's or Bukka White's, beating on the guitar almost

like a drum.

His tunings also derive from Mississippi Fred. "In one way I tune mine like Fred, and in one way I don't," he says. "The same thing he plays in one tuning, I can tune it another way and play the same thing. It's easy to do that. I got 'cross-note' and 'Spanish.' Spanish is like _G_, and cross-note is something like a _D_. Can't use a pick. I just use bare fingers."

His main acoustic is an Epiphone, and his electric is an old Aria Les Paul copy, neither of which is played very often when R.L.'s not performing. "In my way of thinking, I believe you can do a lot of things by thinking about it. If you try, you're trying too hard. Just wait till it comes into your mind, and you'll do it. Part of that album, _Hill Country Blues_, was recorded in Holland in the hotel room. We didn't have enough songs, so I laid down and took a nap, slept a couple of hours, and when I woke up a song came to my mind. Then four or five songs that I didn't know nothing about, I just got up and made them up out of my head right there. Made the whole album the next day. Then I do stuff behind old records I heard—change the lyrics a little, maybe change the type of music with it."

Like Son Thomas, Burnside continued to play local functions until, in his forties, he was discovered and recorded by a blues enthusiast—in R.L.'s case, George Mitchell, author of _Blow My Blues Away_. "George Mitchell was out recording Other Turner—the fife and drum band—in '68," he recounts. "And they knew about me. He asked about anybody else that played blues, and came here. At that time I was living on the plantation, working a sharecrop, and all that stuff. So George and his wife Kathy came and lived at my house there for a whole week, and every night when I'd get out of the field, he'd run the tape recorder, and I'd play some blues. That's what came out on the record [*Mississippi Delta Blues, Vol. 2*]. He was dealing with [Arhoolie Records'] Chris Strachwitz and gave him the record. First album. I never recorded before that. One side of the album was me, and one side was Joe Callicott."

R.L. had played electric guitar, but never in a band context until Tom Boyd, manager and agent for the Mississippi Delta Blues Band, sought him out. "I was living about 15 miles from where I am now. I was working on a plantation, renting my house, but driving a cotton-picking combine. I was making $15 a day, and this guy came up to the house. He had never seen me, but he got the Arhoolie record and had been looking for me. I was in the house, and the kids said, 'Who is this coming to the house?' He knocked on the door and said he was Tom Boyd. I don't know no Tom Boyd. I said, 'Let him in'–because I had an automatic shotgun, a pistol in my pocket and one under the pillow. He said he had that album and was trying to put a band together, and said, 'Do you know a harmonica player out of Jackson called Sam Myers?' I'd heard of him but never met him. Sam was in the band, and they wanted some Muddy Waters-style slide guitar. I said, 'What kind of money you talking about?' And like I said, making $15 a day, $200 a week–playing four nights a week–sounded pretty good. We went to Europe for ten weeks."

"I don't like to go for that long anymore," he continues. "With my family, I can't do that. I'm a poor man; I ain't got nothing. And what's gonna happen while I'm over there? That's what I got to think of. The first time I went overseas in '71, with the Mississippi Delta Blues Band, I told the guys the first week, 'I'll just rock along with what you're doing. And you follow me on what I'm doing.' I can do some slide along with anybody. I'd do ten or 15 minutes by myself, so the promoter in Holland asked me if I'd come over by myself. With the band I went to Denmark, Norway, Switzerland, Sweden, Holland, Germany, and France–for ten weeks. Came back with about $400. Then I went back to Holland by myself for a week or ten days, and I got back with $2,100!"

He has since been overseas 29 times. But when he's home in Holly Springs, it's business as usual. "A friend and I do a little commercial fishing when the weather's right," he says. "But the weather like it is this winter, we ain't doing no work at all. In the summer, when the weather's right, I make three or four hundred dollars a month. He don't pay me no salary; he owns the boat. But if we catch some fish, we just split what we catch. You sell your part, I sell mine. We haven't caught anything in two or three weeks, but sometimes we'll catch 1,800 pounds in a morning. We catch catfish, buffalo, carp. If you catch crappie and bass, you have to throw them back because we're commercial fishing, and those are sports fish."

R.L. is humble but proud of his music, as is his family. "Back when I was about ten, we'd listen to spiritual records," he points out. "Me and my sister started out singing spirituals when I was 12. And that's the first thing I played on guitar–spiritual music. My mom made us go to church every Sunday. I'm religious, but I don't believe you have to go to church every Sunday to be right. I think if you're right, you're right. At that time my mother didn't approve of the blues, but you ought to see her now [*laughs*]. I'll be playing the blues, and she goes, 'That's my boy.' Gets up and starts twisting. She's 82 years old, trying to do the twist."

A SELECTED R.L. BURNSIDE DISCOGRAPHY

Solo albums: *Hill Country Blues*, Swingmaster; *R.L. Burnside*, Swingmaster; *The Blues Of R.L. Burnside*, Swingmaster; *Mississippi Blues* (live in France, '83), Arion; *Sound Machine Groove*, Vogue; *Bad Luck City* ('92), Fat Possum.

Anthologies: *Mississippi Delta Blues, Vol. 2*, Arhoolie; *Deep Blues*, Atlantic.

On film: *Deep Blues*.

THE 1990 KING BISCUIT BLUES FESTIVAL in Helena, Arkansas, cast a mighty impressive lineup, with Albert King and James Cotton fronting powerful bands and Johnny Shines appearing with Robert Lockwood, Jr. One of the absolute highlights, though, came midday when John Hammond took to the stage alone. A harmonica rack around his neck, he sat cradling a beat-up National resophonic guitar. His opening slide into a familiar Robert Johnson riff brought a thunderous roar of appreciation from the sun-drenched crowd. Hammond kept fans on their feet throughout his set, conjuring potent images of Johnson, Son House, Blind Willie McTell, and other country blues greats of generations past. It's a scene John's lived over and over throughout a distinguished career that has brought him in touch with virtually every major bluesman who survived into the '60s.

The son and namesake of the famed Columbia record producer, John discovered early on that the blues provided the perfect antidote for teen angst. By 1960 he had acquired his first acoustic guitar. He quickly taught himself to play, and soon afterwards released his debut album. While Hammond has made a few forays into electric blues and rock bands, solo acoustic blues remains the heart of his art.

You still seem inspired by your original vision.

Yeah, it hasn't gone away. There are times when I feel closer to what I started out to do than even when I was just beginning. I feel a lot more confidence on the stage than I used to. When I began, I had all that energy without a lot of experience.

Is this a good time for blues?

It's a good time for me. There's such a demand, perhaps in reaction to MTV and the phony baloney stuff. There's a real searching for that big feeling and natural sound, like that "MTV Unplugged" segment with Stevie Ray Vaughan playing acoustic into the mike, just like what I do. So I think, far out, maybe it will come to that and there will be solo musicians playing acoustic on TV. Wouldn't that be fantastic, because there's so many great players. Rory Block is really great, man. I've been on a lot of shows with her in the last three years, and she's a real pro. She plays her ass off every night. Paul Geremia is a phenomenal country blues player. The guy is a killer, a great singer and songwriter. He works out of Newport, Rhode Island. He plays little clubs and makes hardly any money, but he's made albums for Flying Fish. He's a sophisticated fingerpicker who does Blind Lemon stuff and Willie McTell songs–wow! I'd go a thou-

John Hammond

July 1991

BY JAS OBRECHT

sand miles to hear him play.

Did you know many of the old-time bluesmen?

I worked on shows with John Hurt, Lightnin' Hopkins, Mance Lipscomb, Fred McDowell, Bukka White, and Arthur Crudup. I played with Son House and Skip James at the Gaslight in New York! Dick Waterman brought Son on a tour of the coffee-house circuit, and he had just recorded an album for Columbia in '63 or so. When I was introduced to Skip James, he was very shy. He was sick and very uptight about it. He had cancer and was really quiet, but what a fantastic voice! What a great vision, and he was so unique.

Oh, man, I was in a show with Furry Lewis. And Lonnie Johnson–I was on some gigs with him at Gerde's! Lonnie wasn't playing blues anymore. He had been found operating an elevator in a hotel in Philadelphia, and he sang sweet gospel-type tunes and jazz standards. He'd lost that edge, but every now and then there'd be moments and flashes. He was such a nice man, a beautiful guy. His early recordings are staggering–the sides where he accompanies Texas Alexander in the late '20s. He played any style. He played with Duke Ellington, Louis Armstrong. He was just phenomenal. I met the Reverend Robert Wilkins briefly, but I didn't get to hang out with him.

Probably my biggest influence when I first started to play was Big Joe Williams. I was on some shows playing harmonica behind him because he liked me; this was 1962 around Chicago. Big Joe played that 9-string guitar and had a little suitcase amplifier, and it was *outrageous*. He was so good, so intense! I used to watch him play with my jaw slack. I was profoundly influenced by Big Joe. Like Robert, he used an open-*A* tuning or open *G* with a capo. Even though I only knew him from hanging out with him for about a week, it was enough to be severely impressed. He was so intense! Big Joe was a character, man. He carried a

"Big Joe Williams," says Hammond, "was probably my biggest influence when I first started to play."

gun that was so big, an Army .45, and he wasn't a tall guy, but he was *big*. I drove him around for a week, and we went to Sylvio's one night. Somebody insulted Joe and he pulled out this gun, and I didn't even know he had a gun. All of a sudden I was more scared of Joe than anything else! But he was cool. He drank schnapps and whiskey and everything all night; it was amazing how much he could consume.

What kind of guitars were the early bluesmen attracted to?

Gibsons, good guitars. Not cheapo stuff, although even the cheapo stuff in those days was really well made. The Stellas and the Kays were all legitimate, well-made instruments in the '20s and '30s. I've seen the photograph of

Robert Johnson playing a Gibson, and that was a beautiful guitar. Even the bottom-of-the-line ones were good. Willie McTell had that Stella 12-string, and it's a *beautiful* instrument. Dave Ray had one when I was beginning to play, and that thing boomed–it was beautiful. So I think the good players had good instruments and a lot of good gigs too. I'm of the opinion that the guys who were really good and who recorded played some fairly sophisticated gigs, not just at the old juke joint out in the back or at a picnic. They actually played at clubs and sophisticated party scenes. These guys were extremely good players, and they knew it. And everybody else knew it too.

Do you see yourself as a continuation of that tradition?

I don't know. I see myself just as having to go through my own reality. I've got so much that I've got to deal with. You know, you get older, you get married, you have kids, you get divorced, you have more kids, you're married again, and all this stuff. I'm working gigs because I love to play, but also I've got to work. This is my life. I don't know how to do anything else, and I'm so fortunate that I've been able to support my family with the money I earn as a player. I'm very proud of that, and I've worked really hard to get to wherever I'm at now. There must have been something like that involved with every guy who got into playing blues as his career. Everybody has to deal with the same kind of stuff when you're traveling, trying to keep your head together so that you don't go nuts. When you're out on the road for two months or whatever, you get a little spacey sometimes.

Plus you're not traveling with a band.

My days of hanging out with the fellows are over. After a while it gets real thin. If you can play as a solo, you really should. There's something much finer about hearing a solo artist than hearing a band. Even if the band is great, all that loud extra stuff diffuses that focus. I would *love* to go back in time and see Robert play and see Lemon and Blind Boy Fuller. These guys were masters, and there was just one person playing.

Did most of the great 1930s bluesmen make it onto record?

I believe so–at least the ones that were so good that everybody just went, "Whoa!" I imagine there were great ones who never got to record, but usually you find a way to get heard. If you're really into it, you find a way to get it. Even given the Jim Crow scene, there was still that same intention to make your mark, to be remembered, to be recorded somehow. It's a universal thing.

Does John Lee Hooker's music strike you as being a continuation of older Delta music?

Hooker is a complete mystery to me, and yet you can hear where he got a lot of stuff. I discovered a guy in Detroit named Baby Boy Warren, and I know John Lee got a lot of stuff from his vocal style. He was impressed with Baby Boy Warren. They recorded about the same time. But John Lee, I think of him as being just unlike anybody else. He's got all of that heavy-duty imagery and that dark, somber kind of magical stuff. I don't have the words to describe it. I was so impressed when I heard him. I thought of him as probably being seven feet tall and having this voice that just went way down in the bottom.

I was on shows with John Lee when he played solo acoustic. He had a board under his feet–*clackity clackity, clackity clack.* Not a sophisticated guitar player, but totally unique. He had his own sound, his own feelings. And when I see guys play who don't stomp their feet, I'm like, how in the hell is that possible? Oh, man, Hooker was so incredible–what a guy! What a voice!

You've worked with many other great electric bluesmen.

I was on shows with Jimmy Reed. Of course, I played with Muddy and Howlin' Wolf. I got to know Howlin' Wolf maybe better than most did at that time. I opened his show at the Ash Grove in 1965, and I was just trembling with the fact that I was going to be on the show with Howlin' Wolf! I came backstage, and it was just him in the dressing room. He said [*in a gravelly, commanding growl*], "Come here and sit down. Where the fuck did you learn to play that?" It was a Robert Johnson song, and I said I learned it off the record. He said, "Play that right now for me!" So I played him the song, and he said, "Man, that's evil." He became real lucid and personal, and I got this rush of being acknowledged by somebody I idolized. He told me he learned to play from Charley Patton. He said, "Did you know that Charley Patton was an Indian? And he was the greatest blues player I ever heard." He told me Patton was a very short guy, half-Cherokee and white and about one-quarter African American. I don't think he was bullshitting me, but he said he was inspired to play by listening to Jimmie Rodgers records. My jaw fell open. I said, "Huh?" And Howlin' Wolf said, "Yep. I wanted to yodel in the worst way, and all that I could do was make a howl." Man, this is the truth. It was a magic moment.

And then he picked up my guitar and played [Patton's] "Stone Pony Blues." At the end, he flipped the guitar, made three turns, and hit the last three notes! It was the most slick thing I've ever seen, and I didn't even know he played the guitar. I said, "How come you don't play the guitar?" He said, "Oh man, I don't like electric guitars. I have my band together, and I play the harmonica. I hire a great guitar player." He had Hubert Sumlin at that time, and Hubert was just so good, so different. He was so attached to Wolf; he was Wolf's hands.

Wolf told me, "If I screwed up, Charley Patton would hit me upside the head." I can't imagine anyone hitting Wolf upside the head! It was just incredible. It made me go out and try to find everything Patton ever recorded. He was a great pre-Robert Johnson bluesman. And in terms of the major influences of Robert Johnson, you also have to look at Lonnie Johnson, Skip James–and Blind Lemon, to the extent that he influenced *everybody*, because his records in the '20s were all over the United States. He was one of the most popular blues and folk artists. His stuff is so varied, and his guitar style was just incredible. He could play almost anything.

What was your introduction to Robert Johnson?

My dad had a 78 of "Milkcow's Calf Blues" and "Terraplane Blues," and he played that for me in 1957–one of the few times he ever played anything for me. He saw how I was into blues and said, "Well, check this one out." It was on a weekend where I was staying with him, and I'll never forget that. And then he and [producer] Frank Driggs made a reel-to-reel tape for me in 1959 with about ten recordings. This was before the Columbia LP was released, so I was into Robert Johnson *heavy* by the time I was 17. I didn't even play the guitar then; I was just a blues fan. I didn't start to play guitar until I was 18.

What attracted you to blues in the first place?

John's breakthrough debut album, 1964.

I was raised in New York City, basically, by my mother and brother Jason. I saw my dad on occasion; my folks were divorced when I was five. And I got into stuff that I had heard on the radio. *The Alan Freed Show* was one of the big influences, and then I went to all the rock and roll shows, which were R&B shows, and got to see guys like Bo Diddley and Chuck Berry in the early days. Back then, everybody went up to Harlem to see shows. I saw Bo Diddley at the Apollo in '56, his first gig in New York. It was Bo Diddley, Jimmy Reed, and Muddy Waters playing with Little Walter, two bucks for a three-hour show. The Alan Freed shows would always have Chuck Berry or Bo Diddley, Jerry Lee Lewis, all these great groups like the Cadillacs, the El Dorados–the list is endless. I saw Gene Vincent & The Blue Caps, and some heavy-duty blues and R&B stuff. So here I was, 14 years old and just checking this out. I began to buy records,

and my blues bent hit by 1957. As soon as they came out, I started to buy all the albums that were being released of the singles of John Lee Hooker and Muddy Waters. Late at night on the AM radio from Nashville, I could get WLAC and hear not only Howlin' Wolf and Muddy, but guys I'd never heard of, like Lonesome Sundown and Slim Harpo. It became another world that sustained me through a heavy-duty adolescence.

How did you figure this stuff out on guitar?

By ear, by just hearing it over and over and over again. When I got the guitar, my friends who had guitars played folk style, so they were no help to me at all, so I worked out shit the best I could. I started simple, and I don't even know how I could play–it happened so fast. Within a year I was playing professionally.

Was your uncle Benny Goodman supportive of your decision to become a musician?

No, man. Uncle Benny was tough. He was a very stand-offish kind of guy. He and my dad had a feud going that I never did understand. He came to hear me play once and didn't even say anything.

Did any of the legendary musicians you met pass along any advice that served you well?

They just said keep doing it. And to a man, all of them were so nice to me, genuinely encouraging. One of my first shows ever was at the Ash Grove in June '62, opening for the four Staples. Pops played the guitar, and that was the only instrument, and it was so great. Pops took me aside after the show and said, "Man, I don't know where you learn this stuff, but don't ever stop doing it. It sounds so good. You know, I used to be a blues singer." And then he played some stuff for me on my guitar. He was so great and such a nice man, and he made me feel like somebody at a very early age. I'm so fortunate that I didn't get my feelings hurt badly, because I was so sensitive at that point, so uptight about playing. And I was walking into the lion's den, in a way, by playing blues. I didn't say I was a folk singer; I said, "I'm a *blues* singer," and this was in the days of Peter, Paul & Mary.

This was years before guys like Mike Bloomfield helped

introduce blues to a larger audience.

That's right, this was early on. I met Michael in Chicago in '61. He was at the University of Chicago, and he was hanging out. He knew all the guys. He took me to hear Little Walter, Sonny Boy Williamson. Michael was my Chicago connection. Oh, I loved Michael. He was a good friend and a funny guy. I miss him a lot. Michael's first recording was behind me, playing a little piano on my *So Many Roads* album. Then he went on to record with Paul Butterfield after that. Yeah, he wouldn't play the guitar on my record because he was so impressed with Robbie Robertson's playing.

Who else was playing country blues around that time?

When I first began playing, Josh White was on the scene. He was playing clubs, and he was very flashy. He wasn't playing a whole lot of blues anymore, but you could tell he had. Among young guys my age there was John Koerner, Dave Ray, Dave Van Ronk, and Eric Von Schmidt, who I didn't see all that often but

"I started simple, and it happened so fast."

I had heard about him. John Fahey was on the West Coast. I began my career in Los Angeles, and I was on gigs with Long Gone Miles, whose guitar player was Willie Chambers.

What has experience taught you about getting a good acoustic guitar sound?

Because I don't use a direct box or anything, I just play into a Shure SM-57 microphone. It's a hot mike. If you sing into it, it'll *pop* with all the p's, but for the guitar it's hot. There are other mikes, but I'm not sophisticated enough to know their names. I've played through Sennheisers that were just fantastic. I used to play in a small club in Florida that had little Bose speakers, but it was a great sound. The room was all wood, so perhaps that made for a great sound.

Any advice for playing outdoors?

Pray. It's hit or miss. If I'm on a show with a lot of electric bands, chances are I'm not going to sound so good. The engineers who know how to do electric bands tend not to know

how to get an acoustic sound, but at a folk festival like the Canadian ones in Winnipeg and Vancouver, they always have the sound just right. I've never talked to sound engineer guys enough to know exactly what they do to make it sound right. I'm spoiled that way; I've lucked out so many times.

Where do you position the mike in relation to the soundhole?

Just at the front of the hole. If you put it right into the hole, it's going to feed back. With a National, you aim the mike right at the cone. I really love playing the National. I like to save it for highlights of the evening because I feel so good playing it. But there are other nights when I feel like I'm really cooking on the Martin, and I'll play that more than the National. Every night is different. Every audience has its own magic, its own body. There are nights when I can do no wrong, and other nights when I don't think I'm playing anything and it's terrible.

Deep, deep blues: John Hammond and John Lee Hooker taping for the BBC, 1992.

The first thing an audience picks up on is how good you feel. You could be playing the greatest stuff that ever was, but if they perceive that you're blasé, down and out, or not feeling well, then they don't hear it. It's amazing. I've seen guys play great sets, and I'll come backstage and say, "Man, that was just a fantastic show!" and they'd say, "Oh, that was terrible." Bonnie Raitt opened for me back when she first started playing. I remember hearing her for the first time at the Gaslight in New York, and I went back and said, "That was just fantastic." And she looked at me and said, "Fuck you, man. Fuck you. That sucked!" And she'd just blown my mind. Bonnie is a fantastic guitar player. I miss her solo stuff with Freebo.

What cuts would have to go on an essential John Hammond anthology?

Oh, I'd love to do that! There's a tune I did with Roosevelt Sykes on the Vanguard album called *Footwork*–"44 Blues." Roosevelt played the piano on his trademark song, and it blew me away. He was so gracious to do that. He was Mr. Wonderful. Oh, what a pisser! That guy just loved life. He exuded charm and elegance, and outrageous bawdy lyrics. He may not have been the greatest piano player, but he had the greatest feeling on the stage. You couldn't help but flip out when he played.

Besides that track, I'd choose "So Many Roads"–Robbie Robertson is phenomenal. The *I Can Tell* album that I did for Atlantic had some cuts on it–"In The Mood," I put a hole in that one too, man. Every now and then somebody will play the first album that I did. There are things that I can't listen to at all, but there's other things that I say, "God!" Because I had only been playing about a year-and-a-half when I recorded that, and I don't know how or where I got this stuff from. To this day, I don't know how I can play what I play because I can't read a note. It's just a matter of ear and inspiration. I feel so inspired. It amazes me that this is my twenty-ninth year on the road.

A SELECTED JOHN HAMMOND DISCOGRAPHY

Solo albums: *John Hammond* ('62), Vanguard; *Big City Blues* ('64), Vanguard; *Country Blues* ('64), Vanguard; *So Many Roads* (backed by Charlie Musselwhite, members of the Band, and Mike Bloomfield on piano, '65), Vanguard; *Mirrors* ('67), Vanguard; *I Can Tell* ('67), Atlantic; *Sooner Or Later* ('68), Atlantic; *Southern Fried* (featuring Duane Allman, '69), Atlantic; *Best Of John Hammond* ('70), Vanguard; *I'm Satisfied* ('72), Columbia; *Triumvirate* (with Mike Bloomfield and Dr. John, '73), Columbia; *Can't Beat The Kid* ('75), Capricorn; *John Hammond Solo* ('76), Vanguard; *Footwork* ('78), Vanguard; *Hot Tracks* (with the Nighthawks, '79), Vanguard; *Mileage* ('80), Rounder; *Frogs For Snakes* ('82), Rounder; *Live* ('83), Rounder; *Spoonful* (reissue of *I Can Tell* and *Southern Fried*), Edsel; *John Hammond Live In Greece* ('84), Lyra; *John Hammond* (reissue of *Mileage* and *Frogs For Snakes*), Rounder; *Nobody But You* ('88), Flying Fish; *I Can Tell* (reissue of '67 LP, plus Allman tracks from *Southern Fried*), Atlantic; *Got Love If You Want It* ('92), Charisma; *Trouble No More* ('93), Charisma.

With others: John Lee Hooker, *Mr. Lucky*, Charisma.

Anthologies: *Blues At Newport* ('63), Vanguard; *Atlantic Blues: Guitar*, Atlantic; *Encore* ('69), Spivey; *Kings And The Queen*, Spivey; *The All Star World Of Spivey Records*, Spivey; *Blues Explosion* (Montreux, '84), Atlantic.

Soundtracks: *Little Big Man* ('71).

On film: *The San Francisco Blues Festival* ('83); *The Search For Robert Johnson* ('92). Hammond has also appeared on PBS' *Lonesome Pine* and *Austin City Limits*, and he has made a blues guitar instructional video for Star Licks.

John Cephas

March 1987

BY JAS OBRECHT

EXQUISITE AND HEARTFELT, Bowling Green John Cephas' acoustic blues hearken back to Blind Boy Fuller, Rev. Gary Davis, Skip James, and other country blues greats of decades past. His rich, resonant voice projects a confidence that rivals Leadbelly's, and he's one of the few musicians on earth who can do a credible Skip James impersonation, complete down to eerie falsetto phrasings. "I play this music because I don't want it to die," says the native Virginian. "The blues is such good music, and it really has something to say. It's not like some of the rock and roll and punk rock and heavy metal and all that repetitious, noisy stuff. The blues is the backbone of all of that other music. It's the grassroots, and that's what people really love."

While his covers of Skip James' "Cherryball" and "Hard Time Killing Floor Blues" echo the Delta originals, Cephas draws another side of his guitar playing from the more sophisticated, ragtime-influenced Piedmont tradition. "The two styles are easily distinguished," he points out. "Mississippi Delta blues has more single-string, harsh progressions, whereas the Piedmont style has a richer, more full-bodied, melodious sound. It features a multitude of strings, just a ringing out of the guitar. Blind Boy Fuller and Rev. Gary Davis are absolutely the essence and the very tops, as far as the Piedmont is concerned. They have had the greatest influence on guitar players. Blind Boy Fuller is a little simpler to catch on to than Rev. Gary Davis. Gary Davis did some stuff that was so fancy that even I can't get it on the guitar. Buddy Moss was another important player."

By trade, John works as a carpenter for the Army National Guard in Washington, D.C. During the past few years, though, his blues have taken him on many European tours, as well as to Africa, Central America, South America, and the Caribbean. He performs the major American folk festivals, conducts seminars, and teaches at Seattle's Puget Sound Guitar Workshop and the Blues Workshop in Elkins, West Virginia. On most gigs, he's accompanied by his partner, Harmonica Phil Wiggins. John made the cover of *Living Blues* magazine in January '85, and five years later he was extensively profiled in Barry Lee Pearson's *Virginia Piedmont Blues*, published by University of Pennsylvania Press.

Born in 1930, Cephas heard his first blues early in life. "I was reared mostly in Washington, D.C.," he says, "but my mother and father used to bring me back and forth to Virginia 'cause that was where most of my mother's family was from. Even when I was at a very early age, I was touched by the blues. There used to be a lot of blues musicians in the

black community—not people that were really known, but it was like a way of life. My aunt used to play, and her boyfriend, Haley Dorsey, used to come around all the time and play. I heard that sound, and that's what got me started off. But even though my family liked the blues, they would always discourage me from pursuing it rather than religious music. They told me it was more like serving the devil." The son of a Baptist minister, the youngster was coached by his mother to sing gospel duets in church with his brother.

At age nine, John made his first attempts to learn guitar: "My father forbade me to play his guitar, because he feared that I would break it up. But when he would leave home, I used to get his guitar and play it. I started in open keys. He used to catch me all the time, just about—he would remember how he put it down, or I might break a string, and boy, I'd get a good lickin' behind that. But that didn't never stop me 'cause I would continue on to play the guitar every chance I got." John's aunt taught him his first chords. In his teens, he played blues and country breakdowns at house parties with his cousin David Talliaferro.

Cephas remembers Talliaferro as an excellent guitarist and credits him with teaching him the three-fingered Piedmont picking style: "I never use a flatpick. I always use a thumbpick and a fingerpick on my index finger. Sometimes I use one on my middle finger too, but I usually play that without a pick. If I want to do a roll, I'll use my other fingers, but mostly it's just the thumb and two fingers." In his early years, he played slide with a knife, laying the guitar flat on his lap.

John's first acoustic guitars of note were Gibsons. Trashed in house-party fights, these were replaced with Yamahas. "I bought three or four of those and wore them out," he says. "Then a few years ago, Fender came out with their [F-270SCE] cutaway acoustic/electric, which I was very fascinated with after playing it. The guy at the music store let me borrow one and take it on tour, and I was so impressed with it that I bought three of them. That's what I'm playing now."

To this day, the influence of John's earliest recording heroes resounds in his playing: "I listened to a lot of Blind Boy Fuller, Rev. Gary Davis, Blind Blake, Buddy Moss, Mississippi John Hurt, and guys like that on one of them old wind-up record players. I guess Blind Boy Fuller and Gary Davis were my real, real heroes. I used to just love playing along to their records, and that's how I learned a whole lot of stuff. I also loved Skip James. I was so enchanted and fas-

"Even though my family liked the blues, they would always discourage me from pursuing it rather than religious music."

cinated with his sound that I practiced and listened to him for hours on end, just trying to figure out what he was doing. Practicing came real easy because I could remember sounds. And, experimenting with the guitar, I would hear sounds myself, or I might concoct them in my own head and just fool with the guitar until I got them out of there." John has fond memories of hanging around outside of Gary Davis and Blind Boy Fuller shows while still a grade-schooler in Virginia. Years later, he played gigs with Buddy Moss.

It wasn't until the '60s that Cephas began turning his blues into cash. "Before that," he remembers, "we played at house parties and a lot of juke joints, where guys used to gather up on weekends. We wouldn't get paid for jobs like that. As we got older, we played for drinks and food and to get high. We were like a band, but we didn't consider ourselves professional musicians." His first recognition came through blues pianist Wilbert "Big Chief" Ellis, who had been a busy New York City sideman during the '40s and early '50s. "I first met him at a house party," John recalls. "We didn't get a penny for it, but the house rocked all night till broad daylight. He played barrelhouse piano in the style of Walter Davis and Otis Spann. I started doing some festivals with Big Chief, and that's when I finally got started getting a little recognition as a pretty good professional player. We never made a lot of money at that time, though—$25 or $50, and we thought we was really getting a whole lot." John worked as Big Chief's accompanist from the late '60s until the pianist's death in 1977. His debut recording—"John Henry"—was done solo in 1973 for the Library of Congress' collection of work songs. His first commercial sessions, though, were with Big Chief Ellis—a 45 of "Fallin' Rain" and the album *Big Chief*, which also featured Brownie McGhee and Tarheel Slim on guitar.

John met Phil Wiggins during a jam session at the 1976 American Folklife Festival in Washington, D.C. At the time, Wiggins was backing street singer Flora Molton. "Chief and I was impressed with his playing," Cephas says, "so we asked him to come on and play with us. We formed a group called the Barrelhouse Rockers. That was Chief, Phil, me, and a guy named James Bellamy on bass. We performed together until Chief died in 1977, which temporarily disbanded the group because he was the leader. People kept calling me to do jobs, though, because they was interested in my guitar playing. So I asked Phil if he wanted to try to go out and do some gigs together because the sound that we had was pretty good. We started to practice, and we've been

"I play this music because I don't want it to die," Cephas says of country blues.

playing together ever since." While their exchanges have often been compared to those of Sonny Terry and Brownie McGhee, Cephas and Wiggins project a distinct personality all their own.

After appearing at the National Folk Festival and the Down Home Blues Festival, the duo participated in the late-'70s Travelling Blues Workshop with John Jackson, Mother Scott, Flora Molton, and Archie Edwards. They cut an album in 1981 for West Germany's L+R label, *Living Country Blues, Vol. 1–Bowling Green John Cephas & Harmonica Phil Wiggins From Virginia, U.S.A.*, and toured Europe several times during the decade. Billed as the Bowling Green Blues Trio, Cephas, Wiggins, and guitarist Barry Pearson also worked as blues ambassadors under the auspices of the U.S. State Department. Their 1982 African journey included concerts in Botswana, Zimbabwe, Ghana, Madagascar, Mali, Mauritania, and the Ivory Coast. The following year, the trio traveled through Central and South America.

Cephas and Wiggins recorded their second LP, *Sweet Bitter Blues*, on April 9, 1983, in Falls Church, Virginia. While less polished than later works, the album contains an outstanding arrangement of "St. James Infirmary," John's "Tribute To Skip James," a couple of fingerpicked instrumentals, and the deep blues "Highway 301" and "Sweet Bitter Blues."

1986's *Dog Days Of August*, cut in a single night at John's home near Bowling Green, has superior sound and performances–so much so that it won that year's W.C. Handy Award for Best Traditional Album. "They brought all the equipment down and set it up in my living room, which just happens to have good acoustics for recording," Cephas reports. "After they set up, we just went for it. I just started playing the guitar, they mixed it, and that beautiful sound came out of it. Most of the songs were done in one shot. There was no re-recording or dubbing-in on any of the songs on the album. The cassette version has an extra cut, Rev. Gary Davis' 'Will Do My Last Singing In The Land,' which was dubbed twice so I could sing a two-part harmony with myself. We did almost 20 songs during that session, so we have enough for maybe two albums."

Although the bluesman holds a Yamaha in the cover photo, a Fender was used for every track: "That Fender cutaway is a very good-sounding guitar. It has a large body and a good, booming bass. What you hear on that album is actually that guitar without amplification." In concert with Wiggins, Cephas often uses one guitar in standard tuning, plus another tuned to open *Dm* for Skip James material. He routes these to a small Peavey amp, finding that "this gives me mobility where I don't have to sit and hold the guitar at a mike that's aimed a special way. I can move around and get the spirit, you know." Like his hero Blind Boy Fuller, he favors an early-'30s steel-bodied National Duolian, open-tuned to *G* or *E* for slide. (He featured this instrument and a Martin D-28 during the 1990 Masters Of The Steel String Guitar tour.)

While he's known as an acoustic player, Cephas has experimented with electrics. "I had plenty of 'em," he laughs, "and I still have an Ibanez. But the acousti-cal guitar has more of a musical sound. It's more natural and sensible than electrified guitars. I just got disenchanted with that loud, repetitious music with that squealing and a-hollerin'. The acoustic music is more down to earth–*real* listening music. It's real-ly saying something. Electric guitar is most-ly a whole lot of noise, as far as I am con-cerned." Although he never uses it onstage, Cephas bought a steel guitar and took lessons for four years from Bud Charlton, former sideman for Ernest Tubb.

On occasion, John ventures outside of the blues: "I can play some of that upbeat stuff, like a few of those old torch songs–'When I Grow Too Old To Dream,' 'Just An Old Shanty'–and some ragtime numbers. Man, I can't even take a stab at telling you how many numbers I know." Cephas and Wiggins have written many songs together, including "Roberta" and the title track

"If you want to play country blues, shut out all of that punk rock, funk rock, and even jazz."

for *Dog Days Of August*. "Phil's more talented as a song-writer than I am," John insists. "I've done some songs, but they haven't been very impressive. I think Phil takes the honors there." While the pair includes a few vocal duets in its repertoire, John does most of the singing.

Cephas' ultimate goal is the preservation of traditional blues: "More than anything else, I would like to see a revival of country blues by more young people learning to play this good music rather than going into all this electrified, loud noise that they're doing. I would like to see them supporting traditional artists–going to concerts, taking workshops and seminars so that they can find the back-bone of all American music. That is why I stay in the field of traditional music and why I won't change and go over into the rock and roll and the upbeat stuff. I don't want it to die.

"If you want to play country blues, you should shut out all the other stuff that is appealing to the younger generations, like all of that punk rock, funk rock, and even jazz, which is wonderful. Get some old records and listen to the old guys. Apply yourself and practice diligently. And don't lose sight of your goal. If your goal is to play that music, then stick with it. Don't change or get discouraged. If you're sincere about it, then you will reach that end."

A SELECTED JOHN CEPHAS DISCOGRAPHY

With Phil Wiggins: *Living Country Blues, Vol. 1–Bowling Green John Cephas & Harmonica Phil Wiggins From Virginia, U.S.A.* ('81), L+R; *Sweet Bitter Blues* ('83), L+R; *Let It Roll* ('85), Marimac; *Dog Days Of August* ('86), Flying Fish; *Walking Blues* ('88), Marimac; *Guitar Man* ('89), Flying Fish; *Flip, Flop, & Fly* ('92), Flying Fish; *Bluesmen* ('93), Chesky.

With others: Big Chief Ellis, *Big Chief Ellis* ('76), Trix; John Woolfork, *Virginia Traditions: Tidewater Blues* ('82), Blue Ridge Institute.

Anthologies: *Virginia Traditions: Non-Blues Secular Black Music* ("John Henry," '73), Library Of Congress; *Songs Of Death And Tragedy* ('78), Library Of Congress; *American Folk Blues Festival '81*, L+R; *East Coast Blues* (two cuts, '83), L+R; *Blues Roots*, World Music Institute.

PRIME MOVERS

Muddy Waters

August 1983

BY JAS OBRECHT

ROLLING HIS EYES TOWARD HEAVEN and shaking his head like a man possessed, Muddy Waters cast a powerful spell. His high cheekbones and Oriental eyes gave him a certain Eastern, inscrutable quality, and at times his face even seemed angelic. He could easily work audiences into a frenzy, marrying the sexual urgency of his lyrics to the vocal slide statements that for 40 years were as much a part of his signature as his voice, which many claim was the best in electric blues.

A Delta-bred bluesman, Muddy instinctively understood the unpretentious beauty and power in simplicity. Time and again, he transformed basic patterns into blues master-pieces. Decades after their introduction, hypnotic stop-time songs such as "Mannish Boy" still electrify listeners. Like the superstitions and voodoo images prominent in his best-known lyrics, Muddy's primal, earthy rhythms contain a deep, almost subconscious appeal.

More than any other performer, Muddy Waters was responsible for forging Delta acoustic music into the electri-fied, band-oriented urban blues of today. And some of his bands were the stuff legends are made of. In the '50s alone, he performed with Jimmy Rogers, Pat Hare, Willie Dixon, pianists Otis Spann and Memphis Slim, and the top names in blues harmonica–Little Walter, Walter Horton, Sonny Boy Williamson II, Junior Wells, and James Cotton among them. British groups copied his songs in the early '60s, one nam-ing themselves after his "Rolling Stone," and guitarists such as Buddy Guy, Mike Bloomfield, Eric Clapton, and Johnny Winter came to share his stage. But through the years and various sidemen, Muddy's music remained intensely his own. His vocals and playing patterns have often been imi-tated, but no one has ever quite captured his touch. By the end of his life, Muddy Waters was hailed as the "Father of Chicago Blues." "It makes me feel very good to be called that," he said. "You know, I feel like I deserve it. I've been through quite a bit, and I've paid my dues."

Old-time bluesmen would insist that to really have an instinctive feel like Muddy's, you'd have to be raised in the Mississippi Delta. A flat plain of former swampland bor-dered on the west by the Mississippi River from Memphis to Vicksburg and on the east by the Yazoo River, the Delta has been predominantly black since it was first drained and cleared. After the Civil War, most of its land was worked by cotton sharecroppers who lived on tenant farms or planta-tions. Many found solace from their physical hardships and low social status in the church's promise of salvation and a

joyous afterlife. Others turned to earthier remedies, such as drinking, gambling, and listening to "the devil's music" or, as it was more commonly known, the blues.

Bandleader W.C. Handy, the self-proclaimed "Father Of The Blues," heard this form of music for the first time in 1903, when he was awakened in the Delta's Tutwiler train station by a ragged slide guitarist. Charley Patton, the most famous progenitor of the Delta style, sometimes cradled his guitar on his lap and played knife-style. The rough-voiced singer moved to Dockery's plantation in the heart of the Delta before World War I, and performed at house parties and local juke joints with two other influential guitarists, Willie Brown and Tommy Johnson. A convicted murderer and failed preacher, Son House developed his ferocious slide style in the late 1920s, and he sometimes played with Brown and Patton. Skip James, Garfield Akers, and Ishman Bracey were also among those who contributed to the Delta blues guitar style. Most of these men knew each other, and all had recorded 78s by 1931.

For sheer finesse, though, Delta blues guitar reached its zenith in the 1936 and '37 recordings of Robert Johnson, who had learned from Son House and Willie Brown. Johnson epitomized the Delta bottleneck style, executing poignant slide phrases or short fills against a steady, damped bass. Several of the 29 songs he recorded became postwar blues standards: "Walkin' Blues," "Kind Hearted Woman Blues," "I Believe I'll Dust My Broom," and "Rambling On My Mind" among them. Of all the Delta bluesmen, Robert Johnson and Son House would have the most profound effect on young Muddy Waters.

***

"The Gypsy woman told my mother,
Before I was born,
'You gotta boy child's coming,
He gonna be a son of a gun'"
–"Hoochie Coochie Man"

The second son of sharecroppers Ollie Morganfield and Bertha Jones, McKinley Morganfield began his Mississippi odyssey in the plantation settlement of Rolling Fork on April 4, 1915. The toddler loved to crawl in the standing water behind his father's two-room shack, so his grandmother nicknamed him Muddy. His sisters added Waters. Ollie Morganfield played blues guitar, but Muddy wasn't around long enough to remember it. With the death of his mother, the three-year-old was bundled off a hundred miles north to be raised by his maternal grandmother, Della Jones, who lived out in the country just northwest of Clarksdale on the Stovall plantation off Highway 1. Here Muddy grew up in a battered one-room cabin, less than a day's walk from where W.C. Handy first heard the blues.

The boy's earliest attempt at music consisted of banging on a kerosene can and singing. He failed at accordion, then took up Jew's harp. At seven, Muddy received his Christmas wish–a "French harp," or harmonica–and by 13 he had fairly mastered the instrument. After finishing the third grade, he was pulled from school and sent to work the fields, plowing and chopping cotton for 50¢ a day. Years later he described his fieldhand days in Paul Oliver's *Conversation With The Blues*: "I do remember I was always singin', 'I cain't be satisfied, I be all troubled in mind.' Seems to me like I was always singin' that, because I was always singin' jest the way I felt. And maybe I didn't exactly *know* it, but I jest didn't like the way things were down there in Mississippi."

"From a kid up," Muddy told Jim O'Neal and Amy van Singel during the extensive interview published in *Living Blues* issue #64, "I wanted to definitely be a musician or a good preacher or a heck of a baseball player. I just had to. I had three choices. I couldn't play ball too good–like I hurt my finger and I stopped that. I couldn't preach, and well, all I had left was getting into the music thing." Even before he could pick "nary a note" on the guitar, Muddy jammed on harmonica with Robert McCollum, a popular musician who later recorded as Robert Nighthawk. Robert and his "brother" Percy played at Muddy's first wedding, to Mabel Berry, on November 20, 1932.

That same year, Muddy saved nickels and dimes until he had the $2.50 needed to buy a secondhand Stella guitar. "The first time I played on it," he told Jim Rooney in *Bossmen*, "I made 50¢ with it at one of those all-night places, and then the man that runned it raised me to $2.50 a night, and I knew I was doing right." The first song he mastered was Leroy Carr's 1928 hit, "How Long–How Long Blues," while the first song he composed, he told Alan Lomax, was "I Don't Want No Black Woman Charley-Hamming My Bones." Muddy's next instrument, a Sears Silvertone obtained via catalog, cost $11. "I had a beautiful box then," he beamed. He watched his friend Scott Bohanner finger chords, and taught himself to pick out little lead patterns. Muddy gave frequent performances, either as a solo artist or as the harp player accompanying Bohanner's guitar. Within a year Muddy surpassed Bohanner on guitar, and the men formed an act patterned after the popular Mississippi Sheiks. Muddy played lead and harmonica, while Bohanner supplied rhythm and Henry "Son" Simms, a former Patton sideman, doubled on guitar and violin. The trio appeared at juke houses, balls, and Saturday night fish fries around Clarksdale, earning a sandwich, moonshine, and 50¢ apiece for playing blues and hillbilly tunes until sunrise. Muddy spent some of his money on 78s by Blind Blake, Blind Lemon Jefferson, Blind Boy Fuller, and Charley Patton. After hearing Robert Johnson's 78s of "Terraplane Blues" and "Walkin' Blues," Muddy said, "I always followed his records right down the line."

The biggest influence on Muddy was Eddie "Son" House, who lived just north of Robinsonville, where he often performed at fish fries and other social events with his cigar-chomping pal Willie Brown. Unlike their sometime playing partner Charley Patton–a "clowning man" with a guitar–Son House took his music mighty seriously. Sitting on a straight-backed chair, he'd suddenly whip his head back, roll his eyes inside his skull, and slide a bottleneck up his guitar strings. Veins bulging in his forehead, he'd moan, thump a bass note, and begin singing with the deep conviction of a sinner on judgment day. His guitar tuned to a chord, he propelled rhyming, strung-together verses with open-handed rhythms, bottleneck wails, and ringing notes pulled pistol-like with his index finger. In person or on 78, Son's blues were intense, anguished, and as powerful as any on record. Seeing him in rural Tunica County, Mississippi, had inspired Robert Johnson, and House likewise cast a lifelong spell over Muddy Waters, who first saw him perform in Clarksdale in 1929.

"One night we went to one of those Saturday night fish fries," Waters explained to *Down Beat* in 1969, "and Son House was playing there. When I heard Son House, I should have broke my bottleneck. Played this same place for about four weeks in a row, and I was there every night. You couldn't get me out of that corner, listening to what he's doing." In the O'Neal interview, Waters remembered, "I thought Son House was the greatest guitar player in the world when I heard him because he was usin' that bottle-neck style, and I loved that sound, man." Son showed Muddy how to tune a guitar in standard and open tunings, taught him his "My Black Mama" riff, and demonstrated how to smooth a bottleneck by holding its jagged end over a hot flame. Big Joe Williams, who'd converted his guitar to a 9-string, reportedly taught Muddy "Baby, Please Don't Go."

While elements of Muddy's guitar tone and vocal style were drawn from House, some of his arrangement techniques and slide embellishments were closer to those heard on Robert Johnson's 78s. "I consider myself to be what you might call a mixture of all three," he explained. "I had part of my own, part of Son House, and a little part of Robert Johnson. I seen him at a distance a couple of times, but never actually seen him to play. I regret that very much, because I liked his style. I thought he was real great from his records, beautiful. Really, though, it was Son House who influenced me to play. I was really behind Son House all the way." Johnny Winter remembers that Muddy looked up to Son as a father figure, adding, "Muddy always said that he learned a lot from Son House, and he always referred to him as the 'old man.'"

Whenever possible, Muddy supplemented his tractor driver income by providing musical performances and, in a way, community services. "I did it all, man," he confided to interviewers Robert Neff and Anthony Connor in *Blues*, published by Godine. "I tried to gamble, and I made and sold whiskey. I didn't stick nobody up, but I was successful with my whiskey. I used to make that jive out on the Stovall plantation. Had me a little still back out in the bushes, man. I never did believe I would get over working, though, and I probably never would have but for music. I'd have worked to 105 years old and saved $10,000–*maybe!* Because they wasn't paying nothing. I made just as much as the guy who worked five days, 75¢ a day. I used to make $2.50 on Saturday night at a frolic or supper with my guitar, and you couldn't make but $3.75 for five days' work. So I laid back and hid from the bossman and made just as much as everyone, and was just as rested as I wanted to be. You got to use your brain." Muddy moved to St. Louis for a few months in '39 or '40, but found the city intimidating and unprofitable.

He returned home and opened a roadhouse on the Stovall plantation, peddling moonshine, reigning over marathon gambling sessions, and performing blues. On occasion he brought over talent from Helena, such as the night Sonny Boy Williamson played at Muddy's shack with young Elmore James on guitar. Sonny Boy returned the favor, featuring Muddy and Son Simms on his radio show. To lure heavyweight talent to his juke, Muddy would drive to Friars Point, catch the Helena ferry, and head to radio station KFFA, home of the popular *King Biscuit Time* show. The cost of hiring a better-known musician–$25 in advance, $25 the night of the show–was offset when the performers announced their appearances over the airwaves.

Muddy had his own string band too, a raucous, drummerless, back-country outfit with Simms on violin, Percy Thomas on guitar, Louis Ford on mandolin, and a huge stand-up bassist named Pittypat. Their repertoire of waltzes and pop hits like "Sitting On Top Of The World" and "Corrina" was similar to one of Muddy's favorite bands, the Mississippi Sheiks. ("Walked 10 miles to see them play," Muddy told O'Neal. "They was high time through there, makin' them good records, man.") Three or four times a year, bossman Howard Stovall would hire Muddy's band to play white parties.

During the summer of '41, Alan Lomax and John Work, members of a joint field recording team sponsored by the Library of Congress and Fisk University, journeyed to the Delta to find Robert Johnson. By then Johnson was dead, and their second choice, Elmore James, couldn't be found.

Locals directed them to a tough young field hand who, they said, played in a manner remarkably similar to Robert Johnson's. He worked under the name of McKinley Morganfield, but everyone called him Muddy Waters.

Muddy had wanted to record since he'd first heard Son House 78s on the jukebox, but he was initially suspicious of Lomax, thinking he was there to bust him for making moonshine. Muddy ended up liking Lomax, though, and agreed to record a couple of songs in exchange for $20 and a copy of the 78. Muddy explained to Jim O'Neal that they then headed back to his shack: "We went down there and we set his stuff up, got it out of the trunk of his car–all his long batteries–and set 'em up on my front porch. And I was in my front room with my guitar, my little microphone, and he ground his wire down through the window and he went to work. And when I played a song and he played it back, then I was *ready* to work. Never heard that voice before, you know, and I was *ready*."

His guitar tuned to open *G*, Waters slipped a bottleneck over his little finger and began playing "Country Blues." With its deliberate pacing, dead-serious vocals, popping bass, and fierce slide chorus, the song was based on Son House's "Walking Blues," which Robert Johnson had also learned from Son. Lomax interviewed Muddy on record immediately after he'd completed the take. Waters calmly described writing his version on or about October 8, 1938, while fixing a tire puncture: "I had been mistreated by a girl, and it looks like that run in my mind to sing this song. I just felt blue, and the song fell into my mind and just come to me just like that and I started singing my own." The song, he added, "come from the cotton field and the boy what put the record out–Robert Johnson. He put out 'Walkin' Blues.' But I knowed the tune 'fore I heard it on the record. I learned it from Son House." Asked whether Johnson or House was the better player, Muddy responded, "I think they both about equal."

The reason he took up guitar, Muddy told Lomax, was "I just loved the music. Saw Son Simms done playin', and I just wanted to do it and I took after it." He remembered practicing an hour-and-a-half to two hours every day when he first started, and described listening to a 78 of "How Long–How Long Blues," the first song he'd ever worked out on guitar: "I just got the song in my ear and went on and just tried to play it." He picked up his bottleneck style, he added, from Son House, and used three tunings–"Spanish" (open *G*), "the natural," and "straight *E*," which he also called "the cross-noting."

Muddy's second selection, "I Be's Troubled," was an original tune he'd made up while walking down the road after hearing a church song. The lyrics provided a good indication of his mental framework at the time:

> *"Well, I feel tomorrow,*
> *Like I feel today,*
> *I'm gonna pack my suitcase,*
> *And make my getaway,*
> *Lord, I'm troubled,*
> *I'm all worried,*
> *And I never be satisfied,*
> *And I just can't keep from crying"*

Asked how he wrote songs, Muddy described: "I make up verses first. After I get my verse made up, then I come get my guitar and try two or three different tunings, see which one would be the better to play it in. Then I starts." Muddy wrapped up the session with "Burr Clover Farm Blues," a song he'd composed at the request of his boss, who grew burr clover on the plantation.

Lomax kept his word and sent a $20 check along with the Library of Congress 78 of "Country Blues"/"I Be's Troubled," which stated "Sung with guitar by McKinley Morganfield at Stovall, Miss., 1941" on the label. A testament to Muddy's great musicianship, these tracks still sound as fresh and vital as the 78s Robert Johnson recorded just a few years earlier.

The following summer Lomax returned and recorded the Son Simms Four–Simms, Percy Thomas, Louis Ford, and Muddy Waters. These raw, exuberant, downhome cuts may seem out of tune to some listeners, but the peculiar tonalities created by playing in improvised tunings on inexpensive instruments were exciting. In the years to come, Muddy would use microtonal excursions outside the standard blues scale to conjure dramatic effects. Waters sang "Ramblin' Kid Blues" and "Rosalie," while Louis Ford fronted "Joe Turner" and Percy Thomas handled vocals on "Pearlie May Blues." Muddy and Simms both played guitars on a recutting of "Burr Clover Farm Blues" and the country swing tune "Take A Walk With Me," which shares melodic similarities with Robert Johnson's "Sweet Home Chicago." Charles Berry, Waters' brother-in-law, came in for a pair of takes of "I Be Bound To Write You," essentially a dual-slide-guitar reworking of "I Be's Troubled" with new lyrics. Robert Johnson's influence was unmistakable in Muddy's unaccompanied "You Gonna Miss Me When I'm Gone."

Muddy borrowed Lomax' Martin acoustic for his final session that summer, probably held in a room off the commissary at Sherard's plantation in Clarksdale. He recorded "You Got To Take Sick And Die Some Of These Days" and "Why Don't You Live Right So God Can Use You" and recut a tune from the summer before, "Country Blues, No. 2." After another take of "You're Gonna Miss Me When I'm Gone," Muddy wrapped up his Library of Congress recordings with "32-20 Blues" featuring Charles Berry on second guitar.

According to Lomax' notes, Muddy's unrecorded repertoire at the time featured pop songs ("Dinah," "I Ain't Got Nobody," and "The House"), country and western faves ("Home On The Range," "Deep In The Heart Of Texas," "Boots And Saddles," "Missouri Waltz," and "Be Honest With Me"), blues by Sonny Boy Williamson and Walter Davis, and Muddy's original numbers "Ramblin' Kid," "Number One Highway," and "Canary Bird Blues." Lomax noted that Muddy kept a table-model Victrola record player at home, along with a few 78s by Arthur Crudup, Peetie Wheatstraw, Tony Hollins, Sonny Boy Williamson, and Jay McShann. Muddy named Fats Waller as his favorite radio star, Walter Davis as his favorite recording artist.

On December 18, 1942, Muddy made his mark–an "X"–on an application for a marriage license in Coahoma County. Five days later, he took 27-year-old Sallie Ann Adams of Stovall, Mississippi, as his second wife. The couple shared a four-room shack in the middle of a cotton field with Muddy's grandmother and his uncle Joe Grant. Sharecropping eight acres, Muddy's family owned only a few hogs and chickens and a small vegetable garden. After paying off debts at the plantation commissary, they hoped to clear between $100 and $300 at the end of the year. Muddy's wife and grandmother were regular churchgoers, and on Saturday nights everyone piled into Muddy's 1934 V-8 Ford to drive to country dances. Waters told Lomax that besides blues, his band played love songs and breakdowns at dances, adding, "I like to play the blues the best." The most popular non-blues numbers at these events, Muddy figured, were "Corrina," "Down By The Riverside," "Chattanooga Choo-Choo," "Blues In The Night," "Darktown Strutters Ball," and "Red Sails In The Sunset."

Muddy drove a tractor for another season, but more than anything he wanted to be a "known person." On occasion he sat in with traveling minstrel shows, and he blew harmonica for a couple of nights when Silas Green From New

The Complete Plantation Recordings

Muddy Waters

THE HISTORIC 1941-42 LIBRARY OF CONGRESS FIELD RECORDINGS

A half-century later, these tracks still sound fresh and vital.

Orleans, the most famous of the Southern vaudeville carnivals still in operation, passed through Clarksdale. Sometimes he drove his band up to Memphis to perform for tips in Handy's Park. Waters was well liked by the plantation hands who came to toss dice or down moonshine in his shack, and his blues performances had already made him a local legend. But the lure of what lay beyond the Delta was too powerful to resist: "I wanted to leave Mississippi in the worst way. I'd had a run-in with my boss on the plantation where I was working. I was driving a tractor and making some big bread–22¢ an hour–and I asked for a raise. He blew his top. I figured if anyone else was living in the city, I could make it there too."

Carrying only a suit of clothes and a guitar, Muddy Waters pulled out of the Clarksdale train station on a hot afternoon in May '43. He changed over to the Illinois Central in Memphis, and arrived in Chicago at 9:30 the next morning. It was a Saturday, but within hours he was hired to unload trucks on the afternoon shift at the Joanna Western Mills paper factory. Muddy stayed with childhood friends on the South Side for a couple of weeks, then moved in with his cousin. Within six months, he had his own apartment a few doors down at 1851 West 13th Street.

The most popular radio shows of the day broadcast big bands fronted by Tommy Dorsey, Harry James, and Glenn Miller. Bebop was making inroads among record buyers, and the rage in Chicago was love ballads by Nat King Cole, Billy Eckstine, and Johnny Moore's Three Blazers. The city's healthy blues community was headed by pianists Big Macco and Memphis Slim and guitarists Big Bill Broonzy, Lonnie Johnson, and Tampa Red, who already owned electrics and favored a smoother, more urbane style than Muddy's deep-bottom Mississippi blues. Still, it was Broonzy who gave Muddy his start by introducing him around Sylvio's club as "a pretty good blues singer" from Mississippi. "My blues, I came to Chicago and I had to work 'em up in there," Muddy told Jim O'Neal. "When I did get it through, boy, I bust Chicago wide open with 'em. Memphis Slim was the big man, Tampa Red and Maceo, Big Maceo–them was the big dudes up in here then. Big Bill, that's the nicest guy I ever met in my life. He really say I had it…. Big Bill was my mainline man. He was one of the greatest in the business. He was just *great* comin' up."

Invitations to play house rent parties for whiskey and tips trickled in, and then Muddy found work backing Sonny Boy Williamson at the Plantation Club. Fingerpicking an acoustic guitar, he could scarcely cut through the din. Switching to metal fingerpicks didn't help much. Finally in 1944 Muddy received a cheap off-brand electric from his uncle. The new instrument expanded Waters' tone, but his style stayed the same. He favored open-*D* or open-*A* tunings and used a sawed-off bottleneck for slide (later in life he switched to a steel tube or Craftsman socket wrench).

Muddy journeyed back to Clarksdale in 1945 for his grandmother's funeral. Meanwhile, another young Mississippi guitarist/harmonicist took a job at a radio cabinet company with Muddy's cousin, Jesse Jones. Upon his return from Mississippi, Muddy was invited over to jam with the new guy, Jimmy Rogers, and thus began an important Chicago blues partnership. Rogers blew harmonica in their earliest lineup, while Muddy and Claude "Blue Smitty" Smith, an acquaintance of Jesse Jones, handled guitars. Playing house parties, Muddy sang original tunes and covers of Robert Johnson and Leroy Carr 78s. His guitar playing consisted mainly of thumped bass notes and bottleneck slides until Smitty, who was adept with boogie-woogie and blues, taught him to finger-fret solos. The trio moved on from one "five dollar a night" club to another.

Sonny Boy Williamson I, who apparently liked Muddy's car as much as his playing, hired Waters for out-of-town dates, such as his weekly gig at the Spot in Gary, Indiana. When Sonny Boy got too drunk to sing, pianist Eddie Boyd would take over as frontman. One night at a club in South Chicago, Sonny Boy slumped into a corner and Boyd grew too tired to sing. He asked Muddy if he could take over. "I said, 'Okay, I can sing,'" Muddy described to O'Neal, "so I pulled the mike to me, opened this big mouth up, boy, and the house went *crazy*, man." Sonny Boy, who loved whiskey more than his work, eventually got the band fired.

Waters' first Chicago recording occurred in 1945 or '46, when he cut a hopping horn version of "Mean Red Spider" that was leased to 20th Century, a subsidiary of Philadelphia's Ballen Record Co. The side is credited to James "Sweet Lucy" Carter And His Orchestra, but the singer/guitarist is certainly Muddy Waters. According to Muddy, supervisor J. Mayo Williams also recorded Jimmy Rogers and Sunnyland Slim at the same session. Ernest "Big" Crawford played bass, while Lee Brown, who arranged the date, probably manned piano on Muddy's side.

Muddy's second session, on September 27, 1946, was organized by blues recording czar Lester Melrose for Columbia Records. Waters was there on the recommendation of James "Beale Street" Clarke. The musicians backed vocalist Homer Harris on three sides, and Muddy fronted on his own "Jitterbug Blues," "Hard Day Blues," and "Burying Ground Blues." Clarke fronted on the session's only issued 78, "Come To Me Baby"/"You Can't Make The Grade." (The Waters tracks remained in the can until '72, when they were included on Testament Records' *Chicago Blues: The Beginning*.) "That country stuff might sound funny to 'em," Muddy speculated. "I'd imagine, you know, they'd say, 'This stuff isn't gonna sell.'"

Thanks to Sunnyland Slim, Muddy joined the roster of Leonard and Phil Chess' Aristocrat Records in 1947. Muddy was driving a truck for the Western Graves Venetian Blinds Co. when word arrived that he was wanted in the studio. Muddy explained to his boss that his cousin had been found dead in an alley, and that he needed time off. "I lied a big old lie that time," he would later smile. Muddy backed Sunnyland on "Johnson Machine Gun" and "Fly Right Little Girl," and then fronted on "Gypsy Woman" and "Little Anna Mae." Big Crawford, Memphis Slim's subtle sideman, thumped string bass. Amplification added new smoothness to Muddy's guitar tone, and perhaps a little of Blue Smitty's coaching echoed in the single lines of "Gypsy Woman." The entire date lasted less than a half-hour.

Leonard Chess was unimpressed by Muddy's first sides and shelved them for several months. After all, he figured, who was interested in old-time Delta blues? Encouraged by Evelyn Aron, his business partner, Chess finally agreed to let Muddy record again the following year. With Big Crawford's backing, Muddy cut "I Can't Be Satisfied" and "Feel Like Going Home." Both were old-fashioned blues, essentially reworkings of his seven-year-old Library of Congress sides. But amplification added sustain to his searing, whining slide, and Muddy intensified his declamatory vocal style by emphasizing vibrato and running words together into quick phrases. Vastly different from the sax jumps and smoky ballads dominating the R&B charts, Muddy's surging Delta rhythms would soon redirect the course of urban blues.

"I Can't Be Satisfied" was released on a Friday afternoon in April '48. Distributed from car trunks to record stores, beauty salons, barber shops, conductors, and train porters, the initial pressing of 3,000 sold out by Saturday evening. Muddy enjoyed recounting how he went to the Maxwell Radio Record Company to buy a couple of copies and found they were charging $1.10 for the 79¢ record and limiting sales to one per customer. Even after exclaiming "But I'm the man who made it," he left clutching only a single copy. "All of a sudden," he told Jim O'Neal, "I became Muddy Waters, you know? People started to speakin', hollerin' across streets at me."

The release of "I Can't Be Satisfied" signaled the beginning of the greatest creative era of Chicago blues. Muddy explained to James Rooney: "To get a name, you had to get a record. People lived right up under me, they didn't know who I was until I got a record out. Then they say, 'He live right there!'–got to get a record. I got a hit thing the first one I got. I calls it luck. It was a big blues seller amongst the black peoples." With just a handshake, Muddy and Leonard Chess sealed their contract. On Muddy's recommendation, Chess signed Robert Nighthawk.

"I Can't Be Satisfied" sold well in Chicago and the South through the summer of '48. The hit's immediate result was to land Muddy and his band–Jimmy Rogers on harp and guitar, Baby Face Leroy Foster on drums and guitar–prestigious gigs at the Du Drop Lounge and Boogie Woogie Inn. A superb, Delta-bred harmonica player, Marion Walter Jacobs–a.k.a. Little Walter–joined later in the year, permanently moving Rogers to guitar and Foster to drums. "There were four of us," Waters confided, "and that's when we began hitting heavy." Barely 18 years old, Little Walter was already an inveterate street jammer. "That boy, I had to chase him out of Jewtown regular," Waters told O'Neal. "He'd see me coming, and grab his mike and *gone!* He done made a lot of money down there. You know, sometimes Walter'd take in $35 or $40. That was good money then. More'n a club was payin' us."

The band didn't limit themselves to any special blues turfs, as Muddy told *Down Beat*: "Little Walter, Jimmy Rogers, and myself, we would go around looking for bands that were playing. We called ourselves 'the headhunters,' 'cause we'd go in and if we got the chance we were gonna burn 'em. Sometimes we'd come in and win the contest– they'd have an amateur contest with a prize–but the guy would come up to me after he found out who I was and say, 'Uh, uh, Muddy–you's *too heavy*. You can work for me if you wants, but you's too heavy to be in the contest.' Of course, I ain't like that no more. I know different now. 'Cause you can't be the best. You can just be a good 'un."

But with the possible exception of Elmore James' Broomdusters later in the '50s, Muddy's lineup was probably the best electric blues band of the era. Their music was raw and physical, each song a taut, emotional plea with Muddy's voice and slide guitar its roaring heart. Playing for all-black audiences, they seldom strayed from the structure of traditional 12-bar blues, outside of occasionally stretching out the count. Muddy was unafraid to sing behind the beat, telling his men: "You don't count it out–you *feel* it."

For transplanted Southerners, Muddy's sets in tiny sawdust clubs conjured the joy and anguish of their own pasts. He was the downhome blues shouter amplified, a commanding presence who could transfix the rowdiest tavern crowd with a patented bottleneck slide to the tonic and fifth and a few words sung in dark baritone. "I used to watch that guy, man," describes Buddy Guy, "and happy tears used to fall out of my eyes when I'd see him play slide. Oh, yeah." Muddy took chances, and his tone had more bite than a scolding shrew. His greatest appeal? "It was sex," Marshall Chess, son of Leonard Chess, insisted. "If you had ever seen Muddy then, the effect he had on women. Blues, you know, has always been a women's market. On Saturday they'd be lined up ten deep."

As tight as Muddy's musicians were, they were not allowed to accompany him in the studio. "Chess wouldn't upset things," Waters explained to Pete Welding. "He wouldn't mess with the harp or the extra guitar. He wanted to keep the combination that had made a hit record–just Big Crawford's bass and my guitar. It was amplified, but I was playing old-style blues." Muddy's final 1948 session produced the slow blues "Train Fare Home," followed by a slightly out-of-tune "Sittin' Here And Drinkin' (Whiskey Blues)." "Down South Blues" linked the Delta's popular "Rollin' And Tumblin'" theme to different lyrics, and "Kind Hearted Woman" was closely patterned after Robert Johnson's recording.

Baby Face Leroy came in on second guitar for four of Muddy's 1949 Aristocrat sides, while the ever-present Crawford played bass. Of special interest, though, were two highly amplified cuts Muddy made with just Crawford: "Little Geneva" blended unusual slide licks into a theme based on Robert Johnson's "Love In Vain," while the bottleneck in "Canary Bird" buzzed around like a bumblebee. Muddy took Jimmy Rogers, Little Walter, and Baby Face Leroy on a tour of the South afterwards, centering on the Delta areas around Clarksdale and Helena. For several weeks he performed daily on KFFA radio, earning five dollars a week and getting bookings via listeners who phoned in.

On his return to Chicago, Muddy stepped outside of his leader's role to record behind his sidemen. Along with Big Crawford, he played on Chess-produced cuts credited to Jimmy Rogers & His Trio. He also clandestinely met Baby Face Leroy and Little Walter over at the Parkway studios to be part of the Little Walter Trio and the Baby Face Leroy Trio. Muddy laid back on most tunes, but couldn't resist tearing loose with slides and moans during Foster's wild two-part "Rollin' And Tumblin'," one of the most powerful downhome sides ever recorded. "People have suggested that Little Walter is the greatest blues player on any instrument, and I'm

Waters in his heyday, thumbpicking a late-'50s Telecaster.

inclined to agree," offers Ry Cooder. "It's just his time and his touch. The most elegant blues. And the rhythm of something like 'Rollin' And Tumblin'' is just awesome, with Muddy Waters on slide. Muddy always played the same way; it always sounds the same–just great! Jesus!

"To me, that track's an example of somebody who transcends anything we think we know about the guitar. I mean, that could've been a one-string there, it could've been a post with a string, it could've been any of my guitars–it wouldn't make any difference. The guy's just playing on two strings, like the *G* and *D* strings, so that tuning must be *G*. What's great about when guys play like that is you don't feel frets and six strings and a scale length. It's beyond construction and principles. He's playing where he knows those notes are, and they are locking into this spirit thing of playing, the movement of the song. And he goes past the note–the note isn't just there at the fret, because there are degrees of the note. It's like Turkish music in some ways–degrees. There's 5,000 notes. The great thing about this is it liberates you from these idiotic frets. So sometimes he's expressing some excitement by alternating between playing a note and going sharp. And that's where all those old guys hear that stuff. There are nuances–no phrases come down the same. When you need a lift, you go sharp, and when you need to sour it up and make it feel a little darker, you go flat. But you don't

think about it. You just do it.

"It is staggering to have that quality of performance on a record, though, knowing what we know. If you listen to Sonny Boy Williamson's 'Little Village' with Leonard Chess, how did records ever get made when assholes like that were running the show? It's amazing to me. They made these records under such duress, conditions that ultimately we see all around us today. They talk about slaves singing code songs–it's hardly any different. But the really amazing thing is that you can get that kind of free expression and excitement and even joy, perhaps, in a white guy's recording studio. It takes a lot of power and amazing strength of personalities. These aren't wimpy guys. They're pretty heavy-duty characters, and it's coming out. They're just blasting away. We're very lucky this shit got recorded at all. It's a miracle that it did, when you look at the record business and the people that ran it.

"Baby Face Leroy's 'Rollin' And Tumblin'' is not chord-based. You don't feel chord in it. And it's greater than anything African. This is taken to another planet. This is the beauty of the American music. Listen to those big string bends–whoa! Slap bass. It's incredible. Nobody in Africa can do that. I mean, as great as African music is, it all comes together in this country. Mister Microtone. I guess that's what you'd have to say, finally, about Muddy: He's Oriental in his approach." Upset at hearing his most prominent artist on another label's release, Chess firmly advised Muddy not to play slide for anyone else.

Johnnie Jones came in on piano and Baby Face Leroy played drums on Muddy's first 78 of the '50s under his own name. "Screamin' And Cryin'" was notable for its extended single-string slide solo. Muddy was then paired with Big Crawford for two takes of "Rollin' And Tumblin'" designed to compete with the Parkway issue. Snappy drums and bass lifted the song into the new decade, while Muddy's verse of moans paid homage to its Delta roots. Around this time, brothers Leonard and Phil Chess bought out their remaining partner at Aristocrat and formed Chess Records.

Muddy provided the first hit for the newly organized

label, "Rolling Stone" backed by "Walkin' Blues." With guitar in the forefront of a bare-bones arrangement, "Rolling Stone" became one of Waters' best-known songs. Despite the distorted electric guitar, "Walkin' Blues" retained the flavor of Robert Johnson's version. The 78 sold exceptionally well in the triangle covering St. Louis, Memphis, and Chicago, and ranks high among Muddy's performances.

Muddy's band consistently packed the house at the Du Drop Lounge, where they were often double-billed in blues contests with Big Bill Broonzy or Memphis Minnie. Encouraged by audience response at these shows, Chess finally let Little Walter back Muddy in the studio. That they could lock so tightly on their earliest effort, 1950's "You're Gonna Need My Help I Said," portended good things to come. Pushed by Little Walter's harp swoops and wails and the drummer's easy rim shots, Muddy's slide stung even harder on the session's remaining cuts, "Sad Letter Blues," "Early Morning Blues," and "Appealing Blues." The final taping of the year produced Muddy's first nationwide hit: "Louisiana Blues," which climbed into the R&B Top 10. A variation of the voodoo "mojo hand" theme with a nice guitar-harmonica unison, this side was backed by "Evans Shuffle," a boogie harp showcase with one of the most effective false endings imaginable.

In sessions that followed, Waters and Walter further forged their instruments into a seamless voice or created stunning call-and-response dialogs. Once Little Walter expanded his presence on record by using a good studio amp, he took over as the band's main soloist. "There's no doubt about it, man," says Buddy Guy, "that guy sent the price of a harmonica from five cents to a hundred-and-some dollars now! Little Walter said once, 'If George Washington Carver could make all his medicine out of a peanut, I can get something out of this harmonica.' And back then they would give harmonicas to you, almost, if you go in a music store. Walter was the one made those big chromatics famous, made all of 'em famous, man. He put that instrument on the market."

Jimmy Rogers, whose supple bass runs and unerring fills were essential to the stage act, was finally brought in to record with Muddy in '51. Before the year was over, Muddy had racked up another Top-10 hit with "Long Distance Call," which he later cited as his favorite of all the songs he recorded. Two other steady sellers, "Honey Bee" (with its brilliant microtonal slidework) and "Still A Fool," featured Little Walter's downhome guitar. Pete Welding explains: "For all his strengths as a supporting guitarist, Rogers was never comfortable with such mixed-meter, Delta-derived pieces as these two; Walter, on the other hand, understood them perfectly. This fact is nowhere more evident than on 'Honey

Bee' and 'Still A Fool,' where his second guitar part seems almost an extension of Muddy's lead. It's a pity Walter didn't record more on guitar, for his work on these two selections is flawless. This is not to take anything away from Rogers—his accomplishments are solid and well-documented on numerous records, both with Muddy and on his own." "She Moves Me," cut in '51 with Leonard Chess beating bass drum, became Muddy's biggest hit the following year.

With gigs nearly every night and widespread black radio play, Muddy now reigned supreme on Chicago's South Side. His amplified Delta music had come to define Chicago blues, and imitators sprung up in the Delta, Memphis, Detroit, and on both coasts. Tours took him to the East and South. "When Muddy would come to Detroit," John Lee Hooker recalls, "him and Genny, his wife, would stay at my house. He never would stay in a hotel. Little Walter would be with him. He was a sideman then, one of the greatest harmonica players ever lived. I think so. We would go on tour together sometimes, me and him and Little Walter, Jimmy Rogers. Remember Jimmy Rogers? He had this old Oldsmobile, brand new. And Little Walter was crazy, and he used to drive. Speedin' it. He'd be boogeyin'! And he'd be laughing 'cause I'd be nervous."

Understandably, the potential of success on their own began to attract Muddy's sidemen. After all, they were all fine soloists, and Waters let them prove it. "I give everybody a chance to play," he told them. "I'm not going to hold you back. *I* love you, but I can't make the people do that. *You* do that." Mary Katherine Aldin wrote in her liner notes for the *Muddy Waters* box set: "Some made it on their own and some didn't, but after you'd been in Muddy's band, you were *professional.* He tolerated no excessive drinking or drug use; he carried himself with enormous dignity always, and his band had to be on time, dressed well, sober and ready to play, and those who couldn't or wouldn't toe the line didn't last long."

Little Walter was the first to leave. He scored a huge 1952 hit on Checker with "Juke" (essentially the Waters band's instrumental signature) and quit to take over Junior Wells' position in the Four Aces. Naturally enough, Muddy hired Junior Wells until the harmonica player's induction notice arrived. At Chess' insistence, Little Walter continued to back Muddy in the studio until '57.

For a while, Little Walter's popularity eclipsed that of his former bandleader, but apparently this caused no bad blood between the musicians. "Muddy was friends with everybody," describes Buddy Guy. "I hear these rumors that he wasn't friends with the Wolf or Little Walter, and I was *there,* man. I never saw or heard a cross word other than what they all call all of us, which was 'motherfuckers.' And that was just a natural name. If you didn't answer, they would just come punch you on the shoulder and say, 'Hey, motherfucker–I'm talkin' to you.' It's like me and Junior Wells now: He don't come up and say, 'Hey, Buddy, how you doin'?' If I don't walk up and call Junior a 'motherfucker,' I think he think I'm mad. And really, that's the way it was then. Muddy would look at Walter and say, 'Motherfucker, you ain't playin' that right! You ain't playin' enough harp,' and Walter would tell Muddy the same thing: 'Motherfucker, you ain't playin' that slide. I don't hear what I want to hear.' And that's how they was. Other than that, these guys was the best of friends. Muddy was the type of guy who'd say, 'If you get a break, go for it.' Until he died, Muddy was like that. If something good happened to any sideman, he'd pat 'em on the back."

Walter Horton, with his wide, sweeping harp style, was brought into the band in 1953 and participated in the session that produced "Hoochie Coochie Man." With its voodoo imagery and commanding vocals, this Willie Dixon composition became one of Muddy's finest efforts. "Muddy changed the style of music,"

Muddy's "half-brother," piano giant Otis Spann.

observed Johnny Shines of Chicago blues in the '50s, "but it was through Willie Dixon. See, a lot of people don't give Willie Dixon no credit for things that happened. Willie Dixon was the man that changed the style of the blues in Chicago. As a songwriter and producer, that man is a genius. Yes, sir. You want a hit song, go to Willie Dixon. Play it like he say play it, and sing it like he say sing it–even Willie Dixon can't sing a lick, but just find out what he's talking about and do it–and you damn near got a hit." According to Dixon, Muddy knew it was a hit the moment he heard it: "I brought 'Hoochie Coochie Man' to him when he was working along 14th Street, and he liked it so well he went in the washroom, practiced a few minutes on his intonation, and he come right out and done it. And he's been doing it ever since."

"Hoochie Coochie Man" sold 4,000 copies the first week and became Muddy's biggest seller. "Muddy Waters crashes through with his strongest sales gatherer in many, many releases," wrote a reviewer for *Cash Box*. "Waters, always a solid salesman, waxes a strong piece of material that should push its way close to the top, if not all the way. The cantor throws every one of his tricks into his job, and receives backing that is certainly not the least important part of the disc's success." It spent weeks in the R&B Top 10. A few months after joining Waters, Horton took a gig under his own name and sent Henry Strong in to substitute. A strict leader, Muddy fired Horton and hired Strong, whose style was close to Little Walter's. Walter himself blew the swinging harp lines in 1953's "Baby Please Don't Go."

Muddy finally actualized his dream of a blues "big band" when pianist Otis Spann joined him later in the year. Spann, whom Muddy lovingly referred to as his half-brother, was an unobtrusive sideman who could accommodate styles ranging from subtle fills to thunderous boogies. His admission into the band completed Muddy's move away from the intimate Delta-inspired sound epitomized by the Big Crawford-Little Walter trio sessions to a smoother, more uptempo style. The Waters lineup of two guitars, harmonica, bass, drums, and piano created an enduring standard for blues bands. "I saw something there between Muddy and Otis Spann that was like father and son–for real," describes Buddy Guy. "I had been in Chicago about a year when I met B.B. King, and then him and Muddy and all of 'em would talk to me and Junior Wells like they was our father. I remember B.B. King saying once, 'Otis Spann–that's Muddy Waters' child.' And I've heard Spann say, 'Muddy come down to Mississippi and got me, and until I die, that's where I'll be.'"

With the added support of Spann, Muddy began concentrating on vocals and quit playing slide guitar. "The band sounded so good to me," he would later say, "I didn't think I had to play." Traditional 12-bar blues gave way to groove-oriented arrangements, and with the new emphasis on harp, drums, and piano, the work of Jimmy Rogers moved into the background. For a while, the formula worked: 1953 and '54 proved to be the heydays of Muddy's commercial success. Following in the wake of "Hoochie Coochie Man," "I Just Want To Make Love To You" reached #4 in the nationwide R&B charts and remained Top 10 for more than three months. The band ventured out of Chicago for one-nighters in St. Louis and Nashville, dates on both coasts, and a full-scale Southern tour with Sarah Vaughan and Nappy Brown. Back home, Muddy and his wife Geneva bought a well-kept two-story brownstone in the heart of Chicago's South Side ghetto.

Just as the Muddy Waters band was riding high on the successes of 1954, tragedy struck mid-summer: Stabbed by a girlfriend, Henry Strong bled to death in the back seat of Muddy's car on the way to the hospital. The incident deeply affected Muddy, who eventually hired West Memphis harmonicist James Cotton for Strong's position. Willie Dixon and drummer Fred Below appeared on Muddy's final 1954 chart entry, Dixon's "I'm Ready," which spotlighted superb chromatic harp riffs and added to the lyrical mystique spun in "Hoochie Coochie Man." "Muddy swings out," described *Cash Box*. "Lyrics are pretty potent, and Waters' delivery is Grade A. Beat is solid, and ork-ing [backing] is torrid. A great bet to make it." And make it, it did: right into the Top 10. It was Muddy's last big hit.

Chicago blues record sales started out strongly in 1954, then dropped 25% in the summer. Some South Side execs blamed the depressed economy. Television was also drawing evening listeners away from radio, the most important medium for blues promotion. But something more urgent was starting to come over the airwaves, a primal blend of R&B, blues, and country that was destined to eclipse the blues and every other popular style. Kids would call it rock and roll.

In Memphis, Elvis Presley paired the country tune "Blue Moon Of Kentucky" with a pulsating R&B version of "That's All Right" and sold over 7,000 copies in one week. Bill Haley & The Comets scored million-sellers with "Shake, Rattle, And Roll" and "Rock Around The Clock." Alerted to the vast new audience of white teenagers, A&R men from black-oriented independent record labels scrambled for rock acts. For many, Elvis' appearance on TV sealed the fate of older bluesmen: After all, how could 40-year-olds hope to compete with the hip-shaking gyrations of a teenage idol? Chess Records jumped on the bandwagon and signed artists recommended by Muddy Waters. Charles Edward Berry shortened his first name to Chuck, changed his country-style "Ida Red" to "Maybelline," and shot to #1 in August '55. Berry became as popular as Little Richard and Bill Haley. Soon another new Chess artist could smile down from the top of the charts: Bo Diddley.

Muddy landed an occasional song on the R&B charts–"Mannish Boy" in '56, "Nineteen Years Old" two years later–but his single sales would never approach those of the rock and rollers. He held onto his audience, though, working six nights a week at Smitty's Corner and other Chicago clubs, and Wednesday night dances in Gary, Indiana. He toured the East and South. Willie Dixon began working with the band, as did guitarist Pat Hare. Muddy's first album, Chess' *The Best Of Muddy Waters*, was released in 1958.

More and more, Muddy came to rely on songs written by Dixon and others, causing a sameness to permeate his music. With dismay, he saw the new generation of city-born blacks abandon blues as low-class gutter music. "Young Negro kids now, they're so used to what they hear on the radio, they just turn away from the old blues," he told Pete Welding. "It's not the music of today; it's the music of yesterday." Muddy still lived comfortably, but his prime gigs were dwindling. Unbeknownst to him, across the Atlantic he was selling records and becoming a legend.

American blues discs had begun appearing in England at the close of World War II. Some were left behind by soldiers; others were U.S. releases repackaged on British labels. Impressed by the vital earthiness of Chess blues, youngsters such as Keith Richards and Mick Jagger sent away to Chicago for releases. By the mid '50s, trad jazz–a recreation of dixieland and Chicago styles of the '20s–and skiffle, a folk-blues hybrid, had become the major British musical trends. Chris Barber, a leading exponent of trad jazz, arranged passage for Big Bill Broonzy, Josh White, and Brownie McGhee to come over and perform traditional acoustic blues in little clubs.

Before his death in August '58, Big Bill recommended that Barber bring Muddy over. Just back from a tour of the South, Muddy flew to England with Otis Spann as his only accompanist. Expecting to hear folk blues, British audiences were shocked by Muddy's tavern-shattering sound. One staid critic at the first show found himself retreating row by row from the volume, until he was finally forced to seek refuge in the men's room. "I didn't have no idea what was going on," Muddy confided to James Rooney. "I was touring with Chris Barber–a dixieland band. They thought I was a Big Bill Broonzy, which I wasn't. I had my amplifier, and Spann and I was going to do a Chicago thing. We opened up in Leeds, England. I was definitely too loud for them. The next morning we were in the

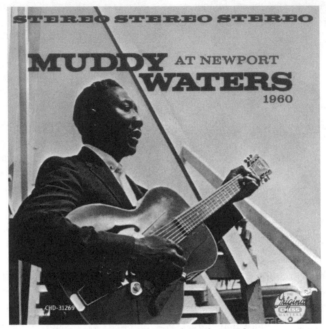
Got my mojo working: Newport '60, with Hooker's archtop.

headlines of the paper–'Screaming Guitar And Howling Piano.' That was when they were into the folk thing before the Rolling Stones." Muddy lowered his settings for the rest of the tour, which reportedly went well.

Much to his surprise, the English tour gained Muddy the attention of American folk and jazz fans. In April '59 he appeared onstage at Carnegie Recital Hall with James Cotton and Memphis Slim. To capitalize on his newfound audience, he was encouraged by Chess to record *Muddy Waters Sings Big Bill*, an undistinguished album of Broonzy material. Muddy's first European release, the French Vogue label's *Mississippi Blues*, took a harder stance, packaging cuts such as "I Can't Be Satisfied," "Evans Shuffle," and "Louisiana Blues."

Meanwhile, the savage power of Muddy's stage presentation remained undiminished. Paul Oliver attended a 1959 show at the F&J Lounge, a blue-collar black club in Gary, Indiana. "His band was his instrument," wrote Oliver in *Jazz Monthly*, "and he sang unhampered, stamping, hollering, his whole body jerking in sheer physical expression of his blues. He would double up, clench his fists, straighten with a

spring like a flick knife, leap in the air, arch his back, and literally punch out his words whilst the perspiration poured down his face and soaked through his clothing." Muddy was in a near-trance when he came offstage at 4:00 in the morning, Oliver added, and spent most of the next day lying in a dark room with an icepack on his forehead.

The Newport Jazz Festival booked the full Waters band to headline its 1960 Fourth of July blues program. Muddy was a sensation, earning standing ovations and being called back to sing "Got My Mojo Working" a second time. Along with Otis Spann and John Lee Hooker, he was filmed at the event for *Jazz USA*, a series of programs by the U.S. Information Agency. Chess issued the performance as *Muddy Waters At Newport*. Muddy returned to England in 1962, once again misjudging his audience. He told James Rooney: "I went back–took my acoustic with me–and everybody's hollering, 'Where's your amplifier?' I said, 'When I was here before, they didn't like my stuff.' But those English groups had picked up on my stuff and went wild with it. I said, 'I never know what's going on.' A bunch of those young kids came around. They could play. They'd pick up my guitar and fool with it. Then the Rolling Stones came out named after my song, you know, and recorded 'Just Make Love To You,' and the next thing I knew they were out there. And that's how people in the States really got to know who Muddy Waters was." Muddy toured England as part of the 1963 American Folk Blues Festival package, appearing on Granada TV's *Blues And Gospel Train*.

Back home, Waters hired Matt Murphy and Earl Hooker to play guitar on sessions. In '63 he contributed tracks to Chess' high-energy *Blues From Big Bill's Copa Cabana*, with Buddy Guy handling electric guitar, and appeared coast-to-coast on CBS' *International Hour*. Encouraged by Otis Spann, Muddy took up guitar again, using his red, late-'50s Fender Telecaster for sessions. Muddy enlisted Buddy Guy as his second guitarist on the unadorned, all-acoustic *Folk Singer*, issued in early '64. Muddy's unaccompanied "Feel Like Going Home" hearkened back to his Stovall days, while "My Home Is In The Delta" featured his unmistakable slide. "I remember that session very well," Buddy Guy describes. "Leonard Chess and Ralph Bass, one of the producers, told Muddy to go in Mississippi and try to find somebody because the colleges was goin' for that acoustic blues. They wanted him to go back and find somebody who really could play the acoustic guitar with him. They wanted no band and no electric instruments. He said, 'Set the session up tomorrow. I got it.' And when I walked in the studio, Leonard Chess and them was lookin' at Muddy like he was crazy. He just told him, 'Shut the fuck up. I got who I wanted.' I went to playin', and man, they're sittin' there with their mouth wide open, saying, 'Now how in the hell you know that?' I said, 'What did you think I learned on?' Even Willie Dixon didn't know it, and he's on there. That was a morning I never will forget. Of course, I love that record. I got that record, and I'll keep it as long as I live."

When British groups began arriving in America circa 1964, they proclaimed Muddy and other black bluesmen their sources of inspiration. Soon after landing, the Beatles announced their desire to see Muddy Waters and Bo Diddley: "Muddy Waters," asked one reporter, "where's that?" An incredulous Paul McCartney answered, "Don't you know who your own famous people are here?" The Rolling Stones were stunned by their first encounter with Waters, as Keith Richards describes: "Muddy was my man. He's the guy I listened to. I felt an immediate affinity when I heard Muddy go [*picks up a guitar and plays the opening lick from 'Rolling Stone'*]. You can't be harder than that, man. He said it all right there.

"So we went into Chess Studios in '64, the first time we came to America. Went to Chicago to record most of our second or third album at Chess, and we walked in. There's Phil Chess and there's Ron Malo, the engineer, and this guy in white overalls painting the ceiling. As we walked by into the studio, somebody said, 'Oh, by the way, this is Muddy Waters, and *he's* painting the ceiling.' He wasn't selling records at the time, and this is the way he got treated. My first meeting with Muddy Waters is over the paintbrush, dripping, covered in white paint. 'This is Muddy Waters.' *I'm dying*, right? I get to meet *The Man*–he's my fucking god, right?–and he's painting the ceiling! And I'm gonna work in his studio. Ouch! Oh, this is the record business, right? Mmmmm. The highs with the lows! Ooh, boy. In that one little meeting, in those few seconds, Muddy taught me more…. [*Imitates Muddy speaking in a gentle voice*] 'It's a pleasure to meet you.' And the look in the eye was saying, 'Well, *you* can be painting the ceiling next year!' Because he had no idea that we revered him or anything. We were just another bunch of creeps."

As Muddy became more famous in the years to come, he often credited the Rolling Stones with helping to renew interest in his music. "Ah, he did, yes, and bless him," Keith continues. "When we started the Rolling Stones, we were just little kids, right? We felt we had some of the licks down, but our aim was to turn other people on to Muddy Waters. I mean, we were carrying flags, idealistic teenage sort of shit. There was no way we thought anybody was really going to seriously listen to us, but we wanted to get a few people interested in listening to the shit we thought they ought to listen to–which is very elitist and arrogant, to think you can tell other people what to listen to. But that was our aim, to turn people on to the blues. If we could turn them on to Muddy and Jimmy Reed and Howlin' Wolf and John Lee Hooker, then our job was done."

Other British blues-rock guitarists paid Muddy homage through imitation, notably Eric Clapton, Jeff Beck, Jimmy Page, and Alvin Lee. Their praise awakened still more white American youths to the fact that the songs credited to one "M. Morganfield" on their favorite albums were indeed by an active performer. "That's a funny damn thing," Waters told Rooney. "Had to get somebody from out of another country to let my white kids over here know where we stand. They're crying for bread and got it in their backyard. They got some of the best blues singers that ever lived right here in the United States–there's nobody else, you know. They sure ain't got no real good blues singers in England. But they got some heck of a players there–guitars, every other thing."

Young white musicians in the U.S. followed suit. Students from the University of Chicago made pilgrimages to nearby South Side clubs and began duplicating what they heard. Foremost among these were a young harmonica student named Paul Butterfield and his guitar-playing pal, Mike Bloomfield. They formed the Butterfield Blues Band, stole the show at Newport, and paved the way for other white Chicago blues acts fronted by Charlie Musselwhite and Steve Miller. Jimi Hendrix unabashedly admitted his debt to Muddy and worked the bluesman's motifs into his repertoire. "The first guitarist I was aware of was Muddy Waters," Jimi told *Rolling Stone*. "I heard one of his records when I was a little boy, and it scared me to death."

As rock and blues became more closely integrated, traditional performers such as Howlin' Wolf, John Lee Hooker, Buddy Guy, and Junior Wells found bookings in white coffee houses and clubs. For the first time, Muddy himself was welcomed full-scale onto the turntables and stages of young white America. And with the possible exception of B.B. King later on, no other bluesman made the transition so easily and gracefully. His new fans found him confident, articulate, and proud: "I wasn't a cat to come in with a big bottle of wine in my pocket and talking loud," Muddy insisted. Billed as the "Living Legend," Muddy discovered his new audience was appreciative of his original style, which enabled him to drop some of the newer songs he tended to dismiss as "commercial gimmicks." With the exception of rare stints at venues such as Harlem's Apollo Theater, Muddy found himself performing before predominantly white audiences at clubs, colleges, and festivals in Monterey, Newport, and Europe. Even New York's Museum of Modern Art and the Illinois Governor's Ball provided him venues. "If you like the blues," Muddy explained, "I can get them over to you no matter what color you are. I do the same thing for white audiences that I do for black audiences. I get down and do real blues. I get the blues, and I just let go in the middle of it."

Chess issued Muddy's *The Real Folk Blues*–a compilation of hits–in January 1966, and then attempted to "update" his sound by casting him as a soul singer on *Brass And The Blues*. Competing with heavy organ and honking, overdubbed horns, Muddy was painfully out of character. Otis Spann's Bluesway album *The Blues Is Where It's At* contained more blues-approved Waters work in the train-like slide effects of "Chicago Blues" and the slide signature in "My Home Is On The Delta." During August '66, Muddy and his band backed John Lee Hooker on *Live At Cafe Au-Go-Go.* "I really enjoyed when we did the Cafe Au-Go-Go in New York, me and Otis Spann and Muddy Waters," Hooker describes. "Otis was one of the greatest piano players of the blues ever. He had the name of the greatest piano player, and he was great. And a good man too. Loyal, friendly, no ego, no nothing, just a perfect gentleman. And Muddy was a really good man." Chess issued more early Waters sides on 1967's *More Real Folk Blues.* Around this time, Muddy hosted the daytime *The Muddy Waters Blues Show* over Chicago's WOPA radio.

For his next appearance on vinyl, Cadet's *Electric Mud,* Waters was submerged in psychedelic fuzztones, wah-wahs, and overbearing drums. It troubled him that the tracks couldn't be reproduced onstage: "If you've got to have big amplifiers and wah-wahs and equipment to make your guitar say different things, well, hell, you can't play no blues." A far more satisfying project from this period was *Fathers And Sons,* a pure blues collaboration with Otis Spann, Paul Butterfield, Mike Bloomfield, drummer Sam Lay, and bassist Duck Dunn. Butterfield and Bloomfield shone on the project, providing smooth, urbane accompaniment, especially on a memorable concert version of "Long Distance Call."

Muddy's popularity with rockers peaked in the late '60s. His '69 appearance at Chicago's Auditorium Theater almost brought the house down–literally. "For nearly ten minutes after he left the stage," wrote Don deMichael in *Rolling Stone,* "the audience roared its delight. They stomped, shouted, clapped, whistled, screamed, jumped up and down the aisles and seats. Pleadings from the stage to calm down were to little avail." Muddy and his band then undertook a tough series of one-nighters at colleges and clubs. On their way home in October, Muddy was in a head-on car accident outside of Champaign, Illinois. The wreck killed his driver, and Muddy suffered a broken leg, fractured ribs, a sprained back, and paralyzed right hand. "They had to lift me out of the car," he described. "I was a lucky man. I was in the hospital for three months. I had numb hands, and they gave me lots of trouble."

For a while, it was rumored he would never play guitar again. "I went places in Europe with Muddy after the accident," recalls Buddy Guy, "and he was very particular about who was driving and the speed they went. In those days there was a lot of two-way highways, and I think that's what he was on when this guy met his driver head-on. To be in a car when the steering wheel gets pushed completely through the driver, I imagine that follows you up to your death. Muddy had all these iron pins in his hip. Before that, he used to sit down and jump up and do his little Muddy dances all the time."

After nearly a year, Waters was able to discard his crutches and begin playing guitar again. He organized a stage band with guitarists Sammy Lawhorn and James "Pee Wee" Madison and drummer Willie Smith, who'd toured with him in the late '60s. Pinetop Perkins replaced Otis Spann, who'd passed away in 1970. The group toured Japan and Australia, stayed active on the college circuit, and made occasional forays into Chicago clubs, where Muddy Waters was invariably revered as the city's foremost statesman of the blues. He and his wife Geneva still lived in the South Side ghetto with their children and grandchildren.

Muddy's kinetic home-turf performances of "Hoochie Coochie Man" and "Nineteen Years Old" were captured in Harley Cokliss' 1970 film *Chicago Blues.* Waters found himself back in front of a camera in '71, singing "Long Distance Call" and "Got My Mojo Working" in *Black, White And Blues.* A collection of Chess sides from '51 through '67, *They Call Me Muddy Waters* won a 1971 Grammy for Best Ethnic/Traditional recording. Muddy flew to London to record his follow-up album with a mixture of Chicago bluesmen and white English rockers such as Rory Gallagher and Rick Grech. *The London Muddy Waters Sessions* won high praise and another Grammy, and Muddy landed a headlining role at the '72 Montreux Jazz Festival. His slide playing was improving, taking on a vocal, almost conversational quality in "Honey Bee" from *Ann Arbor Blues & Jazz Festival 1972.*

In 1973 the McKinley Morganfield family moved to the suburbs; Westmont, Illinois, would remain Muddy's home base for the rest of his life. He featured his touring band on his next studio album, *Can't Get No Grindin'*. 1974's *London Revisited* collected unissued tracks from *The London Muddy Waters Sessions*. Muddy toured Australia and New Zealand, and then crossed the globe to jazz festivals in France and Montreux. In '75 he cut the Grammy-winning *Woodstock Album*, as well as the *Mandingo* film soundtrack. He was then off to festivals in Poland, Germany, and Italy. Stateside, his club gigs were interspersed with stadium and arena appearances with rock bands.

Less frequently, Muddy was called to appear on blues bills with contemporaries such as B.B. King, Albert King, and Bobby Bland. "Ain't too many left that play the real *deep* blues," he explained to Robert Palmer in *Deep Blues*. "There's John Lee Hooker, Lightnin' Hopkins–he have the Texas sound, and Texas blues is very, very good blues–and, let's see, who else? Ain't too many more left. They got all these white kids now. Some of them can play *good* blues. They play so much, run a ring around you playin' guitar, but they cannot vocal like the black man. Now B.B. King plays blues, but his blues is not as deep as my blues. He play a type of blues that can work in a higher class place, like to a higher-class of peoples–they call 'em urban blues. Bobby Blue Bland, the same thing. Albert King play a little deeper blues than they do. Otis Rush is deeper. I don't want to put down nothin' that'll make anybody mad, but it's the truth. There ain't too many left sings the type of blues that I sing."

Thanks in part to Johnny Winter, Muddy Waters created some of his greatest records during the last years of his life. Johnny juggled the roles of friend, bandmate, producer, and protector of the classic sound, and near the end, Muddy came to regard him as a son. Their albums together recast classic material from the 1940s and '50s alongside tough new songs–in effect, reprising Muddy's career–and brought Waters three consecutive Grammy Awards for Best Ethnic or Traditional Recording.

The bluesmen first met in Austin, Texas, during the late '60s. "I can't tell you how excited I was to be on the bill with him," Johnny recalls. "He'd been my idol since I was 11 or 12, so I was there with my camera and my tape recorder. I was so honored just to meet Muddy, I wasn't about to ask to sit in." After the show, Muddy stopped by to admire Johnny's old National, and the two musicians briefly jammed. Muddy too was impressed with their initial meeting. "I see a lot of B.B.-type guitar," he told *Guitar Player* in 1970, "but my style and Lightnin' Hopkins' and John Lee Hooker's, I don't see many people playing. When I played with Johnny Winter in Texas, I knew he had something coming because he was try-

ing to do it the way I did years ago. My sound was pretty hard to get into. It's simple and there's not a lot of notes going on, but it's got a heck of a sound, man."

The musicians met again in '74 while filming PBS' *Soundstage*. "It was then that Muddy and I realized that we could definitely work together," Winter says. "It seems like he had made such bad records, and then when I saw him play, I knew it wasn't because he couldn't still sing and play. It seems like they had tried putting him with all the English guys and recording him nice and clean. Even when he played with his own group, things just weren't sounding as good. But he was still playing and singing the same way. He hadn't changed, but recording techniques and a lot of things had. Those records right before we started working together–I hated hearing them. I thought, 'This guy's still great! Why is he making such terrible records?'

"When I finally got a chance to produce him, my whole thing was to make the record that Muddy wanted to make with the musicians he wanted to work with. If Muddy got pissed off, things would change. He was the boss. My job as producer was to get things sounding right to him. I was trying to not do anything new, but just get back to where he was comfortable and things sounded good and hard, like they were sounding in the late '50s." The final lineup for *Hard Again*, cut for Columbia/Blue Sky during October '76, was James Cotton, Pinetop Perkins, Willie "Big Eyes" Smith on drums, Charles Calmese on bass, and Johnny, Muddy, and Bob Margolin on guitars.

Johnny and Muddy decided upon a live, "back to mono" approach and booked a studio in Connecticut with a room large enough to accommodate the whole band. "We miked everyone," Johnny says, "but we mostly used this one big mike in the middle of the room. It caught a lot of the room's natural echo." Muddy displayed spine-chilling authority as he premiered exciting new material, recut one of his 1941 field recordings, and roared through standards like "Mannish Boy" and "I Want To Be Loved." The album got its title during playback, when Waters uttered that the music "made my little pee pee hard again!"

Since Muddy hadn't played slide for a while, it was up to Johnny to conjure the *Hard Again* bottleneck sounds. "I had studied those records and loved them for so long that I pretty much had gotten everything down before we started working together," Winter explains. "Muddy didn't play a lot at the time. In fact, for a while he'd almost completely quit playing guitar. The blues revival in the late '60s convinced him that he ought to start playing more guitar. But he just had one guitar on the road, and if he'd break a string or something, then you wouldn't hear any slide. But he'd usually just pick a couple of songs a night and play some really

Ain't that a man – Muddy Waters, 1981.

© JON SIEVERT

Satisfied" and "Feel Like Going Home," which was eventually released on *King Bee*. "Boy, he really didn't want to do that," Johnny recalls. "We did those two songs the same night, after the whole record was finished and he was ready to leave. I begged him: 'Please, let's just try a couple of acoustic things.' He did those two songs one time each, and that was it. We could have definitely got a better cut on both of those, but it was that or nothing. He was real conscious about not recording too many songs. He knew how many songs it would take to do an album. The Chess people put out so much of his extra stuff on albums, and he wanted to make sure that that didn't happen. He wanted to get paid for everything he did, and he didn't want a bunch of extra things floating around. So he was real careful." One of Muddy's favorite albums, *Hard Again*, brought the band bookings across the U.S. and Europe.

Johnny produced Muddy's 1977 album *I'm Ready*, with Walter Horton and Jerry Portnoy sharing harp chores and Jimmy Rogers coming in on guitar. Muddy himself played slide on "33 Years," "Mamie," and "Screamin' And Cryin'." "Muddy loved that real trebly Telecaster sound, and he got a great sound out of his treble pickup," Johnny observed. "Muddy would tune his guitar to an *E* chord and just put his capo wherever it needed to go. Though he played in the *A* tuning on a lot of his early records, during the last few years of his life I don't think I ever heard Muddy play in the *A*.

"Muddy didn't really play a lot of stuff. He pretty much had one or two leads, and he would just improvise around with those a little bit. He had it down where it was good and didn't really need to be more than what he did. He definitely had his little licks, like:

burning leads on that, but he didn't seem to want to play all the time like he used to. Maybe it was because he was in that car wreck, and he definitely had pain if he played very long. But on that first record, every time I'd pick up a guitar, Muddy would put his down and just sing. There weren't very many tracks where both of us played guitar at the same time, but there were a couple, finally. I played slide on all that record."

With Johnny bottlenecking a metal-bodied National resophonic, Waters journeyed to his Delta roots for "I Can't Be

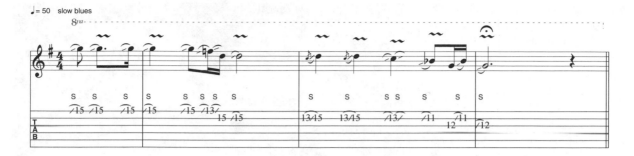

He used to play that in just about everything. He had those signature licks, so you could always tell that it was a Muddy Waters song. Muddy was real modest about his own guitar playing. He didn't feel like he was that great. I remember him saying, 'Well, even an old man probably can outplay me, but I got something now that works.' He knew what he did was cool, but it wasn't about technique. He just had a way of putting it all together."

The band's next tour crisscrossed the U.S., and Muddy was invited to perform at the annual White House staff picnic in August. President Jimmy Carter introduced him to the 700 guests, saying, "As you know, Muddy Waters is one of the great performers of all time. He's won more awards than I could name. His music is well known around the world, comes from a good part of the country, and represents accurately the background and history of the American people." Muddy was featured singing "Mannish Boy" in 1978's *The Last Waltz.* Clips of him singing the same song and "Got My Mojo Working" during a German tour late in the year were presented in the film *Eric Clapton And His Rolling Hotel.* While traveling with Clapton, the widowed bluesman married 25-year-old Marva Jean King.

"Towards the end of his life," wrote Mary Katherine Aldin, "Muddy finally began to enjoy the recognition and honor that he had earned. He discarded the prowling, feral stage presence that had been his hallmark in favor of a more sedate and dignified stance befitting the elder statesman of the blues that he had become. Younger musicians jostled for the chance to play with him, and he became, somewhat to his own puzzled surprise, the darling of the young white rock and roll crowd during the middle to late '70s."

Muddy and Johnny sorted through tapes of their concerts at Detroit's Masonic Temple and Harry Hopes Club in Cary, Illinois, for their stunning *Muddy "Mississippi" Waters Live.* Waters bellowed past hits in fierce, declamatory Delta style and threw cross-sections of his whole stylistic spectrum into amazing slide choruses. His tone was otherworldly. The performances left no doubt that Muddy Waters was still at the height of his powers. The *Live* lineups featured the cast from *Hard Again,* as well as Portnoy, bassist Calvin Smith, and

Luther "Guitar Jr." Johnson. "They wanted me to go on tour with my band and for Muddy's band to open," Winter explains, "and I just couldn't stand doing that. That would have hurt me. I didn't want Muddy to open for me, and I didn't want to be playing with a rock and roll band. I insisted we just had to somehow do this together. It was hard, because Muddy had to keep paying all his guys, I had a band that I had to pay, and James Cotton had his band. So we had to break up three different bands to do that tour. It was expensive, but I really wanted to do it. It was James and the bass player out of his band, while me and Pinetop, Willie Smith, and Bob Margolin were all out of Muddy's band.

"Muddy was real smart about that kind of stuff. Like James wanted to use his drummer, who was good, but Muddy said, 'Man, if we get all those people out of James' band, it's gonna start sounding like James' band.' He really wanted to make sure that didn't happen. And Willie wasn't near as good a technical drummer, but he was a great blues drummer, the kind of guy you'd hear on a good Saturday night. The way we did it, there weren't any little cliques, and everybody was just working for Muddy. It really was a good choice of musicians."

Johnny produced Muddy's swan song, *King Bee,* in '81. Among the songs were recuttings of "Sad, Sad Day," "(My Eyes) Keep Me In Trouble," and "Champagne & Reefer," a pro-marijuana song used to delight concertgoers. "It's too bad Muddy wouldn't do more takes," Johnny sighs, "because that could have been a better record; we had to go back and use some outtakes that weren't quite as great. If we would have had a few extra things to choose from, it definitely could have been better."

Waters toured in support of the album–his slide playing was unspeakably brilliant during his northern California appearances, when he and Johnny were interviewed by Tom Wheeler for their *Guitar Player* magazine cover story. Stricken with cancer, Muddy was preparing for another album when he peacefully passed away at home in his sleep on April 30, 1983. Pops Staples sang "Glory, Glory, Hallelujah, Since I Lay My Burden Down" at Muddy's funeral.

Muddy Waters was survived by his wife Marva, his children, four grandchildren, and seven great-grandchildren. The death of the 68-year-old bluesman added only a post-script to one of the world's great musical legacies. His spirit and influence will live on as long as electric blues are played. Buddy Guy speaks for countless other blues musicians when he says: "Whenever you hear me play, man, there's a part of Muddy Waters, Howlin' Wolf, Little Walter–all those great musicians. The only hard part about it is trying to play as much like them as you can, because nobody will ever fill the shoes of Muddy Waters and Howlin' Wolf and those great people that did that music."

The author thanks Mary Katherine Aldin, Ry Cooder, Willie Dixon, Buddy Guy, John Lee Hooker, Jim O'Neal, Robert Palmer, Keith Richards, Johnny Shines, Pete Welding, Tom Wheeler, Johnny Winter, and Living Blues *and* Down Beat *magazines for their contributions to this article.*

Muddy introduced his new bride Marva during a 1981 California appearance.

A SELECTED MUDDY WATERS DISCOGRAPHY

Early recordings: *The Complete Plantation Recordings* (includes the Lomax/Work interviews), Chess; *Muddy Waters: First Recording Sessions In Chronological Order, 1941-1946* (includes sides with Son Simms Four, Percy Thomas, Homer Harris, and James "Beale Street" Clark), Document; *Down On Stovall's Plantation*, Testament (Library of Congress, '41-'42). Anthologies: *The Greatest In Country Blues, Vol. 3* ("I Be's Troubled" from '41), Story Of Blues; *Chicago Blues: The Beginning* ('46), Testament; *OKeh Chicago Blues* ('46), Epic; *The Roots N' Blues Retrospective 1925-1950* box set ('46 side), Columbia.

On Chess: *Muddy Waters* box set (the essential Muddy Waters anthology, covering 1947 through the early '70s); *Rare And Unissued* ('47-'60); *Trouble No More* (singles, '55-'59); *The Best Of Muddy Waters* ('58; reissued in '69 as *Sail On*); *The Real Folk Blues*; *More Real Folk Blues*; *McKinley Morganfield A/K/A Muddy Waters*; *The Super Super Blues Band* (with Howlin' Wolf and Bo Diddley); *They Call Me Muddy Waters* ('51-'67); *Muddy Waters At Newport* ('60); *Muddy Waters Sings Big Bill* ('60); *Baby Please Don't Go* ('62-'67); *Folk Singer* ('63); *Brass And The Blues* ('66); *Electric Mud* (Cadet, '68); *After The Rain* (Cadet, '69);

Fathers And Sons ('69); *Live At Mr. Kelly's* ('71); *The London Muddy Waters Sessions* ('72); *London Revisited*; *Can't Get No Grindin'* ('73); *"Unk" In Funk* ('74); *The Muddy Waters Woodstock Album* ('75); *Rolling Stone*; *In Memoriam*; *Profile*.

Chess reissues: *Back In The Early Days* ('47-'55), Syndicate Chapter; *Good News* ('55-'58), Syndicate Chapter; *Muddy Waters On Chess 1948-1951*, Vogue (France); *Muddy Waters On Chess 1951-1959*, Vogue; *Baby Please Don't Go*, Vogue; *Sweet Home Chicago* (late '40s-mid '50s), Aura; *The Original Hoochie Coochie Man* ('48-'63), Stack-O-Hits; *Mississippi Rolling Stone* ('48-'65), Stack-O-Hits.

Other labels: *Muddy Waters, 1958* (live in England), Krazy Kat; *Hoochie Coochie Man* (live, '64), LRC; *Live Recordings 1965-1973*, Wolf; *Mud In Your Ear* ('67), Muse; *Muddy Waters Live, 1965-'68*, CFPC; *Live In Paris, 1968*, French Concerts; *Goin' Home* (live in Paris, '70), Fan Club; *Live In Antibes, 1974*, French Concerts; *Live In Concert, 1976* (Europe), Corrine; *The Warsaw Session 1* and *2* (live, '76), Poljazz; *Unreleased In The West* (Poland, '76), Moon; *Hard Again* ('77), Columbia/Blue Sky; *I'm Ready* ('78), Columbia/Blue Sky; *Muddy "Mississippi" Waters Live* ('77-'78), Columbia/Blue Sky; *King Bee* ('81), Columbia/Blue Sky; *Blue Sky* ('76-'80), Columbia.

With Otis Spann: *Half Ain't Been Told* ('64), Black Cat; *The Blues Never Die!* (Prestige, '65, with Muddy listed as "Dirty Rivers"), Original Blues Classics; *The Blues Is Where It's At* ('66), Bluesway/MCA; *Take Me Back Home* ('66), Black Magic; *Heart Loaded With Trouble*, Bluesway; *Bottom Of The Blues*, Bluesway; *Nobody Knows Chicago Like I Do* (Bluesway reissue), Charly; *Rarest Recordings*, JSP.

With Baby Face Leroy Foster: *Chicago Blues: The Early 1950s*, Blues Classics; *The Greatest In Country Blues, Vol. 3 (1929-1956)*, Story Of Blues.

With Little Walter: *Super Blues*, Chess; *The Best Of Little Walter*, Chess; *The Best Of Little Walter, Vol. 2*, Chess; *Boss Blues Harmonica*, Chess; *Little Walter*, Chess; *The Blues World Of Little Walter: The Parkway Sessions*, Delmark.

With Jimmy Rogers: *Chicago Bound*, Chess; *Jimmy Rogers*, Chess.

With Sonny Boy Williamson: *One Way Out*, Chess; *Down And Out Blues*, Chess; *The Chess Years*, Charly.

With others: John Lee Hooker, *Live At Cafe Au-Go-Go*, ABC/Bluesway; Junior Wells, *Blues Hit Big Town*, Delmark; Luther Johnson, *Chicken Shack*, Muse; Johnny Winter, *Nothin' But The Blues*, Blue Sky; *Willie Dixon* box set, Chess.

Anthologies: *Wizards From The South Side*, Chess; *Muddy And The Wolf* (portions of *Fathers And Sons*), Chess; *First Time I Met The Blues*, Chess; *Blues-Rock Cookbook–Montreux Festival*, Chess; *Blues From Big Bill's Copa Cabana*, Chess (first released as *Folk Festival Of The Blues*, Argo); *Chess Blues* box set (includes sides backing Sunnyland Slim and St. Louis Jimmy); *The American Folk Blues Festival, 1963*, L+R; *American Folk Blues Festival, 1963-'67*, L+R; *The Great Blues Men*, Vanguard; *Ann Arbor Blues & Jazz Festival 1972*, Atlantic; *Atlantic Blues: Guitar* ('72), Atlantic; *Blues Deluxe* ('80 Chicagofest), XRT; *Blues Masters, Volume 2: Postwar Chicago*, Rhino; *Blues Masters, Volume 4: Harmonica Classics* (backing George "Harmonica" Smith and Little Walter), Rhino; *Blues Masters, Volume 6: Blues Originals*, Rhino; *Blues Masters, Volume 7: Blues Revival*, Rhino; *Blues Masters, Volume 8: Mississippi Delta Blues*, Rhino; *Legends Of Guitar–Electric Blues, Vol. 1*, Rhino; *Legends Of Guitar–Electric Blues, Vol. 2*, Rhino; *Legends Of The Blues: Volume 1*, Columbia.

Soundtracks: *Dynamite Chicken* ('71); *Mandingo* ('75).

On film: *Jazz USA* ('60); *Blues And Gospel Train* (British TV, '64); *Chicago Blues* ('70); *Black, White And Blues* ('74); *The Last Waltz* ('78); *Eric Clapton And His Rolling Hotel* ('80); *Maintenance Shop Blues: Muddy Waters* (produced by Iowa Public Television, early '80s), Yazoo; *25x5: The Continuing Adventures Of The Rolling Stones* (the band joins Muddy at the Checkerboard Lounge, '81, for "Mannish Boy"), CBS. Waters also appeared on PBS' *Soundstage*, CBS' *International Hour*, Granada TV's *Blues And Gospel Train*, and CBC's *The Blues*.

Muddy Waters & Johnny Winter

August 1983

BY TOM WHEELER

MUDDY WATERS AND JOHNNY WINTER were friends. As onstage performers and studio collaborators, the Mississippi blues bossman and the Texas rock star were also partners. But there were additional bonds perhaps even more profound than their deep, mutual respect as fellow professionals. Johnny's unbounded admiration for his mentor was matched by the appreciation that Muddy felt for his follower's efforts on behalf of the blues. This interview covers the Waters/Winter Grammy-winning album projects, as well as Muddy's techniques, tunings, equipment, and recordings. Throughout the conversation the interplay between the two guitarists reveals a glimpse of their unique relationship, and outlines the historical impact of Muddy Waters' blues odyssey from the Mississippi Delta to Chicago's South Side.

Johnny: Well, the first thing that you've got to understand is that I taught Muddy how to play guitar [*laughs*].

Muddy: Hey, that's right; don't laugh. You're still teaching me now. You play eight notes to my one!

When did you first get together?

Johnny: We met in Austin, Texas. We were on the same bill at a club called the Vulcan Gas Company, which later turned into the Armadillo. I can't tell you how excited I was to be on the bill with Muddy Waters. He's been my idol since I was 11 or 12, so I was there with my camera and my tape recorder. I was so honored just to meet Muddy, I wasn't about to ask to sit in.

Muddy: I asked to sit in with *him* [*laughs*]. I said, "That guy up there onstage–I got to see him up *close*." We didn't play together on the show, but we got together afterward and jammed a little and talked. Johnny had this old National, and I explained that I had played one kind of like that, so right off we had something in common.

Johnny: The first time we ever worked together was in 1974 or '75 on a TV show called *Soundstage*, in Chicago. It was a tribute to Muddy, with a lot of people that Muddy had influenced–Junior Wells, Dr. John, Buddy Miles, me, Mike Bloomfield, Koko Taylor, and a few others. It was then that Muddy and I realized that we could definitely work together. When I finally got a chance to produce records with him, my whole thing was to make the record that Muddy wanted to make, with the musicians he wanted to work with. If Muddy gets pissed off, things change. He's the boss. My job as producer is to get things sounding right to him. And it's been very special and unusual, because we don't disagree.

Muddy: Our first album together was *Hard Again.* I was leaving the Chess label, and my manager went to CBS, and just like that they said, "Well, you should go to Johnny Winter's label, Blue Sky."

Johnny: Epic is part of CBS. They wanted Muddy, but they weren't sure exactly how to produce him. They distributed Blue Sky, so they asked me if I was interested. I said, "Hell yes! Let's do it!" It was that easy.

Muddy: And we didn't practice. We just got in there, and we'd run over a song and put it down. We caught it. The whole album took two days. We would've been done before, but Johnny would get tired and say, "Well, let's come back tomorrow" [*laughs*].

Johnny: I couldn't believe how he was running me ragged. The studio was downstairs and the control room was upstairs, and I was running back and forth saying to myself, "God *damn*, Muddy, you're gonna kill me." I figured we'd play about four hours, take a break, and work some more. But Muddy said, "No, I don't want to take no break, man!" [*Laughs.*] It was one song after another, and they kept getting better and better. They'd run it down once just to go through it, but I'd go upstairs and listen to that first take and know that there was no reason to do it again. That's so rare, when everything's *right* the first time.

And Hard Again *was a Grammy winner in 1977?*

Muddy: *All* of our records were Grammy winners, all three of them. *I'm Ready* was in '78, and then came *Muddy "Mississippi" Waters Live* in '79. *King Bee* is our fourth one together.

You've mentioned that your guitar style was influenced primarily by two people.

Muddy: Son House and Robert Johnson. I can tell you a little bit more about Son House than Robert Johnson. Robert's records were out in 1937, like "Terraplane Blues"

Hard again: Johnny and Muddy with James Cotton, late '70s.

and "Walkin' Blues." I was already doing my thing then, and I never followed him around to hear him or anything like that. But Son House I did follow around and listen to. And I do believe that the way Robert played, you could hear some of Son House in him. Robert was putting in more notes. It was about three notes to one. Robert was one of the greatest of the slide players.

Johnny: Muddy's told me that there were a lot of players to learn from in the Delta–not just the ones you've heard of, but many who never got recorded for whatever reason. Being even as great as Muddy is just isn't enough by itself. He's also very stable and very intelligent, and he held it together for many, many people, always working towards making it. Some good musicians were real itinerant, never worked at the same place twice, just didn't care, couldn't hold a band together...

Muddy: Not with Krazy Glue [*laughs*].

Johnny: But Muddy knew he was damned good, even among all those others. When he was coming up, that music was everywhere.

Muddy: All over the place. Great people you never heard of who just didn't take it for a career. They'd just pick up the guitar and play it like heck and then put it down and forget it. I'd listen, and maybe I'd do some things a little different, maybe learn a few notes to add, and then other people would do it different ways and add more notes till you get up to this boy here–Johnny will stick about 18 notes in there instead of three [*laughs*].

Before you went up to Chicago, were you playing acoustic exclusively?

Muddy: Yes, starting with a Stella, and I had a Silvertone when I came North. First electric I got was in 1944. That's when I hooked into it, and it was a very different sound, not just louder. I thought that I'd come to like it–if I could ever learn to play it. That loud sound would tell everything you were doing. On acoustic you could mess up a lot of stuff and no one would know that you'd ever missed. So electric was really rough.

Johnny: What made you get into electric?

Muddy: People were talking louder in the neighborhood taverns around Chicago, where I'd be sitting and picking my guitar. The people would be drinkin' a little booze and talkin' loud, and you couldn't get your sound over them.

Johnny: Hasn't changed much [*laughs*]. You just have to get bigger amps. Back in Chicago, were they amplifying harps before guitars?

Muddy: Where I was playing, they did it just about the same time. Rice Miller had a little microphone for his harmonica even before Little Walter was doing it.

Johnny: Rice Miller was one of the Sonny Boy Williamsons, the second one.

Muddy: And when I first got to Chicago, the first Sonny Boy [John Lee Williamson] would blow over the house mike sometimes. So the electric thing had started a little bit.

What was the Chicago club scene like when you arrived in 1943?

Muddy: It was going already, with people like Tampa Red, Memphis Slim, Big Maceo, Lonnie Johnson, and Big Bill Broonzy. Those people were heavy in Chicago.

Johnny: But boy, they didn't sound *nothing* like the blues Muddy started up there.

Muddy: No, it was different from what I do. I recorded for Columbia early on, and did a thing for Decca, even

before I started recording with Chess. But I had a hard time trying to get it through.

Why was it difficult at first?

Muddy: Because I brought up the *deep-bottom Mississippi Delta blues*, and blues like Big Bill Broonzy's was entirely different. Mine was a rustier sound, a grittier sound. Big Bill and Memphis Slim and some of the others was singing very clear, and maybe they'd use a saxophone.

Johnny: It's funny that one little area of the Delta would have a sound all its own, but you could go just a few hundred miles one way or the other, and it wouldn't sound the same at all. You can't exaggerate how distinctive Muddy's playing is. In my band, if I stop playing, the main feeling keeps on going, but when Muddy stops, the whole feeling can change, because he's got that Mississippi thing and the Chicago sound all wrapped up together. It's pure style. Muddy Waters *is* Chicago blues, which is electric and has that group sound to it. But he's always kept the feeling of the Delta. And he's a very smart player. He'll do this one hot lead, sort of an Elmore James type of lick that you hear a lot, but Muddy will do it differently and put it in where you don't expect it, and it's just perfect and really grabs you in a new way. Many bluesmen overdo it, but Muddy never does.

What about his impact aside from influencing guitarists?

Johnny: One of the most important things Muddy did was to set up a particular instrumentation–piano, two guitars, bass, drums, and harp. And it became a model, with variations, for many who followed. So this was all part of the thing he did in Chicago. I read in a book once where down in the Delta Muddy asked his sister if she thought anyone would like his kind of music up in Chicago, and she said, "No, they don't want to hear that."

Muddy: When I got up there I had to keep feelin' around, testing out Aristocrat, which became Chess. Before, I had done some things for the Library of Congress. They weren't going to bring it out, but Pete Welding brought it out on his own label, Testament. It's called *Down On Stovall's Plantation*.

Johnny: That's a great record, just amazing.

Muddy: That was made when I was in Mississippi with Son Simms, Louis Ford, and Percy Thomas. We had mandolin, violin, and two guitars. Then I recorded for Aristocrat in '46. I made "I Can't Be Satisfied" and "Feel Like Going Home," and they came out in '47 and went over good and quick. And I was with Chess all the way until I got over with Johnny at Blue Sky just a few years back.

Johnny: We tried to capture the feeling of some of those old sounds on the records that we did together.

Of all your records, which ones stand out, particularly

Blues summit: B.B. King, James Cotton, Muddy Waters, and Johnny Winter at New York's Radio City Music Hall, June '79.

for the guitarist?

Johnny: The first one I ever bought was *Best of Muddy Waters.* That's good, and you can hear him in a small group setting.

Muddy: That record, and the first one I did with Johnny–*Hard Again*–are the two best albums I ever did.

Johnny: *Muddy Waters At Newport* is a real good live one from 1960. But there *aren't* any bad ones.

Muddy: I got some good stuff even on some bad ones [*laughs*].

Johnny: You can't go wrong with a Muddy Waters album. The only thing I didn't care for as well was when they added all that brass.

Muddy: When I did *Brass And The Blues*? Well, I liked that better than that *Electric Mud* record I did.

Wouldn't you consider Electric Mud *a rock and roll album?*

Muddy: I don't know what to consider it [*laughs*]. We ain't even going to get into it.

When it came out about 12 years ago, it made a lot of waves and people took notice, but your own opinion was, "Man, that's dogshit."

Muddy: That's what it was! But you're right–when it first came out it started selling like wild. It got up to around 80,000, and then they started sending them back. They said,

"This *can't* be Muddy Waters with all this shit going on–all this wow-wow and fuzztone."

Johnny: It's worth buying just for the picture on the inside, though. See, the business people thought it'd work, because it had that hippie thing. Those people don't think the same way. They thought they'd take the blues and make it *modern.* You know: "Hey, if Muddy Waters is the big influence behind the Rolling Stones and all these people, all we gotta do is get the real man and put these hot modern players on there." They didn't understand the blues.

Muddy: I think Johnny knows more about my music than I do. When we went to do *Hard Again*, he was bringing up things I had forgot all about, and he was playing them just like they're supposed to be played, and I sat back and said, "*Well!*" He wanted to go back to the old sound, but I didn't know he went so far back. He knew about the tunings, phrasing, slide, picks, and everything.

Johnny: One thing I always wondered was how you got into thumbpicks.

Muddy: It was after I came to Chicago and was having that problem of getting myself heard. I was banging my hand all up, so I went to a thumbpick. That still wasn't loud enough, so I started playing electric. I used to play with a metal thumbpick, but the sound is too tinny to me, so I use a plastic one. No way could I use a regular flatpick.

When you switched to electric, did you change your style?

Muddy: No, no. But I did have to learn how to put that style into an electric guitar. Even today it hasn't changed that much. Only now I play with a band, and I give everybody a chance to play. I tell them, "I'm not going to hold you back. You go out there and make the people love you. *I* love you, but I can't make the people love you. *You* do that."

Johnny: Muddy's a lot different than many leaders. He's proud of his musicians, and he goes out of his way to help them. That's just one of the reasons why he's the father, one of the reasons I just glow when I talk about him. He gave Otis Spann his chance, plus James Cotton and Little Walter, Luther Johnson, and just so many others.

Muddy: Back in Mississippi it was usually just me, or maybe two of us.

Johnny: His style was already worked out by the time he got to Chicago. You did have somebody show you how to fret a little bit, didn't you?

Muddy: Yeah, Blue Smitty [Claude Smith]. See, I was mostly playing slide. When I started working with Blue Smitty and Jimmy Rogers, I learned a few note things. It didn't change my style, just improved it a little by putting some finger work on there. Smitty couldn't slide good, but he showed me how to go up there and do something else, and I put them together. I thank him today for it, because it was a very, very good improvement he did for me, because I didn't have to try to do everything with the slide by itself.

Johnny: A lot of the older guys never would use those other fingers, just the slide.

Did you try actual bottlenecks before you began using a metal slide?

Muddy: Yeah, I learned how to break my bottle. First I'd get me a bottle that I'd think was going to fit my finger. I had the slide in the wrong place at first, on my second finger, and later I put it on my little finger. So I had to get the right pop bottle to fit. Then I'd wrap some string around the neck and soak it in kerosene and light it and let it burn till it go out. Then you just rap it, and it breaks off just right.

Johnny: Every time *I* tried doing it like that I'd make the biggest mess [*laughs*]. There's a real trick to it.

Muddy: It's a short slide, because I don't play as many strings at once as Johnny. I play single strings mostly.

Johnny: I was so amazed to hear Muddy on record, because I couldn't see how in the world he could play slide and then be fretting it at the same time. I thought he was going back and forth between a regular guitar and a steel guitar on his lap or something. As much as I got off his records, I learned a lot more just sitting across from him and watching. It just knocked me out to see these things up close.

Can you tell us some of those things you picked up?

Johnny: Hell no! I don't want nobody else learning them [*laughs*]! No, really, there's a lot, but the main thing is hard to put into words, and that's feeling. And besides, there are some things that you can't learn.

Muddy: No matter what you do, some things come out all different, just your own. It's like singing. Your face, and what you're doing on your face, will change the tone of your voice. That's where my tone is. It's like Johnny will go [*singing, with an ascending melody*], "Goin' down walkin', walkin' through the park." But I'll go way *down* at the end there, because my voice will go down there and Johnny won't go that deep down.

Johnny: Out of all the blues singers, I don't think anyone can do more with one note than Muddy. And every note is blues–whether voice or guitar. Every time I hear him, it's like the first time.

Do you consciously play vocal-style lines on guitar?

Muddy: Yes. I can't make the guitar say as much as my voice, but I try to get it as close as I can. I'm no hell of a guitar player, not the best guitar walkin' around the streets, but one thing I have tried is to make the guitar sound like my voice. See, I could never do like what Johnny does. But the *feeling* that I put into my guitar–a lot of players can't put it there.

Johnny: A typical guy now will play so many notes.

Muddy: That one note of mine will say something that the other guy can't say. The tone that I lay in there, the other guy can't get it out with 12 notes.

Johnny: Muddy will sing a line, and then he'll answer on guitar, almost like a second voice.

Muddy: That's from the Delta style, definitely. Me and my guitar, we have a conversation and talk together.

Is the guitar's tone as important as your vocal tone?

Muddy: Oh yes, it *has* to be there. I think on any guitar, if I could make a note on it, you could still know it's Muddy. But I really can't do nothing with other people's guitars. A lot of the sound is the amp. I'd rather always use my own amplifier. It's the Fender with the four 10-inch speakers, the Super. Even if I forgot my own guitar and had to borrow one, I could make the sound come out of that amplifier. I don't like the Twin–different sound. I like some of Johnny's amps. They're Music Mans, and them little guys is *tough*, man.

Do you ever pick up your acoustic anymore?

Muddy: I got two or three around the house, but I don't even hardly pick them up. You get lazy when you get up in age.

Do you remember your first electric?

Muddy: I really can't remember the name, because I

bought it secondhand. It was one of those off brands. Jimmy Rogers and me were playing a club, and I left it there overnight. We got back and Jimmy's amp was gone and so was my guitar. So we couldn't work. When I actually started making records, I had a Gretsch with a DeArmond pickup on it.

Johnny: What was the archtop you were playing on the cover of *Muddy Waters At Newport*?

Muddy: That was John Lee Hooker's, and I just grabbed it for the picture. My own guitar was up onstage, the same red Telecaster I got now. I got that one in 1957 or 1958.

Johnny: That's Muddy Waters' guitar, and it won't let anyone play it but him. You pick it up and it just says, "No!" You can't believe the action. My own action stays real high, but it's nothing compared to Muddy's.

Muddy: Yeah, I got a heavy hand. Everyone says, "Oh man, the strings are too high! What're you doing?" [*Laughs.*] A lot of guys want to squeeze and bend their strings, like B.B., so they have the strings real low. My strings are *heavy*, like a .012 or a .013 for the first one. I don't need to worry about bending, because I can slide so high up there. But don't let Johnny talk about that slide–he's a dangerous man with a slide!

The King Bee, 1981.

Johnny: My strings aren't so heavy, so I can't quite get that biting sound like Muddy. The heavier the strings, the better your chance of getting a good sound, definitely.

Are you playing mainly in standard tuning now?

Muddy: Mostly standard, 'cause it's tough if you're waiting in between songs to tune to *G* or *A*. And I'm too lazy to carry two or three guitars around like Johnny [*laughs*]. He's still a young boy–he can pull that stuff around. What would I look like with two or three guitars like these kids? I don't need to be bothered with that. I got my one old guitar.

Johnny: I ain't heard no one complain.

Have you ever modified your Telecaster?

Muddy: Yes, in the '50s a guy in Chicago made me a neck for it, a big stout neck with the high nut to raise up the strings for slide. I needed to strengthen it up because of the big strings, and I think that the big neck has a lot to do with the big sound.

Johnny: You switch that thing on the front pickup and it's got so much bass it'll just about blow the amp up.

Sometimes during a verse–maybe just going into the turnaround–you'll switch the toggle from the bass or middle position to full treble and just let 'em have it.

Muddy: Yeah [*laughs*], I like to do that alright.

Johnny: I've never seen anyone do that so effectively, so dynamically. Sometimes he'll go the other way–like from a solo to backing up his voice, and he'll go from the brightest treble to the bass. He'll do it anywhere it works, going back and forth real quick, man, sometimes a couple times in one solo. One thing I always wondered, Muddy–there's a clicking sound you make, like the sound of the slide hitting the frets.

Muddy: I know what you mean. People don't know that I do a lot of this [*pats the strings against the pickup with his right hand*]. I do a lot of *pattin'.*

Johnny: And a lot of times I'll mix it up louder–because it just fits in there perfect. Those little things make a difference.

You've seen the blues go through many changes. Where do you see it going from here?

Muddy: I've seen it go up and down many times. Everything's improved over the years, and it's still changing. But if you're an old standard blues singer like me, my changed sound is still the same basic Muddy Waters style. If you change it too much, it's not blues no more. You can send it into rock and roll or even disco. You don't want to get too far away from it.

Johnny: I think people are moved by the blues because it's communication and emotional expression more than just music. Some people think it's about everybody sitting around and feeling bad together, but it's not at all. We have common problems, and you feel *better* by hearing that other people also have them, and hearing what they think about it and what they're doing about it: I don't have enough rent money, and neither does this guy here. Anybody can understand the blues if they halfway try. It might be braggin' blues about how cool you are, or down-and-out blues. No matter what kind, talking to people is more important than how many notes you play. John Lee Hooker is no Chet Atkins, but he gets up there and gets the point across.

Johnny, you've done a lot to help the blues continue.

Johnny: Well, a lot of people have been working their butts off all their lives, and the major record companies don't seem to care. So my commitment is to help make sure

that people out there who want to play blues music will have a label and a way to be heard. I want to make sure that someone's not just playing great at home by himself because he can't get anyone to record him.

Muddy: And that's a heck of a move Johnny's making, because the big companies forget about the old blues singers, don't care. "What do we want with him? He can't sell enough records. We ain't got time." They look for somebody else.

Johnny: The younger guys can get out there and hustle, like Muddy and I did and everybody else. But you get *tired* of hustling when you're 60 or 70 years old, and people who might have started rock and roll or based their whole careers on what you did just don't even seem to remember. It pisses me off. You see someone who's still great, and during certain periods no one's interested in recording him. There's no excuse for it.

What kind of shape is the blues in right now?

Muddy: It's in good shape.

Johnny: It just keeps going. People say sometimes that they think the blues is dying. But it ain't going to die.

Muddy: It may change around a little bit, but it won't die. See, the groove was here [*long pause*] before time.

Johnny: During the '60s with all the hippie stuff, when the Rolling Stones and all the younger white musicians were acknowledging their gigantic debt to the older blues musicians, kids were listening to the blues. Their idols were telling them how great it is–guys like Eric Clapton and Mick Jagger. In a way it's more real now. They buy it because they really know who Muddy Waters is, not because Mick Jagger recorded a Muddy Waters song. I feel better about it now, but it did help in the '60s–anything to make people aware of where it came from, that's important. Muddy's the father. It's a debt that'll never be repaid in full. Lately I've felt great because he's finally starting to get the kind of recognition he's deserved for so long.

Muddy: Thanks to you.

Johnny: No, no, no. I ain't done anything. [*Johnny leaves the room to get his guitar.*]

Muddy [*whispering*]: That's my son.

John Lee Hooker

November 1989 & August 1992

BY JAS OBRECHT

MORE THAN 40 YEARS AGO, John Lee Hooker sat alone in a Detroit studio and recorded his first songs. One of them–"Boogie Chillun"–was destined to become a million-seller and get the world jumping to a boogie beat that's reverberated through popular music ever since. Over the years, Hook's cut more than a hundred albums and worked with some of the finest musicians in blues, and yet the very heartbeat of his music remains his powerful voice, propulsive guitar, and unique songwriting. Like Lightnin' Hopkins, Muddy Waters, and very few others, he's a musical law unto himself and a direct link to first-generation blues.

Born to sharecroppers in the Delta town of Clarksdale, Mississippi, on August 22, 1917, John Lee Hooker learned guitar from his stepfather, Will Moore. He sang gospel and played blues in Memphis with Robert Nighthawk before moving to Detroit, where he worked in a factory by day and played clubs by night. After his first Modern Records session in the late '40s, Hooker recorded for other labels, using pseudonyms such as Texas Slim, Delta John, Birmingham Sam & His Magic Guitar, Johnny Williams, and Johnny Lee to avoid contractual problems. (It's estimated that between 1949 and '53, he made some 70 singles on 24 different labels, using a dozen different names.) He proved to be as prolific as Lightnin' Hopkins, following "Boogie Chillun" with other big R&B hits such as "Crawling King Snake" in '49 and "I'm In The Mood" in '51. In the '50s Hooker began recording with experienced R&B sidemen such as guitarist Eddie Kirkland, who helped him mold a more disciplined, commercial sound.

Signing with Chicago's Vee Jay Records in 1955, Hooker seldom recorded without guitarist Eddie Taylor and other musicians at his side. "Dimples," cut in March '56, became his first British hit a few years later. Hooker returned to his old style for his 1960 and '63 performances at the Newport Folk Festival, recording solo or with a bassist for the tracks released by Vanguard. He made his first foray into Europe with the American Blues Folk Festival of 1962, and returned home to find that "Boom Boom" had become his first crossover hit, reaching #60 in the charts. The Animals' 1964 cover of the same tune became a huge British Invasion hit and introduced Hooker to white audiences at home. He next signed with ABC, releasing albums on its Impulse and Bluesway subsidiaries. His *House Of The Blues*, a collection of early-'50s Chess sides, reached #34 in the British charts in '67, while 1971's *Hooker 'N' Heat* charted in the U.S. Later

in the '70s Hooker cut for Atlantic, Tomato, Stax, and European labels, and in 1980 he played the role of a street musician in *The Blues Brothers*. Six years later Steven Spielberg featured his music in *The Color Purple*.

Mr. Hooker revitalized his career with 1989's star-studded *The Healer*. (While Carlos Santana, Bonnie Raitt, Robert Cray, Canned Heat, Los Lobos, George Thorogood, Roy Rogers, and Charlie Musselwhite all appeared as guests, the deepest track of all is "Rockin' Chair," a spine-chilling four minutes of ferocious solo guitar and that haunting, unmistakable voice.) He followed this release with *Mr. Lucky* and *Boom Boom*, and in 1993 made guest appearances on albums by John Hammond, Van Morrison, and B.B. King.

Today John Lee Hooker enjoys more trappings of success than perhaps any other bluesman. The walls of his fine homes in the hills of Redwood City and Vallejo, California, are decorated with gold records, music awards, concert posters, letters from governors, and snapshots posed with George Thorogood, Jerry Garcia, Carlos Santana, and promoter Bill Graham. His modest collection of about 50 albums includes titles by Clifton Chenier, Wayne Cochran, Albert King, James Brown, Junior Parker, Champion Jack Dupree, Muddy Waters, Charles Mingus, and a few of his own old albums. The license plate of his white Cadillac reads "Doc Hook," while his sporty red Toyota is registered as "Les Bogy." Our conversation took place in the shade near his hot tub. I left the interview in Hook's exact words.

While The Healer *features many well-known musicians, the strongest tracks are the ones where you're by yourself, especially "Rockin' Chair."*

That's my favorite tune! The others is good for dancing, some of them, but getting right down to the nitty gritty and the real funk, this is it. Just playing the guitar, sittin' there in my old-time rockin' chair. A lot of people like that too. It is *the* closest to my heart. It, and another one on there–I can't think of the name of it, but it's with Musselwhite. Oooh!

"Rockin' Chair" seems to be in the oldest style you play in.

Oh, boy! Whew! That's *direct* to my heart. That's a funky blues. People can just sit there and just *meditate* and think about how it feels sometimes. It'll send a cold chill up and down your spine. It chills you, it's so deep. Sometime when I play stuff like that, tears come out my eyes.

When you were working in Detroit in the early days, you often played like that, with just your guitar, a small amp, and your right foot keeping the beat.

That's the way I used to play. No band, no nothing. Just John Lee Hooker and his feet.

Did that style develop from playing by yourself a lot when you were young?

No, it come from my stepfather, Will Moore, from whom I learnt to play. He taught me how. I used to listen to him. My real father, he didn't care for that kind of music in the house, because he was a minister. My real father and my mother, they wasn't together. They separated or divorced or whatever. My mother, she got remarried.

How much of your style today is similar to Will Moore's?

As the years went by, just a little bit changed with new, young musicians around. Well, maybe my basic style have changed a lot. I listen to my old records, way back, and look at my new stuff, and it's a difference. What I'm doing now is still funky, but my old style was just nothing but me by myself just playing the hard, hard blues. Now with a band, it changes quite a bit.

If someone wanted to hear John Lee Hooker's best guitar work, where should he begin looking?

I would tell him to start lookin' at the years gone by. Back when I was younger coming up, I was playing more hard blues by myself. I could play more guitar and do more by myself. I could do the same thing now if I went on and started playing by myself. But to get the best hard stuff I did, you want to go back to the Detroit days when I was playing by myself in coffeehouses. I played more guitar. I had no band to interfere. I didn't need to give no band no breaks and solos. I could do what I wanted to do when I wanted to do. With the band, it gets in the way a lot.

A band restricts you to playing in a certain format.

Yeah! Now you said it. When you got a band, you got to concentrate on what to do. When I'm by myself, I just do it when I want, change when I want, not change when I don't want. I can sit there and play a whole lot of guitar and just go to it.

Do you see a similarity in your approach and Lightnin' Hopkins'?

Oh, yeah. Lightnin' did it all the time. That's where he was comin'. He didn't believe in all them bands and things.

Are there certain blues albums that you like to listen to a lot?

Oh, yeah. I would start with Albert King and Jimmie Ray Vaughan–well, Stevie Ray Vaughan. Jimmie, too, is nice. Layin' these blues on you. And Muddy Waters and on and on. The great ones have stood here and then have gone, but they still live on in my memory, whom I love so much. Just a great memory.

Right now, it seems like there are tens of thousands of blues guitar players.

Whoo! Well, I hate to say it, but it seems like there's *too* many. And a lot of them is really good! They are good ones, but if you look around, a lot of 'em sound alike. You hear one, you just about done heard them all. So in your mind, they all are good, but if you go in to record with them, you just say, "Hey, this guy sounds like so-and-so. He sound like B.B. He sound like Stevie Ray." They don't have a unique style all to themself, like I got. Some of them play a tremendous lot of guitar–they play much more guitar than I do–but what I play is with a solid drive, a funky beat, and nobody got it but me! That's what make me stand out. In fact, all of them sound almost alike—_do do do do do_ [_mimics stratospheric wailing high on the fingerboard_]. It's good, but…

You know how some guys try to copy another player exactly?

Yeah!

What would you have someone learn from you?

That's a good question. What would I have them learn from me? Just learn to stop trying to make all the fancy chords and a whole lot of guitar all the way down the neck real fast. Forget about the fancy chords and concentrate on just a funky beat and something with a lot of soul and just a feeling to it.

You've played with dozens of great guitarists, from Eddie Kirkland on down to the musicians on your new album. Which of them could send chills up and down your spine?

Albert King [_laughs_]. I don't know why, but there's just something about his guitar. He got a outstanding style of his own, and a lot of people try to copy him too, but they don't get it. I don't know, there's something about Albert–I hear his voice and his guitar, and it just chills me.

He's one of the last guys you'd want mad at you.

[_Laughs._] He sure as big as this house! He's the _last_ guy I want mad at me! Yeah. Well, you know, me and him good buddies. I respect him; he respect me. We're always glad to see each other. B.B.'s the same way. Me and him are really good friends. He's a tremendous guitar player. A lot of 'em try and sound like him. I think he changed over the years too. He's gone to the big-band style, the Las Vegas style. But he can play some hard blues when he just want to. But he don't do too much of that now. He's on the Vegas trip and circles. That's where you make a lot of money, but with me, I just like to please myself.

Throughout your career, you've seemed to remain true to your own vision of music.

Yeah. We all like money, you know, but the main thing is, I want to please myself. I'm doin' alright money-wise, but I want to play what pleases me. I don't want to play Vegas circles. I want to please the other people, but I want to please myself too. And so I just stays in what pleases me. When I was making this record, I had all these good people on it, but it was an entirely different style, like "The Healer" and Los Lobos. But I said, "Hey, I got to play some funky blues on here. I want to play some funk." Now, this other stuff will

sell real fast, like Los Lobos and Carlos Santana–I'm sure they're going to go AM–but I wanted to please myself. I wanted to play some deep funk!

When you were growing up in Mississippi or working in Memphis, did you ever dream about someday being one of the greatest bluesmen in the world?

No, it didn't never occur. I know I had the know-how. I know I had the stuff to do it with. I know I had the voice. I know I had the unique style. But I never would have thought that I would have come to get my foot in the door where I had a chance to prove what I could do. I never knowed that I would come to be this great, this popular on this planet, enjoying these things as one of the greatest bluesmen in my field that is. But I always thought I could be if I had the chance.

Did you work in the Ford Rouge plant after you moved to Detroit?

Yeah, I was a janitor. I pushed a broom. I was so into my music, but I had to work to survive. I always did like to be independent. I wanted to be on my own. I didn't want handouts, and I had to work to support myself. And I didn't want to be doing it in the factory. I would play my guitar at night, be up late, and they would catch me asleep, wake me up. They wouldn't fire me, because at that time it was so union, and then they wanted help so bad, they did give me all kind of chances. They'd wake me up if they found me asleep [_laughs_]: "Little John"–they used to call me Little John–"Little John, get up! Wake up."

Back then, you recorded under a lot of different names– Texas Slim, Delta John, John Lee Cooker, John Lee Booker. Did the record companies give you those names, or were they your idea?

That was me. I want to say this very slowly [_looks carefully around the yard and tips his hat back on his forehead_]. I was the hottest blues singer when I got my foot in the door with, like, "Boogie Chillun," "In The Mood," "Hobo Blues," "Crawlin' King Snake." Everything I did [_snaps fingers_] just turned to gold. I had this manager, Elmer Barbara, and all these record companies would come to him. They said, "This kid got something so different." And I was under contract with Modern Records in L.A., and they was crooked–some of the biggest crooks ever lived. So Barbara would come to me late at night and say, "Man, I got a deal! This record company want to do something with you. I know you under contract, but we can change your name." I said, "I don't care," and this kept going on. Every different little record company would come to me, and I'd say, "Call me what you want to– as long as you got the money." They did give me a name, and I went in the studio late at night.

Would you change your style?

Bluesman's choice: The great Earl Hooker.

CHRIS STRACHWITZ

Sometime, but the company knew. There wasn't nothin' they could do about it.

How would you record guitar back then?

I had an old Stella with a pickup in it. I thought at that time it was a great, great sound. Tremendous sound that was really good until the electric come along. T-Bone [Walker] give me my first electric guitar. Then I thought that was the best I ever seen. It was a Fender–no, no, it was Epiphone [archtop].

Given your choice of any amp, what would you choose?

Fender. I love Fenders and Gibson guitars. I thought two or three times about endorsing Fender amplifiers–get 'em free, 'cause that's all I use. I love the sound of the Twin.

What's your favorite guitar?

A Gibson. I got two Gibsons and two Epiphones. [*Rich Kirch, backup guitarist in Hooker's band, details: "The Gibson ES-335 that John uses now–serial number 26201–was given to him by Carlos Santana on his birthday a few years ago. He plays that one all the time. His blonde Epiphone is his favorite one; it's on a lot of the old records. I'm not sure what year it is, but it's a semi-hollowbody with a single cutaway. He also has a Lucille guitar–the Gibson B.B. King model–and another 335. He gave one of the 335s to Junior, his son."*]

You're holding a Les Paul on one of your early albums.

Yeah, that's when I first started out.

Do you ever use picks?

No.

How do you tune your guitar?

Regular tuning and open tuning. Open *A [E A E A C# E]* and open *G [D G D G B D]*. [*Kirch adds, "John plays most everything in E, except to boogie, when he usually tunes three strings up so he's in open A."*]

Have you ever been interested in playing slide?

No.

Why?

No reason. I just never did care for it myself. I love to hear it, but for myself, I wasn't into it. I didn't want to do it. It wasn't the sound that I wanted, which is good. Oh, I love Bonnie Raitt's slide; she's one of the best slide players I ever heard in a long time. She's one of the unique ladies I ever seen. I love her voice, I love the style of guitar. She can do that slide.

Your cousin Earl Hooker was great too.

Oh, yeah. Well, he was number one. Bonnie Raitt got her style from Fred McDowell. She used to go out there [to Como, Mississippi]. I knew him real well.

If you could put together an all-star blues band, who'd be in it?

That's a good, big, big question. The famous people, like? Well, you can only get so many guitars in one band, so I would say Albert King–the Big Man, I call him. The others, right now I really can't put my hand on it, but number one, I really would pick Albert King to be one of them. There are many, many more that's good–tremendous good. Of course, I don't copy him; I don't do none of his stuff. But I don't do none of nobody's stuff but mine. So I'd get him first, and all the rest of it I'd fill in. If I could pick one who's gone, I'd pick Otis Spann. He was one of the greatest piano men that ever lived. Drummer, I don't know. There's some funky bass players. The guys that I'm used to playing with–and I heard a lot of 'em–one of them's gone, Geno Skaggs. The young kid I got now, Jim Gayette, I never thought he was that good until I really take a good listen to him. He's a funky little bass player–he play funk, play rock, play it all.

Did you know any of the early bluesmen, or were you familiar with the work of, say, Robert Johnson or Blind Lemon Jefferson?

I didn't never know any of those gentlemens; I only know them through my stepfather, so I don't have too much to say. I don't know their background, but all the blues today–they was the root of all that music. It come from them. It come up progressive from those guys, and it could rise and rise and rise, but it was still from them. They was the one who created all of that.

When you began performing, did it seem almost impossible that a blues performer could play to a white audience?

Right. No, you couldn't imagine it. But I had a feeling that it was comin', but when? I know it would come sooner or later. Now it's here in the full. I know back then that the blues was only for the older black people in just a certain area. You get a hit record then, it wouldn't be half of the hit it is now. Just a half a big hit now is *big*, but back then the #1 record didn't make a lot of money 'cause it only went to a certain people, the older black people. But down through the years it all changed.

Is right now a good time for the blues?

Oh, yeah. All over the world. To the non-English-speaking people, Japanese, France, Russia, the Communist countries, the blues have just cut their way into every country in the world, all over the world. Young, old–they found out the true identity of music that is the blues. It is the first music was here. It is the one tells the story. It is the one to tell the life story of a human being or a man and a woman. Who started this? Eve and Adam in the Garden. When the blues was born, it was born with Eve and Adam. Over years and years and years, they beginning to find out the roots of this stuff and what it means to people. The rich, the poor–they all have the blues. No matter how much money you got, when your woman or the one you love have left you or you can't get along with her, all the money in the world cannot fill the place of happiness in your home. Because money can't talk to you. So that's the reason the rich people, they get the blues. They get worried and upset, and then they can't talk to that money at night. They can only spend so much, but they cannot buy happiness. So everybody realizes that now. The young, they study the blues. It's in the library. They read about it.

See, what they call rock and roll haven't been around over 35 or 40 years. What is rock and roll? That was all taken from the blues. Everything that we are saying, they are saying: "My woman done left me [*scat-sings a solo*]." The blues was saying all along, "My woman done left me heartaches," or, "My baby gone, she won't be back no more." Well, rock and roll say the same thing, but they got the really up-to-date form and they call it rock and roll. It's the blues!

Johnny Shines tells of how a guy could walk up to a bus stop and tell people how his house just burned down and his kids died, and most people would walk away.

Right.

And yet that night those same people might spend $10 to hear him sing about it in a club.

Right. Oh yeah! Yeah, you know, that's the blues. The blues is here to stay. That's all I can tell you. And they stronger than ever. I have to admit that when I first started playing the blues and first started making a record, I wasn't making that much money. Just a little bit, but at that time I thought it was big money. You know, you make $1,000 for a week or $500 a night–that was *big* money to me. But now I consider $500–I go out for dinner a couple of times, it's nothing. But back then that was a lot, a lot of money. Now all the kids, especially the young white kids, oh, they eat the blues up. They love 'em. And they playing them too. The young kids, they can play them. It first got big in England. The blues got *real big* in England before it got big here in the '60s. The Stones and Animals and things like that–ooh, boy!

The Animals' cover of "Boom Boom" is probably where most white kids in the '60s heard of you for the first time.

It was! It was! And when I went overseas, it was just like God just let Jesus go over there. That's all you could hear: "John Lee Hooker!" But they had never saw me. But everybody over there was playing my stuff.

Was the audience very different from what you were used to?

Oooh wee! You know, this is the truth: Before I got to the concert hall–even if it was rainin'–the place be full with a line around the block. They had to start puttin' on two shows a night to accommodate those people. Before I got there, the guys was playing all my music–Eric, Jimi, Georgie Fame, Spencer Davis, they all was doing it. John Lee Hooker. And then on the radio it was big over there. When I went over there, oh boy, it was just like the President coming. It made me feel good, you know. That's where it started from, and then I come back over here, and it started catching over here real big. Then everybody in the world got it–the white kids, the black kids.

When the white kids became interested in your music, did you lose some of the black audience?

No. With dedicated fans, no matter who come in, they still are gonna like who they like. Just like a baseball team. I live here and I like the Giants, but I'm a strictly Dodger fan. Although they ain't doin' nothing, but I still like 'em and I'm still with 'em. Oh, I love baseball.

What else do you like outside of music?

I love being home. I'm a regular home person. I like just to lay back.

Do you play guitar much when you're home?

Oh, yeah.

During concerts, it often seems that you compose songs on the spot.

Sometimes, yeah. Sometimes, no.

Do you have a good memory for songs?

I've got a hell of a memory. I don't forget nothing. Once I get it in there [_taps forehead_], I just [_snaps fingers three times_]. I can lay down at night and think of a song, get up, and sing it word by word and don't forget nary a word.

Do you sing songs that aren't blues?

Yeah. Like _The Iron Man_ with Pete Townshend. And I was surprised I did that. He kept telling me I could do it, and I cut it in New York. That was completely out of my style, but it don't sound bad.

You also contributed a version of "Red House" to a Jimi Hendrix project, Variations On A Theme–Red House.

Oh, yeah. I did it real bluesy and funky. That's really nice. Mr. Jimi Hendrix, one of my favorites. He was one of my idols, and I was glad to do it. The guy that used to manage him [Alan Douglas] said Jimi would talk about me a lot, and he was the one who had me do this. It's going to be in music stores for people who like Jimi Hendrix and stuff like that.

Did you know Hendrix at all?

No, I wished I had, because I was a great fan of his.

You seem to have a very smart business sense.

Oh, yeah. I'm very deceptive. Money ain't anything, but I just don't run through it. I know I'm not going to be doing this all my life, and I know that if I live on, I'm going to retire and just have a good life, a good home, and have money to kick back and do what I want to do, go where I want to go. Some of them live so fast when they're making big money, they run right through it. And when they can't do this...

Did you learn that lesson the hard way?

Yeah [_laughs heartily_]. Yeah, yeah, I did. I learned it the hard way. But now I'm very well set. I got a pretty nice home. I'm into real estate. I got three more homes in Oakland that I leased out. But like I said, I learned it the hard way. I could have run through partying, women, whiskey, living the fast life, and I wouldn't have had nothing. You get through, and it's just a dream. It's a dream you went through, and you got nothing–all that stuff's behind you. And then when you're old, that's gone. When all your money and success is gone, all your so-called friends are gone. They ain't friends; they leaches that hangin' on as long as you got something. I learned it the hard way. I _love_ people–don't get me wrong. Oh, I love people. Friendship is the best thing in life. I go out of my way to help people. I'm a kindhearted person. I have a lot of people; I know some of them appreciate it, some of them don't. I hate to say it: Some of them are leaches. _I_ know they are, but I don't tell them. I know what they're thinking before they do it. I _know_. I can look right through people, but I still love 'em.

And you've always got your guitar.

Yeah, always got that! When the women gone, I always got my guitar. My woman can leave me, but my guitar ain't gonna leave me. Always got that. Remember that song "Red House" that Jimi did–"way back yonder 'cross the hill"? He say, "I still got my guitar!" [_Laughs._] Yeah, I still got my guitar.

August 1992

"Ain't a lot of chords to it,
It's just a big beat,
And I sound just like a whole band,
Now you dig it, and dig my feets"
–"Teachin' The Blues," 1961

Our search for the big beat led me to John Lee Hooker's house in Redwood City, California. Mr. Hooker received me graciously, sat down on his couch, and tuned his electric guitar to open A. He quickly launched into an instrumental version of "Boogie Chillun," each foot tapping to a different beat.

Watching you play "Boogie Chillun" close up, it seems like what you're doing is very simple, and yet it's very difficult for others to get it right.

For me, it's simple, but... [_Laughs._]

In the mood: Bonnie Raitt and John Lee make a video, 1989. "She's one of the best slide players," Hook affirms.

That was one of the first songs you recorded.
Uh-huh.

Did you write it when you were a young man in Mississippi?
[*Nods yes.*]

How are you counting time with your feet?
[*Laughs.*] I couldn't tell you. It just boogie. Just go on with it. I don't need drums.

You often played that way in Detroit, using your feet instead of a rhythm section.
Yeah. That first come from my stepfather, Will Moore, from whom I learnt to play when I was 13. John Hammond do it too.

Do you usually keep your guitars tuned to a chord?
Not really. But I use open tuning. "Boogie Chillun," that's in open A. For "Boom Boom," I got to rekey [retune] it.

What do you look for in a tone?
I look for a deep, gutty feelin'. I don't use picks, so I can get that deep gut feelin'. People ask, "How you get that?" It's just there. There's a lot of people try to play real fast chords–*da da da da da*–that's not the blues. It's synthetic. It ain't the hard, solid blues. It's a lot of speed and everything. It's got no feeling to it. You sit down and play some [*whispers*] funky,

funky guitar. Take your time! Don't rush it. Just let it come flowin' through you. I can play guitar so funky, until it bring teardrops to your eyes. It got that funky, funky tone. I'm just me.

While most musicians stick to 12-bar blues, you seldom follow that format.
That's for the birds. People just feel–that's the way the blues supposed to be played. The way you feel those notes or scales. Shut your eyes, and then you'll know what you're doing. I know what notes to hit. I know what notes not to hit. I can do a 12-bar perfect–*perfect.* Oh, yeah. If I did then, I wouldn't be known for John Lee Hooker. See, I'm known for not doing it. When I'm just playing to myself I do it: 8, 12, 4, 16, 24. But ordinarily I don't do it, because it would take away a lot of my feelin'. You cannot learn this in a book. You feel it here [*points to heart and head*], not by what you got writing on a piece of paper. Throw that paper away! When I walk into a studio, I don't need all that stuff. I can go into a studio and in two-hours' time I can record five or six songs. Sometimes it take some people three or four weeks to record one or two songs!

Sometimes it takes a band years to make one album.
[*Laughs.*] Yeah! It do! I can make ten albums in a year, and they come out perfect too.

Can you make up songs on the spot?

Yeah. They're on the spot. I get that good feelin'. But one thing I don't like–what really bugs me–is anybody tellin' me how to play. What to do and how to do. Don't do that.

Has that been a problem on your recent Chameleon and Charisma albums, since so many of the songs feature guest bands? When you recorded with Santana, for instance, you were working in a pretty straight format.

Heavy duty. We get together on it. They know how I do it. With "The Healer" we did two takes–it come out perfect. "Strip Me Naked." [*Laughs.*]

What were you thinking when you wrote that?

Well, I got stripped naked once. She took the house, the Cadillac. And the money in the bank–she took that too.

Did Carlos come to you with the music for that song?

He come to the house, and we set around. Like, he talked and we go with things. Just me and him. I go to his house, we lay the foundation, and then he pass it on to the guys. And it come out perfect every time. "Strip Me Naked," that took just about two takes.

Have your recent albums had a big impact on your career?

Very, very big impact, because it was all-stars. But this one I got comin' out now [*Boom Boom*], I'm not gonna have all-star everyone–just me and my band and some local people. Carlos will probably be on it. We already got a thing called "Chill Out" on the shelf, so we'll probably use that. I'm in the studio now workin', gettin' some pretty good stuff. A lot of the stuff I did a long, long time ago, which is new to the kids now. Some of my classic stuff, but the kids never heard it, so I'm doing it over. I always did want to do it that way. Now that I got a chance, I'm gonna do a lot of it all over, like "Sugar Mama," "Boom Boom," "Dimples."

Those songs turned a generation of kids on to your music during the 1960s.

That "Boom Boom," that "Dimples"–turned a *whole* generation. It went to Europe and told Europe, and then come back here and turned the whole universe on. Then different artists took to doing that song, "Boom Boom"–Bruce Springsteen, all them. Big Joe Turner, he was doin' "Dimples."

© JAY BLAKESBERG

Like Lightnin', Muddy, and very few others, John Lee Hooker is a musical law unto himself.

Is it a compliment when people try to play like you?

Yeah, it is. Because I know I'm doing something to be loved. If he didn't like it, he wouldn't try to do it! So it's very complimentary to me.

Some guys feel very protective...

Not me. I love people that do my stuff. Robert Plant, he did "Dimples." He sing it all the time. He's one of my favorite people. Nice guy. Every time he come over, he try to look me up. He flew me out to New York once to meet him. Paid for my hotel and everything. Had a lady with him called Big Maggie Bell, from Scotland. Met her. But my hero is Bonnie. Me and her just like this [*holds two fingers together*]. I guess you know that. We real close. I've known Bonnie Raitt over the years, and I'm a guest on her tour in L.A.

A lot of your old material has recently come out on CD.

Yeah, you know they comin' out now because we're doin' big things. They just throwin' out everything now–boom. Rhino Records did one.

That has many great tracks, but it's missing "Mad Man Blues."

Yeah. Ohhh, I love the "Mad Man Blues." [*Claps time and sings "I love the Mad Man Blues" and "I'm gonna kill some-*

body" to the original melody.]

Do you play blues when you're alone?

Yeah, around the house I do. Yeah. Sit down in my room and just go with things I want to do, some of that old stuff that I'm trying to revive again and bring back.

Do you work on your own guitars?

No. The little light stuff I do, like adjusting the bridges and raising the saddles. You get beyond that, no.

Why do you play semi-hollowbody guitars?

Well, I like 'em. You got to do that now because the generations come and go, and the young generation, they like to dance and they want it loud. But you still can make it funky loud.

You could play a Fender.

I could, but I don't want to. I'm plainspoken, and I don't want that. This is what I like. You don't got to bring me around the bridge. This is what I like—boom. I like the tone. I always did like Gibson. Even the old style, I did.

Why do you have a guitar with B.B. King's name on it?

I saw it, and I went and bought it. He's a old buddy of mine. I said [to the salesman], "Give me that one." He give me a price—he said, "It's a lot of money." I said, "I don't care! Just give it to me." He said, "Who are you?" I said, "I'm John Lee." He said, "Oooh," and he come down on the price when he found out who I was. I was signing stuff in his store.

What's the greatest amplifier?

I know who got the greatest name—Fender. I got one sittin' right there [*points to an old Concert*]. I got another one back there, man, a Bedrock—boy, that thing is powerful! Whoo. It's not famous, but oh, it's powerful. But Fender is a brand name, and it's the name that sells, and that's what people go for.

How do you set the amp controls?

Different songs, different settings. I don't like it real sharp. I like it kind of medium. Not too much bass, not too much sharp. I get different settings.

Do you like reverb?

Not really. On some of my new stuff I did. About two weeks ago, I got reverb on a couple of my really funky tunes, like "Sugar Mama."

Carlos Santana says a man's tone is his face.

He know.

Albert Collins' tone, for instance, is spiky and sharp…

It is. Oh, it's a thousand miles apart from mine. It's good, but it's his thing. You talkin' in a different world.

Do you like B.B.'s tone?

Whoo! Yeah! Are you kiddin'? Oh, yeah. My old buddy. And Albert King is funky. That old man is funky! He put that pipe in his mouth and rear his head back. He's a good man, and he gonna do things his way or no way! [*Laughs.*] He be

workin' on his own bus right now.

You've used some of the same backup musicians for many years now.

Oh, yeah. My guitar player Rich is nice, nice. Whoo, he's a good guy! Boy, that guy loves me and I love him. I'm the one that brought him to California. He'd been in Chicago all his life. I been knowin' him about 12 years along. I got the guy a ticket, brought him out—he been with me ever since. I talk to him every day. He's a heck of a nice guy and good guitar player. Jim Gayette—oh, he is funky! He's a funky bass player, and funny too. He keep the band laughin' all night.

When you were starting out, would you play for a long time at night?

Before I become famous? When I was a kid? If my parents would let me I would.

You hear about guys playing in Delta juke joints from nightfall until morning…

No, I didn't do that. No. I would've, but I didn't. [*Laughs.*]

What was Hastings Street like when you first came to Detroit?

That was the best street in town. Everything you wanted was right there. Everything you didn't want was right there. It ain't no more now. It's a freeway now, called Chrysler Freeway. But that was a good street, a street known all over the world. But I didn't just play on Hastings—I'd play any club on Russell, Chene, Jefferson. In them days, I was so into my music, but I had to work to survive. I was a janitor. I pushed a broom.

What do you remember of your sessions at United Sound Studio in Detroit?

On West Grand Boulevard and Second? Still there. I would always use my amp, just plug into my old funky amps. It was Ampeg or a Silvertone.

Was your first electric guitar the Les Paul you're seen with in some of the early pictures?

Really, it was. Really good one. Before that I had some round-hole pickups [for amplifying an acoustic guitar]. No, T-Bone Walker give me my first electric guitar. Then I thought that was the best I ever seen. It was a Epiphone.

Did you use an acoustic for early sides like "Mad Man Blues"?

Yeah, that's acoustic. I had an old Stella with a pickup called DeArmond, and it fit across the round hole. You slide it in. I thought at that time it was a great, great sound.

Was Newport '60 your first big concert?

Never been so scared! My first big concert, yeah. Couldn't get my body to stop shaking!

You appeared with Muddy Waters there.

Yeah. I was good friends with Muddy.

Do you have any favorite memories of him?

Yeah, I do. I got so many I couldn't tell 'em all. He'd come to Detroit, he used to stay at my house. I had a big house in Detroit. Matter of fact, I own property there now. He never would stay in a hotel. Him and Genny, his wife, would stay at my house. Little Walter would be with him. He was a sideman then, one of the greatest harmonica players ever lived. I think so. We would go on tour together sometimes, me and him and Little Walter, Jimmy Rogers. Remember Jimmy Rogers? He had this old Oldsmobile, brand new. And Little Walter was crazy, and he used to drive. Speedin' in it. He'd be boogeyin'! And he'd be laughing 'cause I'd be nervous. Just a lot of good remembrances. Things I cannot ever forget. Muddy was a really good man. And he was just beginnin' to come into it really on, like I am now. Just beginnin' to climb up the ladder really high.

His last four albums were terrific.

They was. He was beginnin' to climb up to the top, and it's a hard climb. But, you know, you get there somehow. Some get there and some don't. I be one of the few giants at the top of the ladder. In my travelin' and living in God's world, I love people. My heart go out for people. I'm just a softie. I just give my heart to people, and how can I say no to the people that I know I should? I don't like hurting people. We all like money, don't get me wrong, but it's not the greatest thing in the world, but we have to have it. Friendship, love, peace of mind, and health is the greatest thing in the world. You have to have money to survive, but–and a lot of us do–we can't let money get in the way of friendship and love and the people that put you where you at today. People put me where I'm at today. Weren't for those people, John Lee wouldn't be sittin' on top of the ladder. I'd be sitting down below.

And who put me there? The workin' people, the poor people go out and work five or six days a week, and come out to see me and go out and buy my albums, and stuff like that. Young kids. Old people. Them the people that got me there. Some stars seem to forget–well, they don't forget, but when you get to the high, they say you forget the people that blazed the path for them, the people that put them there. Wasn't no people, you wouldn't be there. So them the people I love. I love to go in them little small clubs, funky bars, get up there singing. I walk into a lot of little clubs, and they surprised to see me in there. Say, "What're you doing in here?" And I say, "I'm just like you. I'm here to have some fun and get down with you." I don't think about I'm a big star, or I got money. I don't think about that. I'm out there at a place I like, get down and have a beer with you. I don't look at me being a big star. I really don't. I really don't.

Who were some of the other bluesmen that you enjoyed playing with?

There's so many of them I enjoy. You sure got me on the spot there. But really I enjoyed it with Muddy when we did the Cafe Au-Go-Go in New York, me and Otis Spann and Muddy Waters. Oh, so many it's hard to say.

What's your opinion of Otis Spann?

One of the greatest piano players of the blues ever. He had the name of the greatest piano player, and he was great. And a good man too. Loyal, friendly, no ego, no nothing. Just a perfect gentleman.

Who would you consider the great slide players?

Whoo! Well, I would say Ry Cooder. He's one of the greatest. Yeah. Right on. I had a cousin, he gone. He's was pretty great–Earl [Hooker]. He was a monster. Nobody could beat him. I got some of his stuff here now, man. We used to work together a lot over the years. Boy, he used to make a wah-wah talk and slide along with it. [Fred] Below's on drums. I got that album here now. We sits around and we play it–it's really funky.

Have you ever played slide guitar?

Nah. I have messed around with it. I could, but I won't be very good. I used to play a little harmonica and drums.

Did you ever see Elmore James?

Once. I was in Chicago. I went to the hotel where we sit there and talk. He was a nice man. A lot of people copied him too. *Lot* of people.

Out of the younger generation of the blues singers, who was my pride and joy? Stevie Ray. I know that kid–I used to go around Austin, Texas, before didn't anybody know about Stevie Ray and Jimmie [Vaughan]. Every time I go there, he sit in and play. We used to talk. He used to come to the dressing room, come to my hotel room. Those days he used to wear a cap. To me, he was one of the greatest young blues singers. He could do anybody, probably–Albert King, Jimi Hendrix–do anybody's thing. George Benson. He played jazz. I sit down and watch him do that. He had his own style–he did, definitely–but he could play anything else anybody could play. He'd say, "I'm gonna play you now," and he play me. And if he can play me, he can play anybody!

Who's come closest to playing like you?

Let's see. Eddie Taylor is *real* close. He can do it. Buddy Guy pretty close. He can play "Boogie Chillun" real good. He plays it on every show. Buddy Guy is playin' so well, and I'm so happy for him. He gettin' a lot of recognition that he should have had a long time ago, like us all should have got. He's such a beautiful person.

Do you admire John Hammond's playing?

Whoo! Who don't? Me and him together over the years a lot too. Now, he can play like me! [*Laughs.*] Yeah, he can. He say, "I'm gonna play like you now, just like you," and then he goes to playin' it and starts laughin'. I say, "If you was outside

"It comes back to you if you do something good."

© JAY BLAKESBERG

On assignment for *Blues Revue Quarterly*, I revisited Mr. Hooker in Redwood City on December 29, 1992. The cover story was to be entitled Spinning The Blues With John Lee Hooker, so I brought along a stack of records that included the earliest 78s made by T-Bone Walker and B.B. King. In some cases, Mr. Hooker's comments were made while the discs were spinning. Other times, he spoke at length following a song's completion. Since Mr. Hooker's speaking voice is as deep and rhythmic as his singing, his words are presented exactly as he spoke them. We began by listening to 1929 T-Bone.

T-BONE WALKER, "TRINITY RIVER BLUES"

Old one there. Oh, yeah. Is that T-Bone? He's one of my favorites. Real favorites. He was the first man to give me my electric guitar–an Epiphone. He was easy to get along with. He was very friendly, very loving, very romantic with the ladies–yeah, like most men, including myself. I can't say enough good things about him. [*Listens intently.*] I didn't know him that far back. What label is that one?

Columbia.

It sure sound different–his voice. Yeah. It sound like old Blind Lemon, almost. T-Bone was such a gentleman.

Did you ever hear him play an acoustic guitar?

I never did. When I knew him, he was playin' electric. He was the first man that made the electric guitar popular around back east in Detroit. Everybody was trying to sound like T-Bone Walker. The guitar players, you'd hear that fancy electric style. It's very up-to-date. That sound he was doin' then would be up-to-date right now in these late years. But this [song] doesn't sound like him to me.

It's a beautiful arrangement.

Yes, it is.

ALBERT KING, "PERSONAL MANAGER BLUES"

Albert King. Yeah. He was a great man. Boy, now he played *the blues!* He's my favorite guitar player.

and you walkin' up, you think it's me in here playin'." He's a really nice gentleman. He's another easygoing person too. He love people. He's a softie. He talk to me about it a lot. We sit down together [*imitates Hammond's voice*]: "John, you know, you love people. We let 'em get away with things we shouldn't, but we don't want to hurt them." That's the way he talk. I said, "They think John Lee don't know any better, but I do. I just love people." You help people. You take 'em in. It all come back to you.

Perhaps the measure of a truly great man is how he treats people day in and day out.

Right! The little things in life, the love. I always believe in "it comes back to you if you do something good." That's the whole thing I believe in. I was taught that, and I think it do too. You do good deeds, somewhere in life it's gonna come back. You can do wrong so long, you gonna get it in some kind of way. That's my belief. So I'm happy with my life. I had a good life, and I had a rough life–I've had both. I don't try to live in the past. I can't bring back those little things. I can't change the rough things that come through, so I look for the future. You can't live in the past–a lot of people try to live in a memory. I live for today and for people today. This is a different world. This world changes all the time.

Why?

He plays the funky blues. He don't go fancy. He stay right where he at. Stevie Ray sound just like this. Oh, I love Stevie Ray! He sound just like Albert, though, when he want to. Albert had a heart attack, and that was a big loss to me. I loved him.

He sure was a character. Did things his own way.

Yeah, his way and no other way! Well, that's the way he was. He didn't let no manager tell him what to do. He'd tell the manager to go fuck off! He'd fire 'em in a minute. He went through managers like rain. That's the way he was. He was a trip! [*Laughs.*] He was right up front. He didn't hold back no punches.

B.B. KING, "MISS MARTHA KING"

Is that B.B.? Yeah, yeah, yeah. One of the nicest men in the world now. Yeah, you can tell that's him. Different style, but it's him. I admire that man so much. I always have admired him. I knowed him when he was a little skinny guy, weighed about 120 or 130 pounds. He's bigger than that now! Yeah, he is. That's what the age and good livin' will do for you, you know. [*Laughs.*] He is a sweetheart man. He love people like me. He don't have special people he love and some he don't–he love 'em all. He got something for everybody. He always friendly, he always ready to talk to people. He's just a hunk of love.

I admit I like his older stuff better. It was more bluesy. I like everything he do now, but go back and get that old stuff he used to do, which he can do now if he really want to. Them hard blues. I guess we all tryin' to update for a while–you got to keep up with the time and what the people want. Like in the race–you got to keep up with this race. So that's what I try to do, and that's what he's doin'.

During the 1940s, why did bluesmen like B.B., T-Bone, and Gatemouth Brown want an orchestra?

Well, why you wanted to have them was some of them little nightclubs was noisy. People drinking. If they sit in there by theyself with just an acoustic guitar, they couldn't be heard unless they playin' a coffee house where people don't drink while you performin'. Coffee houses–that's what I did. Just playin' guitar, and nobody talkin' while I'm performin'. And you could be heard.

I never knowed B.B. or T-Bone Walker to play coffee houses. They played nightclubs where people were noisy, dancing, and they had to have the big band. I don't know if that was their choice or not, but they didn't do what I did by myself at coffee houses. When I was playin', they just quit servin' food and sandwiches until after my show was over. It was quiet, and they could be just sittin' and they could hear me. But bars wasn't like that, you know. Some of 'em come

there to drink and lookin' for women and loud. They like the music, but they ain't payin' it much attention. They just lookin' for what they want, and with the drinkin' they get wild. So they got to have a band to cover that. You follow me?

Sure.

You got to have a band. Come right back to myself: The coffee houses are gone now, and I have to play with a big band at these clubs and concerts, or I wouldn't be heard sometimes. I do it sometimes by myself with the electric guitar–me and Ry Cooder–but mostly for people listening in the concert hall. But nightclubs, you can't do that. They want the music loud, they want to dance, they want to boogie–you got to have a band. But it used to be you could play by yourself at coffee houses like the Chessmate in Detroit, where the people would sit and listen. But now you don't have a choice. All that stuff is gone. But that's the real music. Once you listen to it, you want to hear more and more and more of it. That's the history of American music, because everything come from there. But here lately people get to hear it a lot; they used to sweep it under the carpet. They wouldn't play it on the radio, but now they playin' it. All the young kids, all the young folks love it now. They love it all over the world. But at one time, they didn't know what it was. But when they hear it, they love it.

This next song was recorded by Blind Blake in 1929, and he sings about addresses in Detroit.

I heard of him.

With Charlie Spand on piano. I don't know anything about him.

Me neither.

BLIND BLAKE, "HASTINGS STREET"

Sound like Blind Lemon a little bit. Yeah. This sound like up-to-date music, don't it? [*Laughs at the line "they're doing the boogie, very woogie."*] I never knew where he was from–it sound like he used to live there. I didn't know that. Detroit was jumpin' then. Good piano player. "169 Brady"–yeah, Brady was right off of Gratiot. Brady Street is gone now; I don't think it is no more. Hastings Street is gone, yeah. Jefferson is still there, Gratiot is still there. Chene, St. Auburn, Grand River, and the big main street, Woodward Avenue. When I got to Detroit, Hastings Street was the best street in town.

Do you like Blake's guitar playing?

Yeah, that's the old sound here. Yeah, I do. That's the real blues. You know, it don't take fancy chords. See, all these fancy chords is not real blues. It's just a lot of fast fingers, you know, just sort of 80-, 90-mile-an-hour speed. Which I don't do that. I play the real funky blues in my own style.

And you've got the big beat driving right down the middle of your music.

Driving big beat. Don't get me wrong: These guitar players, they really good in they own way, they own style. They really like just a lot of fancy pickin'–they do–and maybe I couldn't do that. And I don't want to do it. But I don't call it the real blues, though. It's just a lot of speed. What they doin' is good, but not for me. It's the real funk that I play. There's a heck of a lot of fancy guitar players out there, but comin' out of the real blues, it ain't there. I got my own style that ain't nobody else got but John Lee Hooker, and I wouldn't change if I wanted to.

My sound what I got, I don't go by a certain time–8, 12, and 16 [bars], which I can do it *perfect* if I want to–but I'm known not to do it, and I don't do it. I'm allowed to jump here and jump there, because that's the way the blues is. Just lower your head and play the blues–it come from the heart and soul. And then you feel it. And when you feel it, somebody else is feelin' it too. I could play perfect on everything if I wanted to, but then there wouldn't be John Lee Hooker any more: "Oh, he gone to the fancy style" or "He gettin' fancy perfect." I do that on some of my songs–perfect intention–but then I do it unperfect when I don't want to do it perfect. Some of 'em I do perfect, like "Boom Boom." Some of 'em I don't go about perfect changes–I just play my guitar.

Let's hear another famous guitar player–Lonnie Johnson in 1930.

LONNIE JOHNSON, "NO MORE TROUBLES NOW"

Oh, boy. I love that man. Oh, I wish I had that. Send me some of that. I knowed him personally. Nice man. Like he just said [on the record], he like women, wine, and song. He lived in Toronto. That's where he died. I knowed him real good.

It was said that in the early days, he was the most sophisticated blues guitarist.

He is! He got that style, man. He's blues and he's pop–there's some of everything, the way he plays it. He loved everybody. He was a hero to everybody. When he lived in Canada, I'd go see him play, and everybody loved that man. He was so friendly. Always smiling. Nice personality. Everybody loved him–black and white, wherever you are–they loved Lonnie Johnson.

Did you know about him when you were young?

Well, not real young. I knew him when I was pretty young–I was around 30. I used to follow him. Oh, I just can't say enough about the man. He was genius. And he had his own style too; he didn't sound like everybody that pick up a guitar. Nobody sound like Lonnie Johnson. You could tell it was Lonnie Johnson every time he picked it up. Oh, he could play a lot of notes, but you know who he was because he had his own style. [*Listens intently.*] Whoo. Oh, so sad when I hear that.

MEMPHIS MINNIE, "MA RAINEY"

Oh, yeah. Memphis Minnie. I knowed her real good.

Why weren't there more female blues guitarists back then?

That's a question I can't answer. Men is just ahead. Millions of men guitar players, just a few women. I guess it just wasn't… I don't know. That one I can't answer.

Would it have been harder for them to travel around to play?

Yeah, I'm sure it would have been. Memphis Minnie played guitar.

Johnny Shines thought she might have been the first blues performer in Chicago to have an electric guitar.

Could have been. I knowed her when she live in Detroit–her and Son Joe, what played with her.

Can I play you an old song that's really dirty?

I don't care. Get funky. I don't care what it said–pussy, whore, or anything!

LUCILLE BOGAN, "SHAVE 'EM DRY"

[*Laughs at opening verse.*] "Make a dead man come." Who is that?

Lucille Bogan, 1934.

I never heard of her. [*Laughs uproariously at the line, "Say, I fucked all night and all the night before, baby, and I feel just like I want to fuck some more."*] I like that!

Have you heard people play this kind of music?

Yeah.

What about "The Dirty Dozens"?

Yeah. That's a song they used to play, "The Dirty Dozens." "Dozens" means *bad*–something's bad, bad. But playin' "The Dirty Dozens"–I really never did know what they meant by that, but I heard the word a hundred million times.

Was that music around when you were a child?

Oh, no. My parents didn't allow it, no. If I'd heard it, they would kill me! [*Laughs.*]

ROBERT JOHNSON, "PREACHING BLUES"

Oh, yeah. Famous man. And he got to be famous since he been gone. He more famous now than he was when he was alive.

He played around Clarksdale in the 1930s.

I never seen him.

Had you heard his records?

I heard his records when I come to Detroit. I got up to Detroit when I was about 14. I left Mississippi when I was 14.

Were you playing already?

I wasn't famous, but I was foolin' around with the guitar.

Does this Robert Johnson record sound like Mississippi music to you?

It could be any country or any state, and over the years, I guess it would be. Nowadays, he could be any state or any country. But then that was the kind of music in the South.

JOHN LEE HOOKER, "SHAKE YOUR BOOGIE"

That's me. That ain't me singin', though, is it?

It's supposed to be you in 1948. Sounds like you're 14 years old.

Yeah. It's got my name on it, but I think it's somebody else singin'.

You sound like you're bashing your guitar pretty hard.

Yeah, I do that.

JOHN LEE HOOKER, "GOOD BUSINESS"

Yeah, that's me. "You got good business, and I like to trade with you." Yeah.

Do you have a collection of your own old records?

Not that old [*points to the one on the turntable*].

Your latest album, Boom Boom, *covers some of your early hits.*

Some of my classic stuff, but the kids never heard it, so I did it over. I always did want to do it that way. Just me and my band and some local people doing the stuff I did a long, long time ago, which is new to the kids now, like "Sugar Mama," "Boom Boom," "Dimples."

Your career seems more happening now than ever before.

It is. And it hit me by a shock–it was strong, fast, and quick. I'm able to handle it. It don't bother me, success. I'm just a normal person. If you didn't know me as a star, you'd never know it just to see me out in the streets, the way I act with people. I'm really down to earth. I'm more into poor people than I is to people that got a lot of money, rich people. I love 'em all, but my father was just everyday people, just down to earth people. Small nightclubs–I go in and jam and talk to the people. That's the way I am. Success hit me by surprise, but it didn't change me at all. I never thought I would come to be one of the greatest musicians alive, you know. I never thought that. But hey, it happened, and I can't change it, the way people feel about me and love me, which is good. And I give love back to 'em. I really love people, and it shows.

It's just a shame that some musicians don't feel the way I feel. They're real famous, you know, but that's where we come from. The people made us what we are. If it wasn't for the people, we wouldn't be what we are, ridin' in these fine cars and nice homes. The people bought this for us, and I love these people for that. But there are some people I don't associate with. Don't say I hate them, but I don't like what they stand for. As a body and flesh and blood, I love them. But I don't love what comes out of that body, the action and what they stand for. But my door is always open for the right people, because I really love people.

A SELECTED JOHN LEE HOOKER DISCOGRAPHY

Early sides: *Don't You Remember Me* (King and Cobra, '48-'50), Charly; *Half A Stranger* (mostly Modern and Crown, '48-'54), Mainstream; *Detroit Blues* (Gotham and Staff, '50-'52, plus collaborations with Eddie Burns), Flyright/Interstate; *Gotham Golden Classics* ('50-'51), Collectables; *40th Anniversary Album* ('48-'51), Sensation; *Boogie Awhile* (rare acoustic songs, rehearsals, and obscure sides from Danceland, JVB, Acorn, Prize, and Staff, '48-'53), Krazy Kat/Interstate; *No Friend Around* (late '40s-early '50s), Red Lightnin'; *Graveyard Blues* ('48-'50), Specialty; *John Lee Hooker... Alone* ('49-'51), Specialty; *Goin' Down Highway 51* ('48-'51), Specialty; *Blues Brother* ('48-'51), Ace; *Detroit Stuff* (Gotham, '50-'52), P-Vine; *John Lee Hooker Plays & Sings The Blues* ('51-'52), Chess; *House Of The Blues* ('51-'52), Chess; *Detroit Blues, 1950-'51*, Krazy Kat; *Mad Man Blues* (early '50s), Chess; *John Lee Hooker* ('51-'54), Chess Japan; *Don't Turn Me From Your Door* ('53), Atco/Atlantic.

Other labels: *Cold Chills*, Official; *Drifting Through The Blues*, United; *The Blues*, United; *Folk Blues*, United; *The Great Blues Sounds Of John Lee Hooker*, United; *Original Folk Blues*, United; *The Greatest Hits Of John Lee Hooker*, United; *The Legendary Modern Recordings*, Ace; *Moanin' And Stompin' The Blues*, King; *Goin' Down Highway 51*, Specialty; *House Rent Boogie*, Charly; *The Ultimate Collection: 1948-1990*, Rhino.

Mid 1950s-'60s (usually with small group): *I'm John Lee Hooker* (superb debut album, recorded between '55 and '59), Vee Jay. Also on Vee Jay: *Travelin'*; *The Big Soul Of John Lee Hooker*, *Concert At Newport*; *In Person*; *On Campus*; *Soul Meeting Saturday Night*; *Hall Of Fame*; *Is He The World's Greatest Blues Singer?*, *John Lee Hooker Gold*; *The Best Of John Lee Hooker*.

On Archive Of Folk (Vee Jay reissues): *John Lee Hooker*; *Hooked On The Blues*; *John Lee Hooker Sings*. On Charly (Vee Jay reissues, '55 through '64, except where noted): *This Is Hip; Everybody's Rockin'; Moanin' The Blues; Boogie Chillun; Solid Sender; Original Bluesway Sessions* (reissue of Bluesway's *Urban Blues,* '67, with Wayne Bennett and Eddie Taylor, and *Simply The Truth,* '68); *House Rent Boogie; Let's Make It.*

On Ace: *The Folk-Blues Of John Lee Hooker* (solo acoustic, '59); *That's My Story* (Battle trio cuts, '60); *That's My Story/The Folk Blues Of John Lee Hooker* (CD of two albums); *Live At Sugar Hill* (solo in a small club, '62); *Live At Sugar Hill, Volume 2.*

Other labels: *In Person* (Vee Jay reissues, late '50s-early '60s), Dynasty; *Best Of John Lee Hooker* (Vee Jay), GNP; *The Real Blues,* Tradition; *Don't Turn Me From Your Door* ('53/'61), Atlantic; *Sittin' Here Thinkin'* (mid '50s), Muse; *Burning Hell* (Riverside, '59), Original Blues Classics; *Boogie Chillun* (solo, '60s), Fantasy; *Black Snake* (reissue of Riverside's *The Folk-Blues Of John Lee Hooker,* '59, and *John Lee Hooker Sings The Blues,* '60), Fantasy; *Sad And Lonesome* ('60), Vogue; *That's My Story,* Original Blues Classics; *The Country Blues Of John Lee Hooker,* Original Blues Classics; *It Serves You Right To Suffer* (Impulse sides with jazz trio, '65), Jasmine; *Live At Cafe Au-Go-Go* (with Muddy Waters Band, '66), ABC/Bluesway; *The Real Folk Blues* ('66), Chess; *Urban Blues* (Bluesway, '67-'69), MCA; *Tantalizing With The Blues* (Bluesway, '65-'71), MCA; *Original Bluesway Sessions* ('67-'68), Charly; *Lonesome Mood* (Bluesway with Earl Hooker, '69), MCA; *Get Back Home* (solo on Black And Blue, '69), Evidence; *Nothing But The Blues* ('69), Blue Moon; *The Best Of John Lee Hooker, 1965-1974,* MCA.

1970s-'90s: *Hooker 'N' Heat* (solo and with Canned Heat, '70), Rhino; *Infinite Boogie,* Rhino; *Never Get Out Of These Blues Alive* (reissue of '72 album, plus tracks from 1970's *Endless Boogie* and *John Lee Hooker Featuring Earl Hooker*), See For Miles; *Free Beer And Chicken* (ABC, '74), BGO; *Alone, Vol. 1* (powerful '76 solo sides), Labor; *That's Where It's At,* Stax; *Live & Well* (live in Germany, '76), Ornament; *Black Rhythm & Blues* (live in Europe, '70s), Festival; *I'll Play The Blues For You* (half of the cuts are by Albert King, '77), Tomato; *The Cream* (Tomato, '78), Charly; *That's Where It's At!* (a high-water mark of late-'70s Hook), Stax; *Hookered On The Blues* (live, '80s), JSP; *Jealous* ('86), Pausa; *The Healer* ('89), Chameleon; *Mr. Lucky* ('91), Pointblank/Charisma; *Boom Boom* ('92), Pointblank/Charisma.

With others: Big Joe Williams and Lightnin' Hopkins, *Dark Muddy Bottom Blues,* Specialty; Lightnin' Hopkins, *It's A Sin To Be Rich,* Verve; Pete Townshend, *The Iron Man* (Hooker sings two cuts), Atlantic; Sticks McGhee, *Highway Of Blues,* Audio Lab; John Hammond, *Got Love If You Want It,* Charisma; Van Morrison, *Too Long In Exile,* Polydor; B.B. King, *Blues Summit,* MCA.

Anthologies: *Detroit Blues–The Early 1950s,* Blues Classics; *Atlantic Blues: Guitar* ('53), Atlantic; *The Great Bluesmen* (one Newport cut), Vanguard; *Great Bluesmen/Newport,* Vanguard; *Blues At Newport,* Vanguard; *American Folk Blues Festival, 1962,* L+R; *American Folk Blues Festival, 1965,* L+R; *American Folk Blues Festival, 1963-'67,* L+R; *Blues Masters, Volume 7: Blues Revival,* Rhino; *Chess Blues* box set; *The Jewel/Paula Records Story* (only one Hook track, but it's a juke-style "Roll And Tumble," '71), Capricorn; *The Stax Blues Brothers,* Stax; *Legends Of Guitar–Electric Blues, Vol. 2,* Rhino.

Soundtracks: *Mr. Brown* ('72); *The Outsider* ('79); *The Color Purple* ('86); *The Hot Spot* (with Miles Davis, '90), Antilles.

On film: *Jazz USA* ('60); *American Folk Blues Festival* (BBC, '68); *L'Adventure Du Jazz* (France, '69-'70); *Roots Of American Music* ('71); *Gettin' Back* (Ozark Mountain Folk Fair, '74); *The Blues Brothers,* ('80); *Mark Naftalin's Blue Monday Party* ('81).

B.B. King

September 1980 & July 1991

BY TOM WHEELER

& JAS OBRECHT

RILEY B. KING is the world's preeminent blues guitarist. There is hardly a rock, pop, or blues player anywhere who doesn't owe him something, although because much of his influence has been indirectly transmitted through rock stars, more than a few may be unaware of that debt. His dedication is as inspiring as his talent, and it's hard to imagine someone working harder at music, or anything else. For decades Riley, better known as B.B., has worked a staggering 300 nights a year or more, in part because he feels that he must live up to a long-held title. They call him King of the Blues.

"There are days when I don't feel like going onstage," he admits, "but whether I want to go on or not, I *must* go on. Usually when I'm up there, I try and do like an electric eel and throw my little shock through the whole audience, and usually the reaction comes back double-force and pulls me out of it, because the people can *help* you entertain; they become a part of it. It's something like radar: You send out a beam, and it hits and comes back with even more energy."

Sweating in the spotlight, working on the fretboard, B.B. seems like a string-bending surgeon with his deft and confident left-hand technique. Unlike many self-taught guitarists, he plays very efficiently, without the wasted effort that comes from using the wrong fingers. He takes a breath. From his expression you know that in a split second Riley B. King will lay himself bare. He extends an irresistible invitation to share in the simple transfer of joy and pain which he has perfected: He stings Lucille; Lucille stings you. David Bromberg recently put it this way: "Usually in a good concert you'll hear people say 'ooh' or 'aah' at various times, but when B.B. plays they all go 'ooh' at the same time and 'aah' at the same time. He doesn't just play his guitar; he plays his audience."

Many of the post-Beatles guitar stars were of course technically accomplished and innovative, but in most cases, beneath the arrangements and the special effects were guitar licks unmistakably attributable to B.B. King and other American bluesmen who, in the U.S. at least, were then known only to limited numbers of blues buffs. Aside from phrases and blues scales, the dynamics of rock guitar as a communicative vehicle also owe much to the originality of B.B. King. He can make Lucille talk in an almost literal sense, with screams, sassy put-downs, cute little tickles, or an unabashed plea for love. He can articulate the hopelessness of poverty or a love gone wrong with a poetic subtlety rarely matched by mere words.

When he was developing what has become one of the world's most readily identifiable guitar styles, B.B. borrowed from Lonnie Johnson, T-Bone Walker, and others, integrating his precise, vocal-like string bends and his patented left-hand vibrato, both of which have become indispensable components of rock guitar's vocabulary. His economy, his every-note-counts phrasing, has been a model of taste and style for thousands of players. Mike Bloomfield was awestruck upon hearing Eric Clapton in the mid '60s. Later describing his impression, he groped for superlatives: "He was as good as... *B.B. King.*" For Bloomfield, an ardent musicologist, it was the ultimate tribute.

According to one prevalent view, there is some quantum of suffering that must be endured before an entertainer "qualifies" as a blues artist. Under anybody's standard, B.B. King has qualified many times over. He was born on a Mississippi plantation and earned 35¢ for each 100 pounds of cotton he picked; he once calculated that he had walked thousands of miles behind a plow during his years as a farmhand. It was only during the rainy season that he was allowed to leave the farm to attend school, and he walked ten miles to join his 85 classmates in their one-room schoolhouse. For two decades he took his music to scores of obscure and often sleazy bars throughout the South, where isolation crushed the dreams of many a performer.

At age 24 King was performing in a bar in Twist, Arkansas, when two men started a fight, kicking over a barrel-sized kerosene lamp. The building erupted in flames, and the panic-stricken crowd scrambled into the street. Not having enough money to replace his $30 guitar, B.B. raced back in to save it. The man who was later to acquaint much of the world with the blues was almost burned to death, and just after his escape the building collapsed, killing two other men. When he learned that the fight had been over a woman named Lucille, he gave that name to his beloved instrument and its many successors "to remind me never to do a fool thing like that again." The story is the stuff of legends, but legends sometimes spawn stereotypes, and B.B. King is a complex man, one who in the interview that follows disavows several popular images of blues entertainers.

The young B.B. King spent countless hours in the small recording facilities used by Kent (later Kent/Modern), Crown, and Blue Horizon, turning out regional hits in the early '50s. He estimates that he's recorded over 300 sides in all, although because of poor distribution and low retail prices he never reaped much profit on many of them.

He cut more LPs after signing with ABC-Paramount in 1961, one of the best of which is *Live At The Regal*. He was transferred to ABC's now defunct Bluesway label in 1967, and he made the R&B charts a year later with "Paying The Cost To Be The Boss." Producer Bill Szymczyk contributed much energy to *Live And Well* in 1969, and it was hailed in *Down Beat* as "the most important blues recording in many years."

Finally in 1970, over 20 years after cutting his first record, B.B. scored a nationwide hit with "The Thrill Is Gone." Though it employed a string section and thoroughly modern production, he is suspicious of the emphasis so often placed on elaborate recording techniques, noting that many early blues classics were cut in garages or mobile facilities. In fact, his first major R&B hit, RPM's "Three O'Clock Blues," was recorded in 1950 in the Memphis YMCA. It stayed on top of the regional charts for four months, and as he discusses below, it changed his life.

B.B. has been acclaimed in virtually every music poll, and his affection for music of almost all types continues offstage. In his hotel room, a bed or table is usually covered with mounds of cassette tapes, perhaps 50 of them, "just for my own listening enjoyment." He often practices long into the morning hours, even during periods of grueling roadwork, and spends much of his free time listening to the records in his mammoth collection at home.

B.B.'s approach to his art is not only the cornerstone of a distinguished career but also a metaphor for a remarkable philosophy of self-improvement and universal brotherhood. In 1973 he and Fayette, Mississippi, mayor Charles Evers co-sponsored a memorial festival commemorating slain civil rights leader Medgar Evers. B.B. was a founding member of the JFK Performing Arts Center and has received public service awards from B'nai B'rith and many other organizations. He co-founded the Foundation for the Advancement of Inmate Rehabilitation and Recreation. He has played many prison benefits and been cited for his service by the Federal Bureau of Prisons. He is a licensed pilot and an accomplished player of several instruments other than guitar. He received an honorary doctorate from Mississippi's Tougaloo College, and his hometown renamed a park after him and painted a guitar on the street near the corner where the King of the Blues used to play for dimes. The town turned out to see him put his large hands in the wet cement, and the tribute was a highlight of B.B. King's life.

In the following interview B.B. reflects upon his professional standards, his guitar techniques, and his more than 30 years as a bluesman. He rejects certain public perceptions of blues performers and explains the evolution of his relationship to his art. B.B. King is witty, gracious, independent, and significantly more eclectic than his contemporaries. At the core of his career is a dedication to his ideals, to his fans, and to his belief that music is a social tool, a vehicle for bringing people together.

Caught in the act: "As kids, we'd sneak in the church to play with the piano."

Of God In Christ–and the singing and the music in the churches was something that a small boy, even in his fifties today, will never forget.

What did your family think of you playing the blues when you started?

I couldn't play them at home. I was formerly a spiritual singer, and they wouldn't go for the blues, not around the house [*laughs, shakes his head*], not then. That's one thing about the early days of the blues. A few of the spiritual people *liked* blues, but they would play *their* blues after 12:00, when they were in their room and nobody could hear them. But you always had a few devils like myself and a few others that would listen to *anything*. You played it and it sounded good, we would listen to it. I was singing spirituals in my first group, the Elkhorn Singers, but I'd love to go to juke joints at that time.

What made you choose the guitar?

I think that a lot of that has to do with the Sanctified Church, because this preacher played guitar in the church, and that was one thing. But also, guitars were kind of available. The average home had a guitar and a harmonica, usually; you could always find them around. But saxophones, trumpets, pianos, and things like that were rare. Only the middle class families would have a piano. Sometimes a lot of us would like to sneak in the church to play with the piano, and many of us got jobs as janitors, because this enabled us to be near it. We'd be cleaning up the church or something like that, and get a chance to fool with a piano a little bit.

Do you remember your first guitar?

My first one was a Stella, about two-and-a-half feet long, with the big round hole in it, and it was red, one of their little red guitars. I was making $15 a month, so I paid seven-and-a-half the first month and seven-and-a-half the next one. I kept it for a long, long time. It was stolen, but I don't remember when. The next one was a Gibson I bought in

When were you born, and where did you grow up?

I was born in 1925 in the country outside of Itta Bena, Mississippi, which is not too awful far from Indianola. My parents separated when I was around four, and I spent some time in the hills of Mississippi, up around Kilmichael. That's where I lost my mother, when I was nine. I was a farmhand all of my life, until I was inducted into the Army and sent to Camp Shelby near Hattiesburg, Mississippi, in 1943. I was plowing, driving tractors and trucks, chopping cotton–everything that one does on a farm, I did some of it.

When did you first encounter music?

The first music was in church. From that time until now, that... certain something was instilled into me. I had been baptized as a Baptist, then I was in the Holiness–the Church

Memphis with the help of my cousin, Bukka White. It was an acoustic, but we had just learned about DeArmond pickups. I didn't have enough money to buy the regular electric, so we bought that and put a pickup on it that cost $27. The very first Fenders–I had one. I used it when I first went out on the road, '49 or early '50. I also had a little Gibson amplifier that was about a foot wide, and about half a foot thick [_chuckles at the recollection_], with a speaker in it of about eight inches, I suppose, and that was my amplifier, and I kept it for a long time.

When did you begin playing professionally?

In the middle 1940s, in Indianola, on the corner of Church and Second Street. Second Street is like the main part of town, and Church Street crossed it and went into the black area, what we called "across the tracks." I never passed the hat, but the people knew that I'd appreciate a dime if I played a tune they'd requested.

Why had you picked that particular corner?

I was afraid to sit in the square near city hall, because I probably would have been run out of there. I forget the name of the sheriff that we had then [_laughs_], and on my corner both the blacks and the whites would see me. It wasn't something I planned; it was just like a good fishing place–it seemed like a nice spot to be. You'd find me on that corner on Saturdays, and sometimes after I got off work I'd take my bath, get my guitar, and hitchhike to other little towns like Itta Bena or Moorhead or Greenville. Most times I was lucky. I'd make more money that evening than I'd make all week driving tractors. I'd probably have enough money for a movie. Next day, go to church, then back to work. At the time I was making $22.50 a week with the tractors.

Do you remember your first paying job as a musician?

I don't remember my first paid gig, but I remember the first gig where I started working for like a week at a time–1949 that was, in West Memphis, at a place called the 16th Street Grill. That lady was paying me $12 a night, room and board. I was 24 years old, and that was more money–I didn't know there was that much money in the world. So that's how that started. That was me alone up there–sing, and then play, as I normally do. Sing and play. Working there made me think about going on the radio as a disc jockey, because the lady at the grill told me that if I could get my own show like Sonny Boy Williamson and Bobby Nighthawk and quite a few of the guys, she would give me a steady weekly job, and I _loved_ that idea.

How did you acquire the name "B.B."?

The idea came from the local radio station where I was working, WDIA. I was singing some advertisements for Pepticon, one of these cure-all patent medicines. Later, when I became a disc jockey with my own one-hour show, they would call me "the blues boy," or "the boy from Beale Street." A lot of times they'd shorten it to B.B., and I liked that, and it stuck with me all this time.

Before you were nationally recognized, was there much contact between you and your contemporaries such as Muddy Waters? Were you aware of each other; did you have each other's records and so forth?

No. I had _their_ records, but see, Muddy Waters and John Lee Hooker and all of those guys were playing _before_ me, and they didn't know me from Adam. I was _plowin'_ when they was _playin'_ [_laughs_]! I liked them, and I imagine that they were aware of each other. But they didn't know anything about me, no. Like Ike Turner was about 14 years old when I first met him, in Clarksdale, Mississippi. I had this great big band at that time, which consisted of my guitar, a set of drums, and a saxophone. That was a _big band_, wasn't it? When Ike saw me [_laughs_], he said, "Oh, _man_, you need _help!_"

What was it like gigging for years in small, segregated clubs all over the South?

Well, you hear this term "chitlin circuit." That's not one of my terms, but they're talking about the joints where we used to play before we started to play the white establishment. These clubs were small, most of them, and always across the tracks, in the black area. A lot of the promoters couldn't afford to pay you very much money, and if they didn't have a pretty good crowd, sometimes you didn't get paid at all. I only have about $180,000 owed up to me from my playing during my career. I'd say 90% of the promoters were for real, just like they are today. But then you had the other 10%–the young promoter, probably his first time to give a dance or concert. If he didn't make it, that was it, because he had thrown in everything he had to do this one concert, which he felt would be a gold mine. He'd say to himself, "Well, if I can get B.B. King or Junior Parker or whoever, _this_ night they're going to pull me through," and a lot of times that didn't happen, and when it didn't happen for that promoter, you didn't find him. He wasn't around afterwards.

When you started entertaining, did you think of yourself mainly as a singer, as opposed to a guitar player?

When I first started, couldn't nobody tell me I couldn't sing. See, if you told me I couldn't sing then, I would have an argument with you. Later on, I found out how little I really knew, how bad it really sounded. I then found out that my guitar playing wasn't any good either [_laughs_]. It's funny how this happens, because at first, you believe that you _really_ have it, like you're God's great gift. I mean I felt like that, I really did, and had someone told me I wasn't, well, I would just ignore them because I figured they didn't know what they were talking about. My singing was more popular in the early years than my guitar playing. I was crazy about Lonnie

Johnson, Blind Lemon Jefferson, Charlie Christian, Django Reinhardt, T-Bone Walker, Elmore James, and many, many others, and if I could have played like them, I would have, but I've got a thick head that just don't make it, and my fingers–they don't work either. Therefore, I think my playing was very, very, *very* limited, more so than my singing, because I did have a kind of style of singing at that time.

Compared to many electric guitarists, you play few notes.

I was at the Apollo Theater one time, and there was a critic there, and to me what he said was one of the great compliments that people have given me. The critic wrote: "B.B. King sings, and then Lucille sings." That made me feel very good, because I do feel that I'm still singing when I play. That's why I don't play a lot of notes maybe like some people. Maybe that's the reason why most of my music is very simple–that's the way I sing. When I'm playing a solo, I hear me singing through the guitar.

How did people like Django Reinhardt and T-Bone Walker influence you?

In the way they phrase. They still do it today. Even though they may be in different categories, even though some are jazz and some are blues, when I hear them *phrase*, each note to me seems to say something. And it doesn't have to be 64 notes to a bar. Just one note sometimes seems to tell me a whole lot. So that's one of the reasons why I like them. Same thing with Louis Jordan; even though he plays saxophone, the way he phrases seems to tell me something, and that can just stop me cold when I listen.

Did you play rhythm guitar first?

No, I never accompanied myself, still can't. I *cannot* play and sing at the same time; I just can't do it. I've always been featured from the very beginning. I still can't play rhythm worth anything, because I never had the chance to really play in a rhythm section. But I know a few chords.

Did you invent the fingerstyle, perpendicular-to-the-neck vibrato?

Let's put it this way: I won't say I invented it, but they weren't doing it before I started [*laughs*]. I will say that I'm still trying. Bukka White and quite a few other people used bottlenecks. As I said, I got stupid fingers. They won't work. If I get something like that in my hand and try to use it, it just won't work. So my ears told me that when I trilled my hand, I'd get a sound similar to the sound they were getting with a bottleneck. And so for about 32 or 33 years I've been trying to do it, and now they tell me that I'm doing a little better.

> "*I never passed the hat, but the people knew that I'd appreciate a dime if I played a tune they'd requested.*"

What about the idea of hitting the fret a step lower than the intended note and bending it up–were people doing that before you?

Yes, but I'd never heard anybody do it the way I do it. My reason was that my ears don't always hear like they should. I'm always afraid that I might miss a note if I try to hit it right on the head, so if I hit down and slide up to it, my ears tell me when I get there. But also it's more like a violin or a voice; you just gliss up to it.

Were there any milestones in the evolution of your technique, specific experiences or events that made you alter your approach?

I don't think so. It was like this cancer that got hold of me and started to eat on me. Like when I heard T-Bone Walker play the electric guitar, I just had to have one. I had to play, but it's been a gradual thing, and it still goes on. In fact, if you went to my room right now you'd find a Blind Lemon tape that I've been listening to whenever I'm lying around.

Do you take many cassettes on the road?

I take quite a few in order to hear the old things. I listen to the radio to hear the modern music, but I like to go back to some of the old things so that I can keep the same feeling. I like contemporary things with slick changes, but even if I play them I like to put in the feeling of yesterday. You're lost with either extreme, so I try to make a happy medium and do them together.

Your record collection is something of a legend.

Well, I've got over 30,000 records now. You won't believe this, but even though they're not alphabetized I can always tell if one's missing. One day I plan to get me one of these home computers and enter them all into that. Every time I go home I just tape, tape, tape. [*B.B. has since donated his record collection to the Blues Archive at the University of Mississippi.*]

Do you play visualized patterns on the fingerboard, or do you hear a note or phrase in your head before you hit it on the guitar?

I hear it first, sure do. It's like some guys use an electronic tuner and just look at the needle on the meter, but I can't buy that; I have to hear it, and it's the same with a phrase. No one else can set your hat on your head in a way that suits you. I don't think I've ever seen anybody that when you put their hat on their head they didn't take their hand and move it, even if it's just a bit. Well, I'm like that with the guitar. Do it your own way. When I play it's like trying to describe something to someone; it's a conversation where you say something in a certain way. A lot of times I play with my eyes closed, but in my mind I can still see the people paying attention to what I'm doing. I can see them as if they're saying, "Yeah, okay, I get it." Playing the guitar is like telling the truth–you never have to worry about repeating the same thing if you told the truth. You don't have to pretend or cover up. If someone asks you again, you don't have to think about it or worry about it. To me, playing is the same way. If you put yourself into it, instead of something else, then when you get out there on the stage the next time, you don't have to worry, because there it is. It's you.

Today you're doing things on guitar that sound different from what you were doing only six months ago. Your style seems to continue to grow.

Well, I hope so, because I do study. People hold it against me sometimes. They say, "You're not playing the same thing that you played the last time." But I don't *want* to play the same thing I played last time. That would get boring. I always try to add something, or maybe take something away, to give it a little twist.

Do you play instruments other than guitar?

I try. I was doing pretty good on clarinet before I got ripped off for one. I got to where I could read faster on clarinet than I could on guitar. I know a few scales on the violin, and I fool with that a bit. I'm a little better with piano, and better than that with bass. Drums–I did some time with them too. Also harmonica.

Does working with other instruments alter your approach to guitar?

Yes, it affects my phrasing, and it makes me a little more fluent. It's something for me to do when I'm not practicing like I should. I usually practice mentally, but when it comes to physical practice, I'm a little lazy. I don't know how it is with other musicians, but with me sometimes I don't play like I want to, and then I get a little bit disgusted and lay off for a while. Then one day, something happens, and I can't wait to get back to it.

You mentioned mental practice.

Sometimes I hear something–someone will walk by and whistle, or I'll hear it on the music in a restaurant–and I'll start to look at the fingerboard in my mind to see how I'd do it. I visualize the different ways to do it. That's a good thing to do; it helps you learn the guitar. Just don't do it too much when you're driving, or you'll forget where you're going [*laughs*].

Do you ever stick your neck out onstage, or do you usually reassemble a series of notes, a scale perhaps, the structure of which is already known to you?

In my room, you'd be surprised at all the things I try, but I never go out on a limb, not onstage, no, no, no. I make enough mistakes without it. The guys in the band always

tease me. But if you're in the key of C and really don't want a Cmaj7–that B note–if you should hit it, you can flatten it and get the dominant 7th, which sounds all right, and if you make a mistake and hit the A, it's the 6th, so it's still relative. I learned through these many years of being out there and hoping to get everybody working with me that if you make a mistake, *please* work something into it, so that it's *not* a mistake.

There's a very unusual melody line near the end of "Chains And Things" on Indianola Mississippi Seeds, *where…*

I made a mistake. Now you're getting all the secrets. My bandleader and I have laughed about it many times, but I made a mistake and hit the wrong note and worked my way out of it. We liked the way it sounded, so we got the arranger to have the strings follow it. They repeat the phrase the way I played it. If you've got a good take going and then hit one wrong note, you don't want to stop, so I was in the key of Ab, and when I hit [hums E, Db, Eb, Eb], which is #5, 4, 5, 5, we just got the rest of the band to follow right along.

Do you read music?

Reading music is what I call spellin'. I *spell*; I read slowly. If the metronome is not goin' *too* fast, I can do it pretty good.

"Three O'Clock Blues" was your first major R&B hit. How did it change your life?

I could go into the important theaters. As far as the black people were concerned, when you were getting into show business there were three places you *had* to go through to be acclaimed: the Howard Theater in Washington, D.C., the Royal Theater in Baltimore, and the Apollo Theater in New York. "Three O'Clock Blues" enabled me to go into these places, and it opened other areas, like one-nighters. I had been making about $85 a week with my playing and being on the radio and everything else I could do–$85 total–and when I recorded that first big hit, I started making $2,500 a week. I didn't get to keep all of it, but that was the guarantee.

In the early years, how widespread was racial prejudice in show business?

In the *early* years–you mean right now?

Well, I was talking about…

Well, *I* do. It still happens. A lot of things are not happening for us as blacks as they do for the whites. It's a fact. It's a *natural* fact. I've been one of the lucky few. A lot of things have happened for me, yes; a lot of things have happened for a lot of blacks. But when you compare it to what's happening for the whites, it's a big difference, a great big difference. Fortunately, though, it has gotten much better over the past few years. Blacks get better breaks. We're getting there.

Does racism exist predominantly in one field–radio, recording, club work?

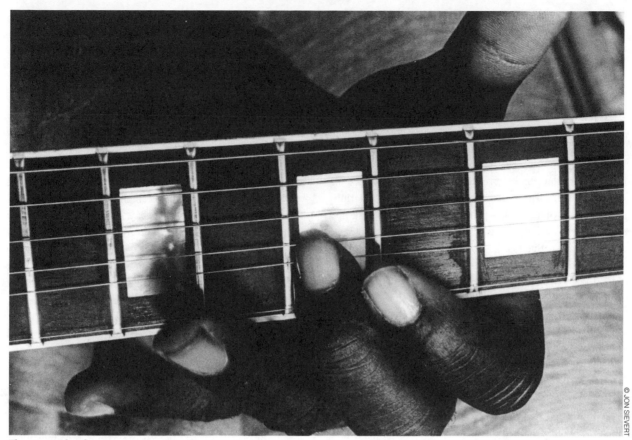

© JON SIEVERT

The master's hands.

You find it in all of them. I can't say which is more, one or the other. But the problem is never with the musicians themselves; it doesn't matter to them. Even when it was very segregated down south, the players always got together and had a good time. Still do. The trouble's been more with the companies, the establishment. Being a blues singer is like being black two times–twice. First you've got to try to get the people to dig the blues, and then to dig you. As a blues singer today, yes, I'm very popular. The FM radio is usually very fair with us, but you won't hear B.B. King or blues very often on AM radio. And I'm not only talking about the white stations. I'm talking about the black ones, too.

Your music is kept off of some white stations because you're black, and off of some black stations because it's blues?

Yeah, of course! I remember once I went to a black dude, a disc jockey that had a program in the South, and he said, "You know, every day we have an hour of blues." I said, "Really? Who do you play?" He said, "Well, I play you, Bobby Bland, Junior Parker, Albert King," and so on. I said, "What about Jimmy Reed, or John Lee Hooker?" "No," he said, "they don't fit my program." And that really got me uptight, you know. This guy is lord and master. He knows what every-

body wants. I guess by being a Virgo, I'm a little sarcastic sometimes, so I said, "Well, how long is your station on the air?" He said 12 hours. And I said, "And you play a *whole hour* of blues?" He says, "Yeah." I said, "Well *look* [*laughs*], why be so nice to us blues singers and give us a whole hour? Why not play a record or two during them *other* 11 hours?" He didn't like what I said, but I didn't really care, because that's the way I felt and that's the way I feel today.

Have the attitudes of black people toward the blues changed over the years?

They're chang*ing*. Today they're not ashamed of it. We've always had black people who like blues, but if I had to try and put it into categories, we had the people that were down here with me, that did the work, you know. Then you had the middle and upper classes, as we called them in Mississippi. The people that worked on the plantations, the regular working class people–*they* understood. They were never ashamed. About 90% of them were a part of it in the beginning; they knew what I was doing. A lot of them could do it even better than I do. But then you had that middle class. A *few* of them would be down with us, and then the others would play our records, but like I said before, they'd only play them after 12:00, you dig? They felt that blues was kind of degrading a bit. They were made to be ashamed of it. They liked blues, but they weren't particular about everybody knowing about it. It's just like me. I like to eat sloppy, and I'd rather eat in my room rather than let people catch me. Among the upper class, the college graduates and the ones who had money, only a precious few would acknowledge my kind of music in the early days. That is changing today, and they're listening.

Early on, were you more popular among youngerlisteners?

Some of the people have stood up and been counted all along, of course. This is a funny thing to say, but it's the truth: When I was young, young people as a mass didn't dig me. When I was, say, like 20 years old, it was always people my age and older. But today, we are gaining ground because black kids will come up to me and say, "Hey, I don't dig the blues, but I dig *you*." So I think we're making progress. At some concerts we'll have all ages and colors. That I like. Lately we're starting to have not just blacks and young whites, but older whites too. I'm surprised, but we have them.

You once complained about the notion that in order to be a blues singer you have to be in torn clothes, you can't be successful, and you've got to be high on something. Do you still encounter that attitude?

I think that that's the one thing that has been *the* big mistake about people in the blues. They seem to think that you have to be high or just completely smashed or stoned out of your head to be able to play blues, and that's *wrong*. And then I don't think that a guy has to be in patched trousers. That image that people seem to put on us is wrong. Blues music is like any other kind of music. Some of us excel, and some of us don't. Some of us are really able to please people, and some of us are not. But we all have the blues. Red, white, black, brown, yellow–rich, poor–we all have these blues. You can be successful and still have the blues. I have been fortunate, and yet now I have more to sing about than I ever did before.

You're referring to the world situation?

Yes. I look around me and I read the papers, and I see what's happening in this country and all over the world. Here, there are money troubles. Food's running low in other places. There's been price fixing, and oil problems. I go to the prisons, and I see what's happening there. Look at what's happening with the people that we pay our taxes to. Look at Asia, at Cambodia. There was bombing going on for years after the Vietnam War was supposedly over. They weren't bombing trees. They weren't bombing ditches. I think of my people, the ones I left behind in Mississippi, and *all* the people in *all* the Mississippis. We are a part of each other, you know. Those problems used to affect me individually, direct-

ly, and now they affect me indirectly. When one person is hurt, it hurts me too. When I see their condition, I know what they feel, and I feel it, and it hurts.

Comparing the earlier years when you were playing to limited blues audiences in the South and in the black theaters in the North to your present success when you are known all over the world, have the blues taken on any new meaning for you? Do you feel the same when singing and playing as you did then?

My blues mean *more* to me now than it did then, because in the early years, sure, I wanted other people to like what I was doing. But at times, I was singing for my own personal amusement. A lot of times I'd get it in my mind that nobody understood me, to be honest with you. A lot of times, the people were there, but they really *weren't* there. The *bodies* were there, but I didn't think they were *with* me. And whenever I felt like that, I would go ahead and sing to amuse myself. I'd close my eyes and visualize all of those beautiful people out there enjoying themselves. But as I kept playing and years started to pass, I started thinking a little different from that. I started to feel that it was my *job* to make people interested in what I was doing, to make them be *able* to understand what I was doing, to make them see that I wasn't just teasing, that I was really for real, you know. And this took a while to do, and it takes time today too.

In purely artistic terms, do you relate to your music any differently?

Yes, it's more of a creative art form now. Before, when I made a record I really didn't think that that's exactly what it is–a record of what you're doing and who you are on that day. And once it's out, it stays. I'm much more conscious of that.

What do you do differently?

It's not just music. It's kind of like a selling job, public relations. Sometimes audiences don't pay attention unless you present it a certain way. No matter how good it is, you seem to need to put a catchy title on it. A lot of people, especially blacks, won't like it if you call it blues, but if you go ahead and play it and call it a different name, they'll like it. That's the truth. So the blues are more important artistically, and also because I feel that I've got a message that should be heard.

What's your message?

Well, here I am. I'm trying to work. I'm trying to bring people together. I'm trying to get people to see that we *are* our brother's keeper. So there are many, many things that go along with it. I still work at it.

You once deliberately chose a spot to perform that was located between black and white neighborhoods of a small Mississippi town so as to draw a racially mixed audience.

Yeah, I got 'em all. We never would have had any segregation if people would've had enough music around. If musicians from all around the world could get together, country to country, that would be a good thing. Like when I toured the Soviet Union in March of '79, the other people who got together thought about politics, but the American and Russian musicians didn't think about anything but music. It was a tremendous experience.

Do you find that your goal of using music in order to bring people together is a common attitude in the entertainment business?

Yeah, I think most of us are doing it. As musicians we feel that if we can get people together just on a social level, having fun, then they can go ahead and get to know each other in other ways too. They can discuss their differences. We get them together and then something good can come from it, because that's when people start communicating.

What brought about your recognition on an international scale?

That has to do with many things, like the changing of times, like the marching, and like the people getting together and trying to stamp out prejudice and all of the many, many things. It seemed to bring people together. It started out to make people think, to see that everybody had something to offer, and that if you listen carefully you could learn something from others. People started searching for the truth…while I've been diggin' all this time. Black awareness–there was a time if you called me black, it was insulting [*nods*], oh yeah, insulting. In Mississippi we always did call white people white people but we, as a whole, really didn't want to be called black. We felt that at the time it was degrading, because it seemed that the person calling you black was really saying *more* than what they said. But later on we started to think about it. If the Indian is a red man, and the Chinese is a yellow man, and you're a white man, then why *not* be a black man? Everybody got aware and became proud of the fact that we are what we are. We began to feel that we *did* have something to be proud of. Like when James Brown made "I'm Black And I'm Proud," this really hit a lot of us, and I think all of this has to do with the blues. There was a time when we felt that nobody else had dirty clothes in the closet, you know–the troubles of life. We were sort of made to feel like we were the only ones that had dirty clothes in the closet, and anytime somebody said something to us or about us, we always felt that we should close the door and not let 'em know what we had in the closet.

And that finally began to change?

Yes. After the early '60s and all that, it's a funny thing, we come to find out that *everybody* has dirty clothes in the closet, and if the people in Nashville and Kentucky can be proud of bluegrass music–which is real music about the way they live, and about their problems, and their happiness and all–why *not* be proud of the blues? This kind of transition caused people to recognize the blues singers. Even the people who don't dig blues come up to me and say that they respect what I'm doing.

Many guitar players discovered you by reading comments by Eric Clapton, Mike Bloomfield, and your other musical descendants.

I talked in terms of black people. Now, as far as the white part of it is concerned, when the Beatles came out, they started people to listening again. See, when Elvis came out in '54, they'd scream–*yaahhh*, you know. They never did hear half of the lyrics. If you could move or shake a bit, if you could twist a bit, rock and roll, that was it. Even though the Beatles' fans used to yell their heads off, their songs said something. People listened again for lyrics. All of this seemed to come back, to be re-imported, in a manner of speaking, because I heard many Beatles tunes that had been recorded by some of the blacks over here. They were re-imported with a different sound. Then Michael Bloomfield, Elvin Bishop, Eric Clapton, and quite a few of the other guys had been listening to myself, Muddy Waters, and many others. *Their* followers started getting inquisitive about their playing, and they said that they had listened to me. That's when the white youth started listening to us. And then another thing: The white youth never did have to feel, say, inferior when they were listening to blues, because they never did have to go through the thing that a lot of the young blacks did–things that made them feel that blues was really degrading to them.

Do you ever get a chance to jam with some of the younger musicians whose careers you've influenced so greatly?

Jamming is something that I rarely do, but we have done it, yes. I have jammed with some of the guys that say they idolize me, but most times I'm rarely around them, or if I am it's just for a short time, like playing the same job. But who knows about the future?

Did you ever jam with Jimi Hendrix?

Yes, we all jammed together at a place called the New Generation in New York City. Any guitar player in town would usually get off work long before us, so they'd come by

> "*Muddy Waters and John Lee Hooker and all of those guys were playing before me, and they didn't know me from Adam. I was plowin' when they was playin'.*"

to see if I was really like someone had told them I was. Everybody would have their guitar out, ready to cut me, you know [*laughs*]. Jimi was one of the front-runners.

Do you ever listen to any of the guitarists who have become famous by playing a style that was originally derived from you? Do you ever find that you are influenced by their playing?

Actually, I'm influenced by anybody that I hear. I don't think that I've ever heard anybody play something that didn't intrigue me at one time or another. If they have been influenced by me, I still find that they have put *their* feelings into what they did, and my things which have influenced them sound different when they come out again. There's only been a few guys that if I could play just like them I would. T-Bone Walker was one, Lonnie Johnson was another. Blind Lemon, Charlie Christian, and Django Reinhardt: Those were the only guys I ever heard–well, there's Barney Kessel, and Kenny Burrell [*laughs*]. If I could have played just like them–not today, but when I first heard them–I would have. And there are also things that they do today that if I *could* do, I probably would, but not the way that they did it. Instead of playing it A, B, C, D, I'd probably play it A, C, D, B–not the exact same thing, because I think that there are very few people that play the same ideas identically as you would feel it yourself.

How long have you been using semi-solid, thin-body guitars?

Since the first one I saw, about '58. I have been using Gibson ES-355s for a long time because they're stereo and I like the highs. I can't hear lows too well–my ears don't tell me much–but highs I can hear very well. My new guitar, which Gibson is planning to release as the Lucille model, is sort of like a 355 but with a few changes.

How has it been modified?

It has a closed body with no f-holes, so you don't get the feedback. I used to have to put towels in my 355 to cut down the resonance, but with the new Lucille I can crank right up. Also, I can tune the tailpiece [a Gibson TP-6] at the back. I usually wear sleeves most of the time, and on the other tailpiece, because of where the strings were wound, I always snagged my sleeves, or I'd wind up hurting my hand a little. With this one, my sleeve doesn't get caught, and when I cup right on the bridge, it doesn't hit the end of the windings, so I don't hang up my sleeve and I don't hurt my hand. Also, the neck is a little bit thinner.

What kind of circuit does it have?

There's a Y cord that lets me bypass the stereo.

Which pickup do you use?

I usually go through the stereo circuitry, with both pickups working against each other. With just a quick shift of the hand I can set the volume or change the tone. To tell you the truth, I'm not even sure which pickup does what. I just put them both on and use my ear.

Did you ever use the vibrato tailpiece on the 355?

No. I think the reason people came out with vibrato tailpieces was because they were trying to duplicate the sound that I was getting with my left hand, and they forgot that I don't need it [*laughs*]. I always took the handle off. The new guitar is really something. I can't put it down, and it has really got me wanting to play again, just like when I started.

Have you had many guitars over the years?

Yes. I was in an accident once, and the insurance company gave me a Gretsch, and then I was in another accident and that one got busted up, and they gave me an Epiphone. Somebody *stole* that. Then I got some Gibsons, and about four of them got busted up. I've been in about 16 accidents. On the thirteenth or fourteenth one, an accident right outside of Shreveport, Louisiana, I remember seeing the bone in my right arm. They took me to the hospital and sewed it up, and the doctor told me that I nearly lost the use of the arm because of some nerve in there. But we drove to Dallas, and I played that night with my left hand. I still made the job.

Weren't you also injured in Israel?

Yes, I fell about nine feet and messed up the side of my face and my shoulder, and busted a blood vessel in my left hand. My teeth went right through my lip–seven more stitches. But I went swimming that evening in the Dead Sea. I couldn't miss it, man, because we were sold out in Jerusalem. The Holy City–I *had* to make that!

What kind of strings and picks do you use?

I use Gibson's 740XL set, with the .009 for the first string. I use a fairly stiff pick. Sometimes it's hard to get good amplifiers, and since I almost always play only with downstrokes, I find that I don't have to hit the strings quite as hard with a stiff pick to get the volume I want.

What kind of amplifiers do you prefer?

Whatever the promoters set up for us ahead of time on the road. I used to request Gibson SG amps, and the second choice was a Fender. Lately I've been trying the Gibson Lab Series amps, and I think we'll be using them from now on.

Of your own records, which ones do you think are the best? Any favorite solos?

I've never made a perfect record, never. Although I'm not ashamed of any of them, there's always something that I could have done better. I know the critics always mention *Live And Well* or *Live At The Regal*, but I think that *Indianola Mississippi Seeds* was the best album I've done artistically.

How seriously were you criticized for using strings and pop songs and more sophisticated chord progressions on some of the recent albums?

I have had some people that weren't thinking. They'd come up and say something about it, but they didn't realize that I was using strings in the early '50s, with things like "My Heart Belongs To Only You," "How Do I Love You," "The Keys To My Kingdom," and quite a few things like that. We were using strings long before "The Thrill Is Gone," many years before. But those critics didn't say much about that. They thought that you were being Mr. Big or you were being jazzy. My answer is this: If the song needs just a guitar and me singing, we use that, and if you need something else to make it, then you should use that. Whether it be a full orchestra or just a harmonica and guitar–whatever's needed, that's what you should use, though I don't think that one should put a lot of stuff in there just to put it in there.

Were you criticized when you decided to have a large stage band with nine or ten pieces?

I have been criticized, yes, but again, a lot of the people who are criticizing didn't know that I had a big band back in the early '50s. It's a great thing to have a big sound from time to time. Years ago, Blood, Sweat & Tears and Chicago showed that if you've got a good band, a band that shouts and plays well, you can get a great thing going. Count Basie and them–that's all they did. They'd swing you to death, man, they'd swing you crazy, and I've always liked that.

What do you look for in a musician who comes to work for you?

A man. I look for a man first, and a musician second. I must respect what he has to offer. I wouldn't say that a guy that can really blow the roof off a building is necessarily the best musician. He may be fiery; he's the type of guy that can really move an audience in a hurry. But an audience don't like to stand on its nose all the time. They want to get down and be something else from time to time. Then you've got another guy that has a touch when he's playing that can really move people, like in a slow groove. Well, you don't want *that* all night. Each guy is good for his one particular thing. Everybody in my group is behind me to push me. I need their cooperation. But I look for someone who's 100% man. If he's only 50% musician, that's okay; we'll turn him into 75% musician after a while. But if he is not 100% man, there's nothing I can do.

Do you have much of a problem with discipline, members not showing up on time and so forth?

I've had guys in the band that screwed up from time to time, but I feel kind of like their father or uncle, and unless

they do it very bad I won't do anything to them. I may fine them today and give it back tomorrow. They can tell you such fantastic lies: "Man, the *train*, like, came by, and one of the cars ran off the track, man, and they wouldn't *allow* nobody to come across." So I laugh, and if he doesn't screw up tomorrow I don't say anything about it. All of the guys are very good musicians and very dependable. I've been fortunate to have dependable men. But I got a thing: Three days of screwing up in a week's time, and you're out. No more fines. So these guys are cool. I tell them that if I can make it, so can they.

You've toured the world and worked 300 nights a year for over three decades. What is the source of your strength and energy?

You've asked me a hard question. I guess one thing is that when I first became popular and started going to many, many places, I always felt kind of bad about stopping school in the tenth grade. I always felt that I wanted to be able to talk to people everywhere I went, to really participate in whatever was around. As I moved about, I found then that my education was really far off. I started learning how much I didn't know. That was one of the reasons why I *really* started to push myself, and I've done it through the years. Sometimes a lot of people wouldn't expect a blues singer to know certain things, and I *do* know them. I won't mention them, being a Virgo, but it just knocks me out for people to cut me short, thinking that I may not know. I work a lot of times just to have that little bit of pleasure. That might not sound like very much, but to me it kind of knocks me out for people to think, okay, the B. didn't go to college or he didn't do this or he didn't do that, and certain things they don't expect me to know–I know *about*. I pay attention, and if I hear something played or hear somebody say something, I'll put it on the tape recorder and listen to it and work with it. I wouldn't say it as he did, but I liked what he was doing and I would do it *this* way, *my* way.

How do you maintain your health and keep up the pace?

It's part of my job. It's like this story about the snake who's lying by the road all cold and muddy. This guy sees him, picks him up, and takes care of him. He gets home, around the fire, and the snake warms up and pokes his head up and says, "You know what? I ought to bite you." The guy says, "You wouldn't do that. I took care of you." And the snake says, "Yeah, but I'm a snake, and that's my job–I'm *supposed* to bite you!" [*Laughs.*] It's the same with being on the road and keeping up with the schedule. Sometimes it's a

> "*People seem to think that you have to be high or just completely smashed or stoned out of your head to play blues, and that's wrong.*"

part of your job to eat, and sometimes it's a part of your job to get some sleep.

Many people call you the King of the Blues. Does that change your outlook on your work or make you feel obligated in some way?

Well, I guess I look at it both ways. First, I never think of myself as King of the Blues; I happen to be a guy named B.B. King, and he plays the blues. Of course, I think I know my job pretty well. What keeps my feet on the ground is that there are people who haven't had the popularity that I've had who are just as talented, or even more so, some of them. But I have so many young fans now, white and black, that come up to me. They trust me; they have faith. You know how it is when you do something and it's appreciated by your girlfriend or your father or mother or whoever it may be. You can see it in their eyes. I can't explain it; it's a feeling that I can't tell you about. You have to see for yourself to know. Maybe like your little brother or your daughter or your son, maybe even like your pet, your little puppy or something. When you look at them, there's something that *tells* you–I know it seems a little deep, and it's hard to explain–but you know that this pet or this person or whoever is really serious about what you've done.

I wish I knew the words–now I'm really at a loss. You're hurting when you can't say what you really want, but there are times when no one else can tell you that they dig you like this special person can. This feeling has happened to me as a musician through the years. It's made me think a lot of times when I go out on the stage and guys come up and want to play guitar with me. You can look in their eyes, the young musicians, and know that you have been something that's going to help them go much further than probably what they would have without you. It's like seeing your own children or your neighbor's children. You don't want to mess up, and this makes you really buckle down and try to do it a little better. I look at my own kids sometimes, and my nephews and nieces. They won't say it around me, but I can tell that they've been whispering, "That's my daddy! That's *my* daddy!" That within itself is enough to make me really go out and try to do better. I try and live and be a certain way so that each day I meet a person, they can't help but say, well, he's just B.B. King. And that's all.

July 1991

A DECADE AFTER Tom Wheeler's B.B. cover story, Billy Gibbons flew up from a break in his ZZ Top tour schedule to join Jas Obrecht and Mr. King for *Guitar Player*'s July '91 cover story interview. The meeting ground was the Embassy Suites in Indianapolis, Indiana. On hand was a cassette of early B.B. King guitar highlights from Ace Records' *The Memphis Masters* and a copy of Stefan Grossman's *Bottleneck Blues Guitar* instructional video, cued to a scene of Bukka White playing a lap-style "Poor Boy" with a metal rod slide. Bedecked in a splendid silk three-piece, B.B. shook our hands warmly and settled into a chair.

Billy: Word's out that you're opening a nightclub on Beale Street.

B.B.: Yes, it's called B.B. King's Blues Club. I'll be playing at the opening soon.

What led you to choose that location?

B.B.: I started from Memphis. Beale Street was very good to me in the beginning. When I came to Memphis from Mississippi, the first place I thought of, because of hearing so much about it, was Beale Street. I come to find out that Beale Street was like a college of learning. You had *everything* goin' on [*laughs*]. Beale Street was like a little town all of its own. Good musicians in the park playing various styles of music. In fact, the first time I ever heard a black guy play a Hawaiian steel guitar was there in Beale Street Park. He was playing the steel like a lot of the country people. It drove me crazy!

Billy: Let's show that little piece of film we peeked at, which shows someone you know playing lap-style slide. [*Starts video.*]

B.B.: Bukka White! That's my cousin. [*Laughs heartily.*] Thank you! Old traditional blues song. I sure appreciate this. You don't know what you're doin' to me.

Billy: He's got some real power in his forearm; the way he's shaking that thing takes some strength.

B.B.: He was a big guy. Not just fat like I am, but *big*.

Had you seen people in the Delta playing that style?

B.B.: Yeah, that's what I grew up with. That's why I feel that I've got stupid fingers, because I could never do it. I could *never* do it. It's sort of like trying to play the piano–my right hand, pretty good. The left hand, it just seems like the only reason I've got it is to help the other one out.

When you first moved to Memphis, you reportedly lived with Bukka for ten months.

B.B.: Yeah, I suppose so. He was working over at Lauderdale and Vance at a place called Newberry Equipment Company. He got me a job working with him. We used to make tanks that they used in service stations, what they put the fuel in down underneath the pumps. Yeah, that's what we were doin'. These big transfer trucks that carry fuel from place to place–we made those too.

Billy: You were playing on the evenings or weekends?

B.B.: Mostly weekends. I would go out with him sometime [*nods to Bukka*]. When I first came to Memphis, I kind of left in a hurry because [*laughs*]... This is a funny story. I was a tractor driver in Mississippi, and there was nine of us that drove the tractors on the whole big plantation. I was considered pretty good. See, if you were a slow learner, you was choppin' cotton–you'd pick cotton by hand. But if you a pretty fast learner or you want to advance, first you plow the mules and then you learn to drive the tractor. Once you drive the tractors, man, you *in*; that's doin' it. You're kind of pampered a little bit when

B.B. King and Billy Gibbons, Indianapolis, April '91.

© BILL REITZEL

you're a tractor driver. You big stuff. Well, I wanted to be a tractor driver, so when I was about 14, man, I was a regular hand at it.

At the beginning in that part of the Delta, the old houses was way up off the ground because the Mississippi River would flood around there. So the boss' house was way up, and when he moved to town, that left this building to be something like a tractor barn, and we'd put the noses of all nine tractors underneath it. The tractor has a big muffler, and exhaust comes up through the top of about the center of the engine.

Billy: The pipe's sticking out.

B.B.: Right. When a tractor has been running a long time, usually it's hot. So you use magnetos on it for your fire. You have a battery to start it, but the magneto runs it. Well, when you cut it off after it's been running a long time, a lot of times it will backfire. It'll do two or three times back or forward. If it's in *gear...*

Billy: Oh, no. I know what's coming.

B.B.: [*Laughs.*] I thought you'd get it. This particular evening, boy, I'd been flyin' all day, man, and everything was cool. I'm thinking about a lady I'm going to go see that night, ran the tractor up like we usually do, cut it off, get off there, and that sucker turned over a few times more. And when it did, under the house it went! That broke off the exhaust. Scared me so bad–I knew my boss was going to have a fit! His name was Johnson Barrett, I love him, but I knew he was going to have a fit. I didn't go to see the girl. I got me a bus, and I left and went to where Bukka was that night. Now, that was the first time I went to Memphis. I stayed away for about ten months, you're right. But then I started to thinking about it, because I missed my family and I missed everything. So I went back down there and told him what happened. He laughed then. I told him, "I'm sorry, and I came back to pay for it," which I did. I stayed there a year. I left legitimately the next year, which was the last of '47. I went back to Memphis, and *that's* when I started living on my own.

I'd been listening to Sonny Boy Williamson, the harmonica player on the radio. He used to be on a station in Helena, but at this time he'd moved to West Memphis, Arkansas. He had his little program on KWEM, I believe. I felt like I knew him. You know how we are with entertainers–you meet a person that you heard so much about...

Billy: You know him.

B.B.: Yeah. So I went over that day, and I begged him to let me go on the radio with him. He made me audition, so I sing one of Ivory Joe Turner's tunes called "Blues At Sunrise," and he liked it. I didn't know anything about chords–still don't. But I had a good loud voice, strong, and I could keep a good beat. But if you thinking in terms of the changes and everything, I was terrible. Still is. [*Laughs.*] But he liked it. And that day, as fate would have it, he had two jobs. One what was payin' him a couple of hundred dollars, maybe, where he was making $15 or $20 down at the 16th Street Grill. The lady's name was Miss Annie. He had 15 minutes, and when he was off the air, he called Miss Annie and asked her did she hear me. She said yes, and he said, "Well, I'm gonna send this boy down in my place tonight, and I'll be back tomorrow." He hadn't asked me anything! She said fine, and when I went there to play for Miss Annie that night, I found that West Memphis was then like a mini Las Vegas. Wide open.

In the front of her place they sold sandwiches, burgers, and stuff like that, but in the back of it they gambled, shoot dice. My job was to try to entertain the people that was up front. Me being young, slim, and crazy about the girls. And I could holler real loud then, man. So she said, "You know, the people seem to like you. If you can get on the radio like Sonny Boy is, I'll give you this job. You play six nights a week, you have a day off. $12 a day, room and board." Well, man, I didn't know there was that much money in the world! Drivin' a tractor, when I thought I was big stuff, you made $22.50 a week. But she was gonna pay me *$12 a night?* And them girls?

Billy: That's why we got into this business!

What were you playing?

B.B.: I was playing anything you mention, but nothin' right. During that time Louis Jordan was very popular, Dinah Washington, Roy Brown. I could mention a lot of people that was popular in the vein of stuff that I could do. I never did any of it right, but my way of doin' it was me, and it came off pretty good.

Were you performing by yourself?

B.B.: Yeah, I had a guitar with a DeArmond pickup.

Billy: Just the add-on kind, wasn't it?

B.B.: Yeah, you just put it on. I had me a Gibson amplifier and an old black Gibson guitar, the first one I ever had with the f-holes in it. And, man, that was the thing at that time.

Not long after that, you started to record.

B.B.: Yeah. After Miss Annie telling me that if I could get on the radio like Sonny Boy was that she would give me the job, that's when I first heard about WDIA in Memphis. That was the first all-black-operated station. So I went over there a couple of days after I had talked with her, and I saw Nat Williams on the air. I actually had started off singing as a gospel singer, so I was pretty up on radio stuff. So I asked for Nat Williams, this black disc jockey in the picture window. His question was, "What can I do for you, young fella?" I said, "Well, I'd like to make a record, and I'd like to go on the radio." So he said, "Maybe we can help you with one; I don't know about the other." So he called Mr. Ferguson, the general manager, and Mr. Ferguson said, "Yeah. I think we can." So that *very evening* they put me on the radio, doing ten minutes with just me and the guitar. Now, that's without the amplifier. And would you know, they was gonna start a competitive product to what Sonny Boy was advertising over in West Memphis.

Billy: Flour?

B.B.: No, no. See, when he left Helena, that was the end of the *King Biscuit Time.* When he came to West Memphis, he was advertising for a tonic called Hadacol. Well, Mr. Ferguson was starting a new tonic called Pepticon. And that's what I was introducing.

What exactly was it?

Billy: A little of everything.

B.B.: Yeah. I never did really find out what Pepticon actually was until about eight years ago; somebody sent me a bottle of it. But I know we used to sell it like there wasn't gonna be no more. Come to find out it was 12 percent alcohol! [*Laughs.*]

Billy: Somebody was feeling good!

B.B.: Some of those church people were having a good time with it. I used to go out on the truck with the salesmen on the weekends, and man, they'd give me like $100, $150 sometimes, according to how much they sell. I'd be on the top of the truck singing:

Pep- ti- con sho' is go- oo-od

Pep- ti- con sho' is good. You can

get it any where in your neigh-bor-hood.

That's how it started, really.

Billy: Going back to West Memphis, I had heard stories about the wildness. I mean, West Memphis was it, man.

B.B.: Yeah, it was really good. I loved it. I really did.

Billy: There are still guys today that talk about it. In fact, you can drive down that old main street, and it hasn't changed too much. You can pick up the feeling. There's still something about it.

B.B.: Memphis was a bit conservative. They didn't believe in having racetracks and all that, so they put it right over in West Memphis, and all the money and everything would go over there on the weekends. So they had gambling and all that, as long as they had a particular sheriff that they kept in there for a long time.

Billy: Was there other live music?

B.B.: Yeah. See, it wasn't just this particular little place. Anybody that was all right with the sheriff and the city government was okay, okay? That make sense? And there was a big white place out there where they really had good music all the time because they could afford to have the best–black, white, or any type of entertainment you could bring. What you have to remember, though, was that during this time it was still segregation, but when we went to that club, there was no segregation. You couldn't get out on the floor and dance, but you could have all the fun you could playing the music. Everybody get together and you talk, spin yarns as we usually did. The people out there was doing their thing, and we did ours in the back. But a few of the better clubs were black clubs where whites would come to them.

Billy: That's so peculiar. Try as you might to keep a lid on a good time, you can't do it. When people want to have a good time…

B.B.: They will have a good time.

Billy: It's gonna be there.

B.B.: And I'll tell you, had it not been for that, my life would have been very slow–very, very slow. I loved it.

Billy: In fact, there is still a faction of people who, if they had their choices, would relive those times in West Memphis, particularly the '40s up to the '50s.

B.B.: Oh, yeah.

Was Beale Street similarly wild?

B.B.: Not really. The guys would have what we called little turn-row crap games or something like that, but if a cop caught you, you were in big trouble! But it was always something going on. You had the One Minute Cafe where you could go in and eat for 15¢, man. I mean, *really* eat: bowl of chili, nickel's worth of crackers [*laughs*], and what we call a bellywash–something like an Orange Crush drink. Man, you could live, I mean, really *live*. Sunbeam Mitchell's was one of the established places for music, so you'd have the best traveling musicians coming through. Let's assume that we were going through town: We'd go to Mitchell's, because we'd have a chance to see the best and find out what's goin' on in the city. That's where you get your information. Kind of like when I used to come to Houston, I'd go to the Fifth Ward and go to Club Matinee.

Well, Memphis was like that. You had several pawnshops. You used to keep a couple of good rings, a good tie pin, and a pair of good shoes, so if you got broke, you go down and pawn them. They know you coming back, because ain't nobody else gonna wear your shoes! Clothing and food and good music of all kinds. You had gospel, find a little spot over here where a guy's preachin', find another over here where some guy's sittin' on the stool playing his guitar, over further some guy's gambling. You may have a few pickpockets. You had some of *everything* going on in the area of three blocks.

Billy: Correct me if I'm wrong, but I've been told that in comparison to West Memphis, which was a different scene, Beale Street was wide open too, but in a stricter sense. There was a police department keeping everybody in line.

B.B.: Yeah.

Billy: You didn't want to act up. Beale Street was controlled.

Did old-time country blues mix with electric blues on Beale Street?

B.B.: Well, see, I didn't know the difference at that time. You had a chance to see people that you'd never seen before; you'd just hear about them. But on Beale Street, he was just another person. It's kind of like if we walked in a room now with Springsteen or the Beatles or U2 or the Rollin' Stones–we all people. You don't see them as if you're out there and don't get a chance to rub elbows with them. On Beale Street, guys like me was lookin' up, but the other guys were just, "Hey, there's old so-and-so. How you doin', man?" But it was a big thing for guys like myself that just came from Mississippi. I had a chance to see Muddy Waters, all the guys that was big then–Sonny Boy Williamson. And then you got a chance to see guys with big bands, like Duke Ellington coming through. Count Basie. And all these people would patronize or fool around on Beale Street.

During that time it was segregated, with the exception of certain places. Now, in the radio station where I worked at, there was no segregation. None. When you came in there, your title was whomever you were. If you was an elderly person, it was Mr. so-and-so or Mrs. so-and-so, but other than that, you were who you are and you was treated with respect. But when you walked out, it was like leaving the Embassy [*laughs*]. It was a different story.

Beale Street was similar, because everybody–white and black–that lived and worked there was accustomed and used to the people being there. Duke Ellington and Count Basie or Louis Armstrong was known not only to the blacks, but to the whites as well. They had the Hippodrome and a few other places where the slick black promoters would bring in one of the big artists, and they would play two shows–one for whites and one for blacks, and they made money. Those were the days, though, man. If you were a little entertainer, you could always stand in the background. Like when the big guys be on the stage, you'd be in the wings lookin'. So it was some beautiful moments, some moments that I'll cherish and forever love.

You think that you got drug problems today, but it was there too. Most of the people would say, "If you want to make it, don't do that there. See what that dude doin' on the corner? Leave it alone," like that. It was sort of controlled, but people did do it.

Some of the jug band musicians fell into that.

B.B.: There was several great jug bands there. You know, in each society of music or whatever, you always got what I call the hierarchy, the people at the top that's the best at what they do, whether it be a boxer or a singer. So whenever one of these guys came around, like the great jug bands, everybody move over there where they can check that one out. I remember, for instance, Lightnin' Hopkins. When I first met Lightnin', it was in Memphis, met him there on Beale Street.

Was there something called headcutting?

B.B.: Well, you could call it that [*laughs*]. People do this now. When a great musician would come to town, like a jazz musician, well, all of the guys would be laying around him trying to cut his head. Well, we had some giant musicians there. The Newborn family was terrific. The old man, which was Phineas [*pronounced fine-us*] Newborn, played drums, and his son Phineas [*pronounced fin-ee-us*], they called him, played the keyboard. And he was *bad*–when I say bad, I mean terrific. And then he had a brother named Calvin, who's still around and plays back in Memphis. Terrible, man, I mean, he plays some guitar! And then you got Fred Ford, Bill Harvin, Herman Green–a lot of people that would be waitin' on you when you come to town. You supposed to be a musician, they want to get you on that stage up at Sunbeam's, and then they started calling Gershwin tunes and stuff like that.

Billy: Oh, lord, look out! The tough stuff.

B.B.: So if you wasn't trained or didn't know tunes pretty well, you'd see a guy start taking his horn down–something was wrong with his horn–and the other guy breaks a string on his guitar, and they move. A guy came to town named

Charles Brown. I'm still crazy about Charles even today. The guy who made "Merry Christmas, Baby" is the one I'm talking about. Well, they knew Charles was a blues singer and a blues player, but they didn't know that Charles had been to college and majored in music. Nobody knew that.

Billy: Whoa!

B.B.: So Charles came to town. He had Wayne Bennett playing guitar, and a few other people. That night after the show they kept begging Charles to come up to Sunbeam's. They get him to get on the stage, and then they started calling "Lady Be Good" and any of the good jammin' Gershwin tunes, because those were the real jazz standards. That night when Charles Brown finally figured out what they was trying to do to him, he called "Body And Soul," which has got *a lot* of changes. When he called the tune, all the guys figured they really gonna cut him now. But then he started to modulate chromatically.

Billy: Giving it to 'em!

B.B.: So a guy done learned it in one key, and now Charles is taking them through it all chromatically. Then I started seeing guys who had something wrong with his horn and such. Finally it wound up with Charles Brown, the bass, and the drums [*laughs*]. That's the best example I ever seen, and it was really fun to see that happen.

You recorded with some of the Newborns early on.

B.B.: My very first record, the whole family was on it. I made my first record for Bullet Recording Company out of Nashville. I had old man Phineas on the drums, his son Phineas Newborn, Jr., was on keyboard, Calvin was on guitar, and a lady was playin' trombone–I can't think of her name now. It had Ben Branch on tenor sax, Thomas Branch on the trumpet, and Tuff Green, bass. It was four sides, and we did them at the radio station in the largest studio, Studio A. "Take A Swing With Me," "How Do You Feel When Your Baby Packed Up To Go," "Miss Martha King," and "I Got The Blues"–the first four sides I ever recorded.

Let's play another one of your early sides, "Mistreated Woman."

B.B.: [*Laughs.*] That's on Modern Records–or RPM, really. That's me. [*At this point the solo starts.*] Yeah, that's the old guy.

Billy: Gibson guitar?

B.B.: Yeah. Crazy about T-Bone Walker. Crazy about Lowell Fulson.

Charlie Christian?

B.B.: Oh, yes. God, yeah. Well, Charlie Christian, Django Reinhardt–those are my jazz players. I don't know, this is going to sound a little weird to you, maybe, but I've always been conscious of being put down as a blues player. So I've had one thing that I always tried to keep in mind: It's always better to know and not need than to need and not know. I always like to know more than people think I know, so I practice hard trying to be able to do things that nobody would expect me to do. That's how I learned to fly airplanes; nobody ever thought that I could be a pilot, so I learned to be a pilot. I learned to do many other things simply because coming from Mississippi usually was the first downer, you know: "Yeah, man, this dude from Mississippi, still got clay mud on his shoes," stuff like that. It's still that way. So I started to say, "Yeah, I'm from Mississippi, and I'm proud of it." And today I'm very proud to be a Mississippian–very, very proud. Because I've been put down for trying to be something else. It wasn't a matter of just being something else–I just wanted to do what I did better than it had been done before. I felt that if I could do it there, I could do it at the White House, do it in New York, do it anyplace, and it could be thought of as being artistically well done.

Billy: Through your graciousness over the years, you've become a cornerstone for so many people by knowing more than what people thought you knew.

B.B.: Well, it was satisfactory to me, in a way of speaking. All right, I don't speak English well, but if I go to Spain, I'll try to learn a couple of words. Any different country, I'll try to learn a couple words. So when I hear people talking in Japan and they say a few things, I'll pick it up. It's the same thing musically. If I hear you play [*indicates Billy*], I may not be able to play what I hear you play, but I'll know a little something about it because I'm *listening*. Got my ears on it. Same thing with him [*indicates Jas*] or whoever. Well, that is a peace of mind for B.B. King–maybe not to anybody else, but to me. And this is not something you do once in a while. Each day I've got my ears kind of cocked, learnin'. If I could do what you do or what somebody else do, I'd find myself saying, "You sound so good like that, but I wouldn't sound that good, so I better try it *this* way." But it's still your idea.

Billy: Let me indulge in a little complimentary flattery by pointing to the single-string soloing on that track we just played. So many have cited the B.B. touch; so many people have made references to the B.B. King influence. I would say that it's your sound and approach to soloing that has made the guitar such a lead instrument. It's really inspired a lot of people to learn how to improvise and solo. Wouldn't you say that was just developing for the guitar around the time you recorded that track in '50?

B.B.: It's a funny thing. During that time, guitars hadn't really come into being, if you will. Excuse the word, but it was a bitch to try to get a good guitar at that time–just to try and *get* one. And when you did get one, you better hold onto it–don't loan it to nobody. If you did, they didn't come back, most of 'em. So yes. Nobody had any idea that the guitar

would become what it is today. Where I grew up at, there was no other instrument that was available to you, really, but maybe a harmonica. And everybody don't want to blow everybody's harmonica. In my area, they couldn't afford keyboards of any kind. You couldn't afford no pianos or organ. I guess I've only seen an organ in maybe three or four homes in an area of 150 homes, and those was what we called–an old word down there–*uppity* [*laughs*]. They had the uppity blacks as well as the whites, see. So very few people had those. Only time I ever seen a piano or organ was when I went to church. So when I would go over to somebody's house, there usually was an old guitar laying on the bed. And the only strings I ever knew about at that time, we bought them at a drugstore, and they was called Black Diamonds.

Red packs.

Billy: Or the glass jar, if you really want to go back.

B.B.: Yeah. And your *E* string, man, was about as big as my *G* string is today. I use a .010 for my *E*, a .013 for my *B*, and a .017 for my *G* string. And those *E* strings then had to be close to .014.

Billy: At least. Somebody gave me a set of Black Diamonds, right out of the box–wires!

B.B.: Now, when you break one of those strings, then you would take baling wire–the wire that you bale hay with–or the wire they used to wrap broomsticks, and we would use that for strings. You take that and tie it onto the string. Once you tie it on, you put that wire on your tuner, so from here to here [*indicates from about the fifth fret to the bridge*] you got string.

Billy: You couldn't play down below that? Oh, man!

B.B.: You could never play down low. But a lot of people didn't do it anyway–in fact, my friend Gatemouth still don't! So you take a clamp [capo]–when you could afford one–and put it on between the end of where the string is broke, so you got good clear string. And if you couldn't do that–in most cases, we didn't–you get a pencil or a piece of stick that's straight across, and you put it on there, take some string, tie it down, and that's your clamp.

A homemade capo.

B.B: Yeah. It's like the nut of your guitar.

Billy: Hope that you sing real high for the rest of the week!

B.B.: [*Laughs.*] Well, we learned to do things. We let [tuned] it down!

As a child, did you ever make a one-string?

B.B.: Yeah. We take the same cord from around that broom, and you put a big nail up there [*points about five feet up the wall*]. Take another one and put it down there [*about three-and-a-half feet lower*], and you put the string on the nails. Then you take something like a brick–we always found that a brick was really good for sustaining tones–put it in down there between the string and the wall, tighten it, put another brick up there on top, tighten it, and then you bang on it.

Would you play with a slide?

B.B.: I can't play slide on my guitar today! [*Laughs.*] Still can't. Another thing we used to do is take an inner tube–you don't find 'em often now, but most of the cars at that time had inner tubes inside of the tire. So when one of those would blow out, you'd take the rubber and stretch it. You'd make a board and put small bricks or pieces of wood on it, just like you do your guitar, and you could play that. You could also take a stick and wet it, put it across, and it sounds similar to a violin. You leave it to kids, boy–we'd find a way to make music!

Was there a moment when it became clear that you were destined to play the blues?

B.B.: Yeah. It was after I had been in the Army when I was 18. Working on the plantation where we lived, we was growing produce for the Armed Forces. You was compelled, you was drafted, as you became 18 during World War II. There wasn't no ifs and ands–you went and signed up for the Armed Forces. Well, in our area they claimed we was doing things for the Armed Forces, and they

"I never think of myself as King Of The Blues. I happen to be a guy named B.B. King, and he plays the blues."

needed us there. So we went and took partial basic training, and then they reclassified you and sent you back home. You couldn't leave; you had to stay there. If you left, then you was reclassified again and went back in. But even if I die tomorrow, I couldn't get a flag, because we didn't complete the basic training. I came back home–I was driving a tractor at this time–and I started to go on the street corners to sit and play on a Saturday evening after I got off work.

I would always try to sit on the corner of main streets, where we get blacks and whites coming right past us. I would sit and play; I didn't ask nobody for anything–I would

hope! Now, I was singing gospel with a quartet; we were pretty good. We were like an opening act for groups like the Soul Stirrers, Spirit Of Memphis, and like that. But for some reason, the guys never seemed to want what I wanted. I wanted to move up a little bit with it, and everybody was very conscious of their families, which I can understand. But I guess I wasn't as family-orientated as they were. I kept thinking that we could go off and do like the Golden Gate Quartet and many of the other groups. Every autumn, after our crops was gathered, I would say, "Hey, now is the time to go," and we'd make plans to leave and go to Memphis or

someplace where we could record. But every time that would happen, they'd say, "No. We didn't do too well. The crops didn't… So we won't do it."

Anyway, while sitting on the street corners playing, people'd ask me to play a gospel song. And when I'd play it, they'd always pat me on the shoulder or something and compliment me very highly: "Son, you're good. If you keep it up, you're gonna be all right one day." But they never tip. But dudes who would ask me to play a *blues* song would always tip, man, give me a beer. Man, they'd yell at everybody else: "Don't you see this boy playin'? Give him something!" Instead of making my $22.50 a week on the plantation, I'd sometimes make, gosh, maybe $100–at least $50 or $60.

Billy: You're speaking of the war years now?

B.B.: Yeah. So these people would always give me nice tips, man. That's when the motivation started. That's when I started deciding I would play the blues.

What were the first blues 78s that knocked you out?

B.B.: My aunt used to buy records like kids do today, and some of her collection was Blind Lemon, Lonnie Johnson. She had Robert Johnson, Bumble Bee Slim, and Charley Patton. I could just go on and name so many she had. But my favorites turned out to be Blind Lemon Jefferson and Lonnie Johnson. I liked Robert and all the rest of them, but those were my favorites.

What's the appeal of Blind Lemon?

B.B.: I wished I could tell you, because if I could, I'd do it! [*Laughs.*] He had something in his phrasing that's so funny. He had a way of double-time playing. Say, like, one-two-three-four, and then he'd go [*in double-time*] one-two-three-four, one-two-three-four. And the time was still right there, but double-time. And he could come out of it so easy. And then when he would resolve something, it was done so well. I've got some of his records now–I keep them on cassette with me. But he'd come out of it so smooth. His touch is different from anybody on the guitar–still is. I've practiced, I tried, I did everything, and still I could never come out with the sound as he did. He was majestic, and he played just a regular little 6-string guitar with a little round hole. It was unbelievable to hear him play. And the way he played with his rhythm patterns, he was way before his time, in my opinion.

Which of his songs would you recommend for guitarists?

B.B.: [*Sings in a gentle voice*]

"See that my grave be kept clean,
See that my grave be kept clean,
See that my grave be kept clean,
See da-da-da-da-da-da"

That's one of them. Lightnin' Hopkins did it, and many people have done it since. But that's where it came from. [*Resumes singing*]

"It's a long road ain't got no end,
Long road ain't got no end,
Long road ain't…"

Oh, one other part:

"Three white horses in a line,
Three white horses in a line,
Three white horses in a line,
Gonna take me to my burying ground"

Something like that.

Billy: Since this interview is centered around Memphis and the early years, I'd like to cite a personal favorite vision that has recently come out. The two B.B. King albums that come over from England that have the picture of you …

B.B.: Wearin' shorts, huh? [*Laughs heartily.*] Well, you know, I used to think that I was kind of hot stuff. My cousin Bukka White told me something that has stayed with me over all these years. I mentioned how we used to be put down as blues singers. I've quite often said if you was a black person singing the blues, you black twice. And if you a white person, you black once. Because people usually will put you down. Like, if you from the country, people was, "Aw, look at the little country dude." And if you from the city, country people won't talk so much about it, but they say, "Well, he from the city, he think he's something." Well, my cousin Bukka White used to say, "You see how I dress? [*Tugs lapels of his suit.*] When you dress like this, it's like you're going to try to borrow some money. The banker don't know who you are, and the people that you're talkin' to don't know what you are. So you always dress like that, and people don't know, because you look clean and neat, and they may loan you the money. But if you come up and you're not dressed nice, you look like you're a beggar. But dressed up, the white people see you, and you look like a preacher or something like that, so you get by a little easier." I started to do it, and I started to notice that made a difference–always. After that I started a trend for my own band, and we sort of set a pace like that. I got used to doing it, and I like it. Anyway, there was something else I started to tell you a little while ago…

Billy: About the Bermuda shorts.

B.B.: Yeah! Thank you. Well, I thought at that time that this was kind of slick, you know.

Billy: It was slick. To this day.

B.B.: Yeah, but if I had realized what my legs looked like then, I probably wouldn't have done it. I had seen guys from Australia wearing short pants, and I thought it was cool.

Billy: In fact, in that photo you're playing a Gibson–it could have been a Switchmaster or the ES-5. Big-bodied.

B.B.: Yeah, I think I had what they called the 400.

Billy: Did the big bodies give you much trouble with feedback?

B.B.: I didn't think of it so much at that time. T-Bone Walker had one that had three pickups, and I was crazy about it. Crazy about him. Well, as I said, during that time it was hard to get and keep a good guitar, so the early '50s is when the Fenders first came out. So I had one of the early Fenders. I had the Gretsch, I even had a Silvertone from Sears, Roebuck. So I had any kind of guitar you can probably think of. But when I found that little Gibson with the long neck, that did it. That's like finding your wife forever. This is she! I've stayed with it from then on. Now, a lot of times you may buy a guitar just to keep at home, but to play–for me, that was it. They had the ES-335, and then they had a new idea for the 355, and I've been crazy again. So that's the one I've held onto. But I've tried guitars through the years–you name them, I've probably had one.

Billy: You've been credited with starting so many fads, trends, crazes, and things that have gone way beyond that now because they're carved in stone as just the way to do it. And people keep digging up relics of the past: Just recently a friend of mine sent me a postcard that's a reprint of a publicity shot of the B.B. King Orchestra. The band members are lined up, and you're leading the pack, standing in front of the bus. Everybody is just natty, neat as a pin. It's the definitive vision of the way an outfit should look. And it's coming back around to this.

B.B.: Yeah, I remember that. We took that picture in front of my first old bus. That was a pretty big band then, about 12 or 13 pieces. I thought myself big stuff because we could play the blues like I thought we should, and then we could venture into other little things from time to time. This was '55.

Billy: Well, you had the strength to be that leader.

B.B.: I've enjoyed doing what I've done. I've had so much happiness from so many people.

Billy: It shows.

B.B.: If you'd ask me 40 years ago–this is 41 years I'm into it now–would I even be living today, I would have bet you odds no. But so many good things have happened. I'm happier today, this very day, than I've ever been in my life. I've had so many wonderful things happen. And I'll tell you what, you've made me happy just sitting here talking with you. This is a real treat. I never dreamed this would ever happen. I really thank you. I've been asked before if there was anything I would do differently if I had this life to start again. And there are only two things I can think of that I would change: I would finish high school and go to college and try to learn more about the music, and I wouldn't marry until after 40!

A SELECTED B.B. KING DISCOGRAPHY

A fine 77-song retrospective, MCA's *B.B. King: King Of The Blues* CD box set collects tracks spanning from 1949's "Miss Martha King" through B.B.'s recent collaborations with U2, Bonnie Raitt, and Gary Moore.

Early recordings: *The Rarest King* ('49), Blues Boy; *Singing The Blues* (early/mid '50s RPM sides), United; *The Blues* (early/mid '50s), United; *Best Of B.B. King* (reissue of first LP), Flair/Virgin; *Singin' The Blues/The Blues* (RPM/Crown/United LPs), Flair/Virgin; *The Feeling They Call The Blues, Vol. 1* (RPM/Kent), Trio; *The Feeling They Call The Blues, Vol. 2* (RPM/Kent), Trio; *Ambassador Of The Blues* (RPM/Kent), Crown.

On Ace: *The Memphis Masters* ('50-'52); *King Of The Blues Guitar* ('50s instrumentals); *Rock Me Baby* (Crown); *The Best Of B.B. King, Volume One* and *Volume Two* (RPM/Kent); *Do The Boogie!* (early '50s); *One Nighter Blues* ('51-'54); *Across The Tracks* ('51-'57); *Lucille Had A Baby* (mid '50s); *The Fabulous B.B. King* (Modern); *My Sweet Little Angel* (Modern); *Heart And Soul* (Kent and Modern).

On Kent: *You Done Lost Your Good Thing Now; Incredible Soul Of B.B. King; I Just Sing The Blues; Better Than Ever; The Unexpected Instrumental B.B. King; Boss Of The Blues; Doing My Thing Lord; From The Beginning; The Jungle; Greatest Hits Of B.B. King; Pure Soul; Let Me Love You; Rock Me Baby; Underground Blues; Turn On With B.B. King; Anthology Of The Blues.*

On United: *The Great B.B. King* (mid to late '50s); *I Love You So* ('58-'59); *The Soul Of B.B. King; Swing Low, Sweet Chariot* (gospel songs); *My Kind Of Blues* ('60); *A Heart Full Of Blues; Easy Listening Blues; Blues For Me; King Of The Blues; Let Me Love You; Onstage–Live; The Jungle; Boss Of The Blues; The Incredible Soul...; Turn On; Better Than Ever; Live; The Original Sweet Sixteen.*

1960s–'90s (on MCA): *Live At The Regal* ('64); *Why I Sing The Blues; Live And Well; Back In The Alley* ('64-'67); *Blues Is King* (live in Chicago, '66); *Great Moments With B.B. King* ('66-'68); *Guitar Player; His Best: The Electric B.B. King; Live In Japan* ('71); *Live At Cook County Jail* ('71); *Indianola Mississippi Seeds* ('72); *To Know You Is To Love You* ('73); *Friends* ('74); *Two On One* (combines *Live At The Regal* and *Live At Cook County Jail*); *Lucille Talks Back* ('75); *The Best Of B.B. King; Completely Well; Midnight Believer* ('78); *Take It Home* ('79); *Now Appearing At Ole Miss* ('80); *There Must Be A Better World Somewhere* ('81); *Blues 'N' Jazz* ('83); *Love Me Tender* ('85); *Six Silver Strings* ('85); *King Of The Blues, 1989; Live At San Quentin* ('91); *Blues Summit* ('93).

Other labels: *Completely Well* (reissue of Bluesway's *Live And Well* and *Completely Well*), Charly; *Spotlight On Lucille* (instrumentals, '60-'61), Flair/Virgin; *Blues Is King* ('67), Bluesway; *Lucille* ('68), BGO; *Blues On Top Of Blues* (Bluesway, '68), BGO; *His Best: The Electric B.B. King* (Bluesway, '69), BGO; *B.B. King In London* (with British rockers, '71), BGO; *Guess Who* ('72), ABC; *B.B. King* (Newport Jazz, '72), Accord; *16 Original Big Hits* (reissue of Galaxy's *B.B. King's 16 Greatest Hits*), Fantasy; *B.B. King Live At The Apollo* ('91), GRP.

With Bobby Bland: *Together For The First Time… Live*, MCA; *Together Again*, MCA; *I Like To Live The Love*, MCA.

With others: Sonny Boy Williamson, *Goin' In Your Direction* ('50s), Trumpet; U2, *Rattle And Hum* ('88), Island.

Anthologies: *Atlantic Blues: Guitar* ('72), Atlantic; *Live At Newport*, Intermedia; *Blues Masters, Volume 7: Blues Revival*, Rhino; *Blues Masters, Volume 8: Mississippi Delta Blues*, Rhino; *Blues Masters, Volume 9: Postmodern Blues*, Rhino; *The Fifties: Juke Joint Blues*, Flair/Virgin; *Juke Box R&B*, Flair/Virgin; *A Sun Blues Collection*, Rhino; *Blues Guitar Blasters*, Ace; *Legends Of Guitar–Electric Blues, Vol. 1* and *Vol. 2*, Rhino.

Soundtracks: *For Love Of Ivy* ('68); *The Seven Minutes* ('71); *Black Rodeo* ('72); *FM* ('78); *When You Coming Back, Red Rider?* ('79); *Into The Night* ('85); *The Color Of Money* ('86); *Air America; Heart & Soul*.

On film: *Monterey Jazz Festival* ('67); *Monterey Jazz* ('68); *Medicine Ball Caravan* ('70), Warner Bros.; *En Remontant Le Mississippi/Out Of The Blacks, Into The Blues* ('71 West German/French film; available from Yazoo Video); *Blues Music In America–From Then 'Til Now* ('71); *Le Blues Entre Les Dents/Blues Between The Teeth* ('72); *Sing Sing Thanksgiving* ('73); *Black, White And Blues* ('74); *Give My Poor Heart Ease* (William Ferris' 1975 documentary features footage on acoustic and electric guitar); *Got Something To Tell You: Sounds Of The Delta Blues* ('77); *Good Mornin' Blues* (King narrates this '78 production by Mississippi ETV; available from Yazoo Video); *Live At Nick's* ('83, Sony Video); *New Orleans Jazz And Heritage Festival; Memories From Beale Street; Let The Good Times Roll With B.B. King, B.B. King & Friends* ('87). B.B. explains his guitar technique in the three-video *B.B. King Blues Master* set available from DCI Music Video. He's also appeared on numerous TV talk shows and sitcoms.

B.B. King
& John Lee
Hooker

September 1993

By Jas Obrecht

J OHN LEE HOOKER AND B.B. KING, the world's preeminent bluesmen, met at Fantasy Studios in Berkeley, California, during March 1993 to record together for the first time. The session was for B.B.'s *Blues Summit* album, a star-studded affair featuring duets with Ruth Brown, Robert Cray, Albert Collins, Lowell Fulson, Buddy Guy, Etta James, and Koko Taylor. No track comes closer to celebrating B.B.'s Mississippi roots, though, than his mesmerizing "You Shook Me" with the Hook.

While B.B. and John Lee have similar backgrounds–both were raised in the Delta, idolized the same musicians, migrated north, and began recording in the late '40s–their styles are remarkably dissimilar. A master of single-note solos punctuated with his signature hummingbird vibrato, B.B. has typically worked with a jumping, well-rehearsed big band. Much more of a lone wolf, John Lee tends to perform solo or with a small, handpicked band, matching his deep, deep voice with propulsive, trance-inducing rhythms or raucous boogies. Performing together, though, the bluesmen easily found common ground during the "You Shook Me" session.

A few weeks later, on April 4th, the B.B. King Band played the Circle Star Theater in San Carlos, California, just a few miles downhill from Mr. Hooker's Redwood City home. We had just 35 minutes between sets to score the interview and photo shoot. After a thrilling performance before a packed house, B.B. cooled down for a few minutes and then settled into an easy chair alongside the couch where John Lee Hooker was holding court. Their exchange began with a hearty handshake.

B.B.: John, you did me a great favor. I owe you one.

John Lee: Look, B.B., there ain't nothin' in the world… I could never give enough to do what I did with you.

B.B.: Same here.

John Lee: All my life, I wanted to sit down with one of the great masters.

B.B.: Oh, listen to that! [*Hitches up pants legs and pretends he's wading.*] Now go ahead, John. [*Both laugh uproariously.*]

John Lee: He's a genius. I been on the stage with him a lot, but this is the first time I recorded with him. That was a pleasure too. I never will forget it as long as I live. We did "She Shook Me, Like The Hurricane Shook The Trees." We played the hell out of that tune.

Was B.B. hard to work with?

John Lee: Just like takin' candy from a baby. I been talkin' about wantin' to do that for years and years. We come up together–I don't want to say how far back–but we were youngsters. We would party, go out together. But something I dreamed of was wantin' to sit down with this man, side to side, face to face, and just play. It was such a tribute, to me, and I just felt it will be with me until the day that I go, tryin' to be with one of the greatest musicians alive, one of the most famous persons alive, and one of the nicest persons. He just like a lamb, he's so easy for people to talk to. He's such a nice gentleman. He'll talk to anybody, anywhere. He's not the kind of person that run, duck, and hide from his fans. That's what I like about him. I said, "Well, here's two *mah-sters.*" You know what a *mah-ster* is? Like two great men.

The two of you have probably made more blues recordings than any other pair of artists in history.

B.B.: I would think so. I think John has made many more than I.

John Lee: Oh, yeah, I have. I did a lot before he did.

B.B.: See, John was playin' when I was plowin'. I was still on…

John Lee: What is a plow? [*Both laugh uproariously.*] You down there in Indianola.

B.B.: I was still in Indianola. Just come to Memphis, and John was makin' records then.

John Lee: You know who I met you through? [Promoter] B.B. Beaman.

B.B.: B.B. Beaman, Atlanta, Georgia.

John Lee: He was *thin* [*points to B.B.*]–weighed about 125, 130 pounds.

B.B.: Yeah.

Is that before you had a hit with "Three O'Clock Blues"?

B.B.: Yeah. That was about the time of [1952's] "Three O'Clock Blues." I'd made about six or seven records before "Three O'Clock Blues." The first four sides I made was for Bullet Record Company out of Nashville. It's funny–when I made those four sides, they went out of business. So I was that bad!

John Lee: You know the first thing I heard from you? "C'mon, Baby, Take A Swing With Me."

B.B.: That was one of the first four sides.

John Lee: [*Sings "C'mon, baby, take a swing with me."*]

B.B.: Yeah! Then after that I recorded several other tunes. I'd been listening to Lowell Fulson. I got his "Three O'Clock Blues," and when I did that, that was the one that did it.

John Lee: Yeah, I love that Lowell Fulson. Still do. "Everyday I Have The Blues"–he really did a good job on that.

B.B.: Yeah. You know, a lot of people don't know it, but after Memphis Slim wrote it and recorded it, Lowell Fulson was the first one that ever made a hit on it. 'Cause I don't think Memphis Slim called it "Everyday I Have The Blues." He called it something else, but it was the same lyrics.

John Lee: It was the same, same thing.

Do you hear traces of the Delta in John Lee Hooker's music?

B.B.: I don't think of John as a lot of people do. I think of John Lee Hooker as John Lee Hooker. And he play the blues like I heard 'em when I first started to play. And he *still* plays 'em. He plays the blues like John Lee Hooker does. It was two or three people that I knew before–in other words, that was older than John–and that was Lonnie Johnson, Robert Johnson, and Blind Lemon. I didn't know them all personally, but I did get a chance to meet Lonnie before he died. But these people, the way they played, they were so themselves. Well, in the modern times–and what I call modern times is the time I started to play–John Lee Hooker was one like that. Lightnin' Hopkins was like that.

John Lee: Oh, yeah.

B.B.: You *know* who they were the minute you hear 'em play. When John Lee Hooker plays, it's like writin' his name: "I'm John Lee Hooker." So I don't necessarily think of it as Delta or city or any other type…

John Lee: No, me neither. It's just blues.

B.B.: I just think of him as John Lee Hooker playin' the blues. It takes me home, of course. Yes!

John Lee: You know people ask me about Mississippi blues, jump blues, big city blues, Mississippi boogie–it's all the blues to me. The blues is all over the world now. People that don't speak English love the blues. I'm so happy for myself and other blues singers out there that the blues is beginning to get so popular.

Is it better now than during the 1950s and '60s?

John Lee: Oh, yeah! Are you kidding?

B.B.: Yeah, because nowadays people don't class you so much. It's not always thumbs-down, as it used to be. It used to be back in that time, in some places, the minute you say you a blues singer, it would be thumbs-down.

John Lee: Yep.

B.B.: It was just like, "Oh, he's a nice guy, but he's a black."

John Lee: Yeah, yeah.

B.B.: "He's a nice guy, but he's white." Nowadays there's not so much of that. You do find it, but…

John Lee: It's very rare.

B.B.: The only thing I kind of take issue with a little bit is when people say, "Oh, that's city blues, that's Delta blues, that's Mississippi, that's Chicago," and so on. Muddy Waters, for example, is to me the first of the so-called Chicago blues.

John Lee: That's right.

B.B.: Muddy left Mississippi, went to Chicago. John left and went to Detroit. I left and went to Memphis. We was still migrating, and wherever we went, our identity was pretty strong, like Muddy's was and the people surroundin' him. So you had a lot of the new guys to be born and started to play later. But to add to that, to me, blues is that label again. For instance, when John Lee made "Boogie Chillun," that wasn't blues. That was get up and get it!

John Lee: Get up and go! That was the first rock!

B.B.: That's right!

John Lee: You get rock and roll from that.

B.B.: So when people say blues and you say "Boogie Chillun," how in the heck could he be blue? He's havin' a ball! He's havin' a good time.

John Lee: That's right.

B.B.: If I sing "I got a sweet little angel," I'm not blue at all.

But when you were growing up, wasn't blues used as party music in the Delta?

B.B.: It still is. You didn't only just hear it in the roadhouses. You could hear it on the streets of Indianola, Sunflower. You could hear it in most of the places around. Even in Memphis, you could find it on Beale Street then. When I first went to Beale Street, there was…

John Lee: Look, B., okay, I want to say something now. The blues was here when the world was born and man and woman got together. That's called the blues. Rock and roll sayin' the same thing that me and this man are saying: "My woman gone, she left me." See, rock and roll, you have the same thing, you just cut 'em in a different form. Cut 'em hopped up and shined and polished up. You sayin' the same thing. You talkin' about a woman that left him. You could make it a ballad. [*Croons "My woman have left me, she gone away."*] You wouldn't call that blues, but we all sayin' the same thing. But I'm gonna tell it in a different way. You understand that, B.?

B.B.: Yeah. Another thing, see, like they use words today that if I'd have used them around home comin' up, I'd get smacked in the mouth.

John Lee: Oh, you get you teeth knocked out!

B.B.: Like, for instance, if a guy say, "Man, make it funky!" If I said "funky" around home, my mother would knock the hell out of me! [*Both laugh.*]

John Lee: [*Like he's talking to his mom*] "I wasn't makin' funky!"

B.B.: Now you hear guys quite often, and nobody pay

"The blues was here when the world was born and man and woman got together."

any attention: "Here, make it a funky beat, man. Put a funky beat." Well, now we accept it. But during the times I was growin' up, man, that was a bad word. That was like a kid swearin' in the house.

John Lee: It sho was. You say "funk" around my mother [*laughs*]…

B.B.: Smack you! "Boy, what are you saying?" Bam!

What can someone gain by listening to B.B. King play guitar?

John Lee: Well, I'll tell you what he just told you about me. There only one B.B. There's a lot of imitations, lot of people pick up the guitar and follow this man—many, many of 'em. Used to be everybody that pick up a guitar try to sound like B.B. King. But you can tell when the *main* person, the main man, hit it. You know it's B.B. There was a boy in Chicago called Little B.B.

Andrew Odom?

John Lee: I think so. Tried to sound just like B.B., but I know it wasn't B.B. He be playin' with my cousin a lot, Earl Hooker.

B.B.: Yeah! That's a bad man. Ain't been but one other person play slide like Earl Hooker. You know who that is, for me?

© BILL REITZEL

"Lot of B.B.s out," claims John Lee, "but it ain't like the real one."

John Lee: What, Bonnie Raitt?

B.B.: Bonnie Raitt. She is the best that is today, in my opinion.

John Lee: Yeah. So let me finish. So you can tell in a minute if you hear B.B. from an imitation–I can. What they don't know, maybe–and I think you know this, B.B., you know it [*points to Jas*], and I know it–anybody can sound like John Lee Hooker, but it ain't the real John Lee Hooker. He make it real good, but I can come along and just *hit it*, and they gone. They'd rather see me. Like B.B.: Lot of B.B.s out, but it ain't like the real one. You can tell it's B.B. King. He had one song I never will forget, but everything he do, I love it. Come to my house, I got stacks of B.B. I've got his six-pack. What they call it?

B.B.: The box set.

John Lee: I got that. And he got one in there: "You breakin' my heart, and there ain't anything I can do."

B.B.: "There ain't nothin' I can do," yeah.

John Lee: Boy, people used to play that thing!

It's interesting that both of you play Gibson's B.B. King guitar.

John Lee: Yeah, I went and bought one.

B.B.: John has played so many different guitars through the years, though. So many different ones, and they all sound like John.

John Lee: I got my identity. I got my style. I got nothin' to regret. I got nothin' to try to gain. I got nothin' to try to change. I wouldn't change for all the tea in China and all the money in the world. Who else you gonna sound like?

B.B.: It's just like one piano that sits over in the corner. If John go and play it, he gonna sound like himself, 'cause that's the way he play. If I go play it, I'm gonna sound like myself, 'cause that's the way I play. Now, if you don't believe it, you can hear Ray Charles play it or Pinetop [Perkins] or Elton John–they gonna sound like themselves. That's just one of the things that we're lucky we were blessed to be able to do–to be ourselves and do our own style. Like, when I heard John, I know it was John. If I hear Jimmy Reed, I know it's Jimmy Reed. My cousin Booker White–know it's him. Even in jazz and rock and roll, *certain* guys–not all–have that identity.

It's just like you as a journalist–certain styles people have of writing, singing, whatever they do. Like an architect or some of the Old Masters painters, da Vinci and all these guys that was doin' whatever they did. You *knew* the way that they did it. Same with the classical musicians–some of 'em you *knew*. Well, that's what I think of John. John couldn't change if he wanted to.

John Lee: No.

B.B.: I couldn't change if I wanted to.

John Lee: I'm like in the old way. I couldn't change if I wanted to. But *if*, like B.B. said, if I did it, it wouldn't be me.

B.B.: It's just like a way of talkin'.

Is it a waste of time for someone to try to play like you?

John Lee: I would think so.

B.B.: Well, not really, John. Think about it. 'Cause when we first started–I know I did–when you first started, you heard somebody you liked.

John Lee: Oh, all the time. I did, I did.

B.B.: So I liked somebody when I first started. We had our idols then, just like kids do today. So there's nothing wrong, I don't think, with listening to or trying to play like someone–*in the beginning*. But then as you learn, you start to think that there's already one of those. So you try to play as you play.

John Lee: Don't play like Jimi Hendrix or B.B. King or somebody else. Play…

B.B.: As you feel yourself. Put you in it. We all like somebody. Everybody did. John, who was your idol? Who did you like when you first started to play?

John Lee: Well, when I first started to playin', T-Bone Walker was my idol.

B.B.: Me too. [*Both laugh.*]

John Lee: Boy, I used to follow him like a little puppy followin' his mama.

B.B.: Yeah, me too. I tell ya somebody else I liked–I was crazy about Lowell Fulson.

John Lee: Whooo weee! "Everyday I Have The Blues," and then "Blue Shadows Fallin'."

B.B.: Even before that, Lonnie Johnson.

John Lee: Oh, man!

B.B.: I was crazy 'bout him. Lonnie Johnson and Blind Lemon. Those were my people, along with T-Bone Walker.

John Lee: Lonnie Johnson, he sing, but it didn't sound like deep blues. What would you call that?

B.B.: I don't know. He was so versatile, he did some of all of it. Lonnie Johnson. Now, most of the kids today are crazy about Robert Johnson. Now, I think Robert was great. I think he was really great, but he wasn't my idol.

John Lee: No, he wasn't mine, either.

Why did Robert Johnson have a gold record in 1990?

B.B.: Well, that's from the same thing I just got through sayin'. Johnny Winter *swears* on him. [*Laughs.*] He says he's the greatest thing ever happened–that's what he told me. And a lot of the kids are crazy about it because they say it's authentic.

John Lee: It's authentic. Let's put it like this: The man has been out of existence so long that they really built him up a lot just talkin' and writin' about it. Then when they did put it out, everybody went for it. He get so much publicity.

B.B.: There you go. You just hit it.

Publicity?

B.B.: Of course!

John Lee: So much publicity!

Do you like Robert Johnson's music?

John Lee: Some of it, yeah. I'm like B.B. I'm not a fan of his, though. But I listen to it.

B.B.: And I like some of the things he did. I just didn't idolize him like I did Lonnie Johnson.

John Lee: Lonnie Johnson and T-Bone Walker. I would have dust his feet if he'd have said so.

B.B.: Here's what happens in a lot of cases. We'll take John as an example. John has been great since I first heard him. He was doin' great things all the time, but he couldn't get the publicity...

John Lee: That's right.

B.B.: Until he got this manager he have today and Bonnie Raitt.

John Lee: This man right there [*points outside of the room to Mike Kappus of San Francisco's Rosebud Agency*].

B.B.: So that was the same thing with me. My manager's name is Sid Seidenberg. So when Sid and I got together, that's when things started to change. Gosh, as great as Bonnie Raitt is–I've known her all her career–and as great as Robert Cray and Roy Rogers and a lot of the people we hear today are, John has been like that since before they were *born.*

John Lee: It's true.

B.B.: You understand? But, thanks to John's manager and other people that know how to package it, the people that knew Robert, that knew Roy, that knew Bonnie–many of the people–now can hear John. Like a guy told me not long ago: He said his son came home and says, "Daddy, you got to hear this guy I just heard!" And his father say, "Who is it, son?" He said, "Oh, you wouldn't know him. You wouldn't know anything about him." Said, "Well, who is it, son?" He says, "You got to hear B.B. King! You just got to hear it!" [*Laughs.*] So his father said, "Son, long before you was thought of, I was listening to him." He said, "Yeah, but dad, you don't know about things like that! This is new!" So it's the same thing. John and myself and a lot of us that's been playing for a long time just never got the break.

John Lee: Never got the breaks, and then they just didn't push the blues like they should. They still don't, like they really should right now. But they pushin' more than they used to. They used to just push it under the cover.

Does recording with rock stars make that big a difference?

B.B.: Oh, yeah. Of course, of course! That's why I mentioned Bonnie Raitt. It's like U2 and myself. Had it not been for U2, a lot of people wouldn't know. But thanks to Sid, we were able to have this happen.

John Lee: The same thing I say about my manager. Thanks to Mike. You know, I had give up recordin'. I said, "I'm not gonna record no more." The record companies, they rob you blind. Like Modern Records and Vee Jay and them– they just robbed you. You know they was takin' everything you had. Well, I think you know that too. [*B.B. nods and laughs.*] They were! I said, "I'm gonna get out of the business." And I had been out for about eight years. I was still with Mike. Mike says, "Let's get you a record deal." He worked *hard,* got me a record deal. Got me pulled together. And that's how I come to be... I never was forgotten, but I got disgusted. I said I wasn't gonna record anymore.

B.B.: See, Mike's a very good man, as Sid is to me. They always lookin' out for things that'll help us, that will get the publicity that we...

John Lee: Never was able to get.

B.B.: Now, don't misunderstand me. Nobody gave Bonnie

nothin'. Nobody gave Robert [Cray] anything. They earned it. But today they are superstars. What I'm trying to say is that had people known John in the beginning as they have known him now, he would have been a superstar years ago.

John Lee: Right. Just wasn't gettin' that push.

Like Muddy Waters, you're both making very good records during the second halves of your careers.

John Lee: Well, Muddy gone now, but he…

B.B.: But he was makin' them then, man!

John Lee: Yeah, he was makin' them, but they wasn't bein' pushed.

B.B.: Even today–take it from me–if I wasn't on the record with U2, nobody would have played B.B. King.

I don't know about that.

B.B.: Can you take my word for it?

Yes, but I'd listen to your record even if it were just you and an acoustic guitar.

John Lee: *You* know he's a monster. You know how good he is. But you're just one.

B.B.: Look, I'm not trying to be false modesty or anything of that sort. But today listen to the radio. Watch the T.V. And every time that you hear a new B.B. King record play… Of course, I don't think it will be like that with this album John and I just got through doin'. I think this is gonna be played.

John Lee: I think so too. I'm prayin'.

B.B.: But prior to that and prior to John and Bonnie Raitt–understand?–I *bet* you wouldn't hear a John Lee Hooker record played.

John Lee: I don't think so either, B.

B.B.: I have to eat my words. I said that if I ever had a record played on MTV, I would eat the cover. [*Both laugh.*] So I had to eat my words because they did play me with U2. We did "When Love Comes To Town," and they played it. I said, "Well, I'll be darned. I might as well go start eatin' covers." [*Laughs.*]

John Lee: Gettin' back to Bonnie Raitt. She was on about 20 years that nobody ever knowed her. Remember that?

B.B.: Yeah. Used to be an opening act for me.

John Lee: Me and her used to party together. She used to drink liquor like water.

B.B.: One of the nicest people I ever met, though. One of the nicest.

John Lee: Oh, she's nice. Whoooo wee.

B.B.: She's a great person. Nobody gave her anything. She earned it. I was so happy to see it.

John Lee: Nobody give her nothin'. She earned it. Like this man here, nobody give him nothin'. He earned it. Nobody give me nothin'. I earned it. But they just beginnin' to play us now, but not like they should.

B.B.: I think what we're talkin' about now is, today the blues is known better. One of the things I take issue with quite a bit, you hear people say, "Oh, the resurging of the blues."

John Lee: Resurgin'! It ain't never went nowhere!

B.B.: It never left, as far as I can tell. I've worked on an average of 300 days a year since '56, many concerts every year. What they fail to realize, though, is that when you have superstars like Eric Clapton or Robert Cray or Jeff Healey or Stevie Ray Vaughan, when they came on the scene, they had their new thing goin' *and* they played the blues, so that made a difference. But they hadn't left nowhere. It's just each time we got a new disciple.

Does it seem like there's something fundamentally wrong with this?

John Lee: No, it don't bother me. Not at all. I don't know what about B.

B.B.: No, the only thing that bothered me is that we didn't have nobody like that at first.

John Lee: That's right.

B.B.: That was the thing that bothered me. We wasn't recognized. So today, to find that we have some people that's playin' the blues and not ashamed to say it…

John Lee: Right. Then they had the right people to push it.

B.B.: That today makes me happy. Very happy.

John Lee: Me too.

B.B.: So today we got superstars. John's a superstar today.

John Lee: B.B. I know could have been…That older stuff we did? It should have been…

B.B.: There was a lot of good stuff done. When you did "Boogie Chillun," man, everybody should have known about it.

John Lee: Yeah. And "Boom, Boom," "Dimples," and stuff like that.

Do you remember creating "Boogie Chillun"?

John Lee: Yeah, I do. I used to hear my stepfather, when I was a kid. My style–I got it from him. He'd do stuff like that [*sings "boom-da-boom, boom-da-boom, boom-da-boom" while snapping fingers*], "Boogie Chillun," different things. I do remember that. I got people to do something like what rested in him. Everything I do is *direct* from Will Moore, my stepfather. He play just like I'm playin' today. I learnt from him. He played that kind of stuff–foot stompin'.

Open G?

John Lee: Yeah. "Mama don't allow me to…"

B.B.: "Stay out all night long."

John Lee: "Boogie Chillun" and all that kind of stuff. It used to be "Boogie Woogie," and I changed it to "Boogie Chillun." I didn't know it was gonna… You know, it was just a old funky lick I found.

B.B.: But it was a monster hit.

Were you writing about your own mom?

John Lee: Nah, it's just a song. There's so many kids, their mama don't allow them to stay out all night long, you know. I couldn't just be talkin' about my mama. Lot of people have kids don't stay out all night long, but they gonna stay out anyway. [*Sings "Mama didn't allow me to stay out all night long."*] I didn't care what she didn't allow, they would stay out anyways! They knew they would get a beatin' when they get home, but they still stay out.

Does playing guitar bring you as much joy and satisfaction as it did when you were younger?

B.B.: Yes. I think it brings even more today…

John Lee: It do.

B.B.: Because I'm more concerned about what I'm trying to do. Then, I was just havin' fun.

John Lee: Havin' fun, drinkin', stayin' out.

B.B.: [*Laughs.*] As you said, stayin' out all night long. But now today I'm concerned about it, because if I get out there now and I hit something that don't sound right, I know that there are a lot of people that are listening to me.

John Lee: Critics.

B.B.: Well, not only that, but a lot of the kids that are listening to me. Reminds me of a story I heard once. There was a trumpet teacher teachin' trumpet to his class. And one little boy, the teacher was tryin' to teach him to play non-pressure, where his jaws wouldn't balloon out. So the teacher was talkin'. So there's one little smart egg in the class [*laughs*], and the teacher say, "Why are you playin' like that? I keep tryin' to tell you that when your jaws pop out like that, that's not good." So the little smart egg, he said, "Well, Dizzy Gillespie plays like that!" So the teacher thought about it for a moment, and he says, "Yeah, but there's only *one* Dizzy Gillespie." So I think about it a lot of times now when I'm playin', that the kids out there idolize me, like me. And not just kids, but people that are starting to play or the people that's already playin' and maybe came out to admire what I do or be critical of what I do. And if I make them wrong notes or put them in the wrong way or hit something I don't intend to hit…

John Lee: B., I have never heard nobody as true as you, man. Nobody.

B.B.: Well, thank you. But I make mistakes, though. So when I make 'em now…

John Lee: Everybody do.

B.B.: Yeah. To answer your question, when I make a mistake now, it hurts [*thumps chest*]. Oh, yes. It hurts.

John Lee: You're right.

B.B.: Because, see, I'm supposed to be professional–that's what I think to myself. I'm supposed to entertain. I'm supposed to rehearse, practice enough to not do that.

John Lee: But some people, when you look out into the audience, they don't even notice what you did, they so excited about lookin' at him. But he know it [*points to B.B.*].

B.B.: Yeah, and that hurts, don't it?

John Lee: Yeah, that's right. They may not know, but you know you made that mistake. And you lookin' back at the fellows, and some of them look like they kind of smile, you know, because they know I did.

B.B.: But when you're able to run it into something else…

John Lee: To cover up.

B.B.: Yeah, like you and I, say we talkin', and we got a male conversation goin' on and all of a sudden a lady walked in, you gotta change it into something else! [*Laughs.*] That's the way it is with playin'. Here's another thing: When guys start to gettin' to be our age, John, they're not quite as fast as they used to be.

John Lee: I know.

B.B.: And as you get a little older, you think more about it. Remember when you was young and somebody said, "Come here," you get up and start running? Now you think about it–do I really want to run, or will I just walk on over there?

John Lee: Yeah, walk to the car!

B.B.: And a lot of the youngsters that come around can play rings around me–this is not false modesty!–but what they do, they think of what I did that gave them a chance to think beyond that. You think Graham Bell thought of what his work would be doin' today? There was that first foundation. I was able to go and see one of my idols, Lonnie Johnson, and I was able to shake his hand and thank him. Because he was one of the people that made me want to play. I don't know. Here I am, still doin' somethin' with it.

John Lee: Well, B., time for me to go.

Is this the first interview you've done together?

B.B.: Yes. The very first.

John Lee: I've did it with a lot of people, but this is the first I ever did with B.B. And I couldn't wait for tonight to come!

B.B.: It's an honor to me. What you are doing for us will even help it to go further. We appreciate it. Thank you. And thanks to a couple of other guys named Mike and Sid.

Elmore & Homesick James

September 1993

By Jas Obrecht

HOMESICK JAMES' throaty, bittersweet sliding conjures images of the late Elmore James and band rollin' and tumblin' in a sweaty Chicago nightclub, playing so damn *hot* that working class people threw money at their feet. Elmore's long gone, but his spirit still surges in the music of his old pal and partner, Homesick James.

Homesick's distinctive tone is a combination of heart and hands, a hunk of conduit, a homemade guitar, and a battered amp. Nearing his eighties, he sings with a vibrant, vibrato-drenched voice somewhat reminiscent of the second Sonny Boy Williamson's. On his new CD *Sweet Home Tennessee*, cut in Nashville with vets of the Gatemouth Brown, Paul Butterfield, and Bo Diddley bands, he projects deep roots and rugged individualism, especially during his mesmerizing reading of "Meet Me In The Bottom." While his new record sticks to tried-and-true electric blues, Homesick points out, "I play anything–reggae, rap, country music, bluegrass. I play calypso, a lot of Latin music. See, I don't have no one-track mind. All of music to me sounds good."

Blues references list Homesick's last name as Williamson, although during our meeting he stated, "I can't tell nobody what my real name is. I never uses it. But my passport says John William Henderson." He was born in Somerville, Tennessee, on May 3, 1914. His father, a cotton worker named Pluz Williamson, played snare in a fife and drum band, and his mother, Mary Cordelia Henderson, performed spirituals on guitar. His churchified mother forbade him to play, fearing he'd learn blues songs, but by age eight the youngster was hauling out her guitar on the sly. A neighbor named Tommy Johnson–not the famous one who made 78s–taught him to play lap-style slide with a pocketknife. Young Homesick met Blind Boy Fuller during a visit to North Carolina, while Mississippi sojourns brought him his first contacts with Howlin' Wolf and Johnny Shines. Visiting a relative in Canton, Mississippi, he met a shy 12-year-old one-string player named Elmore Brooks, who would become famous as Elmore James.

Homesick James and John Lee Williamson (a.k.a. Sonny Boy Williamson I) met as boys and may have been cousins. By 1933, Homesick, Sonny Boy, Yank Rachell, and Sleepy John Estes were working the southwest Tennessee blues circuit, with regular stops in Jackson, Brownsville, Nutbush, Mason, and Somerville. Homesick moved to Chicago in '34 and stayed with Sonny Boy, who'd arrived months before, until he found work at a steel mill. At night he played cov-

Elmore James, 1950s.

ers of Memphis Minnie and Blind Boy Fuller songs with Horace Henderson's group at the Circle Inn. He was quick to electrify his sound; a photo of him at the Square Deal Club, his second extended booking in Chicago, shows him playing a Gibson ES-150, which had just been introduced in 1936.

On occasion Homesick rambled home to play with Yank Rachell, Sleepy John Estes, and Little Buddy Doyle. James says that he was one of the uncredited musicians who played on Doyle's 1939 Vocalion sides. After serving in World War II, Homesick joined Sonny Boy, Big Bill, and pianist Lazy Bill Lucas at Chicago's Purple Cat, with harmonica ace Snooky Pryor sitting in whenever he could get a pass from nearby Fort Sheridan. Later on, Homesick and Snooky worked with Baby Face Leroy Foster in South Chicago. Called up from reserve status, Homesick was wounded during a Korean tour of duty.

Homesick made his first recordings under his own name during 1951. Cutting for Chance Records at the old RCA Victor Studio on South Michigan, he dialed in a thick, distorted tone and traveled downhome, humming and moaning "Lonesome Old Train" to Lazy Bill's rocking barrelhouse piano. With lines like "I ain't gonna chop no more cotton, I ain't gonna plow no more corn," the flip side's "Farmer's Blues" was aimed at ex-sharecroppers who'd migrated north. Homesick says his second Chance session, with Snooky Pryor, was unissued. His next session produced the hit "Homesick," a rollicking romp with Robert Johnson-style turnarounds and slide figures that reappear on Elmore's later recordings. Its B side, "The Woman I Love," featured Johnny Shines on second guitar. (Elmore, who'd been fronting a band since 1939, made his first record down in Jackson, Mississippi, for Trumpet Records in 1951. With Sonny Boy Williamson II on harp, his jacked-up version of Robert Johnson's "Dust My Broom" reached #9 in the national R&B charts. The 78's flip side was Bobo Thomas' "Catfish Blues.")

At subsequent '50s sessions, Homesick backed Lazy Bill on a Chance 78 and covered Memphis Minnie's "Please Set A Date" for Colt. He assumed the pseudonym "Jick And His Trio" for a 78 on the short-lived Atomic H label.

Homesick and Elmore reunited in Chicago while Elmore was backing pianist Johnnie Jones, with whom Homesick was lodging. They began playing together, usually billed in

Homesick James, late '50s.

the *Chicago Defender* as Elmore James–The Broomduster. Elmore had often supplemented his income by moonshining, and his musicians shared his fondness for drink. Fights between Johnnie and Elmore were reportedly a nightly occurrence. At their peak, the Broomdusters featured Odie Payne on drums, tenor saxophonist J.T. Brown, and Homesick playing bass lines and occasional solos on guitar. As Robert Palmer points out in *The Sky Is Crying*'s liner notes, "The Broomdusters were one of the greatest *electric* blues bands. In terms of creating a distinctive and widely influential ensemble–and in terms of sheer longevity–the Broomdusters' only real rival was the Muddy Waters group that included Jimmy Rogers, Little Walter, and Otis Spann. And judging from the recorded evidence, the peaks of intensity reached by the Waters band in full cry were at a level the Broomdusters reached before they'd finished warming up."

Elmore was fresh out of the hospital from his second heart attack when he cut for Chief in '57. "Coming Home" rolled to the "Dust My Broom" theme, with Elmore, Homesick, and Eddie Taylor all reportedly playing through the same amplifier. Wayne Bennett played the elegant lead on its flip side, "The Twelve Year Old Boy." The same date also produced an anguished rendering of Tampa Red's "It Hurts Me Too." Elmore's bookings jumped when the Vee Jay label reissued the sides.

The following year Elmore returned to Jackson, Mississippi, and became a disc jockey, but he was back in Chicago by November '59, when Homesick played bass on the legendary Fire/Fury session that produced "The Sky Is Crying," "Dust My Broom," "Held My Baby Last Night," "Baby Please Set A Date," and an instrumental dance tune, "Bobby's Rock." Earlier that year, the label had a #1 hit in *Billboard's* pop and R&B charts with Wilbert Harrison's "Kansas City," and Bobby Robinson decided to produce Elmore's session in stereo. James' otherworldly slide tone on these records has yet to be duplicated. "Elmore's beautiful sound is the greatest thing in the world," describes Ry Cooder, "but it's only on the Chicago sides that he cut for Fire and Enjoy. Even the Fire and Enjoy sides from New Orleans and New York sound different. He had something else he used on those. I don't think it was his Kay with a pickup, because there's no way a Kay with a pickup can sound like those Chicago sides, like 'It Hurts Me Too.' I am sorry–I've been through everything, and it cannot. That 'unknown amp' is the real mystery." The first release, "The Sky Is Crying"/"Bobby's Rock," reached #14 in the national R&B charts.

Homesick played guitar during Elmore's smoky, saxy April '60 Chess sessions for "I Can't Hold Out (Talk To Me Baby)," "The Sun Is Shining," "Stormy Monday," and "Madison Blues." He switched back to bass for their fourth session together, at Manhattan's Belltone Studios, which produced "Rollin' And Tumblin'," "Done Somebody Wrong," and eight other songs. Homesick did not play on Elmore's subsequent "big band" session in New York, nor at his final dates in New Orleans and New York.

During 1961 Elmore was blacklisted by Chicago's musicians union for nonpayment of dues, and in '62 he returned to Jackson, Mississippi, with Homesick in tow. For a while they stayed with Johnny Temple in Jackson, and then Homesick headed back north. He and Elmore shared their final dates when promoter Big Bill Hill intervened with the union and brought Elmore up in May '63 to open his new Copa Cabana Club. Elmore arrived in Chicago on a Sunday, took his bags to Homesick's house, and played the Copa that night with Homesick and a drummer. Afterwards, they stopped by Sylvio's to see Howlin' Wolf. The musicians played the Copa twice more during the week, and on Friday night the 45-year-old suffered a fatal heart attack just after taking a shower at Homesick's house.

For a while Homesick fronted his own group in the same South Side taverns where he'd begun. He recorded an early-'60s 45 for Colt with Hound Dog Taylor on second guitar, and his reading of Robert Johnson's "Crossroads" b/w "My Baby's Sweet" became a hit 45 for the U.S.A. label. During '64 James made the *Blues On The Southside* album for Prestige, with Eddie Taylor on bass. Homesick James & His Dusters (bassist Willie Dixon and drummer Frank Kirkland) resurrected Elmore's spirit on the 1965 Vanguard anthology *Chicago/The Blues/Today!*, covering "Dust My Broom" and "Set A Date."

During the '70s Homesick played clubs and made forays into Europe, often in partnership with Snooky Pryor. Their 1973 American Blues Legends tours of Europe produced a pair of albums and a review in which a critic described James' "usual tricks–playing guitar behind his back, jumping up and down, laying on the ground while playing." At the time, Homesick was 61. Homesick recorded *Ain't Sick No More* for the Bluesway label shortly after his return, and in '74 played a guitar-bass doubleneck on Roosevelt Sykes' *Hard Drivin' Blues* and cut *Homesick James & Snooky Pryor* for England's Caroline label. He returned to his acoustic roots for Trix' *Goin' Back Home*. He and Snooky worked as a duet during the October '79 Wolf sessions in Vienna that produced *Sad And Lonesome*, with Homesick mixing "Crossroads" and "Last Fair Deal" with shuffles and slow blues.

Since then Homesick James has played the role of elder statesman of the blues, making appearances at blues and jazz festivals, but recording little until *Sweet Home Tennessee*. He earned rave reviews for his performances with Yank Rachell at this year's Chicago Blues Festival.

Who are the best musicians you've worked with?
I'll tell you, the best I worked with was me and Elmore. See, I was Elmore's teacher. And when he passed away, he passed away on my bed. Oh, yeah, he died right there in Chicago at 1503 North Wieland Avenue. He just had come back, and he said that when he died, he was gonna die with me. I wasn't thinkin' nothin' of it. And about two weeks later, he was gone. He was stayin' with me. That was 1963, May the 23rd or 24th. We was gettin' ready to go to a gig too–Club Copa Cabana.
Elmore sure was a fine slide player.
Well... [*Laughs*] He got all that stuff from the old master here.
From you?
Hell, yes! I give him his first guitar when he was about 12 years old. I knowed where he stayed in Mississippi. I worked down there. Him and a guy by the name of Boyd Gilmore was tryin' to play. Elmore had a piece of wire tied up on a coffee can and a board–it had one string on it. He

was tryin' to learn so hard, but Boyd Gilmore, he had an old guitar.

People have speculated whether Elmore James knew Robert Johnson.

Yep. Sure, Elmore knowed Robert Johnson. Well, Elmore and all of them were down in the Delta together. Elmore and Rice Miller, who was Sonny Boy number two–all those guys, they know Robert. I met him. See, I knowed Robert very well. Robert Jr. Lockwood can tell you that. I also knowed another guy that nobody never said anything about–I knowed Charley Patton personally. Now, I ain't thinkin' that I know them, I _know_ these people. I know Ishman Brady [Bracey] perfect. I would associate around together. When I used to come through there, that's what would be playing at the picnics and the barrelhouses and things. I was hoboin' with my guitar, a Stella 6-string.

Were these tough men?

No, no. Nope. They would just drink and gamble, that's all. They run 'round with women and drink and gamble. That's what musicians act. No, they wasn't no mean guys. All of us was drinkers. Every musician drink. Ain't but one time he'll stop–that's when he comes down diabetic. Yeah, then they'll quit because they have to.

Describe your first gigs.

I played many a country supper. I was out runnin' around–picnics and frolics like that, me and Yank Rachell, Sleepy John Estes, and Little Buddy Doyle. We'd play at a picnic right here outside of Oakland, Tennessee, out on Highway 647. Little Buddy Doyle was a midget and I knew him personally, because me and him recorded together. That's sure the truth. Yeah. It was in 1937. Big Walter Horton was on the harmonica. It was at the Hotel Gillsaw in Memphis, right across the street from the Peabody Hotel. It was wire recording machines. But that wasn't really the first song I ever did. I did some stuff back in '29, a song with Victoria Spivey. She's the first person that turned me on to studio stuff. See, I did "Driving Dog" in 1929. Victoria Spivey, she heard me play, and she said I played that "cryin' guitar." Elmore, now he had never started [back then]. See, I had been with the Broomdusters ever since 1937 myself. I had the Dusters.

The expression "dust my broom" means to get out of town in a hurry, right?

Uh, no. It never was "dust my broom." It was "dust my room." And people made a lot of mistakes by sayin' that.

A lot of people heard Robert Johnson's version, which was "dust my broom."

"Dust my room," that's what it was. That was around before Robert Johnson did it. That was around in the '20s–'29 or '30.

How did you and Elmore get back together in Chicago?

What happened, he had an uncle there named Mac. And Elmore had this one record out, and this was that "Dust My Broom" thing with Rice Miller [Sonny Boy II]. He didn't have but one side [of the Trumpet 78]. He didn't do the other side, that "Catfish." Another guy down in Mississippi did that. Elmore just had one riff on guitar. See, I can read music and write it too. And what happened, I sent Elmore a ticket to get him to Chicago, because he had this song out that was so popular. Me and Snooky Pryor were workin' together out of the south of Chicago in the Rainbow Lounge, and when Elmore come, I had to quit and go and get Elmore together, because he didn't have nobody.

On some nights, it's said, you and Elmore were so hot that people threw money at your feet.

Oh, yeah. Heck yeah! Aw, people just give us money, man. When we played, people just come in and throw a twenty or a ten–that's the way it was. We were pretty good musicians, though.

How did you end up playing bass with Elmore?

I always could play bass. Harmonica, bass, guitar–I can play any instrument. But that wasn't no bass with Elmore. That was guitar tuned low. Elmore played bass too. We had a way of playing these guitars that no man would be able to do these things. In the key of _D_, I would keep four strings tuned into that Vastapol [_D, F#, A, D_, from the _D_ string to the high _E_], and we would run those other other two strings, the _A_ and _E_, down lower, just like a bass, so it sounds like a bass. A lot of time when we'd be playin', Elmore would be runnin' that bass like I did while I be runnin' slide. See, all he would do is [_sings the "Dust My Broom" riff_] and run back to the bass pattern. All he could do was go to _D_. But he wasn't able to go to _G_ and _A_ in the _D_ tuning. I'd let him play his part when it got to it, and I'd catch those other chords. We was workin' so good together. We were just a team. He'd run that real high note and then jump to the bass, and I'd jump right there. You couldn't tell when one switched to the other. See, we studied this stuff together, how to come up with ideas. We was the hottest band in Chicago. That's the way we were.

Were you playing loud?

No, no. Never did it loud. I don't allow it now.

Would people be dancing?

Oh, man. That's all they did, was dance. Yeah. Those days were so sweet, man. Everybody come out to drink, dance, and have a good time. Yep.

Did you do much touring outside of Chicago?

We come down to Atlanta, Georgia. We had a station wagon from Chess Records. I'd taken my money and put half, and he'd taken his money and made the payment. We traveled to a country club in Georgia, we played around there, and then we played around Cleveland, Ohio.

Was Elmore pretty quiet offstage?

Well, Elmore was real quiet all the time–until he take a drink. He used to say, "I'm Elmore. After me there won't be no more."

What did he like to do besides music?

Me and him used to set around and tinker with electricity and mess with making guitar stuff. If we wasn't makin' them, I'd be putting them together for him. Did you see that big old Kay guitar he got? I fixed that. I wired it up. He bought that guitar, paid $20 for it at a pawnshop over on Madison Street. It wasn't no electric. He said, "Will you put some electricity on it?" I said, "Yeah." I always knowed about electric. Me and him used to sit together. He stayed at my house all the time. I used to live on 1503 North Wieland, and I used to live at 1407 Northwestern. This was in '59, when we did "The Sky Is Crying," "Bobby's Rock," and all this stuff. And that's where I built his guitar for him.

Bobby Robinson writes that Elmore composed "The Sky Is Crying" the night before the session.

Ah, no. No, no. I know direct, 'cause I was right there. Okay. That's my song. That don't belong to Bobby Robinson or none of 'em. See, it had been rainin' so hard, and we were sittin' alone at 336 South Leavitt in Chicago. See, me and Elmore came up with the idea "The Sky Is Crying," but I told him, "Don't say that. Say 'the cloud is cryin',' because the sky don't know how to cry. The rain come out of the cloud." And when he got in the studio, he forgot. When we got home, he said, "You know, I made a mistake. But it's good, wasn't it?" I said, "Yeah." But no, he didn't write that. "The Sky Is Crying" come out in '59, and then we did "The Sun Is Shining," the "Madison Blues"–all that stuff is mine. I can verify these statements. Ask Gene Goodman at ARC Music–that's the copyright on all those songs. Later on I made "The Cloud Is Crying" for the Prestige label.

Which is the best label you worked for?

Vanguard wasn't too bad.

Besides Elmore's, what are the best records you've played on?

I'll tell you, the best thing I ever did was "I Got To Move," number one. I love that tune. Oh, yeah. I did that for Columbia or Decca, a long way back. I like that, and I like "Set A Date," 'cause all the youngsters are doing it now, like Fleet-

From Homesick's scrapbook: "This is Elmore and a girl named Mary Lee, standin' at the 1815 Club with my amp right there."

wood Mac, George Thorogood. After I had did it, then Elmore did it. He asked me if it was all right. See, Elmore wasn't no writer.

If, as you say, Elmore was taking credit for songs you wrote, didn't that cause trouble between you?

Well, how? No. We had an agreement, man. Nooo. See, every time he would ask me did I have some songs, you know. He say, "Can I do any of your songs?" I said, "Look. You don't have to ask me. Let's do it." Didn't make no difference. Some people, you tell 'em one thing, they'll print another. I seen a lot of things that they said about Elmore, and I said, "No, no, no, no, no. This ain't right." Like when I come up with the "Madison Blues," I played it all up and down Madison Street. That's where I wrote that song. See, we worked on a partnership basis. Like if he were living today, whatever royalty come, we broke it right down. He never was paid no more on no job than I was. Me and him got the same salary. But now the sidemen didn't get what we get. See, that was the agreement with the owners. "Homesick was makin' records way before I was," Elmore would tell them. He said, "Now, you ain't willin' to pay two leaders, I won't be there." I would tell them the same thing. That's the way we worked it. We just shared together.

You must have been really close.

Tell me about it. I never have been that close to nobody, no musician, because we just stayed together. Me and him run into a lot of problems, but we never had a argument. We had problems with our station wagon one time. That was up in Cleveland, Ohio. They repossessed it; they come and got it. Yeah. We got stranded. See, what was happenin', we had an agreement: "I pay this month, you pay next month." So his month come, he told me he had paid, and he didn't. When my month come, I sent my payment in. He got way behind on his, because he loved to play cards. He loved to gamble–drink and gamble. He'd lost all his money. He was always calling me and asking me to give him money, and I'd give it to him. I didn't loan it to him, I just give it to him. I'd say, "Yeah, what you want?" We were just like that.

They come and got the wagon. We was playing at a Cleveland musical bar, and we went out, and he told me somebody else stole it. He wouldn't tell me the facts about it. I called the guy who was booking us, Bill Hill, and asked him. He said, "Didn't you see Ralph Bass?" 'Cause Ralph– you know, the engineer for Chess Records–and Philip Chess, they come in the same night. I thought they was comin' through from New York, but they come there to get that wagon. It was a 1960 Ford Catalina, nice station wagon. It had "Broomdusters" on the side of it.

Anyway, then we had to get a ride back. So what'd we do? Now, Elmore had a contract with Chess Records. He said, "I'm gonna call Bobby Robinson, and I'll see can we get a session." Bobby agreed with it, and we flew in from Cleveland, Ohio, to New York, and that's where we recorded that "Rollin' And Tumblin'" and all those other tunes. That was in 1960. And we take all our money, put it together, and bought another wagon while we were up there. Same model, but it was rust-colored or beige. The first one was solid white. We had chauffeurs to drive us. We wouldn't drive 'cause we be drinkin' too much, carryin' on, talkin'. Me and Elmore we were just always together, man.

What was your favorite drink?

Scotch. We'd drink that, and then we'd drink Kentucky Tideman or anything we could get to get high off [*laughs*]. We'd just sit back and come up with ideas and talk it, how we want this played. I was the leader of that band. Oh, yeah. That was my band all the way. We had J.T. Brown on the horn, Boyd Atkins. That was the best band I ever have worked with. J.T. was good about arrangin' music too. All those guys is dead now.

What did you use for slides?

Before I started making them from conduit pipe, I used the metal slip that goes over the top of tubes in them old radios and old record players. I used to pull that out and put it on my finger and play. This was after I learned how to stand it up [hold the guitar in normal playing position].

What did Elmore use for slide?

The same thing. A tube cover. Elmore used a light piece of metal, and Elmore had some big fingers too. He'd take one of those slips–protector tubes–from an old amplifier and put it on his finger. If he got a smaller one, then he would split it open–take a hacksaw and saw it open. That's what we played with all the time. See, we used to mess with a lot of stuff. But I use that conduit pipe all the time now. I don't like heavy. I don't think no man should use them big old heavy slides. You can't. The sound ain't there. Like you go to a store and buy them–whew, that's too much weight on your hand.

What amplifier did Elmore use at the Fire session in Chicago?

Mine. A Gibson. A big one. A GA-53, I think it was. It's at my house in Flint, Michigan, in the basement. I own a little small farm up there, and a lot of my kids live there. I got it when I was in the Army. The amp is brown on top and gray tweed at the bottom. It had letters on it, but by travelin', someone done knocked them off. It's about two-and-a-half feet high, and it could fit one 10 and one 12 speaker in the cabinet. Elmore didn't have no amplifier, and he didn't have no good guitar.

So to the best of your knowledge, that's the amp "The Sky Is Crying" was cut on?

I know what it was cut on, sure! Yeah, that's what it was cut on. And I got the picture with Elmore standin' with the guitar with my amp right there. Everywhere I go I keep it, so somebody start to try to say something about Elmore, I just straighten them up right quick. Okay, I want to tell you this too: That was a studio sound that people try to figure out. They'll never get that. The people [at the studio] knew how to operate that stereo sound into it. That's what that is. That's an echo sound. And it's two slide players–that's me and him both.

Were you in a big room?

No, not too big. Small studio. Bob Robinson come down and produced that for Fire and Fury Records. Yeah.

Beautiful sound. Open tuning.

The only people I really know who played in open *D* was me and Elmore. He had it in open *D* when he made "Dust My Broom," because Sonny Boy was playing a *G* harmonica. I always told him, "Don't never tune that string up too high," because if you tune that thing up to open *E*, you got too much pressure on your guitar neck. So you just let the strings back down.

See, I can't play a guitar like a lot of peoples could do–I just don't like that sound. Elmore never did like that either.

I always keep a mellow sound. Don't never press down on your strings too hard. Just glide the slide. Take your time slidin', and don't be mashin' down on 'em. See, some people play the strings too high. The slide guitar players, they got to jack the strings up 'cause they always mashin' down, and the slide hit the frets. But my guitar strings are right down on the neck. Muddy had a heavy touch, and Hound Dog Taylor. The sound was brighter; it ain't no mellow sound, man.

What's your favorite electric guitar?

I make my guitars. I build my own guitars and fix them the way I want. But my favorite parts for what's goin' inside the guitar are Gibson. My favorite sound is Gibson. I bought some of those Seymour Duncan pickups, said I was gonna try them, and I don't like 'em. Too bright. I make acoustic guitars–the big ones with f-holes–and then I put electric to it. And then I buy the pickups and the controls and whatever I need–the switches–and put 'em in there. My house is a workshop. I got guitars all over the place. I make 'em, builds 'em. I can go out and see a nice piece of wood, and I'll just take it and make me a solidbody. I ain't made acoustics since I been here [in Nashville] because I ain't got my blocks what I make 'em out of. But they sound better to me than the ones I could buy.

What was your setup on the new record?

I made the guitar I was usin'. You never seen a guitar like that. Everybody wonder how I put it together like that. It got a paint job on it, it got a lot of designs all over it. That was a Twin Reverb amplifier. Yeah, but give me the Gibson.

Some players say that a smaller amp gets a better sound for slide, makes it sound more like a harmonica.

Aw, no. It don't have to be. It depend on the way you set it.

Do you use guitar picks?

No, I play with my hands. I never have in my whole life used no pick. You can't slide like that, no. Nobody will ever be able to get the sound what I get out of the guitar, because I'm usin' my fingers. I wear the slide on my little finger, and I be pickin' the slide too at the same time I'm making chords with my other fingers.

You've been playing music for 70 years…

Over!

What's your secret for longevity in the business?

My advice for all youngsters is have a nice personality–number one. Know how to treat people, and don't let nothing go to your head, because those people, they the ones buyin' your material. They the ones that helped you up the ladder. Just work with the audience, and don't never insult nobody. Be a gentleman about things. And don't hang out all night if you can keep from it. Always try to go home and get you some rest. That's what I do, and I don't age that much. I take it easy, and when I'm not playin', you'll find me right at home.

Thanks for the interview.

Oh, I'm glad to help out. Anybody want me to help out in any way or anybody ask me something, I'm not too proud to do it. I don't like to copy nobody. Everywhere I go, I leave a ball of fire.

A SELECTED HOMESICK JAMES DISCOGRAPHY

Solo albums: *Chance Vintage Blues* ('52), P-Vine; *Blues On The South Side* (Prestige, '64), Original Blues Classics; *The Country Blues* (early '70s), Blues On Blues; *Goin' Back Home* (solo acoustic), Trix; *Ain't Sick No More* ('73), ABC/Bluesway; *Sweet Home Tennessee* ('92), Appaloosa/Ichiban.

Homesick James & Snooky Pryor: *And The Country Blues* ('73), Today; *Homesick James And Snooky Pryor* (Europe, '73), Big Bear; *Shake Your Moneymaker* (Europe, '73), Krazy Kat; *Sad And Lonesome* (Austria, '79), Wolf.

With Elmore James: *Elmore James: King Of The Slide Guitar* (box set of the Fire, Fury, and Enjoy recordings), Capricorn; *Let's Cut It: The Very Best Of Elmore James*, Flair/Virgin; *The Sky Is Crying: The History Of Elmore James*, Rhino. Anthologies backing Elmore: *Blues Masters, Volume 6: Blues Originals*, Rhino; *Blues Masters, Volume 8: Mississippi Delta Blues*, Rhino; *Legends Of Guitar–Electric Blues, Vol. 1*, Rhino; *The Fire/Fury Records Story*, Capricorn; *Bluesville Volume 2: Electric Blues*, Ace; *The Way I Feel–Chicago Blues Of The 1960s*, Flyright. **With others:** Andrew McMahon, *Blueblood*, Dharma; Roosevelt Sykes, *Hard Drivin' Blues*, Delmark.

Anthologies: *Chicago/The Blues/Today!*, Vanguard; *The Great Blues Men*, Vanguard; *Chicago Blues–The Early '50s*, Blues Classics; *Chicago Slickers, 1948-1953*, Nighthawk; *Chicago Blues Sessions, Vol. 1*, Wolf; *Blues In D Natural* ('50s), Red Lightnin'; *Meat And Gravy From Cadillac Baby, Vol. 1*, Red Lightnin'; *Big Boss Men*, Red Lightnin'; *Chicago Blues Anthology Encore*, Spivey Records; *Spivey's Blues Cavalcade*, Spivey; *Chicago Blues: A Quarter Century*, P-Vine; *National Downhome Blues Festival, Vol. 3*, Southland; *The Best Of Chicago Blues*, Wolf.

Jimmy Rogers

August 1987

BY DAN FORTE

MUDDY WATERS, HOWLIN' WOLF, SONNY BOY Williamson, Little Walter, Sunnyland Slim, Willie Dixon–all true pioneers of the raucous, impassioned music known as Chicago blues. But another essential component to any discussion of the genre is a guitarist who played with all of the giants listed above and more. Because he scored first as a sideman and later as a singer/songwriter on some of the most original blues recordings of the '50s, Jimmy Rogers' importance as a guitarist is criminally overlooked. But in the historic, unparalleled Muddy Waters band of the early '50s, Rogers' sinewy bass lines and chordal backups were as integral to the group's powerful, innovative sound as Muddy's soaring vocals, Little Walter's interweaving harmonica, or Otis Spann's meaty piano.

Listen to Waters' classic recordings of "Hoochie Coochie Man," "Standing Around Crying," "40 Days And 40 Nights," and "I Just Want To Make Love To You," not to mention Rogers' own "Ludella," "That's All Right," "Sloppy Drunk," and "Walking By Myself," and it's obvious that one can't play the blues Chicago-style without borrowing heavily from Jimmy. In the words of the Mighty Flyers' Junior Watson, who backed Rogers on his 1984 LP *Feelin' Good*, "His whole thing with Muddy was so precise–those intertwining guitars. I think it was all worked out, like, 'You play this, and I'll play this.' Their styles were so one-dimensional–this one thing is all they'd do–so they could count on the other guy playing a certain thing. That's why it worked–like Eddie Taylor with Jimmy Reed. The timing and rhythm of Jimmy Rogers' licks are what's amazing. And he hasn't lost any of that."

Although he gave up playing music for a living in 1960, not to return until 1971, Rogers is very active today, touring and recording in the U.S. and overseas, still based out of Chicago. His firsthand recollections give a rare insight into one of American music's most important turning points from one of its moving forces.

Born in Atlanta, Georgia, in 1924, Rogers (his real name was James A. Lane) moved to Memphis and later St. Louis while still in his teens. Raised by his grandmother, he would accompany her to Chicago visiting relatives in the late '30s. By the early '40s he had settled there for good. "I was learning to play before I came to Chicago, but I was real young. After I got to town, I played with Sunnyland Slim before Muddy came to Chicago, and with Tampa Red and Big Maceo. And I played harmonica with Memphis Slim some, and I played with Memphis Minnie on guitar. I had an

acoustic. So I played with quite a few people before Muddy even came to Chicago. But Blue Smitty and myself were working together in Chicago the same year that Muddy Waters came to town, which was in 1946. I turned pro in 1946, but I had been playing before that."

He had also begun playing electric guitar. "Before Muddy came, I was playing electric guitar with Sunnyland. When Muddy came to Chicago, he wasn't playing electric. He had a guitar he brought to Chicago with him in 1946, but it was just a hollowbody with the 'S-curves' [f-holes] in it. It was an Epiphone, I think–an Epiphone or Gretsch. It's been so long, I forget. But anyway, he put a DeArmond pickup on it. That was his first electric. But we had DeArmond pickups and amplifiers and all that stuff before he came.

"My first guitar," he points out, "had the big hole in the center–the big soundhole. And I put a DeArmond pickup across that hole. A fellow there called John Henry [Barbee] had one, which give me the idea of getting it. And Blue Smitty had one made up like Muddy's–with the two 'S-cuts' on the sides–and he put a DeArmond pickup on his. I had a Gibson amplifier, the first amp that I owned, and then I went on through a chain of others until Fender came out, and I started buying Fenders."

Like most bluesmen, Jimmy played regularly in the open-air Maxwell Street market known as Jewtown. "Yeah, me and my friends was playing out there," he smiles; "Buddy, Ed Newman, Porkchop, Stovepipe, Satch, John Henry–all those guys, a bunch of them. Most of those guys is dead now. We'd be out there from maybe 8:00 Saturday night until maybe 3:00 or 4:00 Sunday evening. We played a few clubs, but mostly for parties. When we played in a club, at that time, you wasn't paid to play. You would come in, and the guy would furnish the electricity. You'd hook up and play, and make you some money passing the kitty and stuff like that. We'd play in maybe two or three joints a night that way and make pretty good money like that. In fact, we were making more money that way than I made when we started to call ourselves a band and started to be paid by the club owners. When we started playing, we were getting like $8 a night that way, apiece–three or four of us–but before that two guys, maybe three, would go from one place to the other, and you'd make $20 or $25 apiece. You'd make maybe 75 or 80 bucks a night on weekends. That was good money. Like Friday night and then Saturday night, and then we'd play in the street Sunday night until maybe midnight."

Jimmy also had a succession of day jobs, which is how he indirectly hooked up with Muddy Waters. "Off and on I was working days, but I was more interested in playing. The first job I worked on in Chicago was like a packing house–chicken packing in those big 60-gallon drums. Icing them and

loading trucks, over at South Water Market in Chicago, right off Market Street. The next job that I had was at Midwest Shoe Manufacturing Company, on the West Side. Then I worked at some more packing houses–Liberty, Swift, Armour–and from there I went into construction. I was working at a radio cabinet company with Muddy Waters' cousin Jesse. Jesse would take up with us musicians, like me and Smitty; on weekends he would come around where we'd be playing, and he'd buy us whiskey and stuff. He just liked to be with us. So he got me this job at this radio cabinet place where he was working. He told me he had a cousin that was coming to Chicago. So then I did meet him when he came in, and we got to talking, and he said he was playing down south, down in Clarksdale, Mississippi, for house parties and what have you. And so we just started playing for parties. And from that, club owners hired us."

The guitarist details how what started as a modest, casual arrangement grew into the most important blues group in Chicago. "It was like myself and Muddy–at the time I was playing harmonica and some guitar–but Blue Smitty was our regular guitar player. I had been switching from harmonica to guitar with Blue Smitty, so when Muddy came in, he took one of the guitars, Smitty had the other one, and I was on harmonica. It was just three of us playing around like that. Then Blue Smitty wasn't too interested in playing, really, so he soon dropped out of it. And then Sunnyland Slim brought Little Walter to Chicago, and I met him. We'd be playing on the streets there on Maxwell Street, in Jew Town, where I was living at the time. That's where I met Little Walter at, down on Maxwell Street. He was about 17. So I took him down and introduced him to Muddy, and I told him he was a good harmonica player. In fact, Little Walter was about the best harmonica that was in Chicago–for the blues, at that time. I grabbed him right away, and we started practicing with him. We just formed a unit then: Muddy, Walter, and myself. I'd tune my guitar down like a bass, and Muddy was playing the slide. We did all right like that. We added a drummer in there later on, Baby Face Leroy [Foster]. He was a guitar player and could play drums pretty good, too. So we started touring around different places like down to Muddy's home, Clarksdale, Mississippi, and over to Arkansas and around different places, playing little nightclubs, in 1947."

Muddy Waters had recorded a few sides for the Library of Congress as early as 1941, while still in Mississippi. He recorded his first Chicago sides in '46, a year before Little Walter first recorded. (Baby Face Leroy, incidentally, also made a few stirring records under his own name, in 1949 and '50, backed by Muddy and Walter.) "Sunnyland got Muddy started on records," states Rogers. "We were making

During some Chess sessions, Jimmy backed harmonica ace Sonny Boy Williamson II.

onstage, and the record don't sound as good.' And he talked to Chess, and they decided to start letting me record with him. We made 'Sad, Sad Day' and 'Just Make Love To Me' and all that stuff with the full band–Baby Face Leroy and myself, Otis Spann, and Big Crawford. But Big Crawford died shortly after he got into this, and then we started using Willie Dixon on the upright bass. All this stuff was happening like in a two-year period–from around 1948."

Although there was almost always upright bass on the recordings, the Muddy Waters band that played clubs consisted of drums, piano, harmonica, Muddy's slide, and Jimmy's rhythm guitar, playing bass lines. "At that time we didn't have a bass," Rogers points out. "I'd lower the guitar, tune it down and play the bass part. Dixon started playing bass on the records, but he wasn't playing the blues at clubs. He was playing like semi-blues or jazz-blues; they called themselves the Big Three Trio. And he was writing stuff already, but he started mostly helping arrange the blues stuff that Chess guys would do. And he got to the place that he could tell Chess what was going to sell and what wouldn't sell. He got enough good sellers out of it for Chess to start really paying attention to what he was saying."

Incidentally, on one or two sessions for Muddy, Rogers shared guitar chores with Little Walter. "That's how we made 'Still A Fool,'" Jimmy points out. "Muddy was just singing; me and Walter were playing the guitars. Walter wasn't considered a good guitar player; he clowned with it a little bit. But basically we had been playing, and he knew the sound, the way that I played, so 'Still A Fool' wasn't hard for him because he knew a little about the guitar. It was just up and down, the same thing, up and down. I was harmonizing, and he was just squeezing the string when it'd get to that point. So we made that particular side, but he didn't play guitar on any of Muddy's other records. [*Author's Note: Some sources state that Walter also played guitar on "Honey Bee."*] But on

records, but they was on a small label, like underground. They wasn't getting off the ground too good. Sunnyland was working with Aristocrat, and that finally changed over and was the Chess label. Sunny knew Leonard Chess, and Leonard was like a talent scout for blues. Sunnyland said, 'I know a boy that plays hard Delta blues there on the West Side called Muddy Waters.' So they recorded him, just him and a bass player, Big Crawford. Sunny played piano on some, but on others it was just a bass and the guitar."

Waters' earliest recordings for Aristocrat and Chess–songs such as "Gypsy Woman" (1947), "Little Geneva" (1949), and "Rollin' And Tumblin'" (1950)–featured spare backing, usually bassist Big Crawford and/or pianist Sunnyland Slim. "He wasn't getting the sound that he was getting when we were all of us playing together," Jimmy feels. "So he was down there sweating, man, and scuffling, trying to make the records. I told him, 'We have a good sound a lot of songs Muddy would be standing over there in a booth, just singing, and we'd be over there playing. Most of the stuff Muddy played on is when you hear that *keen*–that slide. Sometimes after we would play, then he'd run a track [overdub] with the tape."

With the addition of Otis Spann, the band not only boasted of having arguably the greatest blues pianist of all time, but cut the die for most electric blues and rock bands that followed. "Otis Spann was playing with a fellow I knew over on the West Side, [singer/guitarist] Morris Pejoe. He made a record or two on Chess, but they didn't do too good. Otis was glad to work when I approached him about playing with me and Muddy. And he turned out to be a real good piano player. He was fantastic. He helped put weight behind the band. Then Leroy Foster dropped out of the picture, and we got another drummer called Elgin Evans. There was five of us; we held that five pieces there for a long time."

Whereas Waters' main influences on guitar were fellow Mississippians Son House and Robert Johnson, Rogers leaned more towards Big Bill Broonzy, one of the key figures in the blues' transition from rural to urban and already a big star in Chicago. "Big Bill was my favorite guitar man. Yeah, Bill used to call me his son; I knew him a long time. Tampa Red and Big Bill Broonzy and Big Maceo were really the leading hard blues artists that were in Chicago. And Memphis Minnie, but she was fading. Muddy talked about Robert Johnson, but he didn't know Robert too well. But he would talk about what he heard about Robert, see. Muddy knew Son House, and Son House was playing along this same style that Robert was playing. And so he picked up a lot of stuff from Son House, this Delta blues player. He had a lot of different stories about those guys back there. But, see, Muddy was, I'd say, about 10 years older than I am. So when he got to Chicago, he was like 30 years old."

Another big influence on Rogers' guitar style was Joe Willie Wilkins. "He never got too well known, but he was a good blues guitar player," Jimmy stresses. "He played with Sonny Boy Williamson on the *King Biscuit* show. But he was a home-type fellow. He would stay right around mama, hang around mama's dress tail. You could pull him away from Memphis for maybe a week, then he'd go back. Man, I didn't care *where* it was, I would go. I always was the going type. The further the better for me. I saw Joe Willie in Chicago once. He came to where we was playing at, and sat in with me and Muddy. And he was telling me, 'I'm getting the payback from when you played my guitar when I was with the King Biscuit boys.' He let me play his guitar one night, with Rice [Miller, a.k.a. Sonny Boy Williamson II] and all of them. In fact that was the first electric guitar that I played–Joe Willie's."

Rogers never took up slide guitar because, in his words, "I never really liked it too much. You didn't have enough range with that slide; you're limited. You can't play chords. You've got to retune your guitar. If you've got it natural [tuning], when you play the slide, it's light and you're not executing too well. Muddy was doing enough sliding for me. And I really don't want slide on a record of mine. I'd take a harmonica, but I never wanted a slide in there."

His early influences, combined with the necessity of covering the roles of rhythm guitarist and bassist, accounted for Rogers' unique style, often consisting of bass lines and double-stops or single-note fills behind the vocal. "Yeah, with Muddy, I would do that," he says. "I was mostly a harmony player, see. It was actually mostly background, playing with Muddy. Also, I was used to harmonica because I played one myself. I know what it takes for a harmonica player to play, so I could play it on the guitar. That's the reason why the average harmonica player loved to play with me. I'd play heavy melody tones for the harmonica, to give the harmonica something to drive with. A lot of guitarists don't know how to play very well with a harmonica. You gotta know how to play harmony. You gotta know the changes and harmonize on the guitar to back up a harmonica. But most guys, they don't play that way. Most guys, they play that loud stuff like Albert King or B.B. King–single-stringing all the way through. And that don't leave no opening for a harmonica. That's why they don't like to play with a harmonica."

Rogers' relaxed but solid guitar work was the perfect foil for Muddy's intense vocals and whining slide. "I would pay attention to how he was singing," he stresses. "You got to be very alert. I would know how to phrase and how to change it. At the time that he was thinking of changing, I would watch him–pay close attention to him by ear, and watch what he was going to do. He'd pretty near do the same thing just about every time in the same order. So when I found out that that's the way he worked, well, I'd know then how to bring him. A lot of times he'd be lost–he wouldn't know when to make his change–but I'd change for him, see, and he was right there on the top of it. When he'd get through, he'd laugh, man–say, 'Man, that's good.' Because so many people didn't understand that. That's the good part about it."

Muddy's band wasn't the only electric blues band in Chicago, and not necessarily the first, but it was definitely the strongest. "There was lots of bands around," remembers Jimmy. "The Myerses, who were the Aces, they were playing. They had Junior Wells playing harmonica with them. They were called the Four Aces–Junior Wells, Dave and Louis Myers on guitars, and Fred Below on drums. And then when Walter left us, see, he had taken that band over, and Junior joined me and Muddy on the harmonica. They just changed places. We worked on like that for a couple of years, and then Junior went into the Army and we got another boy playing the harmonica, Henry Strong. Everybody called him Pot. He was learning to be a good harmonica player, but he got killed in Chicago. And then we got this boy who died a few years back in California called George Smith, and he played with us for about eight, nine months. After that, that's when we got James Cotton. Shakey Horton recorded some stuff with us, too, but he didn't play with Muddy as a regular harmonica player, see–not too long. Cotton was working with him when I left the band." (The back cover of the Chess Vintage Series' *Chicago Bound* LP features a backstage photo of one edition of the Waters band, including Muddy, Otis Spann, Elgin Evans, Henry Strong, and Rogers, with an unidentified maracas player. Jimmy clears up the mystery: "That was Tommy Lee Armstrong. He wasn't really in the band, but we'd let him sit in on maracas. Actually, he was a sign painter; he's the one who painted 'Hoochie Coochie Man' on the bass drum.")

Nearly every player who worked in Muddy Waters' band during the '50s has since achieved legendary status. In town the group was intimidating, to say the least. "They called us the headcutters," Rogers laughs. "Anytime we'd go in a club, man, the other musicians had to back down because we had the floor. If some guy was playing over here, when we'd get off work we go to his club–just to have a nice time. But they wouldn't let us rest until they'd get us on the bandstand and tear the house up. Then we'd go to the next club."

The battles of the bands that had begun in the days of Big Bill, Memphis Minnie, and Memphis Slim were still commonplace. "On Sunday afternoons clubs like Sylvio's would have battles. You could win maybe $20 or a fifth of whiskey. We [the Muddy Waters Band] would lay down a lot," Jimmy reveals. "We could win them all, but we would lay down and let somebody else win. The public didn't like that at all–they'd know."

Sylvio's and most of the other South and West Side Chicago clubs were rough-and-tumble joints. "Sometimes the black clubs would be pretty rough," Rogers allows, "but it never harmed any of us. The Zanzibar was the roughest one–at 13th and Ashland, on the West Side. Just about every week somebody would get messed up. But what could you do? We was pumping the blues good and had a big crowd. Somebody'd look at somebody else's girl, and there you go."

By 1955 Rogers had already scored a succession of blues hits, so he left Waters to form his own band. "In Chicago the

clubs that we were playing was too small," he explains. "We would pack the place, but the prices they was getting just wasn't enough to cover. Now, Muddy might've been getting a little more money, but he wasn't kicking it out to us. So then I said, 'Well, I could do this good or better with my own band.' Walter felt the same as me, so he left before I did. He tried to get me to leave when I made 'That's All Right,' because that was a big hit. Walter was going to pull off with me, but I said no, because we were trying to make an all-star unit."

Like Little Walter's early solo hits, Jimmy's recordings utilized Muddy's band and were usually done at the end of Waters sessions. "We made 'Juke' and let that go out under Walter's name. I could've taken it, or Muddy, either one, but we said no. We had made this up between the three of us. I told him to call it 'Juke.' Then we didn't have anything to back it up on the flip side because Walter wasn't singing at the time too much. He would sing a couple of the late Sonny Boy, John Lee Williamson, tunes. One of them was 'Crazy About You, Black Gal.' And we just changed it; instead of saying black gal, he just sang 'crazy about you, baby.' I kept on pumping it to him: 'Don't say *black gal*, say *baby*.' So they had a song to go on each side of the 45."

The most amazing aspect of Rogers' solo recordings, especially considering that the first was done in 1950, was how sophisticated they were. They were much more melodic than the blues that was prevalent at the time, and many, while following three-chord, 12-bar changes, departed from the usual AAB lyrical structure. "I got ideas from big bands," he reveals. "I like a lot of jazz, man–big band stuff. A lot of my songs are just verses and choruses that go on and on, playing the 12-bar changes. But that's a different pattern [vocally]; the average blues player don't play that way. I guess that's why they say that it's different, because it *is* different. It sounds good to me, so we just go on with it like that. 'That's All Right' was already in the making before I started playing with Muddy, but I hadn't recorded it. I always felt that it would be a hit, but I wanted to wait and put it on a national label. It's been recorded a lot of times now. I like that version by Mose Allison."

By the time he was recording his own material, Jimmy had changed guitars. "I had a Silvertone," he recalls, "but when I made 'That's All Right,' I played a Gibson. The Silvertone was a nice little blonde, and that was the sweetest-playing guitar, besides the Gibson, that I'd ever played. I've been using Gibsons ever since–a lot of years."

After Jimmy recorded with Muddy's band, most of his recordings featured his own group, occasionally with Chess

> *"I got ideas from big bands. I like a lot of jazz, man – big band stuff."*

session players brought in. "It would be my band," he explains, "but they had this dude Reggie Boyd who played on some stuff with me. He played the jazzy stuff on 'Rock This House,' and 'My Last Meal' he was on, too."

Jimmy retired from music in 1960 and didn't return to active playing until 1971. "My kids were growing up, and expenses were going higher," he explains. "And I was a family man. Music wasn't doing too much for me at the time, so I had to do other things. I bought into a cab company with another fellow. Then I left that and had a clothing store. I would go around with some of the guys who was playing–Magic Sam or sometimes Muddy–after I closed the store at night. I'd go maybe on a Saturday night and play a number or two. But people would go, 'Where are you playing tonight?' and I'd go, 'Well, I'm not playing right now.'"

In 1971 Jimmy was forced out of retirement: "I started back a while after I got burned out. The store had burned down back when Martin Luther King got killed [in '68], and I lost a lot. They had a riot in Chicago, and they was burning up everything. So I got caught in it real bad. I had to do something. I already had an offer to go to Europe, but I'd refused it. I called back and within a month's time, I was in Europe. And that helped me to get myself started back again. I was getting good pay over there, and people was appreciating what I was doing. So I recorded a couple of records over there, and I was getting a pretty fair shake, I'd say."

Rogers played around Chicago with the Bob Riedy Blues Band, with whom he recorded, but he made his first full-fledged solo album, *Gold Tailed Bird*, in 1973, backed by the great Freddie King. During his years off Jimmy always kept a guitar in the house. "Yes, all the time I had a guitar. The ES-345 I play now I've only had for maybe four or five years. But I got another one at home. I love those 335, 345, and 355 Gibsons; I've got one that stays at Antone's [in Austin, Texas] all the time, and I've got about four guitars at home."

It wasn't too severe a culture shock to come back after a nine-year layoff because, in Jimmy's words, "I stayed in contact with the world. I would be practicing and learning more about what I was doing. So it wasn't bad. Me and Johnny Littlejohn started back together. Johnny was playing some guitar with Wolf, and we started playing gigs together. That was like in '71, '72, and then I went to Europe. I've always had good bands; I picked pretty good musicians all the time. I know what it takes. I had a guitarist named Jim Kahr in my group. He lives in Germany now. He's a Chicago boy."

These days Jimmy's original Chess recordings are available on reissues, and he has several recent LPs out in the States and in Europe. He appeared on a live anthology from Antone's tenth anniversary, featuring Rogers as front man (accompanied by Jimmie Vaughan), as well as backing Snooky Pryor, Eddie Taylor, James Cotton, and Pinetop Perkins. His latest release, 1990's *Ludella*, finds him in superb form working alongside harmonicist Kim Wilson, pianist Pinetop Perkins, and guitarists Hubert Sumlin, Derek O'Brien, and Bill Campbell.

Looking back over his illustrious career, Rogers is both proud and understated when he says, "We really did something for the blues–we all did. At the time when we were doing it, we didn't know; we were just playing to our satisfaction, mostly. We didn't really know how strong the blues was going to become."

A SELECTED JIMMY ROGERS DISCOGRAPHY

Solo albums: *Chicago Bound* ('50-'56), Chess; *Jimmy Rogers* (includes *Chicago Bound*), Chess; *The Classic Chicago Blues*, Chess Japan; *Chicago Blues, Vol. 4*, Chess France; *Left Me With A Broken Heart* ('76/'89), Chess France; *Jimmy Rogers & Left Hand Frank*, JSP; *The Dirty Dozens*, JSP; *Chicago Blues*, JSP; *Feelin' Good*, Murray Brothers; *Chicago's Jimmy Rogers Sings The Blues* ('72-'73), Shelter; *That's All Right*, Chess; *Sloppy Drunk* ('73), Black And Blue; *Gold Tailed Bird* ('73), Shelter; *Ludella* (with members of Muddy's band, '90), Antone's.

With Muddy Waters (on Chess, except as indicated): *Muddy Waters* box set; *Rare And Unissued*; *Rolling Stone*; *Sail On*; *The Real Folk Blues*; *More Real Folk Blues*; *Trouble No More*; *Back In The Early Days*, Syndicate Chapter.

With Sonny Boy Williamson: *Down And Out Blues*, Chess; *One Way Out*, Chess.

With others: Sunnyland Slim, *House Rent Party* (pre-Muddy sides), Delmark; Bob Riedy Chicago Blues Band, *Lake Michigan Ain't No River*, Rounder; *Elmore James, John Brim, Floyd Jones* (six tracks with Floyd Jones, '51-'52), Chess/Vogue.

Anthologies: *Chicago Boogie–1947* (Maxwell Street acetates), St. George; *Chess Blues* box set; *Howlin' Wolf* box set, Chess; *Wizards From The Southside*, Chess; *The Second Time I Met The Blues*, Chess U.K.; *Tenth Anniversary Anthology, Vol. 1–Live From Antone's*, Antone's; *Antone's Anniversary Anthology, Vol. 2*, Antone's; *Drop Down Mama* (backing Floyd Jones and Johnny Shines), Chess; *The Blues, Vol. 6: '50s Rarities* (backing Little Walter), Chess; *Stickshift* (one LP side by Rogers), Teardrop; *American Folk Blues Festival, Live '83* (backing Louisiana Red), L+R; *Blues Masters, Volume 2: Postwar Chicago*, Rhino; *Blues Masters, Volume 6: Blues Originals* (backing Howlin' Wolf), Rhino.

Albert King

September 1977 & April 1993

By Dan "Bob" Forte

ONE OF THE OCCUPATIONAL HAZARDS of being a dyed-in-the-wool blues fanatic is that you become attached to performers who inevitably pass on. One can be philosophical, of course, and realize that "the records will live on forever," but in recent years the blues ranks have narrowed so many times that even the most philosophical buff can't help but feel a bit numb, even jaded, as yet another in an already dying breed leaves with no suitable replacement on the horizon. But the loss of Albert King, who suffered a massive heart attack on December 21, 1992, hit me especially hard, on both artistic and personal levels.

You see, I first met Albert King under what can only be described as unique circumstances. One night in 1969 my father came home from his job as an inspector on the Oakland Police Department and said, "Guess whose trailer full of equipment got stolen?" Albert had been playing in San Francisco, and while parked at his hotel–this was during the days when he still toured in a station wagon with *Albert "Born Under A Bad Sign" King* painted on the side–a thief (one with a trailer hitch) simply unhooked the guitarist's U-Haul, attached it to the rear of *his* station wagon, and drove off, not even knowing what he'd stolen until he got home.

That particular modus operandi was all the OPD needed to home in on the crook; the next task was locating the guitars, amps, drums, and organ at pawnshops throughout the East Bay. Once that was accomplished, I got a call one summer afternoon while mowing the lawn. "If you want to meet Albert King," my dad said, "get up to the police station as soon as you can. He's flying up from L.A. to reclaim his stuff."

As quick as you could say "I'm a crosscut saw, baby, drag me 'cross your log," I was pulling up to the station house, armed with copies of *Born Under A Bad Sign* and *Live Wire/Blues Power*. The 6'4", 250-pound bluesman finally lumbered into my dad's office, wearing a black fedora (with the front brim flipped up, as always) and a lime green, pin-striped suit over a lavender shirt with a diamond stickpin. For the next several hours I pumped my idol with questions about Robert Nighthawk, Little Junior Parker, and T-Bone Walker, and he obliged with anecdotes about each. I rode along with Albert and my dad, from hockshop to hockshop, recovering the fenced property one instrument at a time. I'll never forget the look on Albert's face when the last pawnbroker brought out a rectangular guitar case held together with a brown leather belt. "That's my Lucy," he beamed, cradling his trademark Gibson Flying V as though it were

his baby daughter.

When we said our goodbyes, Albert promised to put me on the guest list the next time he played the Fillmore. A nice offer, I thought, but one that will never come true. And, at any rate, I was already in blues heaven, inspecting my copy of *Born Under A Bad Sign*, now inscribed with a printed "A.B. King."

At a time when most of the select group now known as Guitar Heroes were jockeying for king of the hill, this self-taught southpaw was already *my* guitar hero. One of the advantages of growing up in the San Francisco area in the late '60s was KMPX, the country's first underground FM radio station, and shortly after its release in 1967, *Born Under A Bad Sign* was getting near-constant airplay. With backing by Booker T. & The MG's and the Memphis Horns, the Stax album was a milestone, the hippest thing the blues or rock world had seen in ages. Songs like "Crosscut Saw," "The Hunter," "Laundromat Blues," and "As The Years Go Passing By" were peppered throughout the time slots of Abe "Voco" Kesh, Larry Miller, and "Big Daddy" Tom Donahue.

I first saw Albert perform on February 2, 1968, at San Francisco's Winterland, where he shared billing with England's Soft Machine, John Mayall's Bluesbreakers, and the Jimi Hendrix Experience. That weekend was in fact Albert's first exposure to the hippie throng that underground radio and Bill Graham nurtured, but he played the crowd as skillfully as he played Lucy–as though he knew precisely what to do before even taking the stage. And what he did, wisely enough, was just *be himself*, Albert King. Some accounts actually credit King with stealing the show from Hendrix; I would prefer to call it a draw. I'm not going out on a limb when I state that onstage Jimi Hendrix was quite possibly the most overwhelming phenomenon any rock audience had ever witnessed. But Jimi played *at* the audience; Albert played *to* it. While thousands stood with mouths open and eyes glazed over as Jimi extracted unheard of guitar sounds from his Stratocaster, they laughed and hollered and danced and *participated* in the dialogue that Albert carried on from the stage. As Jerrold Greenberg of *Rolling Stone* wrote, "The least contrived, certainly the most 'old-fashioned' of the three, Albert King was nonetheless the only consummate artist among them, the only one who could play on the full emotional range of his audience with as much facility as he used to sustain a note on his guitar." (No fool when it came to PR, Albert would later recall the bill as himself, Hendrix, and Janis Joplin, since Big Brother & The Holding Company replaced Mayall on the last night of the stint.)

Albert was soon "a permanent member of the Fillmore family," to quote his introduction on *Live Wire/Blues Power*, headlining shows with younger bands like Creedence Clear-

water and recording the aforementioned LP at Graham's new site, Fillmore West.

And after our first meeting he indeed remembered his promise of putting me on the guest list, and my parents held up their end of the bargain, inviting him out to the suburbs for fried chicken or his favorite, Chinese food (with, in Albert's case, plenty of white bread accompanying both). I became Albert's unofficial valet whenever he hit town. Some of you ex-hippies might remember a hyper little redhead carrying a suit bag and a guitar case with no handle, leading the way for a larger-than-life black man–probably saying something very peace-and-love like "Get outta the way, Albert King's coming through!"

There was always a lot of voodoo surrounding Albert's pickless, backwards-strung, oddly tuned technique, but one of his most memorable displays, for me, was when I showed him the '61 Les Paul/SG I'd gotten for my seventeenth birthday. After tossing the case unceremoniously on his hotel bed, he examined the right-handed Gibson, flipped it over left-handed and mashed down on one of his patented perfect-fourth bends. My guitar, standard tuning, no amp. Sounded exactly like–you guessed it–Albert King.

Albert was terrible with names but had a great memory–a combination that resulted in him calling me Ted (never Dan) for several years. Then one day I was no longer Ted; for most of the next decade I was Bob.

Although Albert was perhaps the first bluesman teamed with a symphony orchestra, in St. Louis in 1969, and played at the historic WattStax concert in 1972 and on *American Bandstand*, he will probably be best remembered as the "Flower Power Blues Guitarist," thanks to his success in the late '60s and the rapport he established with that audience. But he was simultaneously one of the few bluesmen scoring hits on contemporary black radio. As Mike Bloomfield told me in 1977, "Between Al Jackson's production, Booker T. & The MG's rhythm section, the choice of material, the Memphis Horns, and Albert's playing, he was the only bluesman I know of who had a completely comfortable synthesis with modern black music–R&B, so to speak–and sold copiously to a black audience as well as the white audience. He was the only singer who had clever, modern arrangements that would fit in with the black radio market *and* with the white market and in no way compromised his style. That's sort of amazing, in that B.B. King never did it, except once with 'The Thrill Is Gone,' but Albert did it time after time."

As with most "overnight successes," Albert's glory days came after years on the chitlin circuit. He was born April 25 in Indianola, Mississippi, and although the liner notes to *Bad Sign* listed the year as 1924, reports at the time of his death put it at 1923; he was 69. (A good rule of thumb when

Albert King at the King Biscuit Festival, 1990.

interviewing Albert, a notorious embellisher, was to double- and triple-check all facts and take any declarations with several grains of salt. For instance, his desire to get out of music and go back to driving a bulldozer, quoted extensively in later years, was a yarn he'd been spinning since arriving on the Fillmore scene.)

He was first attracted to the guitar through his stepfather, Will Nelson. "He had a guitar," King recalled, "but I couldn't play it. I used to climb up on a chair and hit the box hanging upside the wall. Sounded good to me." Because he was left-handed but played right-handed instruments, even picking up licks from watching other players was difficult, let alone any type of formal instruction. (To clear up the mire that often surrounds unorthodox lefties, Jimi Hendrix would restring right-handed guitars so as to be standard for a southpaw–the chassis he was working on may have been right-handed, but his playing was all lefty–while Albert literally played upside-down and backwards, with the lowest strings closest to his toes.)

After fooling with a one-string "diddley bow"–essentially a wire connected to a wall and played with a bottle as a slider–Albert graduated to a homemade guitar. "It was a wooden cigar box for the body," he explained, "and a little tree that I cut off and shaved up to make the neck. And I used

wooden pegs for the keys, with holes in them to wrap the wires around. Years ago they used to make whisk brooms that had real thin stainless steel on them. Sounded good. I had all of the strings tuned different, but I had to use the same grade wire on all six. I kept that guitar for a long time, but it got burned up in a fire."

As a boy, King was exposed to two giants of country blues. "The first one was Blind Lemon Jefferson," he stated. "Later I heard him on records, but I used to see him in these parks, like on Saturday afternoons in these little country towns around Forest City, Arkansas. We'd work till noon on Saturdays, and then my stepdad would hook up the wagon, and sometimes my sister and I and the other kids could go to town. This one particular day he was playing acoustic guitar, and he had his cup. He sounded something like that folk singer, Richie Havens–something on that order. He had a crowd of people around him, and we'd put nickels in his cup, and he'd play a song. It was amazing to me to see him count his money. He could feel the face of the coin and tell you what it was. Then he'd put it in his pocket and play some more. I also heard this lady Memphis Minnie. She used to come to town and sing to the electric piano–they called it the 'self-playing' piano. Not the kind you pump with your feet; the kind you just turn on and it goes to playing the sheet music on a spool. She brought her music with her that would fit right in that. I was a little boy, and I used to sneak and peep in the door before they'd run me away."

Albert's first legitimate guitar, a Guild acoustic, didn't come until he was 18. "See, this guy had a guitar," he recalled in 1977. "He'd paid $2.00 for it. Well, he had a girl, and they wanted to go to the afternoon movie show, but he didn't have the money. I didn't have a little girl, but I had my allowance that my mother gave me. So it was getting close to show time, and this girl was really getting upset to get in to see the movie. I offered him my $1.25 for it. 'No, I ain't gonna sell my guitar. Give me $1.50.' I said, 'You just wait around; that girl's gonna be ready to go to the movies soon.' It was really funny. All the guys who didn't have nobody were gathered around waiting to take her. Well, I had my mind on that blasted guitar. She was getting ready to go in with another guy, and he couldn't stand that, so he came over and said, 'Give me that $1.25, man; you can have the guitar.' So that's how I got my first guitar, and I just started rapping on it from the left side."

The upside-down approach may have presented its share of obstacles, but as a result one of the blues' most distinctive sounds was born. "I knew I was going to have to create my own style," he conceded, "because I couldn't makes the changes and the chords the same as a right-handed man could. I play a few chords, but not many. I always concentrated on my singing guitar sound–more of a sustained note."

Steve Cropper, who played rhythm guitar on many of King's Stax sessions and appears on *Jammed Together* with Albert and Pops Staples, points out that the lefty also had his own tuning. "He tuned to an *E* minor chord, with a low *C* on the bottom. That's a low son of a bitch, like a tuba, but he didn't play it that much; that string got overlooked a whole lot. He mainly concentrated on the top three strings, the highest ones. We were in the studio once, and I said, 'Boy, that sure would sound good if it had Albert King playing on it.' He was out of town, so I took one of my old guitars and strung it backwards and tuned it to his chord and tried it. And it worked, because I'd been around Albert, and I knew how he played–I'd picked up his guitar and goofed with it a couple of times. So I set one up with that action, and it sort of got the Albert King sound."

The "Albert King sound" was almost on a different instrument. After working on construction crews in Osceola and Little Rock, Arkansas, and occasionally singing in a gospel quartet called the Harmony Kings, Albert moved to Gary, Indiana, in 1953. "I stopped playing guitar [an Epiphone electric] and got a job playing drums with Jimmy Reed. We were playing them little small joints, and it got to where Jimmy wouldn't stay sober and wouldn't work half the time,

so I said, 'Hell, I'm going to make a record myself.' Al Benson in Chicago had a label called Parrot, so I went over and auditioned for him. He said, 'Okay, be in the studio tomorrow night.' We recorded 'Bad Luck Blues' and 'Be On Your Merry Way.' He said, 'I've got to see if it's going to sell, then I'll give you a contract later [*laughs*]. I didn't get no contract, I didn't get no statement–the record sold about 350,000 copies. I didn't get any money out of it, but it kind of helped make a name for me, you know."

Following a handful of singles for the Bobbin label, Albert scored his first bona fide hit in 1961. "Don't Throw Your Love On Me So Strong," cut in St. Louis with Ike Turner on piano and released by King Records, went to #14 on the R&B charts. A collection of his King and Bobbin sides was released as Albert's first LP, *The Big Blues.* "Sam Lay, who played drums in the Butterfield band, used to be his drummer, and he gave me that record," remembered Mike Bloomfield. "I'd never heard of him before. I was knocked out; the guy was just a fabulous lead guitar player. His style was superb, comparable to Otis Rush or Buddy Guy or any modern blues guitarist, but it wasn't as well-formed as when his first Stax record, *Born Under A Bad Sign*, came out years later. I could hear that the way he played guitar was different than the other guitarists, but I couldn't figure it out until I saw him in person. Then I realized that he played backwards.

"He was a huge, immense man, and his hands would just dwarf his Flying V guitar. He played with his thumb, and he played horizontally–across the fingerboard, as opposed to vertically. And he approached lead playing more vocally than any guitar player I ever heard in my life; he plays exactly like a singer. As a matter of fact, his guitar playing has almost more of a vocal range than his voice does–which is unusual, because if you look at B.B. or Freddie King or Buddy Guy, their singing is almost equal to their guitar playing. They sing real high falsetto notes, then drop down into the mid-register. Albert just sings in one sort of very mellifluous but monotonous register, with a crooner's vibrato, almost like a lounge singer, but his guitar playing is just as vocal as possible. 'I Love Lucy' is a good example of that. He makes the guitar talk.

"His attack, the timbre, the tone–it's always right," Bloomfield continued, obviously enjoying a chance to talk about one of his favorite subjects. "I can listen to 10 minutes of him playing the same licks over and over and never get bored. He can take four notes and write a volume. He can say more with fewer notes than anybody I've ever known."

As with all of the truly great blues stylists, Albert's influences are virtually undiscernible in his totally individualistic style. Although he mentioned Lightnin' Hopkins, Lonnie Johnson, Elmore James, and Howlin' Wolf as influences (in addition to Blind Lemon), T-Bone Walker topped King's list of favorites. "When T-Bone Walker came," he told me, "I was into that. That really gave me an idea of what I wanted to do; that opened it up. That was the sound I was looking for, because he had an incredible blues sound. But all those licks and things he was making, I couldn't do. I said, 'I'm gonna have to try to do something with these strings.' So I developed that string-squeezing sound." In other words, Albert's style developed as a result of *not* being able to emulate his favorite guitarist–which is why T-Bone relied on chords, linear lines, and half-step bends, while Albert would, to quote Bloomfield again, "bend the guitar seven frets," if that was the note he was shooting for.

As Bloomfield noted, Albert's trademark sound finally jelled on *Born Under A Bad Sign*. As music critic Robert Palmer wrote, "Its impact was as inescapable among blues players as John Coltrane's influence was in jazz." MG's bassist Donald "Duck" Dunn explains, "We took a blues artist and put a few different rhythms behind him; it wasn't just that shuffle type of stuff. You've got to attribute a lot of that to [drummer/producer] Al Jackson and his drum patterns." Cropper adds, "Al gave it a little bit different flavor. Like 'Crosscut Saw' has a sort of bloopy, crazy kind of lick, and that was Al's innovation–which consequently made everybody else play a little different. The only one who didn't play different would be Albert King, who played like Albert King."

Working on the 1977 *Guitar Player* cover story, I found it wasn't difficult to find people eager to sing Albert's praises. As Elvin Bishop said, "Everybody in the world that I know of who plays any kind of blues guitar was affected by him to a small degree at least. A couple of his little pet licks are just part of the language." Johnny Winter pointed to one of Albert's early singles, "I'm A Lonely Man": "I learned that and played it for about five years every night, note for note,

A lot of voodoo surrounded Albert's backwards-strung technique.

man. I got every single record he made." Bill Graham even granted a rare interview, doubtless his only one for a guitar magazine, to talk about the Fillmore's bluesman-in-residence. "In the mid '60s, once the Fillmore got started, I began to speak to a lot of the musicians I respected and ask them where they got whatever they did. I decided to track down some of these artists to see if I could expose their talents to people who didn't know they existed. It may sound corny, but it's almost like dealing with your child. If your child says, 'I want the ice cream,' you say, 'Well, you've got to finish your meat first.' I'd look at the headliner and say, 'Who would I like to expose their audience to?' When you had a Jimi Hendrix, the Hendrix fan, who was into guitar, would listen to a John Mayall or an Albert King. So Albert was the meat, even though they got to enjoy it.

"Albert was one of the artists I used many times for various reasons," Graham continued. "He wasn't just a good guitar player. He had a wonderful stage presence, he was very congenial and warm, he was relaxed onstage, and he related to the public. Also, he never became a shuck-and-jiver. One of the sad things that happened in the '60s–it's not a nice thing to say, but it happens to be true–was that the blues artists began to realize that anything they did onstage, white America would accept. And a lot of them became jive. But Albert remained a guy who just went onstage and said, 'Let's play.'"

Bloomfield concurred: "I've never seen him once when he wasn't vital, exciting, and not shucking. I've seen every blues singer there is shuck at one time or another, but I've never seen Albert do it once. He's always giving 100% of himself–much more than I would."

As indelible as his influence was on white blues-rockers, equally significant was his effect on the black bluesmen who were his contemporaries, many of them, such as Otis Rush and Albert Collins, already distinctive stylists in their own right.

The impact Bishop spoke of is as pervasive today as ever. Compare the Eric Clapton solo on Cream's "Strange Brew" to the source, Albert's break on "Oh, Pretty Woman." Or listen to Mark Knopfler's uncharacteristic tone and phrasing on Dylan's *Slow Train Coming* or Stevie Ray Vaughan's work on David Bowie's *Let's Dance*. In his 1984 cover story Stevie didn't deny the similarity. "I kind of wanted to see how many places Albert King's stuff would fit," he told me. "It *always* does. I love that man."

But Albert was fiercely protective about his signature licks and was the ultimate gunslinger when it came to jamming, as Stevie later found out. "When that album [*Let's Dance*] first came out, Albert heard it. He said, 'Yeah, I heard you doin' all my shit on there. I'm gonna go up there and do some of yours.' We were doing this TV show outside of Toronto, and during the lunch break Albert went around to everybody in there looking for an emery board. I didn't think anything of it. We were jamming on the last song, 'Outskirts Of Town,' and it comes to the solo, and he goes, 'Get it, Stevie!' I started off, and I look over and he's pulling out this damn emery board, filing his nails, sort of giving me this sidelong glance. I loved it! Lookin' at me like, 'Uh, huh. I got you swinging by your toes!'"

One of the ever-quotable Bloomfield's best lines on the subject of Albert King referred to the unenviable position he found himself in one night–jamming with Jimi Hendrix. As he related to Tom Wheeler, "Oh, my God, I was up there just wishing I was Albert King."

I can't imagine who B.B. King wished he was one night in 1970 when he got himself into an onstage battle with his namesake at Fillmore West. There was a lot of anticipation about the double-bill, but Albert shook off any queries about a possible jam as we walked through the crowd. Albert's and B.B.'s dressing rooms were on the opposite sides of the hall, and the two didn't cross paths, let alone discuss a super session, so I'm sure Albert was as surprised as I was to see B.B., guitar in hand, standing at the side of the stage at the end of Albert's second set. "I'm looking for an amp for B.B.," he ad-libbed, as the crowd rushed the stage.

An amp was wheeled out and B.B. plugged in as Albert and his seven-piece band kept cranking out "I Get Evil." Known for playing a few essential notes rather than complex, high-speed runs, Albert nevertheless played over, under, around, and through B.B.'s more subtle licks, until B.B. decided that the answer to his dilemma might be a little showmanship and dropped to his knees. Unaware that the crowd was now screaming for more than just his double-stop bends, Albert continued to play until he noticed his rival on the floor next to him. In an instant, 250 pounds of purple, lime green, and black landed on the floor, knee-to-knee with B.B., and the Kings slugged it out like two gladiators. Bloomfield may have been referring to the same show when he said, "I remember seeing him and B.B. King jam at the Fillmore, and Albert cut B.B. to death, man. He had that big Acoustic amp, and it sounded like bombs exploding."

Regrettably, in later years Albert became as famous for bad moods as for great playing, and too many fans who only saw him once or twice, and only in the past 10 or 12 years, might remember him more as the curmudgeon/bandleader who fired his bassist in mid-song or berated the house soundman for an entire set. Diagnosed as diabetic, Albert did curtail his touring schedule in recent years, although he headlined the 1992 Memphis Arts Festival.

Ultimately, we *are* left with the artist's work, which in Albert King's case is, thankfully, a formidable legacy indeed. *Born Under A Bad Sign* remains a classic, and *Live Wire/Blues Power* is a veritable textbook of licks. Fantasy Records recently added two very welcome discs, *Wednesday Night In San Francisco* and *Thursday Night In San Francisco*, recorded during the same stint as *Live Wire*, as well as his 1973 live set at Montreux, *Blues At Sunrise*. In 1972 Albert teamed with the Bar-Kays and effectively reinvented himself on *I'll Play The Blues For You*, the title emblazoned across the side of the Trailways bus he now took on the road (and drove personally). And his pre-Stax work for the King and Bobbin labels has been reissued on Modern Blues Recordings' *Let's Have A Natural Ball*.

Of all the encounters I had with Albert King over the course of 23 years, the anecdote that sticks in my mind involves a show that I didn't even attend. My two older brothers went to see Albert play San Francisco while I was away on assignment. Exchanging pleasantries after the show, Albert looked around a couple of times and wondered, "Where's Bob?" "You mean Dan," they tried to explain. "He's out of town." "No, Bob," a confused Albert said again, "the little one, the baby." "Yeah, that's Dan. You call

him Bob, but his name's really Dan." Albert sat back and paused for a second and said, "Well, who's Bob?"

Years later, Albert would correct himself ("Bob–I mean Dan") whenever we spoke, until my real name was at last ingrained into his head. After that, deep down, I always kind of missed Bob. But not like I, and the whole blues world, will miss Albert.

A SELECTED ALBERT KING DISCOGRAPHY

Solo albums (on Stax): *Born Under A Bad Sign* ('67); *Live Wire/Blues Power* ('68); *Years Gone By* ('69); *I'll Play The Blues For You* ('70); *The Lost Session* (produced by John Mayall, '71); *Blues At Sunrise; Lovejoy; Chronicle* (one side each by King and Little Milton); *The Best Of Albert King* ('68-'73); *Jammed Together* (with Steve Cropper and Pops Staples); *King Does The King's Thing–Blues For Elvis; I Wanna Get Funky* ('74); *The Pinch* ('77); *The Blues Don't Change*; *Crosscut Saw: Albert King In San Francisco* ('83); *Wednesday Night In San Francisco; Thursday Night In San Francisco*.

Other labels: *The Big Blues* ('62), King; *Travelin' To California* (King and Bobbin, '59-'63), Bellaphon; *Let's Have A Natural Ball* (King and Bobbin, '59-'63, including material from *Travelin' To California* and *The Big Blues*), Modern Blues; *Laundromat Blues* (Stax, '66-'68), Edsel; *Door To Door*, Chess; *Masterworks* (includes Stax sides), Atlantic; *King Of The Blues Guitar* ('68), Atlantic; *Truckload Of Lovin'* ('75), Charly; *Albert Live* (Montreux with Rory Gallagher and Louisiana Red, '77), Charly; *New Orleans Heat* ('77), Charly; *I'll Play The Blues For You* (half by John Lee Hooker, '77), Tomato; *Albert* ('78), Tomato; *King Albert* (disco, '78), Tomato; *San Francisco '83*, Fantasy; *I'm In A Phone Booth, Baby* ('84), Fantasy; *Albert King Masterworks*, Atlantic; *The Blues Don't Change*, Ace.

With others: Toru Oki, *Toru Oki Blues Band*, CBS Japan; Albert Brooks, *A Star Is Bought*, Asylum; Gary Moore, *Still Got The Blues* ('90), Charisma.

Anthologies: *Chess Blues* box set; *Door To Door* ('53-'61), Chess France; *Parrot/Blue Lake #1–Hand Me Down Blues* (mid '50s), Relic; *Atlantic Blues: Guitar* ('66-'67), Atlantic; *Blue Monday*, Stax; *Best Of WattStax*, Stax; *It's Christmas Time Again*, Stax; *The Stax Blues Brothers*, Stax; *Super Blues*, Stax; *Blue Monday*, Stax; *Montreux Festival*, Stax; *1000 Volts Of Stax*, Stax; *2000 Volts Of Stax*, Stax; *Blues Masters, Volume 1: Urban Blues*, Rhino; *Blues Masters, Volume 7: Blues Revival*, Rhino; *Blues Masters, Volume 8: Mississippi Delta Blues*, Rhino; *Blues Masters, Volume 9: Postmodern Blues*, Rhino; *Legends Of Guitar–Electric Blues, Vol. 1*, Rhino; *Blues Guitar Blasters*, Ace.

On film: *WattStax* ('72 concert), Columbia; *The Blues Alive* (with John Mayall's '82 Bluesbreakers reunion tour), RCA/Columbia Home Video; *Maintenance Shop Blues: Albert King* (produced by Iowa Public Television in the early '80s, Yazoo Video); *B.B. King & Friends* ('87), HBO; *An Evening Of Blues With Gary Moore* ('90), Charisma. King also appeared on PBS with Stevie Ray Vaughan.

Freddie King

January 1977

BY DAN FORTE

SK NEARLY ANY ROCK GUITARIST TODAY who his early influences were, and almost as a matter of course you'll hear the names of the three "Kings" of electric blues: B.B., Albert, and Freddie. With highly distinctive approaches to the instrument, each offers the guitarist/student a different technique to master and a different code to decipher–B.B.'s hummingbird-like vibrato, Albert's long, bending phrases, and Freddie's aggressive, piercing attack.

Oddly enough it was Freddie, the youngest of the three (born in Gilmer, Texas, in 1934), who most aspiring white guitarists heard first. Back in 1961, while B.B. continued to record and tour as a top name in the all-black market and Albert split his time between driving a bulldozer by day and playing blues by night, Freddie scored a hit single that was picked up by AM stations, both black and white, all across the country. "Hideaway," an uptempo instrumental recorded a year earlier, was swept up by the wave of twangy guitar instrumentals churned out by people such as the Ventures and Duane Eddy and succeeded in getting Freddie, at least temporarily, out of the chitlin circuit.

Originally a singer/guitarist/bandleader much like B.B. or Albert, Freddie recorded the song as a flip side to his vocal on "I Love The Woman" for the Federal/King label in Cincinnati, Ohio. The pattern of success his flip sides began achieving resulted in his first LP, *Freddie King Sings*, followed by an all-instrumental release, *Let's Hide Away And Dance Away With Freddy King.* (This LP was also repackaged and marketed by King as *Freddy King Goes Surfin'*, with the only difference being some canned applause. During this period his first name was spelled with a "y.")

The Freddie King uptempo instrumental has by now become somewhat of an institution, much like the Elmore James slide guitar shuffle. John Mayall's first three Bluesbreakers albums each included one of Freddie's themes, with Eric Clapton recreating "Hideaway" on *Blues Breakers*, Peter Green plowing through "The Stumble" on *A Hard Road*, and Mick Taylor taking a stab at "Driving Sideways" on *Crusade.*

These songs and several others by Freddie are now standard warm-up or break songs for countless semi-pro bands featuring guitar. And much in the same way that organist Bill Doggett's "Honky Tonk" is in seemingly every R&B band's repertoire with all of Billy Butler's guitar licks left intact, guitarists tend to stay close to Freddie's lines in "Hideaway"–from the open-string hammer-ons to the muted bass

runs to the tongue-in-cheek quotation from "Peter Gunn."

Freddie's relationship with the guitar began at age six, when he began learning some blues and gospel from his uncle and mother, who each played guitar. His first axe was a Silvertone acoustic, and the records he was listening to at this time were by the prominent blues artists of the day–people like Lightnin' Hopkins, T-Bone Walker, Muddy Waters, and John Lee Hooker.

Electric guitars didn't enter the picture until several years later. As he recalls, "I finished school at 16 and went to Chicago. Carried a guitar on my back. I went there to live in 1954, but I'd been there back in '50 and in '49. Muddy Waters, that's who I was looking for. So I found him and Jimmy Rogers. Then I met Howlin' Wolf and all those cats, you know."

It was Muddy's guitar man, Jimmy Rogers, who influenced Freddie to forgo flatpicks. "I never have used one," King states. "I use a steel fingerpick on the index and a plastic thumbpick. Jimmy Rogers and Eddie Taylor taught me how to play like that. Robert Jr. Lockwood can play with all three fingers." King later co-produced and played some guitar on Jimmy Rogers' 1973 comeback LP, *Gold Tailed Bird.*

Goin' down: "I play my guitar like Louis Jordan used to play his horn."

Freddie's Texas roots intertwining with the Chicago blues environment made for his up-to-date musical outlook in comparison to many of the already established South Side bands. King soon became close musical kin to the younger generation of Chicago blues guitarists, including Otis Rush and the late Magic Sam, who gravitated mainly to Chicago's West Side. "We played a whole lot of stuff together," King remembers. "We'd go around and listen to each other; then we'd trade licks. Me, Otis, Magic Sam, Jody Williams–I taught Luther Allison how to play." It was this atmosphere that actually provided Freddie with his initial hit "Hideaway." "Hound Dog Taylor played that," he confesses, "then

me and Magic Sam worked it out."

Whereas Taylor played strictly bottleneck guitar, King has steered clear of the slide technique because, as he explains, "my fingers are too heavy; I play too hard. I wish I could play slide, but I can't. I do some of the same licks, though, as Elmore James, Earl Hooker, and guys like that." While his heavy right-hand attack precludes the use of a slide, it is this factor which Freddie credits as his "gimmick."

During the mid '60s, between the time of his first Federal singles and the white awakening to blues music, Freddie, like virtually every other blues artist, was working hard and gaining little ground, since even the top of the blues heap was still at the bottom of the popular music market. His tunes began turning up on LPs from the English blues scene, and two sessions for Atlantic's Cotillion subsidiary let listeners know that one of the originators was still around.

But it wasn't until rock pianist Leon Russell signed King to the Shelter label that Freddie got his second shot at the masses. "We met," he recounts, "and I told Leon that I wasn't with Atlantic no more. He said, 'I'm starting a company. Would you like to come with it?' So we tried it. And everybody knew me from 'Hideaway,' so the Fillmore circuit wasn't really too hard for me."

The association with Russell did more than merely bring some old tunes out of the closet. Freddie's vocals (something he'd never actually stopped doing) again came to the spotlight. As Freddie states, "It's taken me a long time to get back into the vocals. Everybody wanted to hear the instrumentals. I always did do both, but they wouldn't push the vocals. When I really started singing again was with Shelter."

King is quick to credit the Leon Russells, Eric Claptons, and John Mayalls for reviving interest in blues. "These young whites started people looking at me, B.B. King, and all the rest of them," he declares. "If it wasn't for them, I think the blues would still be in the same old black market. But now it's a bigger market. Johnny Winter, John Hammond, Paul Butterfield, Mike Bloomfield—he hung around us as a kid in Chicago. They're really blues cats. It went okay for me."

Freddie's equipment consists mainly of a Gibson ES-355, wired in stereo and fed into a Fender Quad amplifier. Both pickups are employed, with all controls set at half bass, half treble. The string set is split between Ernie Balls (.010, .011, .012) on the top three and Gibson medium gauge for the bass strings. Freddie favors Gibson guitars and in addition to the 355 owns an ES-335, an ES-345, a Les Paul, and two Firebirds. "I used to use Fenders, but not anymore," he says. "Fender is a good-sounding guitar, but for the way I play I think Gibson is the best."

He sums up his technique, saying, "I play my guitar like Louis Jordan used to play his horn. That's the same sound I get."

Though he has at times easily transcended the boundaries of categorization, and dabbled with funk numbers and tunes like Bill Withers' "Ain't No Sunshine" and Dave Mason's "Feelin' Alright," King is quick to give credit to "all the blues players" for his extensive background. Still, judging by a brief list of contemporary guitarists he enjoys listening to, Freddie is anything but narrow-minded. "I like other guys, too: Steve Cropper, Kenny Burrell, Chet Atkins—he plays with his fingers, too. I listen to a whole lot of people, but the thing *I'm* into is the blues."

[*Freddie King passed away in 1976.*]

A SELECTED FREDDIE KING DISCOGRAPHY

Solo albums: *Freddie King Sings* (reissue of superb King sides, '60), Modern Blues; *Let's Hide Away And Dance Away* ('60-'61), King; *Takin' Care Of Business* (Federal sides, '60-'64), Charly; *Freddy King Gives You A Bonanza Of Instrumentals* (Federal, '61-'64), Crosscut; *Just Pickin'* (King/Federal instrumentals), Modern Blues; *Freddy King Goes Surfin'*, King; *17 Original Greatest Hits*, Federal; *Freddie King Is A Blues Master* ('69), Atlantic; *My Feeling For The Blues* ('70), Atlantic; *Getting Ready* (recorded at Chess Studio, '70), Shelter; *Texas Cannonball* ('72), Shelter; *Woman Across The River* ('73), Shelter; *Key To The Highway* (Shelter, '70-'73), Del Rack; *The Best Of Freddie King*, MCA; *Burglar* ('74), Polydor; *Live In Antibes, 1974*, French Concerts; *Rockin' The Blues–Live* (Germany, '74-'75), Crosscut; *Live In Nancy 1975, Vol. 1* and *Vol. 2*, French Concerts; *Larger Than Life* ('75), Polydor; *1934-1976*, Polydor; *Live At The Texas Opry House*, P-Vine; *Hideaway*, Gusto; *"Texas Cannonball" Live*, Double Dutch; *Live In Germany* ('75), King Biscuit; *Best Of Freddie King*, Island; *Freddie King & Bugs Henderson Band* (live, '76), Blues Interactions.

With others: Jimmy Rogers, *Gold Tailed Bird*, Shelter; Lulu Reed and Sonny Thompson, *Boy-Girl-Boy*, King.

Anthologies: *Atlantic Blues: Chicago* ('68-'72), Atlantic; *Ann Arbor Blues & Jazz Festival 1972*, Atlantic; *Blues Masters, Volume 3: Texas Blues*, Rhino; *Blues Upside Your Head*, Charly; *Legends Of Guitar–Electric Blues, Vol. 2*, Rhino.

Clarence "Gatemouth" Brown

May 1979 and March 1993

BY JAS OBRECHT

WITH JAMES ROTONDI

EPUTY SHERIFF CLARENCE BROWN ambles over to the dresser, pops open his briefcase, and pulls out a snub-nose Rossi .38. He turns around and stares intently at us before flipping open the cylinder and pouring out the bullets. As he hands the ammo to writer James Rotondi, Brown demands in a gruff voice, "Look at these bullets, son. Tell me what they are."

"Uh, they're loaded?" responds Rotondi, who's just grown a shade paler.

"Those are silver bullets," bellows Brown, "and they got a *powerful* recoil!"

From his instruments and arrangements to his cowboy boots, Stetson hat, black pipe, and ancient tour bus, everything about Clarence "Gatemouth" Brown bespeaks fierce individualism. And while Brown is rightfully regarded as the closest heir to the sophisticated electric blues of T-Bone Walker, more than a few journalists have been singed by making the mistake of calling him a bluesman to his face. "I'm a *musician*," Brown clarifies, "not some dirty low-down bluesman. I play American and world music, Texas-style. I play a part of the past with the present and just a taste of the future." Mastered during a half-century on the road, his tools are his voice, electric guitar, violin, viola, bass, drums, and harmonica.

The oldest of seven children, Clarence Brown was born on April 24, 1924, in Vinton, Louisiana. At age one, he was bundled off to Orange, Texas, where he spent his youth. "I started strumming guitar behind my father when I was five," he remembers. "The kind of music I played then wasn't blues, wasn't jazz–it was country, Cajun, and bluegrass. That's what my father played, see. The guitar was bigger than me–it was one of those resophonic guitars with an all-metal body. We would play tunes like 'Boil Them Cabbage Down,' 'Bully Of The Town,' and all that real heavy mountain music. Of course, that music means more to me than any other music because I am more familiar with it. Jazz and blues just came automatically."

Young Gate was soon experimenting with other instruments. "The first set of drums I played cost me a whippin'," he laughs. "I sneaked one of my mom's washtubs out and got me two tree limbs and put 'em to it. Man, I was wailing away, and my mom come out there and tore the tub all to pieces and, of course, she tore me up too. That was my first encounter with a set of drums. And my first fiddle–I tried to make it out of a cigar box and screen wire, and it didn't work."

Armed with his dad's advice–"learn to tune your instrument, don't overplay, and play some of everything so you don't get stuck in one bag"–Gatemouth embarked on his professional career at 16. His first band, the Gay Swingsters, was fronted by a mailman, Howard Spencer, who only knew how to blow sax in one key. "Everything he ever played was in *Bb*," Gate recalls. "I never will forget these guys taking me to Chain's Nightclub in Beaumont, Texas, and we'd play *hard* upstairs all night and got three nickels apiece, and the guy who was handling the thing took all the money. That's what you consider paying dues." The teenager toured with W.M. Bimbo & The Brownskin Models, an old-time traveling road show that left him stranded in Norfolk, Virginia. He took a job there at the El Dorado Club, drumming in the house band until the outbreak of World War II.

After serving his time with Uncle Sam–"five months, ten days, and a few hours"–Brown headed to San Antonio. Billed as "The Singing Drummer," he played with Hort Hudge's 23-piece orchestra at the Keyhole Club for a couple of years. Don Robey, who owned a club in Houston, was intrigued by Brown's act and invited him to Houston. The following morning, Gate was thumbing his way east.

Not longer after his arrival in Houston, Gatemouth had a memorable encounter with T-Bone Walker: "T-Bone was the hot stuff on guitar throughout Texas at that time, and nobody knew I played guitar. So I went in this club–the Bronze Peacock–and sat down aside the bandstand. T-Bone was sick with an ulcer or something, and he laid his guitar down and ran to the dressing room. And so just out of nowhere, I got up and walked up on the stage, picked up his guitar, and invented a boogie–right there onstage. I started this tune with the words 'My name is Gatemouth Brown, I just got in your town, if you don't like my style, I will not hang around.' It was coming to me just out of the clear blue, and the women and men was just pouring money down my bosom and everywhere else. And I made $600 in that period of time. That tune happened to become my first recording, 'Gatemouth Boogie.'

"So all of a sudden T-Bone Walker recovered and come back and snatched his guitar from me, onstage. It kind of hurt my feelings, and he told me that as long as I live, never touch his instrument again. So I said alright. By that time Don Robey heard the commotion and the people screaming, and he came down and told me to come see him. The next day he bought me a Gibson L-5 for $700 and a uniform, and I've been going ever since."

Robey flew Gatemouth to Hollywood to record his first four sides on August 21, 1947, with the Maxwell Davis Orchestra. Gate's roots may have been in the fertile country blues territory of east Texas and southwest Louisiana, but his debut Aladdin 78s jump with progressive orchestrations and seasoned showmanship. "Robey knew nothing about recording," Brown says, "but he was a very smart man. After they recorded my first four sides and he learned more about the business, we formed the Peacock Record Company in Houston, and that was our company for 17 years." Brown's Peacock 78s featured piano, bass, drums, and a jumping horn section, and his exciting treble tone seemed to leap off of sides like 1953's "Boogie Uproar" and 1954's magnificent "Okie Dokie Stomp." By the late '50s, though, Gate's record sales were dwindling. After his final Peacock side in '61, he didn't record again until '64, making a single 45 for Cue.

In 1965, Gatemouth headed for Nashville to try his hand at recording C&W for the Hit Sound label. "I started easing back into what I always loved–country, Cajun, and bluegrass," he explains. "See, the clubs I was working was all Caucasian clubs, and so this music is what I started getting back to. I got to where I didn't want to play the rhythm and blues. I freelanced around for a while, and there was nothing happening because people at that time didn't want *music.* The old doo-wop bunch was out there doing acrobatics, and there was the hard rock and roll, so I just went to playing small clubs around Colorado, Nevada, and Texas. I decided to back off on recording in America."

Unbeknownst to Brown, French fans were raving about his Peacock sides. Promoters persuaded him to tour Europe in '71 with an all-star group. He recorded *The Blues Ain't Nothin', Clarence Gatemouth Brown Sings Louis Jordan,* and *Gate's On The Heat* for France's Black And Blue label and played the Montreux Jazz Festival. He was invited back to Montreux in '73, recording *Cold Storage* during the same trip. In 1977 Brown took his band on a tour of northeast Africa sponsored by the U.S. State Department. "It was one of the greatest chances of my life," he recalls. "We got to see the true grits of Africa, and it's a beautiful country." Upon his return, Gatemouth ended his American recording exile, cutting *Blackjack,* a collection of jazz, blues, Cajun, bluegrass, country, and folk music performed on his guitar, fiddle, electric mandolin, viola, and harmonica. The following year Gate recorded the country LP *Makin' Music* with Roy Clark. Gatemouth cut several albums for the Rounder label during the 1980s, and joined the Alligator Records roster in '89. He delves into jazz, blues, bluegrass, ballads, zydeco, Cajun, and calypso on his latest releases. During our interview in San Francisco, the outspoken Mr. Brown was alternately gruff, charming, and tender.

You've often said that you don't play guitar like guitar, but…

Like a horn. I play horn lines and horn kicks. You know

how a horn would phrase different passages? Well, I do that with my guitar.

Do you always pick with just your fingers?

Always. I got control of my mind with my fingers. I got control of the guitar with my fingers. I can let them ring, or I can smother my strings in a snap and cut it just like a horn would do when your breath run out. The circle of breathing–I can do that by using my fingers. And of course another secret of mine, I pick with both hands. A lot of people don't understand that, and it's hard to explain.

Which fingers do you use?

Depends on what I'm playing. I might use 'em all, and I might use a thumb. I may use an index finger. I might use my ring finger. It's unexplainable. People ask, "How you do that?" I say, "Magic." When they say, "Show me how to do that," I say, "I show no one nothing." Years ago when I was playing along with my father, I said, "Dad, how you do this?" He said, "I'm not going to show you anything." I said, "How shall I learn?" He said, "Pay attention." It's as simple as that. I love my father more than life itself. Of course, I lost him in 1954, and man, that hurt me more than *anything* on earth. He was my life, and it was a great loss to me, but I kept my promise. I promised him that I would be the best in my field that I possibly could, and that's exactly what I'm doing.

"I'm a musician," growls Mr. Brown, "not some dirty, low-down bluesman."

When you arrange your music...

I head-arrange with the guitar. I put it on there, and then I got a guy that writes it–or they memorize it–and you got your take. Other guys in the band help with the filling in spaces too. And once we get them down, we write 'em.

What's the greatest satisfaction when it all comes together?

The greatest satisfaction to me is we don't have the same sound on everything. Most records you hear just strike one medium, and you can't even leave that. You have to stay with it, and that's bad, man, because if you can't grow, you're in trouble.

You've been making records longer than John Lee Hooker and B.B. King.

Why, sure I have. Notice the caliber of the music too.

It stayed high.

It stayed together. You see, friends are one thing, but I cannot shield a man if he's not musical, if he's not creative.

And if you're gonna sound like you did when you first started, there's no point in keeping going.

Is it a compliment when guitarists try to figure out your tone or passages on the Peacock 78s?

Yeah, I think so. I'm not a blues player; I'm a musician. But all blues players, when they play the blues, their minds are in their work. It's what they want out of life—it's not what you need. But I'm different from that. When I walk on that bandstand, I'm giving myself to all of my kids. You are my child, you are too [*points to Jas and Roto*]—all of you. I have no color barrier. Period. And the message I'm trying to give to them will help them rather than make them try to live like these supposedly blues players do. That's why I hate the idea of people labeling me as a blues player, because I'm not.

Although you've played some really great...

I play blues, sure, but don't call me a bluesman. When the white society think of blues, they think further back. See my last album? *No Looking Back.* So forget it.

Don't look back to older musicians?

No. Forget it.

Why? What if that old music still brings pleasure to people?

That's fine if somebody else want to do it, but I don't want them to ask me to do it. I cannot talk for others, but I can always talk for myself. Mostly all you kids do is listen to the beat or listen to how sorrowful a blues is. And it is sorrowful, because it's very negative. And you notice that every white blues player that ever got out there to play what he thinks is the blues, if he tried to live that life, it killed him. I'm serious! That's what I'm trying to get to. Do not tackle something you don't know nothing about!

When you were a kid, how was blues music regarded in your neighborhood?

Well, son, I'm gonna be honest with you. When I was a kid, I listened to very little blues because it made me feel sick inside. It just made me feel physically sick.

Hearing a Lead Belly or Blind Lemon record?

Yeah, man. I wouldn't listen to that stuff. I didn't like it. It made me see disastrous things facing me. You see, my father was a great, great, great musician—three "greats" to it—and I don't ever consider myself better than he. I took what he taught me—just like what the Japanese doing with our inventions—and added to it.

Blues and jazz is not my first music. My first music is country, Cajun, and bluegrass. My daddy sung Cajun, country, and bluegrass, and played it on fiddle, accordion, banjo, and mandolin. He was a heck of a vocalist. But he was a railroad man. When he was coming up, they didn't have nightclubs like they have today. They had what they called "house parties." People who had the biggest houses moved all the

furniture back, they would cook a lot, and they would have all kinds of drinks—it was great days when I was coming up. And another thing—I never been an alcoholic. I drank twice in my life. I got drunk because I was going in the service, and I was scared. The second time was through a woman—it happens to all of us. And I said, "If I ever get over this sickness, I'll never do it no more because I can't stand to be sick of the stomach." I can't, man.

I learned the other person's downfall, but I took advantage of it and didn't do it. Like all the cokeheads and all them people back when I was growing up: They was acting very strange, and I said I would never want to do that, and I never did. I wouldn't even know what cocaine tastes or feels like. It only takes a weak person to want to kill himself. And you can see it kill other people, like Charlie Parker, Gene Ammons—oh, dozens and dozens of other artists. Alcohol and narcotics killed 'em. I knew that's what killed 'em—why should I do it?

Can I ask you something off the record?

You can print anything you want, because I'm not going to give you a negative answer.

Do you think reefer is bad for musicians?

No! It's not, and I've always said that. Marijuana is the only substance on earth that's grown by what we know as God, nature, or whatever, that don't really harm no one. But all this man-made chemicals—that's what killing them. Alcohol is killing us. Whiskey is the most deadly drug on earth; it killed my third brother. Great, great guitarist and vocalist, but he followed people like Lightnin' Hopkins and Guitar Slim, and you see where they all end up: six feet deep. Alcohol is one of the most *devastating* drugs there is. You get too many drinks and run out there and kill everybody including yourself. They're fighting the wrong substance—that's all.

Guys used to say they'd have to drink to play good.

What do you mean *used to*, son? Right now we have what could be some great musicians, but this alcohol and women get in front of it. When you try to go with all these women—you can't do that. I am one of the few entertainers that don't go out there womanizing just because I'm in a position to do it. It means nothing to me. What means something to me is trying to keep families together and trying to keep people with love and concern for each other.

Do you see your music as a positive healing force?

It is. I've stated that all over the world. I do positive music. Even just my music without me opening my mouth is very positive. It tells a story. It tells you something about life. I've had ladies and men come up to me and say, "You know, Brown, when I left the house I felt very bad. But now I feel so good from the inside out." Boy, that's a great statement for people to make to someone. That's a great thing to be honored for.

Can compliments be a distraction?

To some of them. Not me. If I was asked about my Grammy Award, I'd say it was alright, but it wasn't nothing that was going to make me flip out on. It was just a piece of metal. What's important is the people I can get to with my music, not the piece of metal that's going to get to me. What good is that piece of metal? I don't care if I ever got a Grammy, and I've always said that. But I've got one, and very seldom does it ever make it in my write-ups. I just don't bother naming it. I got four or five Handy Blues Awards. I've gotten many documents from mayors all over the country. I'm a deputy sheriff in Louisiana, where I live. I arrest no one, but I'm well bonded by the sheriff's department, and I carry my stuff with me all over the world where I go. And I'm real good with all the policemans that I meet because I became one of them and maybe I have some good influence on them.

Are there certain songs you have to play every night or else people will be disappointed?

Well, they don't say anything about it. [*Laughs.*] I can't possibly play everything that I know in the run of the night. Sometimes they request "Okie Dokie Stomp," but I have ways I can soft them down. I may use the excuse about the band hasn't rehearsed this, and I don't want to do nothin' unless it's rehearsed–that sort of stuff. But basically I keep people so well geared up they forget about what they might want to ask. You have to keep 'em occupied.

What have you learned about performing after being on the road for 50 years?

Well, son, I've learned a lot. I've seen a lot. I've seen failure after failure after failure. I can see why they have failed, but what I've learned beyond that is not to get up on a bandstand trying to please *me*. I get myself on that public. That's why I don't like a heavy spotlight on me where I can't see the public, because I work with my public. That's the name of the game. I want to get a visual of you, so I know exactly what to do to get your response, and I can't do that if I can't see you. Now when you're on TV, that's a different story. You have to think of getting to the people in a different way. And you have to be careful about not making mistakes, because too many out there know when you've made one. And if you happen to make one–as we all will do–be smart enough to cover it. Like a cat–cover up your mistakes.

Do you ever just repeat it, so it seems like that's what you were supposed to do?

That's exactly it a lot of times! And it works. "Okie Dokie Stomp" has one of the biggest boo-boos in the world in it– I made a note that I wasn't supposed to make in it–and it works because I play it over.

We recently saw an old photo of you playing a Fender Telecaster.

Yeah. Fender used to give me a Telecaster every year and a half, but I never could like 'em. But I loved their amplifiers. Now I use Music Man amps–one for my viola and fiddle, and the other one for my two guitars.

What's your all-time favorite setup?

Well, son, let's put it this way: My favorite guitar is the one that sounded good to me at the precise moment I was playing. I'm not cutting you short. Now, I got a Washburn guitar that I bought for $175 brand-new out of a pawnshop. I love pawnshops; I get good stuff out of there. Then, of course, my ['63 Gibson] Firebird has been with me for years. It's famous all over the world–the one with that leather pickguard. I use that with the Music Man, and that's my sound.

What does the fiddle give you that the guitar doesn't?

A different sound, a different feeling, a different avenue, and another planet. When I'm playing fiddle, I feel like my father is standing beneath it with me. It has been written that I'm the most unorthodox fiddle player and guitar player in the world–well, that's good because I'm all out there by myself. No one has ever been able to really copy my music. You can do the horn lines, but when you get to the guitar solo, that's when they all die off. I got my own individual style, and it's hard to explain. I can't explain my feelings to you.

Do you play rock and roll?

I play rock and roll a lot of times. You see, what they call rock and roll today is not rock and roll, son. It's a lot of noise. A lot of string bending and not even making a statement. Remember that tune of mine called "Chicken Shift"? That's rock and roll. "Dolly Got The Blues"–that's rock and roll. Louisiana zydeco is a mixture of rock and roll and Creole music. Then I play straight-ahead Cajun that has nothing to do with nothing else but Cajun.

What can you say to young rockers?

If a guy's a heavy drinker or heavy dope user, don't follow him, because he's in misery in the first place. That's why he's playing that kind of music. And them hard rock players, well, all I can say for those kids is they're being brainwashed to brainwash others. Why play music that loud and ruin yourself before you hit 20 years old? And what they're playing is not understood–no way–because everything is so high volume. Why play something so loud where it's going to tear you up inside? I've seen guys that was so loud, my stomach was hurting!

What do you look for in a tone?

Dynamics. Just what I do. And there's four dynamics, all told: High volume, midrange, soft, and off. See, if you play in a high volume, you've got it goin'. Now, at a certain portion you drop it down and leave it to midrange. I go further than that: I go from a high volume to real soft, but just keep that drive going. And every time I do it, you can hear 'em scream all over the place because it feels good. I can rattle my guitar and almost tear out windows, and drop it to where you just barely hear it. Every man in my band knows when to do this. That makes music.

What should a Gatemouth Brown solo be about?

I don't understand the question.

A lot of guys show off during solos. They play fast licks over and over, but they don't tell a story in the way that you seem to on your records.

You asked that real nicely. In the first place, a guy who's doing that is not playing for people. He's on an ego trip trying to tell hisself he's the greatest guitar player in the world, and not playing nothing! Making a lot of nonsense. You can take a five-year-old kid, give him a pick, and tell him just start hitting all them strings–that's all they're doing. It's not making any sense.

Your solos work so well with the rhythm. If you're doing a nice shuffle, you move right into the rhythm.

Here's one secret about music–I don't care what instrument you're playing. If somewhere in the song you have a solo, every one that's playing with you needs to get *underneath* you–not even with you or over you. Then you do that for them when they solo too. I do nothin' I don't want my men to do. When the piano player is playing, I comp under him where he can be heard. Why? Because he's the one featured at the time. Not you. And every man in my band has got to be a good musician–if he isn't, he can't stay. Because I'm gonna damn sure make him solo. I give every man a chance for the world to hear him as well as me. That's what teamwork is all about.

What are your rules for the band?

Not a beer bottle, not a whiskey glass, or nothing on that bandstand–number one. I don't want no bullshitting and talking to each other on the bandstand unnecessarily. I want everybody to concentrate on his job. I don't want no scrambling about all over the bandstand.

Do you have rehearsals?

Never. I need to, but I don't. Son, I haven't had no time.

How many nights a year do you play?

About 300 or less.

You've been playing Ellington's "C Jam Blues" for a long time.

Yes. I just like the drive of the tune. I like the concept. I don't like all of Ellington's music, no, but that's one of the few I've liked. It's a different blues from the other kind of blues. I put myself into it and just keep the identification. That's the next thing. When somebody does somebody's

music, don't do it note-for-note like that person–that's stupid. Use the head of the tune, and then when you come in, play it yourself. Don't try to play what that other person played, because you can't do it. I wouldn't even attempt to try. That's what you call a copier, and not a rearranger. I rearrange everything. I can kick any big band tune and rearrange it, but you'll know it's the tune because the idea is there. After that it's me, but it's all gonna fit. I used to do the theme from *Dr. Zhivago*, and I never knew that bridge. So I made a bridge up to go with it, and it was perfect. When somebody said that's not right, I said, "Look–what is right? You want me to copy? You want to hear every note that was done in this tune? I'm not going to do it. There's going to be some changes." I'm going to use his head idea, and after that it's me. That's how I'm successful in what I do.

Frank Zappa has said that you're probably his favorite guitar player.

Man, there's 100,000 guitar players around the world say this. But I don't hear me nowhere. Maybe I influenced them to get started. If you notice, a lot of people now are trying to use my type of arrangement, but they can't do it because I never do the same thing twice. All these musicians get right down in front of me...

I'm going to be there tonight.

And I'm gonna get you, son. In concert I say, "How many musicians, guitar players, what have you, are here tonight?" Boy, they all stand up. I say, "I know why you're here. You're here to snatch some licks." Then my final word is, "Snatch on this," and I may come up with a jazz tune, man, and *burn* it. [*Laughs.*] They just sit there like, oh, no. I say, "This is a very easy tune to play." I love to tease the kids. Back in the '60s and '50s, you used to get guitar players from all over the world wanting to have what they called a battle of guitars. And I've never lost one.

What was your secret?

Being myself.

Would you be put up against guys like Guitar Slim?

No, man, they're not guitar players! See, that's what I said a while ago. When they think of blues, you all go right to the bottom of the barrel and scrape off the crud. And you expect me to go along with it, but I'm not. This man killed himself trying to be me. He was so frustrated. He tried to dress like me, he tried to walk like me, he tried to play like me, he tried to sing like me, and he didn't do none of that. But one thing he did that wasn't like me was being a heavy drunk. I played in Kansas City one time, and he come to town. And back in them early days, I was wearin' tails. And he went and bought him tails just like me and changed his Cadillac color every day to suit the tails that he was wearing–that was so stupid. But the ultimate of the story was he was real ignorant, and he went and opened his trunk right on the street with me and a bunch of people standing right there, and he had about ten gallons of wine in that car. And he died a young man–too young. I met his son, who said, "Mr. Brown, I want you to tell me something about my daddy, because I don't know him." And I said, "Son, I would rather you not know."

Which historical musicians would you most like to have seen?

Count Basie and Louis Jordan. Those were my idols as a child. Louis Jordan was one of the greatest gimmick singers in the world. Nobody has ever surpassed this man.

What would you have young players learn from your concerts?

Good question. Here's your answer: What the young people can learn from me through my concert is the positive music. Let's go back to the way that people lived in Mississippi, like with B.B. and all them. During their times, they wrote about the common life that was going on. It was about hardship and working, no money, and that sort of stuff. In Texas, T-Bone was writing about how no good a woman was. Now to me, if the man didn't like no woman, he must have hated his mother. Every song that he's got is against a woman. What caused him to be what he is was a woman.

Your music has a lot of love in it.

Thank you. That's the difference. Now you see what I'm talking about. I've had a few hard times, but no one ever had good times all their life. Somewhere back in your life you did somebody wrong, and you sure gotta pay–it's the truth, but I try to outlive that.

What records are the best introduction to your guitar playing?

Any one you pick will have a good message for you. That's all I can say.

What keeps you growing?

Positive thinking, positive living, treating you like I wished to be treated. I don't look at you because your skin is light. I don't want you to look at me because my skin is dark. We're all people. We need each other. If we don't have each other, what the hell we got? One shouldn't look at one because of the color of his skin. Because there's blacks I don't want around me, and there's whites I don't want around me. There's other nationalities I don't want around me, but I take people as individuals.

You've spent your whole career knocking down racial barriers.

That's right. And if I had to go back and do it all over again, it'd be a *hard* job. Still is. I turned down two movies because I didn't like what they wanted me to portray. I'm not going to be an Uncle Tom for nobody. I came this far by being me; I'll continue going by being me.

A SELECTED GATEMOUTH BROWN DISCOGRAPHY

Solo albums: *Original Peacock Recordings* ('52-'59), Rounder; *Atomic Energy* ('47-'59), Blues Boy; *San Antonio Ballbuster* ('49-'59), Red Lightnin'; *The Nashville Session–1965*, Chess U.K.; *Just Got Lucky* (Black And Blue), Evidence; *The Blues Ain't Nothin'* ('70), Black And Blue; *Clarence Gatemouth Brown Sings Louis Jordan*, Black And Blue; *Gate's On The Heat*, Black And Blue; *Cold Storage* ('73), Black And Blue; *Okie Dokie Stomp*, Black And Blue; *More Stuff*, Black And Blue; *Pressure Cooker* (Black And Blue, '73), Alligator; *Hot Times Tonight*, P-Vine; *Bogalusa Boogie Man*, Barclay; *Blackjack* ('76), Music Is Medicine; *Makin' Music* (with Roy Clark, '78), MCA; *Alright Again!* ('81), Rounder; *One More Mile* ('82), Rounder; *Real Life* ('85), Rounder; *Texas Swing*, Rounder; *Standing My Ground* ('89), Alligator; *No Looking Back* ('92), Alligator. Homespun Tapes offers *The Guitar According To Gatemouth*, a set of three one-hour audio instruction cassettes.

With others: Jimmy Dawkins, *Tribute To Orange*, Black & Blue/Evidence.

Anthologies: *Best Of The Blues–A Summit Meeting* ('73 Newport in New York), Pair; *Best Of The Blues* (Barclay reissues), Polydor; *The Alligator Records 20th Anniversary Collection*, Alligator; *Blues As Big As Texas*, Home Cooking; *Blues Masters, Volume 3: Texas Blues*, Rhino; *Blues Masters, Volume 5: Jump Blues Classics*, Rhino; *The Best Of Duke-Peacock Blues*, MCA; *Legends Of Guitar–Electric Blues, Vol. 2*, Rhino; *Strike A Deep Chord: Blues Guitars For The Homeless*, Justice.

On film: *The San Francisco Blues Festival* ('83).

Eddie "Guitar Slim" Jones

March 1984

BY JEFF HANNUSCH

TWENTY-FOUR YEARS AFTER HIS DEATH, Guitar Slim's extroverted, passionate blues guitar playing can still send chills down one's spine. His highly personal compositions, including the R&B standards "The Things That I Used To Do" and "The Story Of My Life," are still staples in the repertoires of blues, rock, and even zydeco bands. And anyone who ever saw the man perform, be they player or listener, has vivid memories of one of the most colorful figures in the history of New Orleans rhythm and blues.

Fellow New Orleans guitarist Earl King remembers seeing Guitar Slim at the peak of his all-too-short career: "Gatemouth Brown, T-Bone Walker, Lowell Fulson, and Guitar Slim were all performing one night at the White Eagle in Opelousas. Slim was headlining, because 'The Things That I Used To Do' was a scorcher. They were all sitting in the dressing room, and Guitar Slim walked up to 'em all and said, 'Gentlemen, we got the greatest guitar players in the country assembled right here. But when I leave here tonight, ain't nobody gonna realize you even been here.' Well, they all laughed, but that's exactly what happened.

"Slim came out with his hair dyed blue, blue suit, blue pair of shoes. He had 350 feet of mike wire connected to his guitar, and a valet carrying him on his shoulders all through the crowd and out into the parking lot. Man, he was stopping cars driving down the highway. No one could outperform Slim. He was about the performinest man I've ever seen." King's description coincides with that of virtually everyone else who saw Guitar Slim onstage, or knew him personally. Though he's been dead for over two decades, Guitar Slim's legend continues.

When I was researching the Guitar Slim story, I got the telephone number of a guy who supposedly had been his tailor–because Slim was famous for the outlandish suits he wore. I called the number, and an older black lady answered, and I told her I wanted to ask her husband about Guitar Slim. He got on the phone, and I introduced myself, and he proceeded to tell me this story about taking the bus downtown in New Orleans. They got in front of the Dew Drop club on LaSalle Street, and traffic was lined up on both sides of the street. So he got out of the bus to see what was going on, and Guitar Slim was playing out in the neutral ground on the boulevard, walking over the tops of cars while his

valet was spooling out his big, long guitar cord to him. Then I asked the guy to tell me about the suits he made for Slim, and he said, "No, I'm no tailor; I'm a carpenter. You must have the wrong number." In New Orleans, even the wrong numbers have at least one Guitar Slim story.

Even though his music has remained popular all these years, many details concerning his life are still shrouded in mystery, so much so that putting together a concise biography is like completing a complex jigsaw puzzle. Guitar Slim was born Edward Jones on December 10, 1926, and he's known to have at least one sister. Though Slim claimed in his Specialty Records biography that Greenwood, Mississippi, was his birthplace, Hollandale, Mississippi, has also been suggested. No matter, Slim was raised in the Greenwood area, a rural region of intense cotton production in the heart of the Mississippi Delta. Times were probably tough, and likely Slim did his fair share in the fields, visiting Greenwood on weekends.

The first mention of Guitar Slim (he was six feet tall, 160 pounds, so he easily fit the colorful alias) in the *Louisiana Weekly* was during September 1950. It stated: "New Orleans' newest gift to the show world is Guitar Slim, held over at the Dew Drop. The New Orleans blues sensation has made a terrific impact on blues fans in New Orleans. Acclaimed to be an exact carbon copy of Gatemouth Brown, the singing guitarist includes 'My Time Is Expensive,' 'Gatemouth Boogie,' and several other performances made popular by Brown."

The comparison between Guitar Slim and Gatemouth Brown is indeed apt; it is interesting to note that he would draw his greatest influence from the Texas guitar school, rather than the guitar players from his own state, Mississippi. "Gatemouth's 'Boogie Rambler' was Slim's theme," adds Earl King. "He listened to all of them and compiled bits of their style–Gatemouth, T-Bone, B.B. King. But he took a different approach; he had a lot of melodic overtones in his solos. He used to play a solo that had a marriage to the rest of the song, rather than just play something off the top of his head."

Earl also chafes when others suggest Slim was a poor instrumentalist and unable to even play without the aid of a capo, or as Slim referred to it, "a choker." "Slim tuned standard, but he used that capo to get the effect of open strings. You can't do that without a choker. I've seen Slim play many a time without it. He just used it for effect."

Percy Stovall, who booked Slim during his early career, remembers: "I used to worry him sometimes and hide his choker. He'd be runnin' around saying, 'Stove, where's my

choker at? I can't find my choker.' I'd say, 'I ain't seen it, Slim,' and he'd be running around trying to find it everywhere. Then just before he would go on, I'd pull it out of my pocket and hand it to him, and he'd say, 'Stove, I knew you had it all the time.'"

Stovall is the first to admit that Slim was his favorite artist, but also points out he had his share of headaches with him. "Man, he loved to drink," says Stovall, shaking his head. "If I didn't watch him all the time he'd miss his job. If he had a job over in Florida, I'd have to ration him. I'd make sure the valet gave him only a fifth of wine when he left New Orleans, another fifth in Biloxi, and one more by the time he got to Mobile. And don't nobody fool with Slim's wine or he'd be in trouble."

One of Stovall's favorite stories concerning his early days of booking Guitar Slim took place in Monroe, Louisiana. "Fats Domino and Slim played a Battle Of The Blues," he recalls, "at the Monroe Civic Auditorium. Man, the place was packed. Slim had told Fats before the show, 'Fats, I'm gonna run you offa that stage tonight.'

"So Slim went on first because Fats had hit records out. Slim just tore 'em up. The place was goin' wild. Slim walked off the stage with his guitar and went out the back door of the place and got in a car, still playing. Everyone wondered where Slim had gone. When it came time for Fats to come on, Fats just told the people, 'Ain't gonna be no battle tonight. You just saw it.' So Fats just played his regular show."

By 1951, the record companies had been hearing about this wild guitar player in New Orleans. Imperial approached first, and Al Young produced four sides by Eddie Jones at the J&M Studio. The session was rather chaotic, originally producing "Bad Luck Is On Me" and "New Arrival," which sold poorly. Imperial wouldn't ask Slim back to the studio, but still issued the remainder of the session when Slim hit the big time, using his alias instead of Eddie Jones.

Slim's next record was a different story. Percy Stovall arranged a session with Jim Bullet in Nashville, producing the popular "Feelin' Sad" in 1952. David Lastie played sax on the tune and remembered the circumstances that surrounded the session: "We was working at the Kitty Cat Club in Nashville, and me, Huey Piano Smith, Little Eddie Lang, and Willie Nettles did the session with Slim. 'Feelin' Sad' was a good little record; it had a church sound to it. We worked pretty good off it."

When Slim came in off the road, he stayed upstairs at the Dew Drop. "Slim liked to be where the action was," chuck-

> *"Guitar Slim just blew me away...period."*
> – Stevie Ray Vaughan

les King. "In fact, you knew Slim was back in town, because early in the morning, around seven or eight o'clock, if he was tanked up, you'd hear them amps and PAs going off. People'd be calling the police because you could hear Slim three blocks away! And here's Slim up in his room with his shorts on, going through his stage routine.

"And Slim's room was something else, man. If you went up there, there'd always be about seven or eight different women up there. He'd have his songs written with eyebrow pencil on pieces of paper tacked to the wall."

King also recalls that Slim bought the first Les Paul guitar in New Orleans: "Slim was playing one of those big hollow boxes like T-Bone had. But when the solid boxes came out he got one right away. Slim said the hollow boxes were too big, and they didn't give him enough room on the stage. He couldn't control the feedback that was coming out of them. So he dealt with the Les Paul."

By 1953 Guitar Slim was one of the biggest draws on the southern R&B circuit. The responsibilities of managing and booking reverted to Slim's landlord, Frank Pania, who owned the Dew Drop, while Percy Stovall concentrated on building up a larger roster of performers. Pania also took it upon himself to find Slim a new band. He hired the Lloyd Lambert band from Hosea Hill's Sugar Bowl in Thibodaux, Louisiana. Hosea was a friend and business associate of Pania, and paired Slim with the band for a series of road dates. Bassist Lambert claims that Pania was responsible for introducing Slim to Johnny Vincent, then a Specialty Records A&R man. Vincent was impressed enough to convince his boss, Art Rupe, to sign Slim to a recording contract. "Slim was supposed to sign with Atlantic," Vincent recalls, "but this was one artist I just had to get. He was fantastic. Slim wouldn't let anyone outperform him. I wouldn't let him out of my sight until he signed with Specialty."

On October 16, 1953, Slim entered the J&M Studio to record what was to be the biggest record of his career, "The Things That I Used To Do." According to Lloyd Lambert, the personnel on the session was pianist Ray Charles, Gus Fontenette, Charles Burbank, and Joe Tillman on saxophones, Oscar Moore on drums, Frank Mitchell on trumpet, and Lambert on bass, with Jones playing his gold-top. Vincent claims he had to bail one of the musicians out of jail to play on the date.

When Vincent says, "Slim was hard to record," he has lots of support. Tales of Slim's recording sessions are many. Vincent claims that it took "all night" to record "The Things That I Used To Do." Engineer Cosimo Matassa says "all day," and Lloyd Lambert reports it took "two days." Nonetheless, the musicians were obviously gratified when it was over, because Ray Charles is clearly audible yelling "Yeah!" in relief in the last bars of the song.

According to Earl King, the idea for the tune came to Slim in a dream. Slim related to King that in the dream he was confronted by a devil and an angel, both of whom held the lyrics to a song. Naturally, Slim chose the devil's song, and it turned out to be "The Things That I Used To Do."

Vincent sent the tapes of the session to Rupe, who was less than impressed with the result. According to Vincent, "He told me it was the worst piece of shit he'd ever heard. He said, 'I'm gonna put it out, but if it don't sell, you start looking for a job.'"

The public disagreed with Rupe, to say the least. Immediately after its release, both *Billboard* and *Cash Box* made it the pick of the week. *Cash Box* called it "a slow southern blues rhythmically chanted by the blues shouter... great vocal with the proper blues styling, and this side is headed for sales. Top notch."

"The Things That I Used To Do" stormed the charts. It topped the R&B roster for six solid weeks and ended up the biggest-selling R&B record of 1954. The lyrics, sung in Slim's impassioned gospel-like style, struck a chord in the public's imagination. For many, the real appeal of "The Things That I Used To Do" was the novel guitar approach that Slim took. As Earl King explains: "Slim was gettin' a fuzztone distortion way before anyone else. Believe it or not, Slim never used an amplifier. He always used a PA set, never an amplifier. He was an overtone fanatic, and he had those tiny iron-cone speakers and the sound would run through them speakers, and I guess any vibration would create that sound, because Slim always played at peak volume. That's why it was hard to record him—because of the volume he was accustomed to playing at. Let's face it, if Slim was playing you could hear him a mile away."

Lloyd Lambert agrees that Slim played as loud as he could. "He had this tinny sound," says Lambert, "that he'd get by turning all the bass controls as low as they would go, and turning up his treble controls as high as they'd go."

Although Slim was most associated with his gold-top Les Paul (after switching from his hollowbody electric), some

> *"Guitar Slim's solo on 'The Story Of My Life' is one of the best early distorted guitar solos; it really sounds like he's mad at somebody."*
>
> – Frank Zappa

pictures show him playing a white Fender Telecaster. The piercing tone Slim achieved was similar to that of Clarence Gatemouth Brown and Johnny Guitar Watson, and derived in part from the fact that he, like the others, played guitar with his fingers, pulling at the strings. ZZ Top guitarist Billy Gibbons concurs: "Eddie Jones definitely played with his thumb and his fingers. A lot of people could never figure out why R&B had such vicious guitar tones. They forget that most of the rooms that they played in were so loud anyway. I mean, can you imagine going into a black blues joint in 1954 and having it quiet and sedate? They'd just turn those old Fender amps up all the way, man, just to be heard. Slim would, like, aim for 'patent pending' and just blow!"

New Orleans songwriter Al Reed, who backed Slim, Earl King, Smiley Lewis, and others, also credits Jones with pioneering the distorted electric guitar sound. As he told John Broven in *Rhythm & Blues In New Orleans* [Pelican]: "A lot of the electric guitar sound has been attributed to Chuck Berry, but many people aren't aware of the type of guitar that Guitar Slim played. Guitar Slim was a most profound musician. He had an electric sound like you never heard. They would open the club doors wide so that the sound could just go in and out of the club, and he would draw people off the street. Big passing automobiles would stop, and the people would just listen to this guy play and watch him walk. I think he had a greater impact on the electric guitar sound than any other guitarist because he used the electric sound very much as it is used today. And Chuck Berry was not using that sound at the time. Guitar Slim was the finest and about the first. He was a great guy to be around. He was a man you could learn from–not what you heard, but what you saw. Because he could exhilarate you. Man, he would lift you above and beyond the clouds as he played. He could create sensations within your body that really played tricks with your mind. He was the first man to do this."

With the #1 record in the country, Frank Pania booked a full itinerary for Slim through the South, and bought him a brand new Olds Delta 88. Slim promptly got drunk one night and ran into a parked bulldozer, wrecking the car and ending up in the hospital. "Slim weren't too good a driver," laughs Lambert. "He didn't hurt himself too bad; the doctor just told him to take it easy for a month."

Pania decided to send Earl King out to impersonate Slim on a number of dates, and apparently got away with it. Even though King went along with the charade, he admits he was scared to death: "When I got back to town, the first person I saw was Guitar Slim," laughs Earl. "He was walking down LaSalle Street with a hospital gown on, a guitar under one arm and an amp under the other, yelling 'Earl King, I heard you been out there imitatin' me. If you wreck my name, I'm gonna sue and I'm gonna kill you!'"

Slim was soon back on his feet and ready to hit the road for a tour of the northern theater circuit. Since Lambert's band already had Lawrence Cotton on piano, Slim had to split with Huey Smith, an event which likely saddened both of them.

Eventually Slim's popularity became too much for Frank Pania to deal with, so he turned over Slim's management to Hosea Hill, who ran his own popular nightspot in Thibodaux, the Sugar Bowl. Consequently, Slim spent a good amount of his time in Thibodaux, which nestles Bayou Lafourche, Louisiana.

Guitar Slim's next release, "The Story Of My Life," was a powerful follow-up and came from his initial Specialty session. Once again *Cash Box* spotlighted it by giving it its weekly award and calling it "another powerful item. His mournful tale is accentuated by the chanter's stylings and impressive guitar work."

His guitar work was indeed impressive, less lyrical but more visceral than his solo on "The Things That I Used To Do." Frank Zappa, one of Guitar Slim's biggest fans, ranks it as one of his favorite guitar solos of all time. In the February '82 *Guitar Player* he elaborated: "It's got that 'I don't give a fuck about nothin', I'm gonna play whatever I want in here, and you guys can hang it in your ass' kind of primitive abandonment."

Lambert still relishes the days of the mid '50s, barnstorming the country. "We had the best band out there," he affirms. "Fats, B.B. King, even Lionel Hampton–we could cut 'em all. We had trouble following Slim at first, because he'd always jump meter, but it got to where we'd just jump right with him and it would sound fine. Slim was a showman and a musician. He'd have purple suits, orange suits, green suits, with shoes and hair to match. He'd make motions and faces that would drive people berserk. You couldn't hardly get into the place when he was playing."

Earl King agrees: "Slim could play at the Dew Drop and get a mob of people, and the next night play in Shrewsbury [in adjacent Jefferson Parish] and get the same mob. Even

"We had trouble following him at first, because he would always jump meter, but it got to where we'd just jump right with him and it would sound fine."

– Lloyd Lambert

the people who knew him to say 'hi' in the streets would think nothing of driving 100 miles to go see him that same night."

When the first electric Fender basses came on the market, Slim wanted one for his band and talked Lambert into buying it. Although Lambert became one of the first electric bass players, Earl King says that it took a lot of convincing on Slim's part to prod him into buying the new bass. "When he saw that B.B. King's band had one, that was it. Slim wanted everything electric. If Slim would have seen all the gadgetry that's out today, it would be ridiculous. When the Cadillacs came out with all that gadgetry he was just like a little kid. He just marveled over that–seats moving, water shooting." Slim stayed so busy that Specialty had to arrange to record while the group was touring. Lambert recalled that the second Specialty session took place at Chess Studios in Chicago, and produced "Sufferin' Mind" in 1955, with Art Rupe flying in from L.A. to produce.

Rupe, however, took it upon himself to bury Slim's guitar way down in the mix, and even added a Hammond organ. The session lost a little of the New Orleans feel, but it was identifiable Slim just the same. His final Specialty session took place in early 1956 and was recorded in Los Angeles, before he switched to the Atlantic/Atco label.

Even though Slim's record sales began dipping, he was still a top attraction. He and the band criss-crossed the country, playing to overflow houses. When he came in off the road, he would spend the days in a lazy manner, usually drinking with friends at the Dew Drop or the Sugar Bowl.

Atlantic recorded Slim both in New York and at Cosimo's in New Orleans, according to Lambert. There was little departure from the last Specialty sessions (although voices were occasionally added and the horn section beefed up), largely due to the strength of Lloyd Lambert's tight band. However, on a previously unissued track, "Along About Midnight" (available on *Texas Guitar–From Dallas To L.A.*), Slim is backed by a host of New York jazz heavyweights, including bassist Percy Heath, saxophonist Johnny Griffin, pianist Elmo Hope, and drummer Philly Joe Jones.

Atlantic must have been somewhat disappointed, though, in their attempts with Slim. They had visions of crossing his records into the teenage market on the same scale Chess had done with Chuck Berry, but had little success. As it would turn out, his last Atco session in 1958 would produce the prophetically titled "When There's No Way Out" and "If I Had My Life To Live Over."

> *"I live three days to y'all's one. The world won't owe me a thing when I'm gone."*
> – Guitar Slim

Despite doctors' warnings about his heavy drinking, by 1958 Slim was really sick and getting weaker, so much so that he was unable to travel and forced to stay in Thibodaux. "I wouldn't say he was a pretty good drinker," says Lambert. "He was the best! Slim just wouldn't take care of himself. He lived fast; different women every night. I'd try and tell him to eat good and get his rest, but he'd say, 'Lloyd, I live three days to y'all's one. The world won't owe me a thing when I'm gone.'"

Earl King gives some insight into the last days of Guitar Slim: "Slim got ruptured [from riding the guitar onstage], and I think that's what caused him to drink more than he ever had. Man, when he came in off that last tour, he almost had to wear a truss. I went over to visit him in Thibodaux when he was sick, and he had empty 100 proof bottles laying all over his room. The doctor told him to stay off that hard liquor, but what are you gonna tell a guy who drinks a pint of gin and chases it with a fifth of black port every day?"

Strangely enough, Slim had quit drinking the last months of his life, according to some. "Slim was getting ready to go on another tour," continues Earl. "Slim sat in the Dew Drop one night and was talking very straight and serious. He told me, 'Earl, all this liquor I been drinkin', all the wrong things I been thinkin', you know my body's been slowly sinkin'.' That's when I went over and asked Hosea Hill, 'Is there something wrong with Slim?' He said, 'No, he's fine. He just got out of the hospital, and he's not even drinking. Why do you ask that?' I said, 'Because Slim talks too straight tonight; he's not funny. He's never under the weather about anything.' That was the last time I saw him."

In February 1959, the group embarked on a tour of dances and nightclubs in New York State. "We went up to Rochester," recalls Lambert, "and Slim came up to me and said, 'Lloyd, I'm tired, I don't think I can make it no more. Y'all got a good band; you can get another singer.' I said, 'Come on, Slim, you can make it. You just been with a broad or something.' He said, 'No, Lloyd, my time is up.' So we played the dance, and when it came time for Slim to come on, he could only do part of the first song and couldn't finish.

"We drove to Newark to play the next night, and Slim played the gig but he collapsed right after. One of the valets ran and got a doctor, and the doctor looked at Slim and said, 'Check this man into a hospital; he's really sick.' We were gonna stay in New York, because that's where our next date was. So we drove up to the Cecil Hotel, and I sent the valet across to take Slim to the doctor while I checked into the hotel. When I got to the desk, there was a telephone call waiting for me from the valet. He said, 'Lloyd, Slim's dead.' I didn't believe it, because I'd seen him not more than five minutes before. We got in the station wagon and drove 'round the corner to the doctor's. But sure enough Slim was layin' up on the table, gone."

Word of Slim's death was slow getting back to New Orleans. The *Louisiana Weekly* was a full week late in its announcement. "Somebody knocked up on my door and said 'Slim's dead,'" remembers King. "I said, 'Man, that can't be true. People like Slim don't die. They're still here when I'm gone.'"

"It wasn't liquor that killed him," specifies Lambert. "The doctor said it was bronchial pneumonia. Today, they might have saved him, but all that drinking and hard living brought his resistance down."

Slim's body was kept in New York by authorities to see if drugs were involved in his death. Hosea Hill eventually paid the fare to fly Slim's body back to Thibodaux for a massive funeral at the Mt. Zion Baptist Church. Guitar Slim now lies in an unmarked grave next to his benefactor, Hosea Hill. He was buried with his gold-top Gibson Les Paul.

So ended the all-too-short life of the 32-year-old Guitar Slim. He is survived by several common-law wives, and a number of children, one of whom plays guitar in the small clubs around New Orleans and who keeps Slim's name alive. Hardly a year has passed since his death that someone hasn't re-recorded one of his songs. Earl King's 1982 version of Slim's anthem, "It Hurts To Love Someone," only reinforces the timelessness of his work.

Almost everyone is adamant about what would have happened if Slim were alive today. "He'd have been on the scale of a B.B. King or a Ray Charles," says Earl King.

Lloyd Lambert states simply, "No question about it. Guitar Slim would have been the biggest."

A SELECTED GUITAR SLIM DISCOGRAPHY

Solo albums: *The Things That I Used To Do* ('54-'56), Ace; *Guitar Slim & Earl King: Battle Of The Blues* (nine Specialty sides), Ace; *Red Cadillacs & Crazy Chicks* ('51-'58), Sundown; *Atco Sessions* ('56-'58), Atlantic; *Sufferin' Mind*, Specialty.

Anthologies: *Atlantic Blues: Guitar* ('56-'57), Atlantic; *Texas Guitar–From Dallas To L.A.*, Atlantic; *Blues Masters, Volume 1: Urban Blues*, Rhino; *Legends Of Guitar–Electric Blues, Vol. 1*, Rhino; *Blues Guitar Blasters*, Ace; *Kings Of The Blues*, Ace.

Buddy Guy

April 1990 & February 1993

BY JAS OBRECHT

IT'S ALMOST MIDNIGHT AT LEGENDS, Buddy Guy's popular Chicago blues club, and our host is two-and-a-half hours into his set. He whoops, shouts, and sings with the passion of a country preacher faced with the fires of perdition. A quick jerk of his left hand, and his band drops to a *whisper*. He raises his eyebrows, grins charismatically, and careens into a solo like a runaway Mack.

The crowd roars wildly as Guy leaps from the stage to prowl the house. Surrounded by fans, he wails from the aisles, the pool tables and video machines, even from *inside* the ladies' room. His band pumps hard as he journeys outside the front door onto the icy corner of 8th and South Wabash, never missing a lick. A nearby El roars past, momentarily drowning out the band. Guy looks up and laughs: "That train is messing my time up!" He rushes back inside to finish his solo on tiptoe, his back against a wall as overhand runs and choked bends segue into a patented Muddy Waters lick.

Long before the sweat dries, you're sure of one thing: Like hurricanes, tornadoes, and earthquakes, there's no holding back Buddy Guy.

Jimi Hendrix sat at his feet. Eric Clapton insisted in *Musician* magazine that "Buddy Guy is by far and without a doubt the best guitar player alive.... If you see him in person, the way he plays is beyond anyone. Total freedom of spirit." Jeff Beck recalls the night he stopped by Legends with Stevie Ray Vaughan: "That was just the most incredible stuff I ever heard in my life. We all jammed, and it was *so* thrilling. That is as close as you can come to the heart of the blues."

Opened in 1989, Buddy Guy's Legends has become a mecca for rockers and bluesmen. During our visit, saxophone great A.C. Reed got up to sing a dirty blues, and B.B. Odom plowed through a set of his namesake's best-known tunes. Other famous drop-ins include Hubert Sumlin, Robert Lockwood, Jr., Eric Clapton, Bill Wyman and Ron Wood, Joe Walsh, Jimmy Vaughan, and Buddy's longtime playing partner, harmonica ace Junior Wells. (Blues-approved players preferred! Staffers still smirk about the night a batch of puffheads from the nearby NAMM Show stopped by and cleared the stage–and audience–with pyrotechnic blazing.)

What's going to happen on any given night is anyone's guess. Greg Rzab, a 30-year-old bassist who cut his teeth with James Cotton and Otis Rush before becoming the mainstay of Buddy's band, explains: "We've had this particular group about a month; Buddy just hires people and we

play. I've seen him do this many times, like a snake moulting. In fact, during the four years I've been with him, there hasn't been one rehearsal–ever. And with all the bands that have been here, I've never heard him direct any musician. There's no script. Buddy comes onstage and just starts playing. Sometimes it's like he's plugged into a 240-volt socket–all of a sudden, he'll burst into some stuff, and no one knows where it comes from! He plays some things with the same tone and feel, but there's no pattern in his playing, so we just wing it. I keep the groove happening, so he keeps me around. It's a great gig, and a lot of fun."

At 53, Buddy Guy still looks remarkably young. Face to face in Legends' small, bare-bulb back office, he sometimes bears an unnerving resemblance to Jimi Hendrix. Despite his supreme talent, he's criminally under-recorded. Raised in Louisiana, he cut his first sides in Baton Rouge in 1957; within a year, he was recording in Chicago with Otis Rush and Willie Dixon sitting in as his sidemen. He became a house guitarist for Chess Records in the early '60s, backing Muddy Waters and Howlin' Wolf, among others, but didn't release a full-fledged solo album until 1968's *A Man & The Blues*. His solo sessions escalated in the late '60s and early '70s, when he was frequently paired with Junior Wells. Since the mid '70s, though, he's been poorly represented on vinyl, except for portions of *Stone Crazy* (recorded in France during the late '70s) and a few live tracks released by Antone's Records. His ambition at the time of this 1990 interview was to someday record an album of the *real* Buddy Guy.

You're really a gentleman towards other players. You move to the side of the stage when they solo. You play great chords behind them.

[*Smiles.*] Yes. You know, I was taught by the greatest musicians that ever lived. And that was Muddy Waters and the Wolf and [Little] Walter and them. And they never did *dominate*, although they were, in my book, dominating musicians. I had a chance to come up there with them. Junior, James Cotton–we all taking lessons from those people. And in order for someone else to carry on, we have to just say, "Okay, here's your shot." I didn't get that. There's this young kid I got, Scott Holt; he's out of Tennessee, and his dad and his mama thanks me now, because I had to *fight* my way up. There was so many guitar players when I came to Chicago, you were just one out of the bucket. And there was so many places.

Your bandmates claim that you never try to cut other guitarists.

No, I don't, but I don't hold back. I was shy all of my life, up until I really got here [in Chicago], and Muddy Waters slapped me in the face. Him and Wolf and Walter and them

told me there ain't no such thing as that. I'm going to tell you exactly like they said: "There ain't no such thing as that shit." They said, "We know you can play, and you gonna play." Because I didn't want to get in their way. That's why I got a chance to make quite a few records with those guys. And I was so nervous at them asking me to play, I would lose a lot. I was afraid to even play what I knew, because I'd say, "How can I show who *I* am, sitting behind Muddy Waters, Wolf, or Walter," or any of the other greats that I played with–John Lee Hooker, Big Mama Thornton, just to name a few. And it all flashes back to me now when I'm playing onstage with these young kids. Sure, I feel proud letting them see what I'm doing, because I'm self-taught. It's a God-gifted talent that I have, because I've never been taught guitar by anybody.

John Lee Hooker says that a lot of young players can play flashy solos, but have trouble keeping a groove.

Music is just like the automobile: You get in it, you look for air conditioning, you look for heat, and you look for that thing to almost take care of you. These young people are saying, "I'm playing what's gonna take me to videos and MTV," whereas I suppose John Lee–and I'm not speaking for him–I suppose John Lee and myself and Muddy and all of us were just playing for what we like. When I learned how to play guitar, I wasn't looking forward to making a decent living at it, because there wasn't no such thing as that. We were playing for the love of blues. And the kind of blues that John Lee and I play, young people are going to take it and improve it. This is what they're doing. Our music don't take us into bigger spotlights as these young kids' music do. You know, the record companies are looking for young, good-looking, talented musicians doing something different, and the young people are record buyers. And the way they're playing those guitars is being sold to those young people, and that's what it's all about.

I would like to be commercially successful, but the love I have for blues sometimes makes me forget about how successful I could be–or wealthy, should I say–at my music. A lot of great friends have did a lot for me just by speaking about me, or speaking about my playing, which has helped me a lot. And I owe them a lot of big thanks for that.

Does having people like Clapton claiming you're the greatest living guitar player cause any pressure?

I feel good about him saying that, because it helped me with who I am. I don't have albums out that compare to Stevie and Eric and Beck and the rest of those people. My albums come seldom and *very* seldom, because I'm not with a company or anything now. I haven't had an album out in going on 12 years. And when someone like Eric makes a statement like that, it's great, but I don't want to pat myself on the back and try and live up to that. I don't let that cross my mind. I still just want to be Buddy Guy. I thank him for saying something like that, but man, you've got him for number one, Stevie, and quite a few more. That's a big question mark there–how good I am, or the best one alive. Now, I don't know about that. Because if you go catch him, he can make you almost forget about what he said, because he can play.

You own Legends, where you could control your sound. Why not tape a live album here?

I wish I could. I'd jump in Lake Michigan on a night like tonight and swim if someone would come say, "I want to do an album on you live." I just want to be treated right. I want to be Buddy Guy on an album. The closest I've ever come is *Stone Crazy*, and I had to do that in France. The guy I did it for named the label after my mother, Isabel, and he said, "I want you to do what you've wanted to do all your life." I said, "What's that?" He said, "Be Buddy Guy." I said, "I'd be glad, then, to do an album for you."

I guess this is why I don't have a company giving me a shot at it now, because I really wants to be Buddy Guy. I wants to play the

West Side soul: Young Buddy tearing it up during the Chess era.

things that never came out of me that I know I have. And if I get that opportunity next time I go into the studio, I'm going to give it. If it sells, fine. If it don't, I will please myself inside because I know what I *can* do, and I'm not going to be shy with it anymore. I don't want anybody teaching me how to play when the tapes are rolling; I've had that happen to me a lot in the past. I've got to play what I already know.

You do have your own style. No one plays like Buddy Guy.

Thank you, but that leads back to being self-taught. I've got some bad habits in the way I play. That's the way I taught myself, and I can't get away from it.

What bad habits?

I play a stiff hand. My right hand is very stiff; it's not relaxed. My picking is very hard. I tears up a lot of my Ernie

Ball strings at night. I have to keep them by the stack. I tears into my guitar with my whole heart, soul, and body. When I decided in 1967 to go professional, traveling as a leader, I left a day job driving a tow truck. And my boss told me, "Whenever you feel like coming back, you don't have to ask for a job. Just come in here and punch your time clock." And I do my guitar the same way. I feel towards my music just like I did when I was working. If I'm going to do it, I want to do it to death.

Was that your last day job?

Yeah. I went on vacation in 1967, and the manager I had then, Dick Waterman, told me, "The people love you out there." I said, "How could they love me? They don't know who I am. I just want to make sure I don't starve." My mother and father were living then, and I wanted to try to help them. I didn't trust myself on the road, as sometimes now I doubt my playing, even though Eric and them make those statements about it. But I think it's proven itself now. When I go places, quite a few people will be there saying, "I want to hear you." That lifts me a lot. And when I left on vacation that time, I went to Ann Arbor, Michigan. I had three pieces. I started playing some of my wild licks, and you could hear the kids between songs saying, "He's been listening to Hendrix." And then another guy would say, "No, that's who Hendrix got his influence from." So, they got to me and said, "You listen to Hendrix?" And I said, "Who is Hendrix?" And this kid looks like, "You've got to be crazy, if you don't know who that is." So I said, "I've got to find out who this is."

So I go to Toronto, my next stop, at an outdoor festival called Mariposa. There was about 30,000 people there, and naturally I got shaky nervous. A.C. Reed said, "Man, go burn them. If they don't know you now, they'll know you when you finished." So I said, "Okay, man, if you say so, I'm going to *try*." And I decided to jump off the stage. I thought there was a brace to brace myself back when I leaped off, but there wasn't nothing there but a curtain. But it so happened that I didn't fall; the curtain saved me. So I said to myself, "The best thing to do is don't stop playing." When I came from under there, there was 30,000 people hollering, "That's Buddy Guy! That's the real Buddy Guy."

Did you ever meet Hendrix?

Yes, I did. I've got a film of it now. The night Dr. Martin Luther King got assassinated, I saw a kid come in with a big hat on and ease up to the stage with a tape recorder. And some amateur cameraman was spotting his video on him. This was in New York City, and they were yelling about him being Jimi Hendrix. I was just doing what I had to do, and he said, "Pay them no mind. I've been trying to catch you. I canceled a show in London just to come see you play, because I'd never seen you. But I heard you, and I stole a lot of licks from you." As a matter of fact, a kid just came in the club and said, "I've got a tape I want to show you: Hendrix on his knees, taping your licks and watching you play with your mouth, with the guitar under your feets, and different things like that."

Did you get some of that from Guitar Slim?

I got all of it from Guitar Slim. I don't want to make a comment about what some other guitar players would say, but Guitar Slim and T-Bone Walker are some of the people I copied for *showmanship*. B.B. King, he don't have to do nothing but just shake his left hand and everybody will listen. But the first time I saw Guitar Slim, a guy brought him in on his shoulders like a little baby. And he had on a red suit–I got one back there now for tonight–with some white shoes. And when I heard him, I said, "My God! This is the

way a guitar should be played."

If you're not going to give it all you've got, you shouldn't play anymore, because you owe this to the people. Your fans are your supporters. Don't hold nothing back from them. You owe them everything that they come to see. And strangely enough, since I've been professional, I haven't missed a gig yet. I had the flu last night enough for the average guitar player to say, "Get somebody in my place," and stay at home. But I think somebody was sitting there last night saying, "I wants to see Buddy. I wants to see him play." And I owe that to him. I'm going to come if I have to come on my knees and play.

What should a Buddy Guy solo be all about?

Muddy Waters, T-Bone, Guitar Slim, and B.B. King, and Eric Clapton. I could name them for an hour.

And yet you don't sound like any of them.

I guess that's the Buddy Guy coming out in me then, but I be hitting the same strings, the same fingering of the board, that they do. And the same thing goes for them. You know, I can't be a B.B. King. I can't be an Eric, even though I try a lot. I wonder a lot–what's my problem about not getting records out? So I try to be everybody up there at once–even John Lee Hooker and Lightnin' Hopkins. And please believe me, I'm not lying: Even before I go out tonight, all of these people will cross my mind just as I pick up my guitar. It looks like they're telling me, "Go get it, Buddy. Do it!" Because without those people, I don't even know if I would be playing. Yes, they were sending a message to me while they were alive, and I think they're still sending it to me now, saying, "You've got to play. We left this load on your shoulders, and you've got to carry on." Matter of fact, Muddy told me that two weeks before he passed. I heard he was sick, and Junior Wells and I called him. I said, "We're on our way to your house." He said, "Don't come, because I'm doing fine. Just don't let the blues die." And the next time I heard, it was the international press saying, "How do you feel about Muddy passing?" And I couldn't say nothing for a day. I just sat there. I just couldn't believe it. You know, those things are going to happen to all of us.

Do any conversations with Muddy stand out in your mind?

Yes. I was very shy when I started. I wouldn't sing, but I would play if you'd corner me off, and I'd play well. And Muddy went out there one night and said, "Gee, that guy can play," but when he called me out of the room, I just shied back in the corner and said, "Pay him no mind, man. He's just talking like that." And he just turned around and slapped me, man! And it was hard enough for me to say, "Why are you doing that?" He said, "I don't want to hear that from you. You gonna play." After that he just took over like a daddy to me, man.

As a matter of fact, Muddy was the one… I was going on my third day without eating in Chicago, trying to borrow a dime to call my mom to get back to Louisiana. And Muddy Waters bought me a salami sandwich and put me in the back of his 1958 Chevy station wagon. He said, "You're hungry, and I know it." And talking to Muddy Waters, I wasn't hungry anymore; I was full just for him to say, "Hey." I was so overjoyed about it, my stomach wasn't cramping anymore. I told him that, and Muddy said, "Get in the goddamn car." Yes, he's dead and gone, and that's exactly what he told me. This happened at the famous 708 Club, and he was parked in front of the club. And then he said, "Sit down and eat." I said, "Yes, sir!" [*Laughs.*] I wish he were here now. I thanked him many times before he passed away, and told him how much better I felt after he slapped me and made me eat that sandwich that night.

And then later he just walked up to Junior and grabbed him in the collar and went to slapping him. Junior said, "Why are you doing that to me?" And Muddy said, "Remember you used to stay at my house? And remember you pulled your knife on me?" Junior had pulled a knife on him because the whole band was staying at his house, and he found out that the drummer or somebody didn't pay him rent, so Junior felt that he shouldn't pay no rent. [*Laughs.*] Muddy said, "I got you where you don't have the knife now, and I'll whoop your ass!" And he starts spanking Junior all in the face. Junior wasn't saying nothing, just holding his head down. I said, "You going to fight back, Junior?" He said, "No, I ain't going to fool with that old man." [*Laughs.*]

Yeah, good old man. He could spank me now if he was here. I wouldn't say nothing but laugh and go drink me some beer behind that man. [*Laughs.*] Yeah, I deserve a spanking from somebody that great, man, because those people paved the way for the electric music that we play now. I don't know if anybody else would give them that credit, but them, and the Chess Records, left a great trail for us to follow. Yes, they did.

You recorded with Muddy early in your career.

Yes, I did. He had heard about me because I'd played a set or two with a horn player by the name of Rufus Foreman, and Magic Sam had seen me play. And the word was just getting around: "This little black guy from Louisiana can play, man. He's playing these Muddy Waters tunes." Naturally, that's what I was playing–B.B. or Muddy or Jimmy Reed. It just caught on, and they took me in like a kid. For instance, for one of Muddy's albums, Leonard Chess said, "I want to go way back and have an acoustic album," and I got to play on that [*Folk Singer*]. As a matter of fact, I'm fixing to do some things with Eric Clapton the first week in February

[1990], and from then on I'm going to do two or three songs each and every night with my acoustic. Because it takes me back to the sound that you can't take away from the guitar.

Is Folk Singer *one of your favorite albums?*

Yes, but everything I did with Muddy Waters is my favorite. Everything I ever did with that guy, man, was like an experience to me. I often tell young people right now that those are some shoes that never will be fulfilled. I used to listen to that guy sing "Got My Mojo Working," and it was like my mother sewing on a sewing machine. She would make her feet make the stitches, and she never would stick her finger when she pushed under that needle. And that's just the way he would sing "Mojo Working." And whatever he sang, he could make me sit there all night. During those days, there wasn't hardly a club in Chicago that didn't stay open until 5:00 in the morning. And you better believe they had to kick me out of it, because I couldn't miss a lick of it. [*Laughs.*] My manager gave me an album of everything he ever recorded [*Muddy Waters* box set], and I can go lie down on my floor now and put them on one by one, and don't miss nothing he said or what he played.

Do you own a lot of records?

Not so much of the new stuff. Not much of my stuff. But him, and B.B. King, and the Wolf.

What records do you treasure the most?

"Sweet Little Angel" by B.B. King, and Muddy Waters' catalog. And I got everything Eric ever played, him and Stevie, and all of the guys. I think we listen to each other a lot. And when we meet, that makes us communicate better too.

Stevie Ray covered your "Leave My Girl Alone" during his tour with Jeff Beck.

Yeah, he's a great friend of mine. Matter of fact, he came here as a special guest on my birthday. He walks in the door, and these people just go crazy. And now he tells me just call him; anytime he's available, he will come sit in here with me to help keep the club going.

Your version of "Leave My Girl Alone" has one of your characteristic sounds–the double-stop with a constant high note over a hammer-on in the lower voice.

It's kind of like an octave with two fingers. You pick the two strings at the same time, but they're different notes. I could probably show you better than I could explain it to you. I don't have long fingers, but I can stretch over almost five frets. I can play the *A* note on the *E* string, and take the *G* string and go five frets down and drag the little finger back up and play those octaves all the way back up until the fingers go together, plucking two strings at the same time.

What's the secret to playing those Buddy Guy wildman bends?

I use my third finger. It seems to be the strongest one. It's hard for me to explain what I'll be doing, but when I'm up there trying to please that audience, I can bend it from here to the front door of this place [*laughs*]. Eric mentioned something about that once. I just will bend it until it breaks. I'll make the little *E* kiss the big *E*. Yes, and if it sounds good, I'll keep getting it. And if it sounds bad, I just try to make it sound good.

Do you back that ring finger up with other fingers?

I don't have to. You just have to practice and get your fingers real strong. I'm not the best guitar player. I've got a lot I should learn, or could learn, but I always thought that other finger has to be ready for something else. I can't just depend on it on that string, because if you stay on that one string, you'll wear your welcome out. So I have to stretch it, make it kiss the *E*, and go grab another one and take it somewhere else. I try to make the best that I can out of it.

Describe how you add vibrato.

You mean with the left hand? It's similar to what B.B. King does, rocking back and forth with the hand, but I'm not as good as him. I don't think anybody can do that as well as he can, and we talked about that. As a matter of fact, last year [1989] was the first time I opened the show for him—twice—and you better believe I had to hurry up and get my front-row seat so I could try to get some tips on that man. This guy invented the squeezing. T-Bone was playing the neck of the guitar, but when B.B. started squeezing that guitar, we *all* started squeezing that thing. I have to give it to him, because I got more into guitar than I'd ever been. I was just so in love with playing blues, I would play Lightnin' Hopkins and T-Bone. And then when he squeezed the guitar, I said, "Jesus Christ! Who is this?" And when I saw him, I thought I had a lot to learn. And I'm still like that [*laughs*].

How far back does your knowledge of blues go? Are you familiar with players from the 1920s?

Yes. Strangely enough, I'm one of the luckiest blues guitar players alive in that respect, because I had a chance to play with Arthur Crudup in Australia. We went on tour together. I had a chance to play with Fred McDowell. And Son House, who just passed a year-and-a-half ago; I understand he taught Muddy. So what else can you ask for if you're a guitar player and had a chance to sit down with *this* guy and play? Those are the kind of things that keep us all going.

When do you play your best?

When I'm not trying to be my best. When I'm not pressing myself to try to make this audience get into what I'm doing. I feel like I'm not doing a good job if I don't see them smiling or saying, "Yes." For example, when we first started going to Europe playing blues, the Europeans were like, "We take this as a *serious* music, almost like opera." Nobody said

anything or patted their feet—nothing. I was thinking, "Oh, Jesus. I'm not doing nothing right now. Maybe I got to flip out or do something." Then I got booed. I talked to Muddy again, and he said, "Don't feel bad. It happened to me." When Chris Barber took Muddy back to England for the first time, they booed him for playing this loud stuff through the amp! They invited him back the next year, and he left the amp and took the acoustic guitar, and they booed him for not playing the amp! [*Laughs.*] The same thing happened to me in Germany. I had to go stepping out in front of Roosevelt Sykes, John Lee Hooker, and Big Mama Thornton, and they would just boo every time they'd see me. I said, "Oh, my God!" Me being shy, man, I was just like going under the table. And then when I went back, I said, "I know what I'll do. I'll get me a chair and sit down like John Lee and them and play." I went back, and they got me the same way they did Muddy. They said, "No, no. You've got to get out there and move around. That's what we're looking for now." It takes you so long to figure out what they're saying, unless someone comes up and translates it for you.

You're said to be one of the first Chicago blues guitarists to play standing up.

When I came to Chicago, everybody was sitting down: Muddy, Junior, the Wolf, Walter, and all of them were in chairs playing this beautiful music that still is the best blues you ever heard of. And we used to have the Battle of the Guitars. I was the poorest, and I told them I needed the more-est [*laughs*]. Most of the bandstands used to be behind the bar, and Muddy, Wolf, or Walter would play in their chairs. So I said, "Oh, jeez, these guys is playing way more than I can play. I got to figure out something else to do to be a winner." The winner got a bottle of whiskey, and at that time I didn't drink whiskey. I had a little friend who weighed about 300, and he said, "I'll make you win this whiskey, because I don't have a nickel." It was snowing, and he said, "You remember that thing you told me Guitar Slim used to do?" I had this 150-foot lead wire, and he said, "I'm going to take this wire outside, and you sit in the car. I'm going to plug it in while you're in the car. You come out of this car playing and sliding in the snow, and we got the whiskey." I said, "That's not going to win it, but I'm going to do it."

And when they called me, I stepped out of the car. He opened the door and said, "You all want to see him, come out here." The place was packed, and I had the streets full. So when I walked in, there was Magic Sam and a few more guitar players—including Earl Hooker, who is the greatest guitar player that I ever saw. They had the bottle of whiskey, and it was empty. They told me, "You won it, but we done drinked it all!" [*Laughs.*] The club owner came out and picked me up and stood me on the bar, and I walked straight down the bar. And then he said, "Here's another bottle of whiskey." And that little guy looked at me and said, "Let's go to the bathroom." And I went in the men's bathroom and played for about 45 minutes solo!

Wasn't that called "headcutting"?

Yes, but I don't think I would outplay anybody. It was just like a winner in a contest. We didn't have just one judge saying, "Buddy, you won it." The audience would clap, and it was kind of like something on TV a long time ago, when they'd show a gauge needle move according to how loud the audience clapped. After a while it got to the point where they'd say,

"I was taught by the greatest musicians that ever lived. And that was Muddy Waters and the Wolf and Little Walter and them."

"Well, I don't care who wins it, we're going to drink it anyway, because he doesn't drink!" [*Laughs.*] So I learned a lot from that, and I got a lot of experience from it. Those guys like Earl Hooker, man, they couldn't jump around and run up and down the bar like I did, and that's the advantage I took of them.

No one ever played slide like Earl Hooker.

No. I found one of Muddy's tunes in this collection I've got, and he had Hooker playing on it. As it struck, my guitar player said, "Listen to Muddy!" I said, "That's not Muddy; that's Earl Hooker. Nobody plays it that clean, and you don't hear nothing but the strings."

What did he use for a slide?

I got it! I got his slide in my pocket at home, and I sleep with that thing. It's just a piece of pipe like anybody else used.

You're not usually associated with slide guitar.

I learned a little of Muddy's slide, but it don't ever come out. I'm embarrassed to come out with it. After I heard Earl Hooker play slide, I put that thing I was using in my pocket–it was a bottleneck–and I said, "I don't even want to see that no more, the way this guy plays."

Did you ever play in open tuning?

No, I never did. When I finally met B.B. King, he took me to his hotel room–I didn't even use a straight pick then, I was using fingerpicks–and he told me, "If you want to get a little faster, you have to start practicing with a straight pick." And from him telling me that, I would have one ever since.

You hold the pick with your thumb and two fingers.

Because I can switch it into my palm, and you won't miss it. All of a sudden, I'm picking with my fingers. My pick's like a small triangle. I have to buy them by the thousands because I break them. [*Pulls a Gibson medium rounded-triangle from his pocket.*] That's a heavyweight; the thin is the one I use mostly. I also have a [coffee-colored] Buddy Guy pick that I give away to people as souvenirs.

Do you always know what you're doing in musical terms?

No.

Do you know the names of chords?

A few. F, F#, and flats, and so on like that. You learn that through the years.

Do you always know what key you're playing in?

Yes. You have to know that. But if you'd asked me what did I just play before I left the stage, each note–no, I couldn't tell you. But I could go back and get the guitar and find it and tell you what note I played.

If you're in the key of A, for instance, will you automatically solo in a certain area of the fingerboard?

Yes. I know exactly where I want to be. On all of the new guitars–except the acoustics–you've got several places you can play A. I play A in the middle of the neck on the 5th fret, and then you can go to the high A, which is *way* up there. You start all over again at E when you get higher [at the 12th fret]. It goes, E, F, the same as it is at the beginning of the neck. I don't run enough in the different positions on my guitar like a lot of people do. For instance, George Benson is one of the greatest I've seen; he can do that from top to bottom. I have a tendency to stay there and wear a hole in the neck of my guitar [*laughs*] and just play one sound. Oh, that sounds so good! Someone stole my first Strat from me, and Eric had asked me about buying it. I had wore that neck almost through, and I didn't want to get it redone because I wanted it to stay original, just like it was.

You're now endorsing Fender and Guild.

Yes. I started with a Strat in the beginning. Guitar Slim was tearing 'em up every time I saw him–that's just the kind of wild man he was–and I wanted to be like him so much, I just went into that. And that guitar was built to take it. I finally went to Newport in 1967, and the owner of Guild offered me an endorsement. What else could I ask for? He walks up and says, "You come over to the factory tomorrow; we're going to give you a guitar." And I started playing the Guild guitar. Then B.B. King walked in in New York and said, "I see you got a little Lucille." [*Laughs.*] It was red, and that was enough to make me stick with playing that. It was a semi-hollow Starfire. Now I have a Nightingale. They made one for Eric and one for me. Mine is number 002.

I pop so many strings from playing so darn hard that I have to keep two or three guitars up there to make sure the few fans I got don't miss anything. When I break a string, I don't want to take that time in between and have them missing that note. My guy just hands me another guitar while he puts the string on the other one.

What's your favorite guitar?

The two I'm playing, the Fender and the Guild.

Does your tone change when you use a wireless?

Yes, a bit. Actually, a cord is as true as the acoustic guitar. It gives you the truer sound.

What's your favorite setup from the guitar?

I'm using a Marshall amp. Different clubs will call for you to do different sets on the amp. Sometimes you can be too loud, and normally I will ask the audience, "Am I too loud, or am I too soft?" because I do play very soft sometimes. And then you get the mixed emotions. Some will say, "You're too loud," and then the other half will say, "You're not loud enough." So then I just back up from the mike and tell a big lie, like, "I'm going to do it my way anyway!" I usually use a Marshall 800 amp, but they just sent me the new two-piece head. My soundman hooked it up for me last night and said, "Go for it!" I kind of liked it, but I've got to learn it and play with it for a while. Then I'll be able to get my different sounds and things that *I* like best out of that myself. I play for the people, and if it calls for it, I'll use a wah-wah or an octave [divider]. I'm not trying to be like anybody else.

Do you modify your Strats?

No, this one I have now is special-made for me. They made one for Eric Clapton, and they called me in there to pick out the neck and the kind I want. And without even knowing what he had, I just went for this. They said it was too close to put out a Buddy Guy model or something like that, but it's a bit different from what he picked out.

Some players insist that old Strats are the best.

Well, I've talked to quite a few of the engineers, and they will tell you it's just like the car now compared to the cars in the '40s and '50s. You could run one of those old cars into these things we got now, and that car out of the '50s is going to have a scratch and the one we're riding in now is going to have the grille knocked out because it's plastic. So what they told me is that it's the same thing as talking about guitars. The material's not the same. The wood that they're making them out of now is not the same. And why is that? I don't know.

Actually, I was in Africa in 1969 with my original Strat. We were riding in a station wagon, and it was tied on the top of the station wagon. They was driving 85 and 90 miles an hour, and the guitar flew off and fell out of the case. We backed up to get it, and a car was coming. I laid in the street to make sure the car would go around. The guy said, "African people will run over you, man! They don't care nothing about it." And the only string that was out of tune was the *E.* [*Laughs.*] It got scratched all up, but it was still in tune.

That guitar got stolen?

Yes, some kid broke into my house when I was living here in Chicago, and I guess I cried as long as I did when my mother passed. The lady next door was a nice old lady, which was the kid's mother, and I guess he was so embarrassed. I even asked him why did he sell it–I would've bought it again. I would even give the guy more than what he got for it. He left his mother's keys in the apartment, and the police said, "Whoever broke into here left the keys," and his mother said, "Those are my keys, and my son did it." Her husband was very sick, and I was loaning her money every month, and she owed me. She said, "Well, I'll have to pay you," and I cried more then. I said, "There's no way you could pay me." I wouldn't even accept it from her, because she didn't do it; she was a very nice lady. As a matter of fact, I talked to her a couple of days ago.

Do you have a guitar at home?

Yeah, a lot of them. I got one in the bed with me now, 12-string acoustic. I use heavier strings at home; that keeps the muscles in my fingers a little stronger.

What do you play when you're by yourself?

I will put the slide on sometimes. If you catch me practicing at home, I hit a few licks that I hit here onstage. And to be honest with you, a lot of stuff you see me do onstage, I've never done it before. Everything I do onstage comes to me right then. I just have this good feeling about blues music and what I'm doing, and I feel like I should *try* it, man, try it. Actually, a lot of the sustained notes that you hear us all doing now–and Hendrix said he was getting this from me–I was doing out in the public early on. Chess Records called it *noise*; they wouldn't let me cut it. They was telling me, "Who's going to listen to that noise?" And where did I get the idea from? Once I took a break and forgot to cut my guitar off, and this lady passed by with a wide skirt. The jukebox was going with a tune I liked–I had punched it–and her dress tail hit the *G* string, and this guitar just stayed there, humming in *G*, the whole time that record was going. I got the idea from that to just hold this sustained note. That had to be '59, or something like that. If you love it like I do, boom! I can just be sitting there listening, and all of a sudden somebody will hit something, and I'll jump and say, "What was that?" It's just like a good-looking woman will pass, and you can't keep your eyes off.

What's the best band you ever had?

If I had to name the best people that I ever played with in my life, I would name the guys traveling with me in about 1967: A.C. Reed, [tenor saxophonist] Bobby Fields, who passed away, a bass player named Jack Meyers, and a drummer named Glen McTeer. But I would have to put Fred Below and Otis Spann in too. Those guys taught me a whole lot, just about being a musician. Below used to look up and curse at me, and he would be counting. You could hear him playing drums, "A-one, two, three…" And when I'd make a mistake, he would tell me right then [*laughs*]. A funny story: When we used to be recording at Chess, they built a pen to put Below in, because Below would interfere with the other musicians, telling them what to play! Oh, man, how I wish nobody had to die, when it comes to something like Below and Otis Spann. Otis Spann would set a bottle of whiskey on a piano and tell me, "If you don't take a drink of this, you ain't going to let the soul out of you." Yeah, they was the best I ever seen, man. They corrected me in so many *wrong* things I was doing in my earlier days. If I was playing a bad time, they would tell me, "You got to clean that up."

Is that where your good sense of rhythm comes from?

I don't know if that's the case. I would listen to them. And right now, I listen to these kids if they tell me something. I've never gotten to the point of, "You can't tell me nothing!" In anything I do, I'm listening. There's people working for me in the club right now. If they tell me something, I don't jump up and say, "Oh, no, this is *my* club. I want it this way; I want it that way." They'll hear, and I've got to listen. That's the way it should be.

You never rehearse your band.

[*Laughs.*] You know, that's a bad habit. But I like for my guys to be free. I don't hold anybody *down* back there

behind me. And tonight I'm going to do the same thing. Let them go, let them loose. On a given night, they're going to give me the best that they can. I didn't ever rehearse with Muddy or any of them. They would tell me, "Go get it, Buddy." Matter of fact, I was playing with B.B. King at Bill Graham's Fillmore West one night, and he said, "I'm going to play, but I want *you* to put on a show."

Do any of your children play guitar?

I got one son, 19 years old. He came to me about a year-and-a-half ago and said, "Daddy, give me one of them guitars. I'm going to play Prince." I gave him a big amplifier and a guitar, and two weeks later I went over, and this guy was playing this thing about the doves on Prince ["When Doves Cry"]. And he looked at me and laughed. He's as much shy as I was when I was a youngster. He said, "I got Prince, now who else should I listen to, Daddy?" I said, "Well, if you like Prince that well, you better find Hendrix. I'll look out for some stuff for you." And before I found anything, he had found a Hendrix show on an educational channel. He came back; he was crying. He said, "Daddy, you know the first thing Hendrix said?" I said, "What?" He said, "He said he learned something from you. I didn't know you could play that." I said, "You didn't ever ask me, son. If you had, I could've told you I gets wild." He never could just see me in person, and I don't have anything on television that he could see. I finally sneaked him in a club and he saw me play, and he cried a little more. I done wrote a song like that, too: My child don't know who I am, so how could I expect other young people to know who I am? That's because I don't have records out.

I just hope to hit something one of these days. Maybe somebody will get back to some record company and say, "You better listen to him, and give him another shot at another album." I don't know. If I knew what my problem was, I would correct it. I would like to do a little better financially, because I'm not getting any younger. I want to play as long as I'm alive, and there'll come a time when you need something to carry you as a musician. I've been lucky enough to buy a couple of raggedy buildings, and I pay a retirement-type insurance, because I don't want to be a burden on nobody if I live long enough to survive this. I don't want nobody to say, "We got to take care of him," make collections for me, and different things like that. And in order to do that, you have to make it while you're in good health and try to save some of it for a later day. My mother used to tell me, "Son, always put up a dry stick for a wet day." A blues player like myself has so many ups and downs–more downs than ups.

Despite this, you seem to love your work.

I love it so much, man, I even forgot what down is like.

Even when I'm down, I think I'm up. If anybody in the business loves it better than me, they must eat it! [*Laughs*.] All my life, I've been doing what I love, and I'm not going to change that for nothing in the world. I'm having a lot of fun, and I've never been angry enough to do something to somebody in a way that would hurt them. All of my life, I've been in between people. When I'm in clubs and two people are disagreeing and it looks like it's going to get physical, I can get in between them and say, "Why? What do you gain by doing this to each other? Tomorrow you could be best friends. Tomorrow he could do something to save your life. But if you hurt him or kill him, who knows what he could have done? He's not there to do it."

The world is so tangled with so much craziness. I think we need to be loved a little more than we do. That's why I'm so thankful for my music. At least I draw people together and try to put smiles on their faces. I'm so tired of frowns and fighting. One day I hope the whole world could just look and smile. Yes, especially when I play a note on my guitar!

February 1993

The sun's barely risen, and the wind howls as if the only thing separating Chicago and the Arctic is a strand of barbed wire. Buddy Guy, though, has been up for hours, shoveling snow, talking to friends, and voraciously poring over a newspaper while sipping steaming coffee in his suburban home. Just back from a video shoot in L.A., he seems happier than a grand prize winner of the Illinois Lotto.

Buddy's new album, *Feels Like Rain*, is ready to ship, and it follows on the heels of the most critically acclaimed release of his career, *Damn Right, I've Got The Blues*. Rowdy and spontaneous, stinging and tough, Buddy's playing on the new disc parries any notions of the old "he can't play like he used to," while his gospel-shout vocals deliver a knockout wallop. He's especially proud of having shuffled Muddy Waters' "Nineteen Years Old" and a couple of his own hard-hitting originals among James Brown, Marvin Gaye, and John Hiatt covers and airways-approved collaborations with Bonnie Raitt, Paul Rodgers, Travis Tritt, and John Mayall.

Like Carlos Santana, Eric Clapton, and precious few others, the 57-year-old Guy is lightning-quick to honor those who inspired him. "Whenever you hear me play, man," he starts the interview, "there's always a part of Muddy Waters, Howlin' Wolf, Little Walter, T-Bone Walker, and all those great musicians. Everybody comes out in me."

During our 1990 interview, you said you'd jump into Lake Michigan in exchange for being able to make the album you wanted to make.

Yeah, but don't make me jump in there this morning–it's zero outside!

Have you come close to that goal?

I think some of the things behind *Damn Right, I've Got The Blues* are. I won a Grammy with it, and I feel very proud of Silvertone Records for giving me the chance. Bonnie Raitt–she's on my next album–she felt the same way. Before that, people were coming up to me and saying, "You got it. I see it. What's *wrong*?" My late friend Stevie, Eric, Beck, Keith [Richards], and all of them, they was coming up to me and saying, "I can't understand. We come out and we play with you, and you're like blowing people off the stage, and won't nobody record you." I didn't let that send me down into the basement and forget about myself. I just kept saying that sooner or later, somebody gonna hear me. I'm just gonna keep on. You don't give up. My parents taught me to try, and I just been trying and trying. It's better late than never. It's very late in the day for me, but...

You're still a young man.

[*Laughs*.] Well, you know, you need glasses, I'll tell you that. Then you'll see what I'm talkin' about. But I'm enjoying it. I'm just very proud, thankful to God that I'm still around to see this thing finally happening to me at this late day and age, but I'm not looking at that. I'm just looking at the fun I'm having and knowing that I'm a part, hopefully, of trying to keep the blues alive. That makes me the happiest man alive.

Feels Like Rain *has some nice covers, but the real guitar genius seems to be in the two songs you wrote.*

[*Laughs*.] Ah, well, this is what we talkin' about. You know, throughout my whole musical career, I've always wanted to just cut loose. And I have been told from the time I came here to Chicago that didn't nobody want to hear that. But, as Albert King says, as the years go passing by, somebody was listening. And if it wasn't Eric, it was Stevie or somebody else who was selling enough records for somebody sooner or later to say, "What the hell they talkin' about? They keep talking about Buddy Guy, but I never heard him. I gotta check him out." I owe the biggest thanks in the world to Eric, the late Stevie, Keith, Beck, and all these people, because they was sellin' records and I wasn't. Finally Silvertone said, "I gotta check this out," and they came to me and said, "Listen, we want you to go in and make a record of Buddy Guy, and we gonna support you." I said, "This is what I been waiting for." At the time I signed, I had an offer from two or three more labels, and the first thing they asked me was, "What have you got new?" And I'm like saying to myself, "I don't need nothin' new. Whatever I got old will sell, if you let me do it." Yeah.

What's the story behind "Country Man"?

I left home with that, man. I had kind of written a song before *Damn Right, I've Got The Blues*, but I wasn't through with the song. It goes through your mind, and if it happens you're out there. I just wanted the fans and the people in general to know that I am a country man. I was born and raised on a farm [in Louisiana]. I'm a sharecropper's son. I know how to pick cotton, feed the chickens, and milk the cows. I want to be famous, but I don't want to be so famous that I forget the people who knew me before I was famous. And this is my expression of lettin' people know I'm gonna stay the same as long as I'm alive. Just come and see me or call me, even if it's early in the morning. I'm not gonna say, "To hell with you." I'm up. I'm walkin' the dog. I'm havin' coffee. I'm out here shovelin' snow, cuttin' grass, washin' the car. I'm no different from nobody else, man. And it's not gonna go to my head because I won a Grammy. Hopefully, if I can win another one it's not gonna change me at all. I wanna talk to you, I want you to come and see me, I want you to drink out of the same beer can with me, and we'll

"I'm gonna stay the same as long as I live," says Buddy, seen here in 1986.

just have fun. You'll say, "That's just another guy" after I leave the stage or before I get to the stage.

You've always seemed to be that way.

Yes, and I'm gonna stay that way. Because I got friends very famous, and it look like something happen to you when you can't just relax. I own the largest blues club here in Chicago, and I go set on the bar. Sometime I have to take my rings off because some people say, "I can't believe I'm shakin' your hand," but they be *breakin'* it. [*Laughs.*] So that's the way I want to live. Some people isolate themselves after they get to be known, but people make you. And people also can break you.

Your other blues original, "She's A Superstar," has a very positive attitude towards women.

That's the general idea of the song. The way I was raised was, "Without a woman, what would we do?" [*Laughs.*] With her, what do we do? That's one of those things: You can't get along with her, but you can't do without her. This song goes out to my sisters, my aunties, my wife, my family, my daughter, and every woman I know. I just want to let them know I got the respect and love for them that I wished everybody had. They stand out. You can't get along with 'em, you can't live without 'em, so what do you do, man? I just come out and let you know. They're superstars in my book.

That solo has some unusual tones.

Yeah, I was using an octave pedal and a wah-wah. That's it. You know, young people are record buyers. Blues records can't crash the big AM stations always, so I'm trying to get some licks. I'm trying to say, okay, if I can get one or two tunes on this album to make you play it, somebody go out and listen to it, they gonna get a taste of the blues right behind that. So I'm trying to get slick enough to trick somebody who's eight or nine or thirteen years old into saying, "Who the hell is that? I went to buy it for this effects he was givin', and he done hit me with this Muddy Waters thing behind it. Who was Muddy Waters?" So I'm trying to keep this music alive through my way of saying I'm gonna outsmart you with the blues. As long as I live, I'm gonna get it in that door one way or another.

Is that why you did a soul cover and some rock and roll?

Ah, no. In a way that could be the truth, but before you're Buddy Guy, before you're Muddy Waters, before you're B.B. King, you have to play everybody. You know, when they was throwin' songs at me, they was looking at me like, "You're a blues player, but look at this." And I said, "Let's cut it." They was looking at me: "You know how to do that?" I said, "Man, what you think I did before I was Buddy Guy?" I had to play everybody's music in Chicago to keep the little $5-a-night gig in the club. I couldn't go in and play all of Buddy Guy's stuff. I didn't have nothin'. I had to play a large variety–Little Richard, Fats Domino, Guitar Slim, and maybe a country and western, which I never did learn that well–so the guy would say, "You can bring him in here on a Friday and a Saturday, because he's playin' what these people want to hear." And that's what made who Buddy Guy is today. And then you get in the studio, and you go for yourself.

You arranged Guitar Slim's "Suffering Mind" like a gospel tune. Have you performed gospel?

I tried to sing gospel. My family is very Baptist, and you know, I'm not a baby. Before the electric guitar, I was listening to Lou Rawls with the Pilgrim Travelers and Sam Cooke with the Soul Stirrers, stuff like that. They didn't have no drums or stuff like that. They was using four, five, six guys, and making that musical sound. Then they came upon the amplified guitars and things and put them into the churches and into the blues. Of course I was singing spiritual stuff, yeah. Not in the church, but I was walkin' in the streets. Not on the corners–it was on the road, where I come from–but I would take a walk and belt it out.

Besides Bonnie Raitt, does anyone else play guitar solos on the record?

Bonnie's guitar player on "Feels Like Rain" [Johnny Lee Schell], he was hittin' some of those notes there with me. Bonnie played the slide, and he was playing most of the rhythm guitar on there.

You're also paired with John Mayall.

[*Laughs.*] Yeah. Well, John is an old friend, man. You know, Eric got kicked out there with John as a very youngster [Clapton played in Mayall's 1967 Bluesbreakers]. John is one of those old pros in blues, man. He's one of the originals that was diggin' that stuff up in England.

Were you aware of his music during the '60s?

Yes, I was, but only by records. My first trip to London was February of 1965, and every time I see Eric and Beck, they tell me they heard about me because they had one record, the record I had made live at the Copa Cabana with Muddy Waters and Howlin' Wolf. They shake this record at me every time I see 'em. I was going crazy with it [in England], and Eric said, "I was out there in the truck, about to give up. I didn't know a Strat would sound like that." That's the time him and John were fittin' to explode that music. Actually, I didn't know who I was. When I got to London, they were saying, "Buddy Guy!" And I'm saying, "How the hell do *you* know me as a musician, and I don't know me?" Next thing I know, they were saying Hendrix, Eric, the Cream, and all that, and they're coming to me saying, "I got this from you." I told Eric once, "'Strange Brew,' man, that note runs me crazy." He said, "It should. It's yours." Yeah.

It must have seemed strange the first time you heard British kids playing your music.

Well, not really. The strangest thing was I didn't know nobody was payin' attention to me. In a club, yeah, I'm gonna put on a show. But my records were just a lost cause. I was doing my biggest work *behind* Muddy, Junior Wells, and whoever else would ask me to come in and make a session with them. I was just happy, man, to be invited to a Muddy Waters session or Wolf session or Little Walter session or Sonny Boy session. See, my dream had come true. I didn't give a damn about no hit record. I didn't give a damn who hear me. I had achieved what I left Louisiana to do, which is meet these great blues musicians. Then when Eric and Beck or whoever say, "I got something from you," I said, "Hell, I didn't know it." Yeah. That's just how lost I was with that. I was just havin' fun.

When you worked with Muddy on Folk Singer, *did he give you directions on what he wanted you to play?*

No. He knew. Actually, I remember that very well. Leonard Chess and Ralph Bass, one of the producers, told Muddy to go in Mississippi and try to find somebody because the colleges was goin' for that acoustic blues. They wanted him to go back and find somebody who really could play the acoustic guitar with him. They wanted no band and no electric instruments. He said, "Set the session up tomorrow. I got it." And when I walked in the studio, Leonard

Chess and them was lookin' at Muddy like he was crazy. He just told him, "Shut the fuck up. I got who I wanted." I went to playin', and man, they're sittin' there with their mouth wide open, saying, "Now how in the hell you know that?" I said, "What did you think I learn on?" Even Willie Dixon didn't know it, and he's on there. That was a morning I never will forget. Of course, I love that record. I got that record, and I'll keep it as long as I live.

Your new version of Muddy's "Nineteen Years Old" dives straight into the heart of the blues.

[*Laughs.*] Who wouldn't want to do something by Muddy Waters? Nobody can wear his shoes, but it's an honor to even try and do one of Muddy Waters' songs, man. They came up in the studio and said, "What do you got real bluesy?" I said, "Man, this 'Nineteen Years Old.'" And they just said, "Roll the tape." No rehearsal or nothing. I just wanted to play the blues the way he used to. Muddy didn't come in and say, "I wanna rehearse." He used to look at me and say, "If I rehearse it, I'm gonna mess it up. Let's just play the blues. That's all you need to do."

Your fingerstyle solo parallels Muddy's slide solo.

Well, I used to watch that guy, man, and happy tears used to fall out of my eyes when I'd see him do it. Oh yeah. When I came to Chicago I had a slide, and I think I got the late Earl Hooker's somewhere with me now. I saw them guys play that slide, man, and I gave it to them! [*Laughs.*] I said, "Ain't no sense in me even tryin'," the way they was playin' that slide–Muddy, Elmore James, Earl Hooker, and all these people. And the way Earl Hooker could make a slide talk, I said, "I'm through."

Do you ever play slide when you're alone?

No, but I'm thinking about now maybe I should just try it once in a while. But now you got people like Bonnie Raitt and that little kid in Florida. He's only about 11 years old, and when you hear this kid–man! They brought him on the stage with me in Florida, and I thought, well, okay, he's gonna hit two or three licks. That guy come out there, man, and I was cuttin' loose. Every time I played something, I heard somebody answering me. I looked down, and he just wasn't even paying me no attention. Man, he was playin' the hell out of his guitar. I said, "Hey, man, you got to be heard of." His name is Derek Trucks, and I'm trying to bring him to a few festivals. Another kid that plays straight fingers is down there in Austin [Guitar Jake], and I'm gonna try to have both of them at my club.

Who chose the title song of the new record?

That's a John Hiatt tune. I think this guy is the Willie Dixon of the last of the '80s and the '90s. This guy, man–I gotta meet him. I understand he's a guitar player, and I did one of his songs on *Damn Right, I've Got The Blues.* This guy is outrageous as a writer. Bonnie done did some of his stuff, and I'm lookin' to meet him, because I'm trying to gets ideas how he can come up with such great, great material. They sent me "Feels Like Rain," and I'm from Louisiana, and some of the lyrics are speaking about where the river pours into the sea.

What are your feelings about doing videos?

Well, it's almost like what's happenin' today is what's happenin' today. That's music now. We just finished a video for "Some Kind Of Wonderful" with Paul Rodgers. I had a great time doing it. I made a video for *Damn Right, I've Got The Blues* with "Mustang Sally." I got a grandbaby, and he didn't know who the hell I was until I come out with the video. He saw it and said, "I wanna be like granddaddy. 'Mustang Sally'!" And he was only about three-and-a-half. But without the video, he wouldn't have come and told me that. So it's a good exposure for young people to see blues, because the average blues clubs where we been playin' all our lives, you gotta be 21 to come in there. You gotta wait till you turn 21 before you can find out who I was, or when Muddy was living, to see what he looked like. So this exposes a little bit for blues people.

Any chance you'll make a country video for "Change In The Weather"?

Whatever it calls for, man, I'm here. I'm like B.B. King–he's one of my great teachers. And he says, "Whatever opportunity you have to expose anything, don't ever take no." Whatever they want me to do, I'm for it.

Does your variety in tones come more from your guitars or amps?

No. I just stay with my guitar and my amps, man. I tried a few pedals on that album, and if this works, I'll try a few more. Actually, I think the amplifiers back in the '40s and '50s used to get all of this stuff we use; it didn't get the wah-wah, but we got a lot of different sounds out of amps without the effects. And now it seems the effects are being taken out of the amplifiers and being sold to you secondly. Because all the distortion and stuff–you've got to almost buy it now. I got an old Fender Bassman, and I can plug that up and people ask me, "Well, what are you using?" I say, "Just an amp."

That ferocious solo in "Country Man" has a penetrating tone.

It was the wah-wah with the octave pedal on it. What I'm trying to do is keep up with the times, and if that helps me, look out–I'm coming back with more.

You talk about keeping up with the times, but these devices often make guitarists sound like Jimi Hendrix 25 years ago.

Well, actually, I was going through that stuff before he

really exploded with that stuff. Earl Hooker came up to me with the first wah-wah before I ever heard of Hendrix. We would go down to the music store and run people out with that. But Leonard Chess and them never would let me come in the studio with stuff like that. Aw, no.

What do you expect from your second guitarist?

When I came to Chicago, man, that second guitar took the place of a piano player. Besides my records, I use a second guitarist in most of my personal appearances. And I like to stand back sometimes and play rhythm. I just don't want to be a lead guitar player; I enjoy playing behind other people. When Scott [Holt] comes out there, man, I like to get back there and make a pretty sound. Music to me, man, is let's make it sound good. It don't have to be Buddy Guy out there in front. Let's make everybody happy when they go home, man. Let me see a smile on the faces of these people who thought enough to come out there and spend some time with us. Let's make 'em happy.

What do you tell the musicians in your band?

I have only one rule for the guys in my band: play. I've seen tough bandleaders, but I don't do that, man. I figure men are men. They could probably get out of hand, and I'd have to say something. But all I tell my men is, "I hired you according to your ability–not because of who you are–and you know you got a job to do, and I got a job to do. Let's do it. Just play for me to the best of your ability, and I'm satisfied. If you're not gonna do it, then we can depart on a friendly basis."

What guitar do you play the most?

My personal signature model Strat. I got two of them, including a polka-dot one.

Did you have special requests when Fender built them?

Yeah. I had to go in there and feel around and give them what I was looking for, for which Eric had did the same. I come out so close to what he had, some minor changes gotta be made before they really put mine on the market. They can't put two identical guitars out there and call one Eric's model and one the Buddy Guy model. I guess him and I's taste is too close to call.

What's your amp?

I'm using reissue Fender Bassmans now. That's about as close as you can come to getting the original stuff from back during the '50s and '60s. I don't think you can ever reproduce that Leo [Fender] stuff no way, but they did a good job on this, and it's about as close as I can get to what I really want.

When you hit the stage, what's between your guitar and amp?

Just a wah-wah and an octave, that's all. Sometime I don't even use that. I think the octave is a Boss; the wah-wah is a Dunlop. I endorse for Dunlop too, and he's got one they're workin' on now. I don't know if you know it, but all wah-wah pedals came to me kind of left-handed, because of Hendrix. I told him, "You gotta stick my wah in the other side, because my wah-wah pedal is to my right." He looked at me and said, "You know, I never thought of it." Yeah.

Stacks of Buddy Guy CDs are now available–everything from Chicago Boss Guitars, _which has your first solo recordings in Chicago, to_ Feels Like Rain. _Which of your own records would you recommend for struggling blues guitarists?_

It all depend. Some of my early stuff is a much slower blues, and I was a very slow learner. So when I got ready to learn, that's what I needed–the slow blues–so I could understand it. I picked up speed on the last several albums–_Stone Crazy_ and _Damn Right, I've Got The Blues._ But I would listen to all of 'em, because if you don't, you're gonna get set on one thing. Like when I was learning, I didn't just sit and listen to B.B., Muddy, and say, "That's all I want." I listened to Howlin' Wolf, Lightnin' Hopkins, T-Bone Walker, and a lot of jazz. I listen to a lot of jazz right now. When I get in my car and drive out today, I got it on a jazz station, trying to steal some jazz lickin' and convert it into blues. And that's what it's all about. So I would recommend a kid not only to listen just to Buddy Guy, but if you like Buddy Guy, listen to many more other great guitar players. Beck, Eric, the late Stevie, George Benson, and all these guitar players. You should listen to everybody.

A SELECTED BUDDY GUY DISCOGRAPHY

Solo albums: *A Man & The Blues* ('67), Vanguard; *Hold That Plane* ('69), Vanguard; *This Is Buddy Guy*, Vanguard; *My Time After A While*, Vanguard; *I Was Walking Through The Woods* ('70), Chess; *Left My Blues In San Francisco*, Chess; *Buddy Guy*, Chess; *Buddy Guy–The Complete Chess Studio Recordings* ('60-'66), Chess; *In The Beginning* (Chess and Artistic), Red Lightnin'; *The Blues Giant* ('79), Isabel; *Stone Crazy* (Isabel, '79), Alligator; *The Dollar Done Fell*, JSP; *Breaking Out*, JSP; *Buddy & Philip Guy*, JSP; *D.J. Play My Blues*, JSP; *Live At The Checkerboard Lounge*, JSP; *Ten Blue Fingers*, JSP; *The Very Best Of Buddy Guy*, Rhino; *Damn Right, I've Got The Blues* ('91), Silvertone; *Feels Like Rain* ('93), Silvertone.

Buddy Guy & Junior Wells: *Buddy And The Juniors* (Blue Thumb, '70), MCA; *Buddy Guy & Junior Wells Play The Blues* ('72), Atco; *Drinkin' TNT, Smokin' Dynamite* ('74), Blind Pig; *Live Recording At Yuhbin-Chokin Hall In March 1975*, Bourbon; *The Original Blues Brothers*, Intermedia; *Live In Montreux* (Black And Blue, '77), Evidence; *Going Back* (acoustic in Paris, '81), Isabel (reissued by Alligator as *Alone & Acoustic*).

Backing Junior Wells: *Hoodoo Man Blues*, Delmark; *Southside Blues Jam*, Delmark; *It's My Life, Baby*, Vanguard; *Coming At You*, Vanguard; *Live Recording*, Bourbon; and the anthologies *Chicago/The Blues/Today! Vol. 1*, Vanguard; *Blues Masters, Volume 4: Harmonica Classics*, Rhino; *Blues Masters, Volume 7: Blues Revival*, Rhino; *Legends Of Guitar–Electric Blues, Vol. 2*, Rhino.

With Muddy Waters: *Folk Singer*, Chess; *Muddy Waters* box set; *Baby Please Don't Go*, Chess France; *Super Blues*, Chess; *The Super Super Blues Band* (Buddy plays bass), Chess.

With Howlin' Wolf: *Chester Burnett A.K.A. Howlin' Wolf*, Chess; *The Real Folk Blues* (Buddy plays bass on "Built For Comfort" and "Three Hundred Pounds Of Joy"), Chess; *Howlin' Wolf* box set, Chess.

With Sonny Boy Williamson: *More Real Folk Blues*, Chess; *The Chess Years*, Charly.

With Koko Taylor: *Koko Taylor*, Chess; *What It Takes*, Chess.

With others: Big Mama Thornton, *In Europe*, Arhoolie; Shakey Horton, *The Soul Of Blues Harmonica*, Chess; Eric Clapton, *24 Nights*, Reprise; John Mayall, *Wake Up Call* ('93), Silvertone; B.B. King, *Blues Summit* ('93), MCA.

Anthologies (on Chess): *Chess Blues* box set; *The Blues, Volume 1*; *The Blues, Volume 2*; *Folk Festival Of The Blues*; *Chess Masters*; *Blues From Big Bill's Copa Cabana*; *Chicago Blues Anthology*; *Chess Blues Rarities*; *The Golden Age Of Chicago Blues*; *The First Time I Met The Blues*; *Second Time I Met The Blues*.

Other labels: *The Best Of The Chicago Blues*, Vanguard; *Chicago Blues*, Red Lightnin'; *Chicago Boss Guitars* ('58 recordings), Paula; *The Cobra Records Story* box set ('58), Capricorn; *Atlantic Blues: Chicago*, Atlantic; *American Folk Blues Festival, 1965* (backing Walter Horton), L+R; *American Folk Blues Festival, 1963-'67* (fronting and with Big Mama Thornton), L+R; *Best Of The Blues* (Barclay, '70s), Polydor; *Guitar Workshop*, Pausa; *Chicago Blues: A Quarter Century*, P-Vine; *Tenth Anniversary Anthology, Vol. 1–Live From Antone's*, Antone's; *Antone's Anniversary Anthology, Vol. 2*, Antone's; *Bringing You All The Best In Blues*, Antone's; *Blues Masters, Volume 2: Postwar Chicago*, Rhino; *The Second Burnley National Blues Festival* ('90), JSP; *Muddy Waters Blues–A Tribute To Muddy Waters* ('93), Victory.

On film: *Supershow* ('69, three cuts); *Chicago Blues* ('70, solo and with Muddy Waters); *En Remontant Le Mississippi/Out Of The Blacks, Into The Blues* ('71 West German/French film featuring "Ships On The Ocean" with Junior Wells; available from Yazoo Video); *The Blues Alive* (with John Mayall's '82 Bluesbreakers reunion tour), RCA/Columbia; *Rainin' In My Heart* (PBS documentary, '87); Eric Clapton's *24 Nights* ('90-'91), Reprise; *I Was There When The Blues Was Red Hot* ('93). During the late '60s, Buddy appeared on a B&W *Camera Three* TV segment, playing with his band and in an acoustic duet with Son House.

Otis Rush

October 1987 & November 1993

BY DAN FORTE

& JAS OBRECHT

IRONY IS AN ESSENTIAL INGREDIENT OF THE BLUES, be it Muddy Waters belting out "You Can't Lose What You Never Had" or Robert Cray singing "Right Next Door." But Otis Rush's career has had more than its share of ironic twists.

After storming onto the Chicago scene in 1956 with "I Can't Quit You, Baby," Rush recorded a short but impressive string of classics for the Cobra label, including "All Your Love (I Miss Loving)," "My Love Will Never Die," and "Double Trouble." Anyone familiar with the work of Eric Clapton or Stevie Ray Vaughan will recognize that this handful of sides cut for Cobra over a two-year period sealed Rush's status as a major influence. Clapton's milestone *Blues Breakers* album with John Mayall included a version of "All Your Love," and he later recorded "Double Trouble," the song after which Vaughan named his band. Otis' influence goes much further, however; just listen to Peter Green's composition "Black Magic Woman" with the original Fleetwood Mac on *Black Magic Woman*–not to mention the playing of Robert Cray, Jimmie Vaughan, Ronnie Earl, Anson Funderburgh, Luther Allison, and the late Magic Sam. As Allison once told *Guitar Player*, "I'll put Otis Rush next to any guitar player or any vocalist in *any* bag of music."

Although Rush was signed to the mighty Chess label, home of Bo Diddley, Muddy Waters, and Chuck Berry, the company had its hands full with its established early-'60s hitmakers and recorded only eight songs by Otis in the three years he was under contract–most of them unissued until much later. Rush moved to the Duke label, which had done well for Bobby Blue Bland and Junior Parker, but it released only *one* single–"Homework"–in three years. In late '65 Otis recorded five stunning tracks for Vanguard's fine *Chicago/The Blues/Today!* series, including a more dramatic arrangement of "I Can't Quit You, Baby," which served as the blueprint for versions by John Mayall (the *Crusade* album, with Mick Taylor on guitar) and Led Zeppelin's self-titled debut, with Jimmy Page copping Otis' solo note-for-note. As the British blues movement was coming on strong, one of its biggest influences didn't even have a recording contract–in fact, had never even released an album under his own name.

Atlantic's Cotillion subsidiary remedied that situation in 1969 with the release of *Mourning In The Morning*. But while it had its moments, the album served to frustrate Otis and loyal fans even more, due to rather heavy-handed production and songwriting by Mike Bloomfield and Nick Gravenites. In 1971, though, Rush signed with Capitol and went into the studio with a liberal budget and a well-

rehearsed San Francisco band. The results amounted to his highest points since his Cobra days, with even more consistency. The trouble was, Capitol never released *Right Place, Wrong Time*, which didn't see the light of day until 1976, on the small Bullfrog label. In the liner notes to that package, blues enthusiast Dick Shurman wrote, "His ability as a vocalist and instrumentalist are each remarkable enough separately; the combination of the two is devastating."

A handful of Otis Rush albums were recorded in the following decade, with respectable if not overwhelming results, and in the early '80s frustrations got the better of Otis, who quit performing for nearly two years. Upon his return it was immediately apparent that even while inactive professionally, he had continued to practice and search for new sounds.

Born in Philadelphia, Mississippi, in 1934, Otis began fooling with an acoustic guitar at age ten. "I had an uncle who I used to see play–for his own amusement, not in clubs," he recalls. "I'd be happy when he picked the guitar up. I'm left-handed, see, so I'd take the guitar and flip it over." Like Albert King, Otis crafted his mind-boggling style playing upside-down with the guitar's low strings closest to the floor. He made a couple of attempts at switching to a standard left-handed instrument, but was met with "a lot of confusion."

Cobra Records publicity shot, mid '50s.

If Otis has been underrated as a guitarist, it's only because his singing is so powerful. Oddly enough, the gut-wrenching blues singer first sang country music as a child. "I would listen to other people sing on the radio," he points out, "like Eddy Arnold, the country music singer, and Bill Monroe And The Blue Grass Boys. I'd sing that too. Maybe I'll record some of that one day, but for now I'm trying to find *my* way. My mother was a church lady, so I sang in church a little bit, and I played guitar in church too."

A few years after moving to Chicago in 1948, Otis began checking out the local club scene. "Muddy was the first guy I saw–with Elgin Evans on drums, Jimmy Rogers on guitar, and Junior Wells or maybe Little Walter on harmonica. I said, 'Whoa! I got to do that.'"

Eventually he lucked into a steady gig of his own. "I'd just be practicing," he relates, "and the neighbors would lean out the window and say, 'Would you please get out of here with that noise?' But I was really progressing, practicing, and learning–stuff like Muddy Waters, Howlin' Wolf, Jimmy Rogers, John Lee Hooker, B.B. King, T-Bone Walker. I was just listening to everybody back when I was trying to play. One night some guy came and said, 'Who's that guy making that noise up there? I need a guy to come and play at my club tonight. My band stood me up.' So he offered me four or five dollars, and I went and played–at 2711 Wentworth in Chicago. It was by myself, just stomping my foot and playing. He said, 'Come back tomorrow night.' And I came back three or four nights. I was working a day job in a warehouse, and I wasn't getting any sleep, playing nights and working days, so I just turned to the blues. I'd been making a couple hundred dollars a week, and I gave it up to make forty or fifty–just to play."

In 1956 blues songwriter Willie Dixon hooked Otis up with Cobra Records. "He was scouting for them," Rush explains, "and I was playing at the 708 Club with Louis Myers as the Four Aces. Matter of fact, Junior Wells was a part of it for a while. We were playing together two or three years before I cut 'I Can't Quit You, Baby.' A lot of good things happened at that club; that's where I saw Robert Nighthawk."

Otis' first several recordings found him backed by Dixon, pianist Lafayette Leake, and guitarists Wayne Bennett, Reggie Boyd, or Jody Williams, but for the session that yielded "Double Trouble" he was teamed with the Ike Turner band. "Ike was up there trying to get Cobra to let him do a record. He was there, and I needed musicians to record. They made a little money–helped me out." On "Double Trouble" Turner's exaggerated wang-bar vibrato contrasted with Rush's own distinctive hand-vibrato technique. "He played lead and I played lead, in different places," Otis clarifies.

After recording Dixon's "I Can't Quit You, Baby" and "Groaning The Blues," in Otis' words, "I said, 'Damn, if the people accept that, I can write one better than that.'" He was inspired to write "Double Trouble" after overhearing a woman use the phrase in line at a grocery store. Of his anguished vocal, Mike Rowe wrote in *Chicago Breakdown*, "He approaches the harrowing poetic terror of a Robert Johnson."

From the very start Rush had a more modern, urban sound than the status quo of Chicago blues–Muddy Waters, Howlin' Wolf, and Little Walter. "I was listening to Albert King and B.B. King, really," he shrugs, "and I just sort of went that way–between that and T-Bone Walker and Gatemouth Brown." Songs such as "My Love Will Never Die" anticipated '60s soul ballads. "That was pretty much a church sound," says the guitarist, "a sad sound." Even more progressive was "All Your Love," with its shifting rhythms–from bastardized calypso to shuffle.

After Cobra came a frustrating period of inactivity with Chess, although at least one classic, "So Many Roads," was released. "Chess didn't really need me when they signed me up," he states. "But they get you and handcuff you, you know, where you can't be making records for no one else. They weren't too interested in pushing me; they just wanted con-

trol. That's America. After three years with Chess I signed with Duke. I didn't know what I was doing. They promised me the moon and only put out one single. Now I don't sign nothing–just one LP at a time."

Vanguard's three-volume *Chicago/The Blues/Today!* series, with three artists presented per disc, still ranks as one of the best by-products of the mid-'60s blues resurgence. With stellar performances by J.B. Hutto, Homesick James, James Cotton, Walter Horton, Johnny Shines, Johnny Young, Junior Wells, and Otis Spann, Otis Rush's five selections easily rank as the lineup's most progressive and modern. Of particular interest is his instrumental arrangement of Ike & Tina Turner's hit "Think It's Gonna Work Out Fine" (here dubbed "Everything's Going To Turn Out Alright"), with Luther Tucker on rhythm guitar, a position he held with Otis for ten years, off and on.

Asked about his progressive leanings, Otis downplays his groundbreaking efforts. "That's for people like you to decide," he laughs. "I just play, and I've got sounds–I hear things onstage–and I go home and try to figure them out. I know I'm gonna mess up in places, but sometimes I get away with it. To me, I'm trying to learn how to play. I'm not ashamed to let people know I'm trying to learn. I'm scuffling, trying to find something new, trying to make it off the ground. I'll be reaching for sounds–right onstage. I know I'm going to get caught; that's why you hear a lot of bad notes. I can't just play straight. If I hear something, I go after it. Sometimes it works out; then again, you get some bad collisions [*laughs*], so I try to cover it up. Just like a boxer: You get hit, you got to try to recuperate. I've got some sounds coming around. I got some other things that sound like piano. I'm not bragging; I've just been working on them."

Unlike a lot of "upside-down" players who are strictly soloists, such as Albert King, Rush commands an impressive chord vocabulary. "That's true," he says with uncharacteristic pride. "I went to school a little bit, you know, for chords–just to make me understand my thing. But the guy who was teaching me, Reggie Boyd, wanted to teach me country, which wasn't what I wanted to learn. So I walked out. But he did show me some things." Probably Otis' most distinctive stylistic elements are his full-chord bending and his fast, shimmering vibrato, which Jimmie Vaughan dubbed the "singing string" sound. Both techniques were developed from listening to slide players. "I practiced to get that sound without using the slide," Rush explains. "I'm still trying to develop it. I get out a slide in the hotel room sometimes and do a little. My favorite slide players were Earl Hooker and Robert Nighthawk. There were a lot of them, but I listened to those guys' touch. I don't have the touch they had with a slide, so in order for me to get that sound, I'm trying to just get it with my hands." Otis' instrumental "Easy Go" from *Right Place, Wrong Time* is reminiscent of the Earl Hooker slide approach, and onstage he often performs Hooker's "Will My Woman Be Home Tonight?"

Even though he sometimes plays tremolo-equipped guitars, such as a Stratocaster, Otis prefers to achieve wang bar-like effects with just his hands. "I use the bar a little bit, but would shake my strings [with my hands] if I wanted to. I can shake them without the bar. I can shake a whole chord. I guess by me being left-handed, it's a little bit of an advantage for that style, and then there's other advantages for a right-handed player. No one has it over the other."

To demonstrate some of the advantages, Otis gets out his guitar. "If I hear a chord, I can play it," he begins. "There are some chords that a right-handed player can finger that I can't–because it might have a note I can't reach–but there are other chords I can do that a right-handed guy can't do. It works both ways." He plays a Jimmy Reed shuffle, arching his fingers to stay out of the way of the lower adjacent string, and then launches into Kenny Burrell's "Chitlins Con Carne" in several different positions. "I thought that was one of the most beautiful things I ever heard," he smiles. "I'm working on these piano runs now, and Oscar Moore and Johnny Moore things. As a kid I listened to 'Driftin' Blues' and 'Black Night' by [pianist] Charles Brown. You don't listen to one person, though; you listen to everybody." He then proceeds to play note- (and rhythm-) perfect T-Bone Walker lines. "T-Bone had his shit very well-placed, playing all those horn parts. I just put 'em all together–even Ray Charles," he concludes, playing a pianistic lick obviously indebted to Brother Ray.

One technique that definitely sounds different because of Otis' upside-down approach is his bending–grabbing and pulling *down* on the strings, instead of pushing upwards. Physics might suggest that bending a string in either direction would yield the same sound, but with Otis it's definitely not the case. "Pulling down is easy for me," he states. "I pull the high *E* all the way down to the other *E*. Sometimes I push mine up too–even the *G* and the *B*."

Although he employs fairly light-gauge strings these days, Otis accomplished the same effect in the old days with heavy strings. "I used to use the heavy strings, with a wound *G*," he smiles. "Then they came out with .010s and .009s and all these different strings, so why suffer, you know? I use .010s now, and I can squeeze them quite a bit. With .009s, I break them." (Of his picking-hand technique, guitarist Derek O'Brien of the Lou Ann Barton Band, who has backed Otis on numerous occasions, says, "The first time I worked with Otis, he played the first night all with a pick, and then he played the next night all with his fingers." "It just depends on how I feel," says Rush.)

Referring to his belated debut album as "good-intentioned," the guitarist feels "it was a little bit too much of Bloomfield's and Gravenites' ideas and not enough of mine. I don't think the public accepted it, because it wasn't me. They'd prefer I was going back to the stuff that I usually did." Recorded at Fame Studios in Muscle Shoals, Alabama, the project featured such studio luminaries as Duane Allman and Jimmy Johnson on guitars, Jerry Jemmott on bass, Barry Beckett on keyboards, and Roger Hawkins on drums, although Otis points out, "The leads are by me."

The appropriately titled *Right Place, Wrong Time*, with its title track reminiscent of Albert King, marked Otis' maturation as singer, songwriter, guitarist, and producer. Although songwriter Nick Gravenites was credited as co-producer, Otis stresses, "I put that stuff together–Nick don't know that stuff. I also put [1975's] *Cold Day In Hell* together, although I was high as a kite–drinking heavy at that time. It was okay, but I wasn't getting a good sound. *Right Place, Wrong Time* wasn't a bad album, as far as sounds. We did some gigs in San Francisco with the studio band first, to get our confidence up. I'll give Nick credit for that–setting up the gigs. That stuff really wasn't even mixed; it was just straight playing and straight playback. It's just like we recorded it, because Bullfrog just took the masters and released it." Resigned but still frustrated over the years that the album remained in the can, Otis shrugs, "And in the meantime Dr. John came out with a song called 'Right Place, Wrong Time' and got a gold record for it. All the time my record was laying up on the shelf. If I had come out with that record when I first recorded it, I'd be in better shape today. I'd be more popular."

Although his old promo pictures from the Cobra days show him with a Stratocaster, Otis has used a wide array of guitars. "First I recorded with an old acoustic Gibson with a pickup on it," he begins. "I played a Kay also. After some records came out, I switched to a Strat. I watched Earl Hooker; he had every gimmick or gadget that came out. He had a Strat, so I bought one. He had an old Fender Bassman, so I got that, put them together, and developed a hell of a sound. I used to sing *and* play through that amp; it takes a lot of punishment. My old Strat got stolen, so I got a Fender Jaguar, and then I used an Epiphone Riviera. The Epiphone got broken, and somebody gave me another Strat. Then I switched to a Gibson ES-345. I still use my Strat for different things. [Vintage guitar authority] Danny Thorpe gave me a 1965 ES-355 and a 1962 *left-handed* ES-355 [with the nut and strings reversed], so the controls would be out of the way. That's a problem with the right-handed models. I can get by, but I have to keep reaching up and resetting the

Otis' pal Magic Sam Maghett passed away in 1969. "He was a good-time dude," Rush remembers, "and he had a lot of fun. Hey, he was just an all-around great guy."

Like when you make a chord, man, you've got to hear it."

1986 marked Otis' first, albeit long overdue, meeting with one of his most devoted disciples, Eric Clapton. "I met him when I was in England," he says. "Great guitar player." What did it feel like when the struggling Chicagoan first heard a young English kid playing his songs and style? "Well, everybody plays like somebody. It's good to know that somebody's listening. To me, I'm just a guitar player. I'm not trying to influence nobody, I'm just trying to play, and play well. And hopefully I can sell some records. I've got a better chance now–I'm in a better position–than 10 or 20 years ago. People are listening. Blues today is mostly white people. A lot of black people passed it over. That's strange, I swear. I hear people say, 'I don't like blues.' Well, I be looking under the table at their feet–to find something to get them going. Because blues is the foundation of *all* music."

During his self-imposed hiatus, Otis was never far from his guitar. "I listened to records a lot, listened to sounds, and practiced," he says somberly. "I've sat up 24 hours with it. You've got to get it mentally, and you've got to get it mechanically. It's just like the Lord's Prayer: You've got to know that and get

knobs onstage.

"There's a lot of Strats out there, but all of them don't sound good. I'm always searching for a better tone. I still occasionally play my white Strat that was given to me about three years ago. It sounds good. A Telecaster also sounds great. Magic Sam had one, and I used it. I play the blues on the Strat; if I want to play some Jimmy Smith stuff or some Kenny Burrell chords, I use the Gibson."

These days Otis is still looking for the right amplifier. "I'm searching for an amp, because the last time I was in the studio, I didn't like the sound. I cut some new stuff for Rooster Blues, but the sound was too fuzzy. I'd like to try a Mesa/Boogie. I've got a Fender, but you can only turn it up so loud, and then it doesn't get any louder. The old Twin Reverb comes through pretty good, though. I try to play with a clean sound. I can do a little bit of that Chuck Berry stuff, but not like some guys, who can use that fuzzy sound. I'd rather mine be clean.

that from the heart. I've been down and up. I quit for two years, and I suffered. These companies screw you around, and I got to the point where I was real angry. To be that angry is not good, so I quit for two years. I had to figure out if I wanted to play or not. I needed to get myself together and either accept what's going on or quit.

"But what I have, He gave it to me. 'You gonna quit, huh? What are you gonna do?' [*Laughs.*] So, yeah, I suffered. I'm back at it–for good or bad. I'm not gonna quit no more. I just want to play the guitar the best I can and survive."

November 1993

During the early '90s Buddy Guy struck pay dirt with *Damn Right, I've Got The Blues* and *Feels Like Rain*, and in 1993 Otis Rush was ready to follow suit with a new album that, at press time, was titled *Ain't*

Enough Comin' In. The project features the same production team and core musicians as *Feels Like Rain*, but unlike Buddy's album, with its airwaves-approved duets with star names, Otis is cast as a man alone with the blues. His powerful, big-vibrato playing on the project moves with a confidence and elasticity second to none, while his fever-and-chills vocals travel from passionate pleas to gritty soul and sanctified screams. Jas Obrecht interviewed Otis twice in Chicago that summer, and an edited version of their exchange appeared in the November '93 *Guitar Player* as "Otis Rush–Right Place, Right Time." Here's the full transcript of those conversations:

We want to call our story "Right Place, Right Time," since your new album is so strong.

Sure thing! Well, thank you. Thank you. [*Laughs.*] I'll let you be the judge. I don't know too much. I just appreciate your sayin' what you're sayin'.

Plus all your Cobra material has recently come out in a box set…

Yeah, yeah. I heard about it. Look like it's open season on me. Everybody is releasing my old records.

Are you getting royalties?

Well, some of 'em. And some of 'em, no.

You're credited with starting the so-called West Side sound.

I've heard it, among me and some others.

Does that term have meaning to you?

Not really. I don't even know what they're talkin' about. [*Laughs.*]

It's used to describe your music, Buddy Guy's, Magic Sam's…

Well, I was playin' before Buddy and Magic Sam. Buddy, the first time he went onstage was on my show. He came by to sit in. Buddy always says, "Hey, you the first guy that let me get onstage"–that's what he tells me now.

And you played on his first records.

Yeah, and I got Magic Sam on the Cobra label. Magic Sam was a nice guy, man. Him and Buddy–they both nice guys. Buddy and Sam played different, but both of 'em was tough, man. We play on shows together, you know.

Did you do much playing together offstage?

No, we didn't jam together that way. It was just whenever we see each other, we'd go up and play.

How did you meet Magic Sam?

Sam came by where I was playin' at, and then he got a job down the street. I was playin' at 2711 Wentworth, and Sam was somewhere around 63rd and State. Now, I had made a record already, but Sam hadn't. Him and some other peoples was together, and they come out and sit in.

Were you impressed?

Oh, yeah! Him and Buddy were about the same way. Sam and I used to hang out together, you know. We was playin' at 4:00 [A.M.], and they got off at 2:00, and they would come by. We'd all sit around and drink and play music. I had my band, and sometime I'd go by to listen to them play, and sit in. So we knew each other for a long time. Sam had a special sound, but believe me, I don't know how he got that.

He had more reverb…

He liked gimmicks. He was messin' around with them gimmicks too–him and Earl Hooker.

Earl had a wah-wah early on.

Right.

Did you ever want to go that route?

Yeah. I didn't have the money to buy one at that time when they come out. I never did get one until a few years ago.

Were Telecasters and Stratocasters hard to get during the '50s?

Now, I don't really know about the Telecaster, but I knew it played good. Yeah, it does. It was hard to get a guitar because we was so poor, man, but I had scuffled and got enough money to buy me one. Everybody bought Fenders and Fender Bassmans. The first one Magic Sam had was a Telecaster, and then he bought a Stratocaster.

Was Sam a family man?

Yes, he was. He had a wife and some children.

What was he like offstage?

Sam was sort of a lively guy. He wasn't quiet–he was just lively! [*Laughs.*] He might walk up and say, "President, you got a bug on your head!" President, "Where?" "It's me!" [*Laughs.*] That's the kind of guy he were!

Was he much of a drinker?

Yeah, yeah. No need of me lying. You know, that's a shame. I drinked too, but he was *really* on it. Yeah, he was drinkin'. He just a good-time guy–he don't know when to go home, you know. No sleep, then you gotta work the next night. He'd go take a nap over in the corner, then get up and go play, nap, then get ready and go out again before he go home. That's the wear and tear. That'll get you. He was a good-time dude, and he had a lot of fun, far as I know. Hey, he was just an all-around great guy.

Do you know what killed him?

No, I don't. All I know, they say a heart attack.

Did your Cobra releases lead to any tours?

Yes. The very first record I made was "I Can't Quit You, Baby, I Got To Put You Down For A While," and I started travelin' behind that. That was the first work I ever had behind that record.

What kind of studio were your Cobra sessions held in?

I don't know what it were before I went there, but it was a building, two or three rooms together there. The amps was sittin' on the floor, and they had little shields and things up around the walls, little booths. The whole band recorded at the same time. Ike Turner was on one of the records we recorded in that same room. Sam recorded in there, Buddy. It was on Roosevelt Street. Now it's all torn down.

The Cobra box set credits Ike Turner with playing some of the guitar on "All Your Love."

Well, that's "Double Troubles." That was "Double Troubles" and "Keep Lovin' Me." That was the two he was on.

Did you teach him the parts?

No, I did not. Ike was playin' when I met him. I met Ike in St. Louis before he ever played on my record.

Were you aware of blues music when you were growing up in Philadelphia, Mississippi?

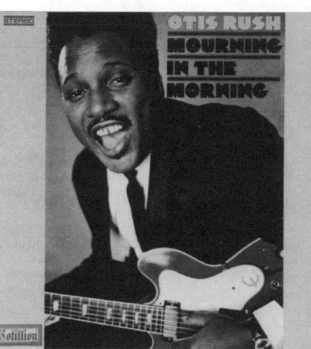

Blues with an Epiphone, 1969.

Yes, yes. You know, I was listening to a guy like Charles Brown, the piano player, and John Lee Hooker. Muddy Waters had some records out, and Howlin' Wolf. I was in Philadelphia then.

Were people performing blues in your town?

No. They was playin' those records on the jukebox. Philadelphia is... You can take a baseball and throw it all the way across it, you know. [*Laughs.*] That's the town—well, it's more like a county.

Your vocals seem to have a lot in common with gospel singing.

Yeah, yeah, yeah, yeah, yeah, yeah. I used to play guitar, matter of fact, in church–and sing. It was a Sanctified Baptist Church or something. I don't know how I was playin'. [*Laughs.*] I was a good guy, but hey, I didn't know what it was all about.

When you started playing clubs, was anyone especially inspirational?

Yes! That was Muddy Waters. He didn't do anything. He just sit there and play. My sister took me to listen to him at the Zanzibar, on the West Side here in Chicago. Okay. I'd just

arrived, and I don't know nothin' about guitar. I just had one at home. So I'd come here to visit my sister and then go back to Philadelphia, Mississippi–that's my home. I came here and said, "Whoa. This is for me!" I heard Muddy, and I said, "Give me a guitar!" So I went and started practicin'.

Did he have Little Walter with him at the time?

Yes, he did. He had Little Walter. Junior Wells was sittin' in with him also, Jimmy Rogers on second guitar, Elgin on the drums, Muddy on lead guitar. Aw, man, it was so great! So I started listenin' to these guys, and I started off workin' for five dollars a night. I quit my day job here in Chicago.

Did any of the older musicians give you good advice?

No, no, no, no. I've always been out there by myself. No one helped me to get out here. I've always had my own band, just a guitar around me, and I would always choose a guy to come sit down and play with me. I just started out that way. It wasn't nothin' big or small. As far as bein' a leader, I just had to do it. Somebody had to do it.

So they never helped you.

Well, yeah, after I made a record. But damn, before I made a record, I'm catchin' hell! [*Laughs.*] You know, all this time they raisin' hell. They got a nice record out and they jammin', you know, but nobody helped me. It's just once... Well, Willie Dixon helped me out a little bit there. He wrote "I Can't Quit You, Baby," and I sit down and try to play it so many times. And it was a pretty nice record for me. Big Willie Dixon.

How did he teach you the song?

He just had it on paper. It's a blues, a 12-bar blues, so I choose the way I want to sing it. He can't sing for me. He'd hum, and I said, "Well, I'll try it this way." So I changed some of the words in it, but that's Willie's song. But I did it my way. Well, I saw Willie writin' 'em, you know, and I'm lookin' at these records and I'm listening at what peoples wrote. I said, "Well, damn, I can do this too," you know. [*Laughs.*] So I went at it. I'm lucky I had a few records out there.

Do you remember writing "All Your Love (I Miss Loving)"?

Yes. I was on my way to the studio for Eli Toscano [of Cobra Records], and I needed two songs. So I did "All Your Love" and that other one–what the hell was it? "Every day I" do somethin'–I forgot the title of it, and I wrote it! [*Laughs heartily.*] Oh, yeah–"Checkin' In On My Baby." "Every day I look for sunshine and know it rain, every time I check on my baby, she's out with another man," or something like that.

Do you compose songs on paper?

Yeah, yeah, yeah. You gotta put it down. Sometime you hear the music first, sometime you hear the words. Sometime you add the words to your music that you hear. Sometime you add your music to your words. Yeah.

Have you saved your song manuscripts?

Oh, no, no, no. I wouldn't know.

What are your favorite of your own songs?

Well, I like "Double Troubles," and I like "All Your Love." Some of the songs. *Right Place, Wrong Time*–that was an album that I thought was pretty good. We recorded it in '71, and they didn't release it until '77 or '76.

What songs would have to go on a best of Otis Rush collection?

Oh, I'd have to get some new songs on there. That's one thing. I gots some new songs. Pretty soon you'll hear them. Some of them are on the new record, like "It Ain't Enough Comin' In To Take Care Of What's Got To Go Out."

Your new album has the same production team and many of the same musicians as Buddy Guy's Feels Like Rain.

Yeah.

But you don't have a lot of famous people sitting in.

No. I didn't do it my way. That's the way the promoter/producer did it. That wasn't my idea. I thought Eric Clapton was gonna be on there, which was said many times. All these same peoples that was on Buddy's was gonna be on mine. It didn't happen. When I got to the studios, it was a different thing.

Your solos on the record seem to tell a story.

Yeah. Sometime, you know, you feel like playin', and it is a story. But it doesn't say any words. It's a feelin'.

Do you think out solos before recording them?

Yeah, you do have to go over it a few times.

Do you have ways of psyching yourself up to deliver an intense performance?

Well, yeah. I'm listening. Like if I'm going to work, I listen to tapes. I'm listening all day, most of the time. I listen to that guitar and singin'. Yeah.

Have you got a record collection?

Yes, yes. All kinds. I have a big stereo here.

What records could you recommend for aspiring blues guitarists?

Well, you would choose your favorite artist, who you love to hear play. You know what I mean? And if it's B.B. King, choose B.B. If it's Albert, choose Albert. If it's me, choose me. It's up to the individual, what he loves to play. It might be Kenny Burrell, if he like a little jazzy guitarin'. I like Kenny Burrell. Matter of fact, I play some of his stuff, but I didn't get a chance to put it on the records, because we're not tryin' to do too much at one time. Next record, maybe some of it may be on there.

Who are your favorite blues performers?

Well, I like Albert King. I like his playin' and his singin'. I like Bobby Blue Bland's singin', and I like B.B. I like Buddy Guy. I like all the guys, man! There's nobody I can't say I don't like, because you can always learn somethin' from anyone. Yeah! But if a guy wants to learn to play the blues, if he can, go around the guy that he really likes to listen to. And if he can't, get the records. Get him a record player and sit down and *play it*. Slow it down. In the beginning it's difficult.

Did you learn this way?

Yeah, yeah. This is what I'm tellin' you. They used to have 78s, 45s, and all that stuff. Say the notes is too fast for you, right? So you bring it down to 33. That's gonna put you in another key, but you learn it in the other key, and then you turn the speed back up and then play along. You learn your notes like that. I did a lot of that with Kenny Burrell. I usually play "Chili Con Carne" by him.

You also play country music.

Yeah, a little bit.

Do you enjoy playing guitar as much as you did when you were younger?

I can't say. I still enjoy playin'–when I think I'm soundin' alright. [*Laughs.*] 'Cause sometimes I like to take an elevator, you know, right through the stage to the basement.

Sounds self-critical.

That's just the truth. Sometimes you sound so bad! You got a bad amp or a bad speaker or something wrong with your amp. Sometime the weather change and you get these bad sounds. This is what I'm talkin' about. And then again, your backup band sometime is not playin' right. All that goes together.

Albert King used to have strong reactions onstage.

Yeah. Well, I understand his reaction. He might come down a little strong, from what I hear, but I feel the same way onstage when something is wrong and I'm listenin' at it. Sometimes musicians are assing off, you know. Sometime a musician is not payin' attention.

What do you expect from the musicians who perform

Otis and John Lee Hooker share a laugh backstage at the 1985 San Francisco Blues Festival.

with you?

I have rules. You know, when show time come, go to the stage. I don't need to be lookin' for you. And don't get drunk onstage during the show. And be on time comin' to work.

Has new equipment changed the way you make records?

Yes, yes, my goodness, yes. Yeah, you know, hey, they got so much stuff, man, I don't know whether to scratch my watch or wind my head! [*Laughs.*] I'm telling you, it's a hell of a thing to look at all this equipment that they have–amplifiers, guitars. You really don't know what to do no more. You just pick up something–if it sound good, you keep it!

What's your all-time favorite setup?

Well, I like the old Fender Bassman. And I like the one I have now–I'm playin' on a Mesa/Boogie now. For guitars, number one, I like Fender. But I like Gibson too.

You've played a number of Stratocasters.

That's right. Like the Cobra stuff? That was Fender. Some of my *Tops* LP was recorded alive with a Gibson 355–that real old one.

Is it easier to bend on either of these types of guitar?

Yeah, I think the Fender's got an edge. But Gibson is good for many things, man. You just can't explain it–like chords and jazz, stuff like that.

What guitar is on the new record?

You're hearin' Fender guitar. I just got a new guitar. John English gave it to me, and I want to give him all the credit that he deserve. The guy is a wonderful guy, and he don't know me and I don't know him. He just made me a guitar.

Is it like other Fenders you've owned?

No, it's different. It plays different. It's the best Fender I ever played–best guitar I ever played, really. It's got some special tone or something. It has the straight pickups, like the old Fender. It'd be good to talk to John English, 'cause I don't know one end of the guitar from the other.

Yeah, sure.

[*Laughs.*] But he knows about it. He made me a purple one, and he's sort of got these little Christmas tints in there, you know. And it changes colors under the lights–it changes green, gold, purple, then it looks black. It's a trip, man. It's really a trip-out! Hey, this might be some hell of an idea, you know. Yeah, he know what he doin'. This guitar look better than Christmas, I swear. Yeah! [*John English of the Fender Custom Shop clarifies that Otis' new guitar is a close copy of an authentic '62 Strat, with custom-wound Vintage Reissue pickups and a finish by Alan Hamel.*]

Do you still have any of the gear you used during the '50s?

I got a couple of red guitars, which are Gibson. But I didn't have them at that time; they was given to me.

What happened to your old amps and guitars?

Somebody stole my guitar. I still got an old Fender Bassman in the closet.

Does playing a flipped-over guitar change your sound, since you're bending strings the opposite way from most players?

Yes, it's different. 'Cause you're pullin' down on it, and the right-hand guy got to push it up. It's got to be different there. Albert King play that way too. As a matter of fact, last time we did a gig was San Francisco, and he was checkin' my guitar out.

He used a different tuning on his own guitar, though.

He plays open tuning, yeah. But he play my guitar, and he played the way he play.

Do you ever use open tunings?

Yeah, sometime.

Which ones?

I can't explain that to you. [*Laughs.*] It's just a way to tune that guitar, though. Different ways to tune your guitars. Still learnin'. [*Laughs.*]

Have you played slide?

Yep. I have a slide, but I just try to play without the slide, so that's what I work on. I don't use the slide. I play just with my hands.

Sometimes with a pick and sometimes without.

Right. It's the sound. You pluck with your thumb, and then the pick is a different sound.

How can you tell a good amp?

Well, you cannot judge it, really. You can go in the store and play it all you want to, but you really got to take it to the gig and check it out with the peoples around you. You gotta have an audience just like you gonna play–that's the way you gotta check your amp. So, many of the stores will let you do that, let you take it and check it. By you playin' in a club with peoples in there, you can tell if it's good. You know if you got enough volume. You know how loud you got to go for distortion, so you know if the speaker is good or blowed. You can tell all kind of things.

Do you know of any great unknown blues guitarists in Chicago?

No, I don't. I really don't. I think just about all the guitar players is out here. I go to work at Kingston Mines and Blues Etcetera and Blues On Halsted–you know, the guys meet up around here.

Who would you go out of your way to watch perform?

I listen to anybody. Like I say, you can always learn somethin'. I'm always out here tryin' to learn somethin', and I'm still tryin' to learn.

Who's your favorite blues piano player?

I tell you, I listen to Charles Brown. As the blues, he strikes some nice chords and runs and notes for me. He's not a big jazz or he's not a hell of a damn piano player, but the way he plays notes, I like it. And I like Ray Charles, yeah.

I bet Charles Brown drove women crazy in the '50s.

I'm sure he did. You know, Ray Charles was tryin' to sing like Charles Brown there for a while. Yeah, some of those old tunes. Everybody was tryin' to sing like Charles Brown–even myself.

Have you had a chance to work with him?

Sure, he played with me in New York for a whole week–as a backup keyboard. Oh, it were a thrill! Here this guy is sittin' with me for a whole week–playin' piano for me! Also, he had his own show in Europe and Sweden, and I had my own show. I had my own band, he had his own band over there. So hey, he's a swell guy, man.

Do you play acoustic guitar?

I can. It's about the same thing, except you can't squeeze the guitar strings on it. You can't go down there and hit them high notes.

How would you answer someone who says you have to be unhappy to perform blues music?

Who said that? You don't have to be unhappy to play blues. [*Laughs.*] I mean, I'm happy sometime. Sometime I'm not, no matter what I do. The blues is my livin'. I play 'em because it's a livin', just like a job. But I get the blues, yeah, more so than other times, like anybody does, man. I play the blues, but not because I'm sad–it's a livin'!

Do you ever play blues when you're home alone?

Yes. I been pickin' and playin' today and just about every day.

Do you need to practice?

Well, what I did is just sort of laid back for a while, because of the recordings. And now I'm beginning to go back into what I was doin'. Hopefully this record will work, and I can get straightened out on some good jobs. I don't have a personal manager right now. Me and my wife Masaki are doing it.

It seems like the perfect time for musicians like you and Buddy Guy to step forward.

You're absolutely right. I'm tryin' to make an effort, tryin' to make a start right here. And I intend to be consistent.

A SELECTED OTIS RUSH DISCOGRAPHY

Solo albums: *Groaning The Blues* (Cobra sides, '56-'58), Flyright; *Otis Rush, 1956-1958*, Paula; *Cobra Alternates*, P-Vine; *The Classic Recordings*, Charly R&B; *Otis Rush And Magic Sam–The Other Takes, 1956–'58* (ten outtakes by each), Flyright; *Albert King/Otis Rush: Door To Door* ('60), Chess France; *Blues Masters, Vol. 2* (also issued as *This One's A Good 'Un*), Blue Horizon/Polydor; *Little Walter & Otis Rush: Live In Chicago* (mid '60s), Intermedia; *Right Place, Wrong Time*, Hightone; *Mourning In The Morning*, Atlantic; *Screamin' And Cryin'* (Black And Blue, '74), Evidence; *So Many Roads* (live in Japan, '75), Delmark (issued in Japan as *Blues Live!*, Trio); *Cold Day In Hell* ('75), Delmark; *Troubles, Troubles* (live in Europe, '77), Sonet; *Lost Blues* ('77), Alligator; *Live In Europe* (France, '77), Isabel; *Tops* (San Francisco Blues Festival, '85), Blind Pig.

With others: Eddy Clearwater, *Flim Doozie*, Rooster Blues; *Willie Dixon* box set, Chess; Jimmy Dawkins, *Tribute To Orange*, Black & Blue/Evidence.

Anthologies: *Chicago Boss Guitars* ('56-'57 recordings), Paula; *The Cobra Records Story* box set ('57-'58), Capricorn; *The Story Of The Blues, Vol. Two* (one Cobra side), CBS; *American Folk Blues Festival, '66* (solo and backing Junior Wells), L+R; *Otis Rush And Little Walter–Live At The Chicago Blues Festival* (includes separate tracks by each), Cleo; *Chicago/The Blues/Today!*, Vanguard; *Atlantic Blues: Chicago* ('69 sessions), Atlantic; *The Great Blues Men*, Vanguard; *Ann Arbor Blues & Jazz Festival 1972*, Atlantic; *Back To The Blues*, Zeta; *Tenth Anniversary Anthology, Vol. 1–Live From Antone's*, Antone's; *Antone's Anniversary Anthology, Vol. 2*, Antone's; *Blues Masters, Volume 1: Urban Blues*, Rhino; *Blues Masters, Volume 2: Postwar Chicago*, Rhino; *Blues Masters, Volume 6: Blues Originals*, Rhino; *Chicago Blues: A Quarter Century*, P-Vine; *Blues Town Story, Volume 2*, Wolf; *The Best Of Duke-Peacock Blues*, MCA.

J.B. Hutto

March 1979

BY DAN FORTE

PAUL OLIVER'S BOOK *The Story Of The Blues* is probably as close to a definitive source as has been written about the idiom. But almost as valuable as the painstakingly comprehensive text is the extensive selection of photographs—each offering a rare insight into the lifestyle and environment surrounding the people who played or listened to the blues. For example, there's a 1966 glimpse of slide guitarist J.B. Hutto playing at Turner's Blue Lounge on 39th and Indiana in Chicago's South Side, a club which Oliver describes as "a rough joint."

Judging by the picture, the late author must have been a master of understatement. Hutto, in short sleeves and sunglasses, sits on a tiny stage barely a couple of feet higher than dance floor level. The reason he's not standing is obvious: If he did, his head might bump the low ceiling. Next to him a middle-aged black couple, dressed as informally as the musician, are boogie woogie-ing. On the stark back wall hangs a burned-out Schlitz sign next to some crude ventilation system. Hutto doesn't seem to be too excited about whatever he's playing on his cheap Kay electric; his expression is more like that of a graveyard-shift fry cook flipping hamburgers—just someone doing his job. But in spite of his weary countenance, J.B. Hutto was and is one of the most inventive and individual slide guitarists to emerge from the school popularized by his chief mentor, the late Elmore James.

The blues has been J.B.'s occupation off and on for nearly 30 years. Born Joseph Benjamin Hutto in Blackville, South Carolina, J.B. was raised in Augusta, Georgia, from the age of three. With his three brothers and three sisters, J.B. formed a gospel group, the Golden Crowns, and sang at the local Galilee Baptist and Holy Trinity churches; J.B. sang lead or second lead.

As far as the blues was concerned, Hutto recalls, "I listened to the majority of the blues records out then, but I wasn't playing that. I guess I was too young, anyway. I listened to them and liked them, but I wasn't really attracted to no kind of music until I hit Chicago." This is evidenced by the fact that J.B.'s resultant style sounds basically like electrified Mississippi Delta blues—whining guitar, percussive attack, and hollering vocals—and reflects none of the qualities found in the sort of ragtime blues played on the Eastern Seaboard.

When J.B.'s father died in 1949, the family moved to Chicago, and it was there at the age of 20 that Hutto became involved with the blues. "I was kind of young," admits J.B., "and I didn't know about people playing in clubs and things

of that nature–so I was still looking for house parties, fish fries, and things like that. But there wasn't nothing happening. I began to make a few friends and began to talk, and they showed me around, and I started going to the clubs, seeing bands."

Hutto's first instrument was drums, which he played with Johnny Ferguson And His Twisters. "I played drums, but I was singing, too," he reminisces. "Johnny was the leader, and he had a guitar. But when he'd lay it down I had it." J.B. met one-man band Eddie Hines, better known as "Porkchop," and the two (with Hutto on guitar) played on Maxwell Street at the open-air flea market known as Jewtown.

From the very start, J.B. played strictly electric guitar. Asked to describe his early style, he shrugs, "I can't explain it; I'll have to show you. [*He plays a dirge-like blues in standard tuning using a lot of open strings and sounding a bit like Lightnin' Hopkins.*] I didn't know how to come up here and maybe bend a string, then get back down here to catch it. But that's where I was coming from."

After hearing Elmore James, Hutto became enchanted with the sound of the electric slide guitar and set out to play it almost exclusively. "He was the cat who made me see what I wanted to do," declares the pupil. "He raised me. He could pick some, but he didn't do too much picking. I think he was like me–he liked that slide. If I could make this thing slide and cry like I want to, maybe I wouldn't do so much picking."

Hutto and Porkchop soon formed a band, and during the early '50s they played clubs like the Globetrotter and the 1015 Club. As Mike Rowe describes it in his book *Chicago Breakdown*: "J.B. blew upon the Chicago scene with one of the noisiest and toughest bands ever. Singing in the fierce, declamatory style of his idol, Elmore James, and backed by the heavily amplified guitar of Joe Custom, the crude harp of George Maywether, and the elemental percussion of Maxwell Street's Porkchop, they sounded ready to devour anything in sight!"

J.B. spent a lot of time with James, listening and learning, but while virtually every blues slide player owes a huge debt to Elmore, Hutto soon found his own voice–with a more varied single-note guitar approach and a more primitive, wild vocal style. In 1954 Hutto got his first opportunity to record, for the Chance label, under the name J.B. And His Hawks, a moniker his various groups have carried over the years. With his first 78, "Now She's Gone," the guitarist established himself as a powerful bandleader and a highly personal lyricist.

But almost as quickly as he had appeared on the scene, J.B. vanished from it around 1954 after recording a mere nine sides for Chance, only six of which were ever issued. The reason for his hiatus can perhaps be found in an anec-

dote related in Mike Rowe's book: "J.B. lost his guitar when a woman broke it over her husband's head, and he quit music for the quieter life of an undertaker."

Not until the mid '60s did Hutto re-emerge, but he seemed none the worse for the 10-year layoff. Producer Sam Charters recorded the Hawks–Hutto, bassist Herlan Hassell, and drummer Frank Kirkland–in 1965 for Vanguard Records' *Chicago/The Blues/Today!* The session featured J.B.'s composition "Too Much Alcohol." Recordings for Testament, Delmark, and other independent labels followed, and the early '70s found Hutto touring blues festivals across the country and overseas (where he also recorded a couple of albums).

A number of different guitars have gone through J.B.'s hands over the years, and he doesn't seem overly concerned with model names and numbers. Until recently J.B.'s main axe was a Fender Telecaster with the finish worn away at the top frets, near the cutaway, due to Hutto's habit of riding the slide up past the neck (near the rhythm pickup) to obtain higher notes. That problem was partially alleviated with J.B.'s most recent change in guitars, when he purchased a solidbody Epiphone with a longer neck and deeper cutaway. The two-pickup model is usually set with just the treble pickup or both pickups on.

After some experimentation, Hutto settled on an open-*D* tuning. "I used to be a one-key man," he confesses. "Tuned it in open *E* [*E B E G# B E*, low to high], and for anything else I used a clamp, a capo. But I had to tune it *up* to *E*, so now I tune it down to *D* [same as open *E* but one whole-step lower on each string]. I don't like my action too high; I don't move the strings up or down. If they're too high, I get a kind of grating sound; if they're too low, naturally you're going to hit the frets."

J.B.'s current amp is a Fender Super Reverb, and as for his slide, he explains, "I used to cut off a piece of pipe with a hacksaw. Now they're selling slides all over in music stores, so I bought one. I tried playing with a glass slide, but it didn't work. I play with it on my little finger, and now I've got two metal slides, a thin one and a heavier one that has a great tone–that really brings the sound out; it almost sounds like two notes. I can't find any as heavy as this one."

Unlike Elmore James, who used a flatpick, Hutto plays with a plastic fingerpick on his index finger, along with a thumbpick. "Elmore played with a flatpick," J.B. explains, "but he could use anything–flatpick or finger and thumb. But I think playing slide is good for playing with the thumb–Hound Dog Taylor used to play with the thumb. You can always catch the strings better. If I play very long without a pick, a knot will swell up on that finger. One night overseas our stuff was late, and we had to play a college gig with new instruments–no picks, no nothing. The next day I had to stick my finger in alcohol to cool it off."

J.B.'s current repertoire includes many of his old favorites, new tunes (which he's writing all the time), and blues standards–all played with Hutto's indelible stamp. "I learned to play like nobody," he boasts. "And anything I play, I have to play my way because that's how I learned. Now, you can play just like the other man–that's fine–but in this open tuning it ain't gonna sound the same. So I just kick off my songs in my beat. Like 'Thrill Is Gone'–it's a beautiful song by B.B. King, and I can do it B.B.'s original way, or I can do it in my version. I'll tell you something about me–I just do my thing. Now, when I play with someone else, what the other man do, I got nothing to do with that. I don't try to out-do him, because we're playing together, making music for the public. When you get over-anxious trying to outdo some-body, you always mess up."

Since the death of Hound Dog Taylor, Hutto has been one of the leaders in a very select group carrying on the Elmore James tradition. J.B. and Homesick James are the obvious keepers of the flame. Of his rival, Hutto feels, "Well, Homesick is a good slide player–or he would be if he played in time, let's put it that way. Time means a whole lot in music. And Homesick James has no time [*laughs*]. I've seen Floyd Jones sit up on the bandstand with Homesick and *sweat*. You got to jump in here and here and here. Home-

sick's all right by himself. When he can play like he wants to, he's a good guitarist, but put him with a band…[*laughs*]."

Of J.B.'s admiration for Hound Dog Taylor, there is no better indication than the fact that for a time after Taylor's death, Hutto inherited his band, the Houserockers, which was the only time J.B. traveled under a name other than the Hawks.

As for current favorites, though, and younger blues-rock sliders, Hutto sighs, "You hear one, you just about heard them all–the way they're playing now. Black musicians are trying to slip into the disco, trying to put the blues into something else and give it another name. They're carrying the same beat, the same sound, and you got nothing. The older blues, you can hear the changes and feel the changes, you know."

As for J.B. trying to update *his* style or cash in on current trends, purists have little to worry about. Today Hutto is playing the blues in the same loud, raucous, beautifully sim-ple style that has been his trademark since the beginning. "When I got this here guitar," he states, "I loved it. This is what I liked; this is what I wanted. I have to have it with me. Sometimes you can wake up in the morning, and you'll find it laying right there on the pillow beside me."

[*J.B. Hutto passed away in 1983.*]

A SELECTED J.B. HUTTO DISCOGRAPHY

Solo albums: *Hawk Squat* ('60s and '70s), Delmark; *J.B. Hutto & The Hawks* ('66), Testament; *Slidewinder* ('72), Delmark; *Blues For Fonessa* ('76), Amigo; *Live, Vol. 1* ('77), Charly; *J.B. Hutto And The Houserockers Live 1977*, Wolf; *Live At Shaboo Inn, Conn. 1979*, Fan Club; *Keeper Of The Flame* ('79-'80), Baron; *Boogie With J.B. Hutto And The Houserockers*, Baron; *Slideslinger*, Varrick; *Slippin' And Slidin'* ('83), Varrick; *Bluesmaster*, JSP.

Anthologies: *Chicago Blues–The Early 1950s*, Blues Classics; *Chicago/The Blues/Today!*, Vanguard; *Best Of Chicago Blues, Vol. 1*, Vanguard; *Great Bluesmen*, Vanguard; *Goin' To Chicago* ('66), Testament; *Chicago Slickers, Vol. 2*, Nighthawk; *Atlantic Blues: Chicago*, Atlantic; *Out Of The Blue*, Rounder; *Blues Explosion* (Montreux, '84), Atlantic.

Soundtracks: *Blue Collar*; *Homeboy*.

On film: *Chicago Blues* (Hutto appears briefly).

Jimmy Reed

December 1976

BY DAN FORTE

THIS NATION'S BICENTENNIAL YEAR was relentlessly harsh on one of America's few unequivocally indigenous musical forms, the blues. The year started off with the deaths of three of the idiom's longtime leaders in rapid succession–Howlin' Wolf, Jesse Fuller, and Mance Lipscomb. All this while the deaths of T-Bone Walker and Hound Dog Taylor a year earlier were still fresh in the blues fan's mind. Still, Wolf had been suffering from kidney trouble for several years (in fact, his death had been reported prematurely more than once), and Fuller and Lipscomb were 79 and 80, respectively.

But perhaps the worst shock came on August 29, when the blues world lost a veritable institution, Jimmy Reed. Born in Leland, Mississippi, Reed was not quite 50 years old and seemed to be at the beginning of a strong comeback when he died of respiratory stoppage apparently caused by an epileptic seizure during his sleep.

After having spent several years hospitalized due to problems of epilepsy compounded by alcoholism, Jimmy had returned to performing with regained health and an optimistic attitude. By this time the Reed repertoire sounded like a "Greatest Hits" album (or two or three). Songs like "Bright Lights, Big City," "You Don't Have To Go," "Baby, What You Want Me To Do," "Take Out Some Insurance," "Caress Me Baby," "Honest I Do," "Going To New York," "Ain't That Loving You, Baby," and "Big Boss Man" poured out, one after the other, all with that immediately identifiable shuffling, walking bass–relaxed but heavy on the backbeat. (As guitarist Albert King, who played drums behind Reed for a short time, once said, "All I could play was a shuffle with a backbeat"–which was about all that was required for the gig.)

Jimmy's guitar playing was primitive, to say the least, but nonetheless bluesy, and as recognizable as his whining, nasal vocals. While repeating his usual song formula, in every possible variation, Jimmy Reed provided countless rock, jazz, pop, and R&B artists with a good portion of their material. The Rolling Stones, Elvis Presley, Count Basie, Muddy Waters, the Animals, Chuck Berry, Johnny and Edgar Winter, Charlie Rich, the Grateful Dead, John Hammond, Jerry Lee Lewis, the Blues Project, James Cotton, the Persuasions, Sonny James, Hot Tuna, Jimmy Witherspoon, Etta James, Bill Cosby, Ike and Tina Turner, Aretha Franklin, and others all turned to Reed's simple but effective music.

Here, in an interview taped just two months before his death, "The Boss Man" reflects on his early development on

guitar, his recordings, his career-long partnership with blues guitarist Eddie Taylor, his years in a V.A. hospital, and his subsequent short-lived comeback.

Didn't nobody teach me how to play the guitar. I just started off trying to fool with a box ever since I was about nine or ten years old. I wasn't making too much progress at it then, but I just kept on trying to do it. Eddie Taylor and me were raised up in the cotton patch together in Mississippi, and we'd fool around with guitars when we got off work in the fields.

But I really didn't get interested in it till after I'd done been up in Chicago. When I was 18 I went into the service, and when I come out, at about 20, I wanted to try it all over again. I was working in the steel mill and listening to that old Muddy Waters, Little Walter, Howlin' Wolf, the Aces, all of them. There was a tavern—it wasn't no "club"—across the street from my house when I was living out in South Chicago. I never did worry about going in the place or nothing; I would stand out there and listen to them playing a little while—but *I* couldn't play nothing. I said to myself, "Well, if these guys can play in here—I don't see too much that they're doing—I think I could do some of the same thing."

I went and bought me an old piece of guitar and just sat out in the alley right in back of my house. I bought me a little amplifier and plugged it in on the patio where I could hear myself.

And at that time you could buy them old 78-size dubs [blank recording discs] that didn't have nothing on them; and I bought one of these old record players where what you was playing on the guitar, you could take this dub and turn it over, and it would play back to you what you had just got through playing. I tried a couple of those, and it seemed like the junk sounded pretty good to me. But it didn't sound like I was getting enough in there—you know, just *me*. So this friend, Willie Joe Duncan, had this piece of wire. Him and me used to get together and just fool around in the alley, drinking and going on.

Then it got around to the point where after I cut about two or three of these old crazy dubs into records, I took them down to Leonard Chess [of Chess/Checker Records]. I asked him what he thought about them. He said, "Well, I tell you what: They sound nice. But I'm so tied up now with Muddy Waters and Walter and Wolf, I can't accept nothing else right now. You're going to have to catch me again later." This was around 1953.

And Vivian Carter was a DJ in Gary, Indiana, and she had a record shop on 16th and Broadway in Gary. Her old man, Jimmy Bracken, was working for Leonard Chess, and he was taking all this in when he heard those dubs, and he

told her what he'd overheard. She sent me a telegram that I had an appointment with her for that coming Sunday. So I went over there and took these dubs along with me and my little piece of guitar and little old amplifier, too. I played a couple of the records for her and got my guitar and amp, so she could see me do it. She said, "How would you like to cut some records for me if I could get you started?" I didn't know anything about cutting no records; I just wanted to hear myself either over the radio or in the jukebox. So we arranged to do a session, but I didn't have no band. She said she'd get the musicians to play behind me and asked me if I wanted pianos or horns or what in there. I never did bother about having piano on no records; it just didn't sound right to me. At the speed of the background I had, it seemed like it was always betwixt and between—wasn't fast enough or slow enough, either.

And when I got to the studio the next week, she had Eddie Taylor there to play background behind me! So on some of them records there was him, me, [guitarist] Lefty Bates, a drummer—and my son [Jimmy "Boonie" Reed, Jr.] had been fooling with my guitar and got pretty good himself. So I had something like four guitars, and the drums made five, and I was blowing harmonica, too, just like I do it now. The one that made me want to get a harmonica was old man Sonny Boy Williamson—the original [John Lee Williamson], the one that did "Good Morning Little Schoolgirl." He could play some stuff! I was fooling with it in Mississippi and started playing with a harness in about '52.

So we did the session, and it sounded pretty good. The first record was "Found My Baby Gone." They named the company Vee Jay—"V" for Vivian and "J" for Jimmy Bracken. Their first records was mine. When I first started making records I thought everything was going to be all right. And everything *was* all right until the thing started making money. I was supposed to be getting royalties, but I didn't get none. But I been thinking about cutting some more records, and a lot of people have been on me to do some more.

But anyway, back in 1954 Vee Jay put out this thing I had cut about "You Don't Have To Go" with "Boogie In The Dark," a stone instrumental, on the reverse side. One evening I was coming home from the Armour Packing Company—I'd quit the iron foundry and was working as a butcher—and I heard this old number about "You Don't Have To Go" over the air. The guy on the radio said, "That's Jimmy Reed; he's going to be out in Atlanta, Georgia, this Friday and Saturday night"—and this was Thursday evening! I didn't know that I was booked in Atlanta. I headed home, grabbed my junk, headed to the studio to cut a couple of numbers, and told Eddie Taylor, "Eddie, I'm supposed to be in Atlanta, Georgia. You going down there with me?" He

Jimmy Reed in San Francisco, a month before his death.

wanted to speak to them. Muddy Waters, B.B. King, all of them big cats–"Oh, you're Jimmy Reed? I'm so glad you come down here to see me. How much they charge you to come in?" "Oh, they let me come in for nothing." "Well, come back in the dressing room." And I'd go back and listen to them talking about this, that, and the other, but it didn't mean too much to me; I didn't know nothing.

I was working one-nighters mostly in Texas, Alabama, Florida, Louisiana, Georgia, and out on the West Coast–while I was still living in Chicago. I might be playing in California one night and have to be in Washington, D.C., practically the next night. I had a little stage fright about playing before the public, but I was drinking liquor at the time. I wasn't never no pot smoker, and I never did fool with any of that cocaine or junk or crazy pills, but I'd drink me some liquor.

Then in the '60s some time I started having these [epileptic] seizures. I remember one time I went on the stage, and I didn't even know when I came off. I must have collapsed on the stage, and they carried me off. After they found out I had been in the service, the V.A. hospital in Downey, Illinois, accepted me in 1969.

The doctor said my nerves had got shook up, and the liquor I was drinking just kept *pushing* me. He said he thought it would be a good idea for me to quit playing music for a while, quit cutting records and everything. He said, "You need to just lay down and rest a while; let your nerves get together." Used to be I could feel those things coming on, and I'd go sit down. But then they started coming on me in my sleep; then I'd have a heck of a time. Because you're capable of coming out from under them things, and you're capable of not coming out. If there ain't nobody there to stick something in your mouth, you might swallow your tongue or something.

said, "Yeah, wherever you want to go!" So we bought a little jug and struck out driving to Atlanta.

And I never did go back to the packing company to even give them back my knife or my clothes or to get my check or nothing. That was the first time I had went on the road or played *anywhere* before the public. I'd just been playing up and down the alley or at friends' houses. I went to see *other* guys in Chicago playing in clubs–go by just to holler at them. I didn't want to play or see the show either; I just

Then I left the hospital and lived in one of these registration [convalescent] homes until the doctor said, "Jimmy, you can go home when you get ready." So they'd mail me a supply of medicine about once a month after I left in '72. I gave up music for about four or five years; I didn't cut no records or do nothing.

I played guitar a lot in the hospital, though. They had a big old music center up there where I would go and get me a guitar and amplifier and just lock up in a room all day. And I didn't have nobody to help me out and back me up. See, during my first two or three records I wasn't doing nothing but blowing the solo on the harmonica and starting off the intro on the guitar. Then the rest of the band would haul off and head into it. But after I got in the hospital, my style changed in a way: I started trying to play my intro part, as much of the lead part as I could get in, do my singing part, blow the solo on the harmonica, and play the bass part all the way through, too. I started doing all that myself, which was a pretty hard thing. But it got me to the place where if I *ain't* playing the lead part, it don't sound right now, since I been doing it a few years.

I used to do all my numbers with a *Bb* harmonica, which would cause the guitar to be in *F*. But after so long it started to strain my voice, so I started playing *A* harmonica, which caused the guitar to be *E*. I put a clamp [capo] on the 5th fret when I blow on the high part of the harmonica, and the band will be playing in *A* then. Of course you don't *have* to put a clamp on it–there's a whole lot can be played up there without one. Eddie Taylor, he don't fool with a clamp. He's played with everybody, and you don't ever catch him putting a clamp on. I imagine if I hadn't tried to play the harmonica and done nothing but play guitar with everybody, I'd probably have been like him. Eddie, I don't care how many records he's made or who he's played with, when he plays somewhere with me, he don't worry about playing nothing he ever did on anyone else's junk. He helped me on all my records but about two.

I can't play behind anybody else. I have to start my own thing and let everybody push me. You can put me up there with somebody else playing, and I can't get in tune or keep up with them. But let me start *my* stuff, and I can go ahead on.

My son also played on all my records, except the first couple and the last couple. He's a stone musician. I ain't nothing, but he can play music, write music, read music, arrange music–he's just long gone with it. But he can't sing worth nothing, and he don't like the blues. He's a rock and roll type. He learned the guitar just from being around me–I ain't taught him nothing. Sometimes I'd go down in the basement and be up all night, trying to see what I could play on the thing. He wasn't nothing but a little kid, and he'd sit down there with me till him and the dog would fall asleep in the corner. I think he was, I should say, 10 or 11 years old when he first played on a record of mine. He plays rock and roll, but me, myself, I play the blues. I don't play no rock and roll stuff, but my records made it on the rock stations, because the background just had some kind of a beat to it that just got everybody to moving.

When me and Eddie used to fool around in Mississippi, they wasn't making no electric guitars. I started off with one of those "folk" boxes with the hole in the middle. But when I got to recording I had me an electric. I played some of everything–I never did have no special brand. Then in '72, after I got out of the V.A. hospital, I was at a music shop getting some picks and strings, and I saw this guitar [a Japanese Les Paul copy made by Ariel]. It had the type of feel I like in a box. So the guy let me have it for $42 or $52–I thought it was a pretty good deal.

My amp is an old Fender Concert; I think it was one of the first ones they made. I had a newer Fender amp, but I got this Concert for $90. The average cats on the bandstand, they turn their box wide open and have them blasting. I don't call that music; you can't hear what the other guy's doing. I can see them doing that if they're reading everything off sheet music, but when you're just playing by ear, you have to listen to who's doing what.

When I started out, I used a flatpick. But with the straight pick, in my style, the wrist will get tired. So then I started using the fingerpick and thumbpick, so there ain't nothing to get tired out but just my thumb. If I wanted to come off the bass with the lead notes, that's when the index finger comes in. This song I made about "Big Boss Man," I've tried to show a lot of guys who was stone musicians, pretty well professionals, how to play the intro to that, and they can't do it so it sounds right.

I just do my one straight thing. But it seems to work out pretty good like it is.

A SELECTED JIMMY REED DISCOGRAPHY

Solo albums (on Vee Jay): *I'm Jimmy Reed; Found Love; Now Appearing; Just Jimmy Reed; Blues Is My Business; Jimmy Reed At Carnegie Hall* (reissued by Mobile Fidelity); *The Best Of Jimmy Reed; Jimmy Reed Sings The Best Of The Blues; Jimmy Reed At Soul City; The Legend, The Man; T'ain't No Big Thing... But He Is.*

Vee Jay reissues: *Rockin' With Reed* ('55-'64), Charly; *Jimmy Reed* ('66-'71), Flyright; *Ride 'Em On Down* ('53-'64), Charly; *Upside Your Head* ('55-'64), Charly; *I'm The Man Down There*, Charly; *Got Me Dizzy*, Charly; *Big Boss Blues*, Charly; *The Best Of Jimmy Reed*, GNP/Crescendo; *I'm Jimmy Reed/Just Jimmy Reed*, P-Vine.

Other labels: *Down In Virginia*, ABC/Bluesway; *The New Jimmy Reed Album*, ABC/Bluesway; *Soulin'*, MCA; *I Ain't From Chicago*, ABC/Bluesway; *Jimmy Reed*, Archive Of Folk; *Cold Chills* ('66-'71), Krazy Kat; *High And Lonesome*, Charly; *Live At Liberty Hall, Houston, TX, 1972* (with Johnny Winter), Fan Club; *Wailing The Blues*, Tradition; *The History Of Jimmy Reed, Vol. 1* and *Vol. 2*, Trip; *Boogie In The Dark*, Aura; *Shame Shame Shame*, Krazy Kat; *Cold Chills*, Krazy Kat; *Jimmy Reed Is Back*, Roots; *Street Talkin'*, Muse; *Down In Mississippi* (Vee Jay material, plus ten sides from '70), Vogue.

Anthologies: *All Them Blues*, DJM; *Blues Masters, Volume 2: Postwar Chicago*, Rhino; *Blues Masters, Volume 4: Harmonica Classics*, Rhino; *Blues Masters, Volume 6: Blues Originals*, Rhino; *Blues Masters, Volume 7: Blues Revival*, Rhino; *The Fifties: Juke Joint Blues*, Flair/Virgin; *The Real Blues Brothers*, DCC; *Super Blues*, Stax; *Blues Upside Your Head*, Charly; *Big Boss Men*, Red Lightnin'.

Little Milton

July 1991

BY DAN FORTE

I

F IT'S POSSIBLE TO BE A SUPERSTAR and an unsung hero at the same time, Little Milton fills the bill. His recording career now encompasses five decades and countless R&B hits featuring his expressive, stinging guitar and deep and overwhelmingly powerful voice. But the blues revival of the late '60s virtually passed him by, and only in recent years has he been embraced by the blues festival circuit. The first edition of *Blues Records, 1943–1966* (by English historians Mike Leadbitter and Neil Slaven) left out his stunning discography, and this is his first *Guitar Player* feature.

Born Milton Campbell in Inverness, Mississippi, in September 1934, "Little Milton" (his father was "Big Milton") first recorded under his own name in 1953, for Memphis' famed Sun label–then home of Howlin' Wolf, Little Junior Parker, Roscoe Gordon, and James Cotton. There and briefly at Meteor Records he displayed much talent but not much individuality; his style didn't emerge until he moved to East St. Louis, Illinois, and scored a regional hit with "I'm A Lonely Man" on the Bobbin label.

Moving to Chicago's Chess/Checker mecca in the early '60s, he leaned towards a sophisticated, horn-bolstered, big band approach a la Bobby Blue Bland, racking up a string of black radio hits. "So Mean To Me" made the charts in 1962, followed by a chilling remake of Bland's "Blind Man" in '64. "We're Gonna Make It" hit #1 on the R&B roster in '65, followed by "Who's Cheating Who," the classic "Feel So Bad," "If Walls Could Talk," "More And More," and "Grits Ain't Groceries" ("Blind Man" and the last two were covered by Traffic, Blood, Sweat & Tears, and Savoy Brown, respectively). He's as comfortable singing a soul ballad as a 12-bar blues, but it's Campbell's versatility, ironically, that has kept him from being fully accepted by many blues purists.

Signing with Memphis' Stax label in 1972, Milton began featuring more of his guitar work, which had evolved from the primitive, distorted abandon of his Sun days (particularly when backing obscure blues singer Houston Boines) to sweet B.B. King bends and finally to his own unique method of percussive muting. He appeared at Los Angeles' enormous WattStax concert that year and soon scored possibly his biggest hit of all, "Walkin' The Back Streets And Crying."

After leaving Stax and bouncing from Florida's TK to tiny Golden Ear to MCA, Little Milton landed back in Mississippi (this time in Jackson) on Malaco in '85. Success on his own terms continues; he tours with his eight-piece All Stars and the Miltonettes backup singers, and in '91 released *Too Much Pain.* As Don Palmer wrote in the liner notes to

just one of the singer/guitarist's greatest-hits packages, "Milton is the consummate chitlin' circuit artist–an entertainer comfortable with several musical moods, and a brilliant showman."

Did your style change depending on which label you were on and what they were looking for?

I don't think so. The only thing it would be safe to say is that I sort of grew and graduated to where I am today. My style is only expressed in my feeling, I guess you could say. So I have always had a versatile feeling for the different types of music I do. I've never been hung up into the 12-bar blues thing. I'm all across the board, and as I learned to feel it deeply I also learned to express it a little wider.

Even though many of your hits, such as "More And More" and "We're Gonna Make It," weren't 12-bar blues, would you agree that blues has always been essential to your style?

Yeah. You know, it's hard to define what's blues and what's not. I'm not ashamed to be billed as a bluesman–if that's what you call it, then that's what it is–but I just feel what I do, however it turns out. I'm just somebody who plays and sings what they feel. And who is there to say what blues is? So many people have different definitions. It's an individual's output of what they feel–happy, sad, comical, or whatever. I'm satisfied as long as I'm making somebody else feel what I'm feeling.

When you first took up guitar, which players did you listen to?

I idolized T-Bone Walker. To me, he was the greatest. He didn't just play all 12-bars, either; his thing was more progressive. He did a lot of chords and frailing. To me, his guitar was like singing. You could really grab just one string and let it express how you felt. He was my favorite. After him, of course, along came B.B., but I believe everybody that picked up a guitar was listening to T-Bone, and everybody wanted to sort of imitate him and had a little bit of him in them–even today. You could recognize T-Bone for the treble he used in his tone. It was electric, but it made it sound more acoustic, semi-raw.

Did you get to see him live?

He and I got to be friends. That was one of the greatest thrills and an honor. We worked some gigs together, and I was really beside myself. Not everybody gets a chance to meet–let alone be friends with–their idol.

Were there additional influences–guitar or otherwise?

Oh yeah. Lowell Fulson, Roy Brown, Joe Turner, Little Willie John, Nat King Cole, Frank Sinatra, and like I said, a lot of country and western. I sort of went to college on all of these people. I guess it would be safe to say I graduated with a little of all of them in me. And somewhere along the way I woke up one morning and discovered that I had molded a Little Milton, and here I am today.

In turn, you've also influenced many singers and guitarists, among them Magic Sam and Albert King.

It gives you a good feeling to know that somebody thinks you're good enough to influence them too. I don't run around gloating about it; I'm just happy that somebody thinks I'm good enough.

Did you hook up with Sun through Ike Turner?

That's correct. Ike Turner took me to Sun Records. At that time Ike was like an independent scout–someone with a lot of acquaintances who had record companies–and he would check out young artists to see if they wanted to make records. And, of course, that was all of our dreams.

How did you come to his attention?

I honestly don't know, but we're from the same area. My hometown and his are about 65 miles apart. His was Clarksdale, Mississippi, and mine are Greenville and Leland. As local musicians, we would bump into each other occasionally. My first exposure was when he and Jackie Brenston had this tune called "Rocket 88." The word probably got around; if there's another kid on the block doing what you're doing, you get to be each other's competition. Anyway, we got to be friends. Naturally, I wanted to make records, and he knew somebody that wanted us, so he took me in. In fact, Ike played piano on my very first recordings. Very talented. But I want to clear this up: I never worked for Ike Turner. We never worked in each other's group. He took me into the studio, but when we left, that was the end of it.

Were you influenced by the music coming out of Memphis?

Well, it wasn't coming out of Memphis too much. The main thing we had to listen to was a radio station out of Nashville called WLAC. The legendary Gene Nobles and Hoss Man were sponsored by one of the biggest record sellers at that time, Randy's Record Shop. Anybody that was recording any kind of record that we would know about, they were playing it. The format was basically R&B, even on the local stations. I can remember listening to Louis Jordan & His Tympany Five every evening at 6:15. With that and the jukeboxes, it sort of gave me the incentive to learn and perform music.

Did you record anything for Trumpet Records before recording for Sun?

Never as Little Milton, but I played guitar with Willie Love, and that possibly predated Sun. I don't know for sure; it's been a long time, and I didn't keep tabs on my career too much back then.

On the Sun stuff you had a loud, distorted tone, espe-

cially backing up Houston Boines. Do you remember your equipment?

Probably a Silvertone. That's about all I was able to afford. But the distortion, I think, was coming from the inaccuracy of the recording equipment or whoever was engineering it, probably Sam Phillips. It wasn't sophisticated like it is today.

Before becoming a bandleader and recording artist, were you a sideman?

I played for a gentleman who had a local band in Greenville by the name of Cleanhead Love, who played drums, and a guy named Eddie Cusic. They had big bands– you know, it was the big band era–and I learned quite a bit from them. They did a great variety of stuff. I came up in a good era, as far as learning different avenues.

Did you play mostly rhythm, as opposed to the lead work you're now known for?

Yes, in the big band thing that's what you had to do. Basically, the horns would solo. Once in a while you might get a solo, but other than that you laid back and played the rhythm feels.

Did that give you a pretty decent chord vocabulary?

Well, I did pretty well.

You also worked with Sonny Boy Williamson?

Yeah. Sometimes he and Willie Love and Joe Willie Wilkins would be like an "all for one, one for all" thing. They hired me, so it was just the four of us. That was a great experience and an honor too, to work with these great guys.

Who produced your Sun sides–Ike Turner or Sam Phillips?

There was no such thing as producing back then, not where we were. You'd go in and strike up a tune. And unfortunately, whoever had hit records on the jukeboxes, you'd jump on the bandwagon. That's why so many of the songs sound just like somebody else's hit.

Many comments about your records from that period describe you as a chameleon–sounding like Fats Domino

Little Milton at the 1992 Chicago Blues Festival: "I'm satisfied as long as I'm making somebody else feel what I'm feeling."

one minute and Elmore James the next.

Yeah. Some sound like B.B. King. Whoever had hit records, that's who you'd sound like. You got away with it because you'd change the lyrics around, but we didn't really write anything before we went into the studio. That's why a lot of the tunes have the same lyrics somewhere in there. But nobody really produced anything. I don't even know if they gave credit for producer. You just went in there and started singing, and they'd turn the tape on. Whatever came up, that's what you had.

When did you begin to develop your own sound?

Oh, I guess it had to be when I moved from Mississippi to East St. Louis, Illinois. We're talking about the latter '50s.

The Bobbin recordings?

Right. I had really come into the Little Milton sound. "Same Old Blues" was for Bobbin, and "Lonely Man" was the very first recording–the birth of Bobbin Records. Bob Lyons, the general manager of KATZ in St. Louis, knew the president of Mercury Records. Bob and I got to be pretty decent friends, so he called his friend and told him we'd send him a tape. We went into the radio station and recorded "I'm A Lonely Man" and sent it to the gentleman at Mercury. He sent it back and said not to send "junk" to him–don't "waste his time." That sort of pissed us both off, so Bob started his own label. "I'm a Lonely Man" must have sold about 50,000 copies. Then the guy from Mercury wanted us to let him have it–the same guy who turned it down. That catalog has been passed through so many hands.

There's a collection of those sides and some of the Sun things on Red Lightnin' called Raise A Little Sand.

Yeah. once we got a check from that company, and by the time we deposited it, it came back–they had gone out of business. That's the same type of underhanded stuff that Sam Phillips did. Once there was Elvis Presley, he never mentioned any of the black artists who actually were the foundation of Sun Records, even today when interviews come up. It's only Elvis, Jerry Lee Lewis, Carl Perkins, Charlie Rich, Johnny Cash; he never mentions the Junior Parkers, the Little Miltons, the Ike Turners, the Billy Gayleses–a whole bunch of artists. When you start talking about an organization, how can you have a history without having a foundation? I don't know how they got all this stuff mixed up. You know, a lot of it is bootleg. Some of the stuff on Bobbin wound up on *Raise A Little Sand,* so I know that Sam Phillips could not have been the sole perpetrator of that. After Sun Records we did a little thing for Meteor, with one of the Bihari brothers, based in Memphis–Lester Bihari. It was pretty decent stuff. I'd just begun writing things before I'd go into the studio. That was the beginning of my graduating period.

Who backed you up on the Bobbin recordings?

That was my band, and Oliver Sain was the bandleader. On some of the stuff Fontella Bass did a hell of a job on piano.

Some of the Bobbin things, like "My Baby Pleases Me," feature vibes–unusual for a '50s blues record.

That's Oliver Sain. See, again, he and I have never been hung up on just that 12-bar stuff. He and I were talking at the 1990 St. Louis Blues Festival. When I got to East St. Louis, it was somewhat of a jazz surrounding. You know, that's Miles Davis' hometown. They were playing all types of stuff, but it was basically standards, pretty tunes. Even though we played some of the hard stuff, we had to mix it up because that's what the audience wanted. So fortunately for Oliver and myself, we were never hung up on the 12-bar blues–even though we could play it, and we did play it. When I had the opportunity to work for people like Sonny

Boy Williamson, Elmo James, Willie Love, who was Oliver Sain's stepfather, and a very dear friend of mine, Joe Willie Wilkins, you know that's what they played. They would call some of the stuff jump music, but it was all basically 12-bar blues. But when they would leave the bandstand, and it was just Oliver and me sitting up there, we'd play the kind of stuff we wanted to play.

Were you into country music at all?

Most certainly, in the very beginning. I've always loved country. In fact, that's almost all you could get. You'd listen to the *Grand Ole Opry* out of Nashville, before WLAC started playing the blues. Nashville was the lifeline, so to speak, for the music for everybody in the South. The radio stations were very powerful, and the distances they would reach were incredible. I was into Eddy Arnold, George Morgan, Hank Williams–just name 'em, I'd be glued to the radio.

One of your Sun tunes, "Re-beat," sounds a little country.

That was the kind of stuff that Willie Love and them called jump time, or jump music–sort of rockabilly.

Obviously, moving to Chess in the early '60s was another big change. Were the big horn arrangements, more of a Bobby Blue Bland approach, something you'd been leaning towards?

Well, back then I was really getting into my own thing. You grow, and it's literally impossible to miss everybody. Unfortunately in one way, but fortunately in another, Bobby Bland and I began to bump, as far as the styles and the power. At that time Bobby was not doing the little [*mimics Bland's guttural cough*] thing that he does now; he had a lot of power. And I had a lot of power. I think the thing that really linked us together was the fact that I recorded one of his songs, "Blind Man." At that time Bobby Bland could do no wrong. Every song he recorded was a smash hit. It seemed like he was untouchable. When I recorded "Blind Man," it turned some ears, and people started saying, "Oh, he's not so untouchable after all." People thought I was a newcomer–which I was not. And the late Don Robey of Duke Records decided to express his greed by re-releasing Bobby's "Blind Man" in order to knock us out of the box. But I think instead of hurting me, it helped me more. That's when things happened for me, because the disc jockeys would make comparisons.

The Chess recordings sounded like producers were definitely involved.

Of course, yes. I produced *Little Milton Sings Big Blues,* but I worked with Billy Davis, then Calvin Carter, and then Eugene Barge.

With your voice as your strong suit, did you ever downplay your guitar?

Yes. For one thing, I've never really considered myself a

hell of a guitar player. I sort of ad-lib. I play for me. As I said earlier, I express what I feel. It's sort of an accent type of thing–the coordination from the voice to the guitar. But when you're talking about the big band sound, I didn't feel like I could play it the way I really wanted to, so I would leave it up to another player–unless they didn't play exactly what I wanted; then I would overdub. On my live shows I would always play the guitar.

Who did you use on the Chess recordings?

Gerald Sims, who I believe is now the owner of the old Chess studio in Chicago on South Michigan, and a guy named Bryce, or Phil Upchurch, or myself. On the Malaco stuff I play most of the leads, sometimes Michael Toles–one hell of a player–and Jimmy Johnson plays rhythm.

Who played on "Feel So Bad"?

That's me. Bryce was on "Sneakin' Around."

What's your main guitar these days?

A very old Gibson ES-345, the first year they made a stereo [1959]. I've got about three of the old ones; they're my treasures. I had one redone green and gold. I don't even play it, it's sort of a showpiece.

What about amplifiers?

You know, strange as it might sound, I'm still holding on to one of those old Acoustics. They don't even make them anymore. When it goes, I don't know what I'll do. I was fortunate to have two speakers in an extra cabinet.

In the late '60s and early '70s, when Albert and B.B. and Freddie King started crossing over to the white, hippie audience, you continued to have hits on black radio but never crossed over to the Fillmore crowd.

You're right. Again, I can't be comfortable doing a show night after night of nothing but 12-bar blues–fast, slow, or medium. I don't know if it's hurt me or helped me, but I refuse to sell myself out. I just keep doing what I enjoy, and hope I can still reach people. I never shot for something because it was what everybody else was doing. I've never been a good follower.

A SELECTED LITTLE MILTON DISCOGRAPHY

Solo albums: *Sun Masters* (early '50s), Rounder; *Hittin' The Boogie* (Sun, '53-'54), Zu Zazz; *Raise A Little Sand* ('53-'59), Red Lightnin'; *We're Gonna Make It* (reissue of '65 Checker LP), Chess; *If Walls Could Talk*, Chess; *Little Milton Sings Big Blues* (Checker, '66), Chess; *His Greatest Sides* ('62-'71), Chess; *Chicago Blues, Vol. 5*, Chess France; *If Walls Could Talk*, Chess France; *The TK Sessions* (reissue of *Friend Of Mine* and *Me For You, You For Me*), Sequel; *Chronicle* (one side each by Albert King and Little Milton), Stax; *Grits Ain't Groceries* (live in Los Angeles, '72), Stax; *Walking The Back Streets*, Stax; *Blues 'N' Soul*, Stax; *What It Is–Live At Montreux*, Stax; *Waiting For Little Milton/Blues 'N' Soul* (Stax reissues), Ace; *Age Ain't Nothin' But A Number* ('83), Mobile Fidelity; *Annie Mae's Cafe*, Malaco; *Little Milton Plays For Keeps*, Malaco; *I Will Survive*, Malaco; *Movin' To The Country*, Malaco; *Strugglin' Lady*, Malaco; *Too Much Pain* ('91), Malaco; *Reality* ('91), Malaco; *Back To Back*, Malaco; *Who's Cheating Who*, Blues Journey.

With others: Willie Love, *Delta Blues–1951*, Trumpet.

Anthologies: *Big Road Blues–The Real Thing From Mississippi 1951-1967*, Collectables; *The Stax Blues Brothers*, Stax; *Super Blues*, Stax; *Blue Monday*, Stax; *Chess Blues* box set; *The Blues Is Alright, Vol. 1* and *Vol. 3*, Malaco; *Sun Records–The Blues Years, 1950–1956*, Charly; *Black Music Originals, Vol. 2* and *Vol. 3*, Sun.

Hubert Sumlin

April 1980 & February 1987

By Dan Forte

& Jas Obrecht

W
HEN IT COMES TO THE UNSUNG HEROES of the blues–of which there are hundreds–Hubert Sumlin would have to be among the main contenders for top honors. For 23 years he played guitar behind Howlin' Wolf, the scariest blues singer of all. His classic parts in "Spoonful," "Smokestack Lightnin'," "Wang Dang Doodle," and "I Ain't Superstitious" influenced a generation of blues-based rockers, including Peter Green, Frank Zappa, the brothers Vaughan, and the Rolling Stones. Jimi Hendrix once cited him as his favorite guitarist, and Eric Clapton told *Guitar Player* in 1976: "For a long time I'd really wanted to meet Hubert because he did some things that freaked me out when I was picking up the guitar–that stuff on 'Goin' Down Slow,' just the weirdest playing. He's truly amazing."

"Weird" and "amazing" are good summations of Sumlin's style. His staccato attacks, extroverted slides, and unique use of fills, bass lines, and mantra-like riffs interspersed with only an occasional chord were perfect complements to Howlin' Wolf's rhythmic style and penchant for songs with no chord changes at all. Wolf's gravelly, demonic growl coupled with Sumlin's hypnotic riffs and occasional solo outbursts could only be described as haunting. Today, more than a decade after Wolf's death, Hubert is keeping the spirit alive on his well-received solo albums and in the film *Hubert Sumlin–Livin' The Blues*.

One of 13 children, Hubert was born on November 16, 1931, in Greenwood, Mississippi, and raised in Hughes, Arkansas–a town about 35 minutes from West Memphis, Arkansas. He started playing drums at age ten, and took up the guitar a year later with an $8 acoustic his mother bought him. "I got an older brother named A.D. Smith on my father's side," Sumlin recalls, "and he was playing way before me. So I tried to get him to learn me how to play. But he wouldn't learn me a tune or nothing, and we got to fighting four or five times because of that. Of course, I got whupped every time because I was small [*laughs*]. So I watched what he was doing and got me one tune. Then my mind started getting together, you know, so I ended up with four or five tunes."

Although the first musicians he listened to were jazz players such as Louis Armstrong, one of the first guitarists Hubert was exposed to as a child was the man he would later spend 23 years of his performing life with. He remembers, "When I first went to see Wolf, he put me out of the place. I'd crawl up under people's legs and get thrown out the door. That didn't stop me, though; I got some Coca-Cola

crates as tall as I could get them, and I was sitting up there, rocking and reeling, until somebody pulled the crates out from under me [*laughs*]. I was just a little dude who wanted to play and hear. I was maybe 12 years old when this started. I did this around Wolf for about two or three years. Finally he knew who I was. He said, 'Let him alone.' He set me in a chair beside [guitarist] Willie Johnson, the drummer, and him. I just sat right there, boy, rockin'. He made me sit in the chair where I wouldn't see no booze or nothing.

"One night he said, 'How'd you get out here tonight?' I just thumbed me a ride, you know. Then he said, 'Does your mama know you're out here? I'm gonna take you home.' I knew if I went back home I'd get two whuppings, but I loved the Wolf anyway. He took me back to my mama and talked to her, so I didn't get no whupping. Then I went back the next Friday night! I asked the lady at the door to ask Wolf if I could come in, and he said okay. Got a chair and sat up there with him. Stayed with him for more than 20 years later on."

A plantation field worker by day, young Hubert got in the habit of taking his guitar with him when he went to work. Ultimately, he remembers, this led to his getting a better instrument: "I'd put my guitar on my back, get on the tractor, and go down to the field. I'd plow about maybe two acres, then I'd just cut the tractor off and sit and play [*laughs*]. So this guy caught me playing the guitar behind the wheel. And he was so mad because I didn't plow but two acres, he took my guitar and broke it across the tractor. I got so mad I hit him upside the head, but that didn't do no good–he was bigger than I was. I was only about 14 years old. So I wasn't gonna work no more until I got me another guitar. Later my mother told this guy, 'What did you do that for?' He said, 'He should have been working.' My mother was sanctified, you know, really religious. And that was the first time I ever heard her *start* to cuss. So then this guy went and bought me a $20 guitar, but I had to promise that I wouldn't play it on my job. I still got the guitar; the strings are way up on it now. You can't even play it–I just look at it."

By the time Hubert was a couple of years into learning the guitar, he considered himself a jazz player. Circumstances, however, prompted his move to the blues. "I found I couldn't get jobs," he explains, "and I had to eat and sleep. So this is when I started thinking about playing something else." At age 18 he found his first professional job, playing second guitar for James Cotton. Cotton's first guitarist at the time was Pat Hare, who later in the '50s was part of Muddy Waters' Chicago-based band. Hubert spent close to three years in the Cotton band, touring Arkansas and Tennessee. He accompanied the harmonicist on a session for the Memphis-based Sun label, recording "I Ain't Gonna Pick No More Cotton" sometime in 1953 or '54.

In early '54 Sumlin joined Howlin' Wolf's band for three weeks, playing in Louisiana, Mississippi, Tennessee, and a stint at the Silkhairs Club in West Memphis. "These guys he had working with him, such as Willie Johnson, was his regular band," he recalls. "I didn't know at the time that they was quitting. My first night of playing with him was in New Orleans. Then we played another job, still with his same old band, down south in Mississippi. We stayed in Memphis and then went through Tennessee. Then Wolf come by in this big old long limousine. He said, 'Hubert, I'm fixing to go to Chicago. I sold the band boys all my equipment. When I get to Chicago, if I need you, can I send for you?' I said yeah, but I didn't believe it. I went on. Sure enough, about two weeks later he sent for me."

On his arrival in Chicago, Sumlin was greeted by Wolf and Muddy Waters. He soon met many of the best-known bluesmen around town, including pianists Eddie Boyd, Memphis Slim, and Sunnyland Slim, harmonicist Little Walter, and guitarists Big Bill Broonzy, Elmore James, and Johnny Shines. Hubert became the second guitarist in Wolf's band. The other members included Jody Williams, a lead guitarist who could also double on bass, piano, or drums; tenor saxophonist Abe Locke; drummer Early Phillips; and pianist Hosea Lee Kennard. At the time, Hubert remembers, Howlin' Wolf mainly sang and played harmonica, although he did pick up a guitar from time to time to teach the band new material.

Howlin' Wolf had signed a long-term recording contract with the Chess label, and in May 1954 Hubert accompanied him on "All Night Boogie," "Mr. Highway Man," "I'm The Wolf," "No Place To Go," "Baby, How Long," "Evil Is Going On," and several other sides. For a brief period later on in the year, Sumlin attended the Chicago Conservatory of Music: "I went to school for my scales and to know where I was on the guitar, to find out if I was right or not. The Chicago Conservatory was the only place I could find when I got there. They taught everything–jazz, blues, rock and roll, and so forth. I was kind of taught by different people before I made it to this school. So I went there and I really knew a little bit too much about guitar. I was sitting there playing and the teacher said, 'What did you come down here for?' I said, 'Well, I come down to learn my scales.' It didn't take too long, about four months. Then I just went back in my bag. I did learn how to read music, so I can read now if it's necessary. If it ain't necessary, I don't [*laughs*]. It's a thing that comes to any musician if he's interested and wants to go the right route–just like you're driving a car: You don't want to go two blocks down when you could go right through where you are."

With Wolf, Hubert found he needed to modify his playing

approach: "With the straight pick, I was running all over myself. I was playing some stuff that I think was before my time, and so I put it down. I sat down in the basement one day and said, 'Well, I gotta find Hubert; I gotta see where I am.' I had to get me a tone. It seemed like it come to me just like I was dreamin'– I found out that I could get a feeling with my fingers better than I could with a pick. I found out that I had more soul in me without the picks. The tone fitted Wolf, and from then on it was a natural thing." To this day, the fingers-only approach is a hallmark of Sumlin's style.

In 1955 and '56 Hubert recorded several more sides with Wolf, among them the now classic "Forty-Four," "Don't Mess With My Baby," and "Smokestack Lightnin'." Hubert explains that oftentimes he and Wolf would get together with Willie Dixon to work out material: "We would run a number down like this–with nobody but me and Willie and Wolf. It was quiet and we didn't have nobody else, so we knew what was gonna happen when we got the rest of the group in there." Friction, however, developed between Sumlin and Wolf, which led to Sumlin's quitting the band in 1956 to go on the road with Muddy Waters. "You know how musicians is," he says. "They have their little faults. I thought I had done got good enough to play what I want to play. And so Wolf was tryin' to help me all the time by telling me, 'No, you ain't–don't think you are the greatest, don't do this and don't do that.' I just got mad and quit.

"So I joined Muddy Waters' outfit and stayed with him a little more than a year. The music was nice; I enjoyed every minute of it. I was kind of young at the time–in my twenties–and what happened was I worked 41 nights in a row. It was a job here tonight, then you had to go 400 miles to do the next job, the next night maybe 250, the next night maybe 350. Well, we was beat on some of the jobs, I'll tell you. When we got back to Chicago we thought we was gonna rest, which we didn't. This is the reason I quit–we couldn't rest. I just had my little fling and come back and told Wolf, 'Hey, man, make room.'"

Sumlin rejoined Wolf's band, and from 1957 until the '70s he almost continually worked the clubs and taverns around Chicago, as well as out-of-town venues ranging from segregated Southern roadhouses to New York's Apollo Theater. In 1957 he played on "Sitting On Top Of The World," and two years later (this time as the band's only guitarist) recorded "Howlin' Blues." His first album with Wolf, 1959's *Moanin' In The Moonlight*, was destined to become a classic.

The following year, with Otis Spann on piano, Willie

© AXEL KÜSTNER

"If you got something of your own, you ain't got to be worried about nobody."

Dixon on bass, and Fred Below on drums, Howlin' Wolf's band recorded three tunes that have since become blues standards, "Wang Dang Doodle," "Back Door Man," and "Spoonful." Hubert used a Gretsch electric for some records during this period, and an early model Gibson Les Paul for others ("Spoonful," he recalls, was done with the Les Paul). By this time he had developed a style of playing that was a combination of lead and rhythm, or as he describes it, "'twixt and between." His relationship with Wolf had also improved to the point where he could second-guess his leader's next musical move: "I became the only one in the group he didn't come right down on and say, 'You didn't do this right,' because I could feel the man. Like we knowed what the other was going to do, what the other one was thinking. I never would get away from him where I couldn't watch him, and we got to communicate so well that I knew what he was gonna do before he did. That's the way we were."

Sumlin and the Wolf band continued recording during the early '60s, producing "The Red Rooster" (this is one of Hubert's rare appearances on slide guitar), "Down In The Bottom," "Shake For Me," "I Ain't Superstitious," and "Goin'

Down Slow" in 1961, "Do The Do" in '62, and "Tail Dragger," "Built For Comfort," and "Three Hundred Pounds Of Joy" in '63. The following year the band toured Europe as part of the American Folk Blues Festival. Once there, Hubert finally had an opportunity to record as a leader. In this context, he not only proved an expressive blues singer–with his plaintive vocal style mirroring his bashful offstage demeanor–but also showed that his roots reached back to his rural beginnings in Mississippi. On acoustic guitar he displayed a rhythmic style recalling John Lee Hooker.

Hubert appeared on some Amiga sides with Sunnyland Slim, and then in 1966 he toured briefly with Muddy Waters and made club performances around Chicago with the Magic Sam Band. His main guitar at this time was a Rickenbacker electric. During the late '60s Chess recorded some new Howlin' Wolf material featuring Sumlin, including _More Real Blues_. In April 1969 the Cadet label released _The Howlin' Wolf Album_, which was subtitled _This is Howlin' Wolf's new album. He doesn't like it. He didn't like his electric guitar at first either._

Howlin' Wolf, Sumlin, and other members of the band journeyed back to England in the early '70s to record _The London Howlin' Wolf Sessions_ for Chess. Appearing on the LP is a host of well-known rock and rollers, among them keyboardists Stevie Winwood and Ian Stewart, Rolling Stones bassist Bill Wyman and drummer Charlie Watts, and, on lead and slide guitar, Eric Clapton. "I didn't know I was gonna meet all these people from famous groups, such as Charlie Watts," Hubert says. "It was a great thing for me to do. I thought they were the greatest; I still think they are.

"I didn't know Eric Clapton until we came in the studio together. He didn't look like I pictured. I was sittin' down, and he got him a chair and sat down by me. We recorded two numbers together before we even reached over and made names together. He said, 'My name is Eric,' and I said, 'My name's Hubert.' And he said, 'I know about you,' and I said, 'Well, man, I heard about you too.' So we got to talking and he invited me to dinner. I went outside the studio and he had a Rolls Royce out there with a chauffeur. We went way up from London in some woods. Man, it was a big old place–I ain't been over it all yet; I've just walked through some of it. The first thing he did was take me down in the basement and show me his guitars. 'Have one,' he said. I picked out a Fender Stratocaster. He had about 140 guitars, maybe more than that. He was surrounded. In fact, I'm using that guitar right now. It's a nice instrument that plays good. I like Fenders, period. They give you a better sound. My amp is a Fender Twin Reverb. When amplifiers first came out, I had an old Wabash amp. I still got it, but it's not workin.'"

During the last few years of his life, Howlin' Wolf was a sick man. In 1973 he was injured in an auto accident that caused kidney damage. Still, the veteran bluesman continued to appear in concert until just before his death in January 1976. "About four months before Wolf really got sick, I thought I had better start looking out for Hubert," Sumlin says. "The thing about it is when you love a person, you stay with him as long as I stayed with the Wolf. You say, 'He ain't gonna die; he's forever.' But you can't think like that. I don't believe the good Lord would have just taken him away from here like that for no reason. After he died, a gang of people was talking about me: 'Oh, yeah, what's he gonna do now? Wolf is gone.' And I got home one day and my wife told me people was callin', wanting to know if I would still work. I said, 'You tell them I'm gonna be working as long as there's a Hubert. I'm gonna do just like the Wolf.' He worked up until the end, so I'm gonna be working as long as I can."

Sumlin assumed leadership of the Howlin' Wolf Band in 1976, and also began working clubs around the Chicago area with Sunnyland Slim. He recorded a solo album, _Groove_, for the European Black And Blue label. In 1978 he was featured on five songs on the first volume of Alligator Records' _Living Chicago Blues_ series, performing with Eddie Shaw And The Wolf Gang. By then, his original Les Paul was enshrined in a glass case in his living room, and his main stage guitars were a Gibson ES-335 and a recent-model Les Paul, both strung with light-gauge strings.

In recent years, the quiet, bespectacled guitarist has concentrated on playing under his own name. His career resurged with 1986's _Hubert Sumlin's Blues Party_, his first American recording under his own name. "I'm 55 years old," Hubert said upon its release, "and I ain't never had a record out in the United States since I been playing all these years with Wolf. This will be my first recording on any kind of major label. I'm very happy about it. It's been too long."

"Singing-wise, Hubert's most effective when he does downhome stuff," producer Hammond Scott noticed during the sessions. "He gets sort of a Lightnin' Hopkins or Jimmy Reed type of sound by himself. But I didn't want to do the whole LP like that, so I brought Mighty Sam McClain to sing songs that bring out another side of Hubert's playing. Hubert's a little absentminded, but he's one of those on-the-spot kind of guys who's a true artist. If you can set up a framework for him to work with, then right off the cuff he'll come up with something wild that sounds really great. But if you go into a session expecting to just lay everything on him–the tunes, the arrangements, and all that–you're in trouble, because he won't do something the same way twice. You never know what to expect, and you can't rehearse his part too much. He's strongest when he can just go in there and blow." _Blues Party_ was followed a couple of years later by *Heart & Soul*, featuring James Cotton and Little Mike And The Tornadoes.

For a long while Hubert was reluctant to cover Wolf tunes, but he's recently added "Down In The Bottom," "Hidden Charms," and a few others to the show. His Abilene Cafe performances a few summers ago inspired Jon Pareles to report in *The New York Times*: "Mr. Sumlin is a guitarist of few notes, masterfully placed. With his raw tone and an extraordinary variety of attacks, he mixes singing blues phrases and slashes of sheer texture–plunking out low riffs, squeezing out delicate sighs in the upper register, making single notes moan, or suddenly swooping down for a metallic shriek. Melodically, his solos are almost abstract; against the chugging rhythms of the band, they are terse and cutting."

Three years in the making, the 72-minute film *Hubert Sumlin–Livin' The Blues* was shot on location in Chicago, Boston, Texas, and Mississippi, with concert footage from the 1984 Delta Blues Festival. In addition to extensive Sumlin interviews and archival photographs and film clips, the documentary features guest appearances by Ronnie Earl, Stevie Ray Vaughan, and James Cotton.

It is interesting to note that when Sumlin looks back over a long career and encounters with most of the best-known bluesmen of the second half of the 20th century, he cites as his favorite guitarist none other than Jimi Hendrix: "I was fortunate enough to meet this guy, and I thought he was wonderful. He was already famous when I met him, and he said, 'I've been hearing about you, Hubert. They tell me you're a fine guitar player.' I said, 'Well, you know, I try to play.' We jammed together in this club in the Village in New York. Richie Havens was there too. Jimi played a whole set with me and Wolf's band. This was pretty close to 1970. I didn't know I liked him that much until I saw him play. This drummer, Buddy Miles, played too. Jimi was a swell guy, one of the best guitar players I've ever seen."

When talking with young guitarists, Hubert's first instinct is to advise them to find their own voice: "When you go on the bandstand, be yourself. Although you may be doing things just like other people do them, be yourself while doing them. You can't just say, 'I'm gonna play just like this man here; he ain't doin' nothing but making money.' If you got something of your own, you ain't got to be worried about nobody. They ain't gonna mess with you. Find that vibration, that feeling, that soul. If you play any instrument, that is it. If you do well, I figure it's like this: You gonna be thought of."

A SELECTED HUBERT SUMLIN DISCOGRAPHY

Solo albums: *Groove*, Black And Blue; *My Guitar And Me* ('75), Black And Blue; *Gotta Run*, Paris; *Hubert Sumlin & Carey Bell* (Sumlin plays acoustic on most cuts), L+R; *Funky Roots*, Vogue; *Hubert Sumlin's Blues Party* ('86), Black Top; *Healing Feeling*, Black Top; *Heart & Soul*, Blind Pig.

With Howlin' Wolf (on Chess, except as noted): *Howlin' Wolf* (a.k.a. "The Rocking Chair Album," '57-'61); *Moanin' In The Moonlight* ('59); *His Greatest Sides, Vol. 1* ('54-'63); *Change My Way* ('59-'66); *Chicago–26 Golden Years*; *Muddy & The Wolf*; *The London Howlin' Wolf Sessions*; *The Real Folk Blues* ('56-'65); *More Real Folk Blues* ('53-'59); *Live In Europe, 1964*, Sundown; *Chester Burnett AKA Howlin' Wolf*; *The Back Door Wolf*; *The Super, Super Blues Band*; *Howlin' Wolf, Vol. 1, 2,* and *3*, Chess U.K.; *From Early To Late*, Blue Night; *Live In Cambridge, MA., 1966*, Fan Club; *Live And Cookin' At Alice's Revisited* ('72), Chess; *Live At Joe's Place, 1973*, Wolf; *Live, 1975!*, Wolf; *The Howlin' Wolf Album*, Cadet; *Howlin' Wolf* box set.

With others: Eddie Shaw And The Wolf Gang, *Living Chicago Blues, Vol. 1*, Alligator.

Anthologies (with Howlin' Wolf and as leader): *Chess Blues* box set; *Blues Anytime* (Europe, '64), L+R; *American Folk Blues Festival, 1964*, L+R; *Atlantic Blues: Chicago* ('72), Atlantic; *Ann Arbor Blues & Jazz Festival 1972*, Atlantic; *Anthology Of The Blues: Memphis*, Kent; *Twenty Greatest R&B Hits*, Kent; *Blues Masters, Volume 4: Harmonica Classics*, Rhino; *Blues Masters, Volume 6: Blues Originals*, Rhino; *Blues Masters, Volume 8: Mississippi Delta Blues*, Rhino; *Legends Of Guitar–Electric Blues, Vol. 1*, Rhino; *The Best Of Chicago Blues, Vol. 2* (backing Sunnyland Slim), Wolf; *The Greatest In Country Blues, Vol. 3 (1929-1956)*, Story Of Blues; *Willie Dixon* box set, Chess; *Antone's Anniversary Anthology, Vol. 2*, Antone's; *American Folk Blues Festival, 1980*, L+R; *American Folk Blues Festival, 1981*, L+R; *Blues With The Girls* (backing singers, '82), EPM; *Back To The Blues*, Zeta; *Blues Guitar Spotlight*, Black Top; *Black Top Blues Pajama Party*, Black Top; *Black Top Blues-A-Rama, Vol. 6: Live At Tipitina's*, Black Top.

On film: *Wolf* (half-hour documentary by Ralph Bass, '71); *Hubert Sumlin–Livin' The Blues* ('87).

Albert Collins

May 1988 & July 1993

BY DAN FORTE
& JAS OBRECHT

ONSTAGE THE ANTONE'S HOUSE BAND is cranking out a shuffle in *C,* and the capacity crowd is buzzing with anticipation. Austin guitarist Derek O'Brien, test-driving a '50s Telecaster he acquired specifically for the gig, sounds amazingly close to Albert Collins, who is backstage playing blackjack with some Austin buddies. Albert's opponent says, "Hit me," checks his cards, and raises the stakes. Albert stares into his eyes and then slams a wad of ones onto the table.

Meanwhile, Albert's valet, Elroy, readies one of the most recognizable axes on the blues circuit, Collins' blonde Telecaster. Albert stands up but still appears to be paying more attention to the cards shuffling backstage than to the blues shuffle *on*stage. Elroy drapes the Fender over Albert's right shoulder and follows the trail of its cord out the door and towards the stage. The guitarist quietly checks his tuning and extracts a roadweary capo, wrapped with electrician's tape, from his pocket and places it at the seventh fret. He quickly twirls the volume knob to 10 and blasts a massive double-stop bend into the next room, punctuating it with stinging vibrato and a wicked smile.

Onstage O'Brien winces, as though he were just Sunday-punched, then smiles, shaking his head and shifting to rhythm guitar. The audience is now on its feet, craning to see where the tone of doom is coming from. Collins rakes the kitty of crumpled dollar bills off the table with mock politeness and stuffs it into his pocket before catapulting another volley of blues runs into the nightclub. By the time he has made his way to the stage, Albert Collins has reeled off a textbook of his patented licks–descending slide jumps, muted staccato triplets, some chicken pickin', arpeggios, octaves, double-stops, and crying bends that can only be described as painful. He strides onto the stage holding a single high note while hammering it over and over in every conceivable way–quarter-notes, eighths, muted, then sustained with shimmering vibrato.

Throughout the set O'Brien and Collins spar, with Derek shaking his head in disbelief more than a few times and Albert running through his entire repertoire of grunts, groans, and grimaces. Other local guitarslingers line up at the side of the stage, and the next contender, David Murray of the Marcia Ball Band, plugs in a white Stratocaster. Albert gives him the floor, reading his licks like a road map before getting behind the wheel and accelerating into each turn. Murray also smiles and shakes his head.

Long after last call, David Grissom, Joe Ely's young Tele

ace, is coiled in front of his Fender Bassman amp, feedback streaming into his face, while Collins fans him with a white towel. Albert does the musical equivalent of Ali's rope-a-dope before delivering a final roundhouse blow–reaching down and bending up a minor third, which hits home like a left hook that began in the next county. The guitarists at the side of the stage try to blend in with the wallpaper before the master can say, "Next?"

Albert Collins may not be the fastest blues guitarist around, or the most versatile. He is, however, the most powerful. And even though he enjoys playing at maximum volume, the power is still there when his solidbody isn't even plugged in (as evidenced during the following interview, when he repeatedly demonstrated the tricks of his trade). The fat, full tone comes from the man's hands, and the biting sting comes from the types of licks he plays–as well as knowing just *when* to unleash them.

As with many bluesmen, virtually everything about Collins' style is unorthodox. For starters, he tunes to a minor chord, instead of standard tuning. (It's an *F* minor triad, or a *Dm7b5* without a root.) Playing essentially in first position at all times, he uses his capo to locate the song's key up and down the neck–hence, using only about a third of the fretboard at times. He picks with his bare thumb and first two fingers, often snapping and yanking up on the strings for emphasis. And while he was inspired by guitarists as diverse as Lightnin' Hopkins and George Benson, his main influences are horn and organ players.

Likewise, Albert's admirers and disciples are spread out all over the stylistic landscape. Robben Ford, Jimmie and Stevie Ray Vaughan, Larry Carlton, Savoy Brown's Kim Simmonds, and most notably Robert Cray have all dipped into Collins' bag of tricks and incorporated his pet licks into their own styles. (Cray's traditional encore, from his days in small clubs to sold-out stadiums, is Collins' "Don't Lose Your Cool.") Still more guitarists have burned the midnight oil trying to capture that massive tone of his. As Grissom said in the video *Further On Down The Road* (which documented Collins' historic Carnegie Hall concert with Lonnie Mack and Roy Buchanan), "That tone! There's something about that tone that just kills you. I like to think of it like a Louisville Slugger, a baseball bat. Somebody hitting a home run and that bat crackin'. When Albert hits the strings, that's what it reminds me of. I've broken a lot of fingernails trying to play like Albert Collins."

When Albert's first singles–"The Freeze" and then his signature tune, "Frosty"–hit the scene almost three decades ago, his was termed the "cool sound of Albert Collins." In fact, although the gimmicky titles worked, few bluesmen sound as downright *hot*. The only thing cool about Albert's sound is the chills it can send up your spine.

Albert Collins was born in 1932 in a log cabin in Leona, Texas, a small town about 13 miles from Normangee, where he was raised. From there, his family moved to Marquez, when he was six, and finally to Houston, when Albert was nine. After a brief period of piano lessons and a twist of fate that found his organ stolen, Albert took up guitar. After stints with an Alamo acoustic and an Epiphone, he got his first Fender, an Esquire, in 1952, the year he finally could call himself a professional. He cut his first 45, "The Freeze," in '58. Though it was a regional success, he didn't follow it up until 1962, when he recorded "Frosty," to this day his most enduring and influential tune. (Freddie King and Collins were virtually the only blues guitarists to consistently record catchy instrumental sides.)

With the help of Los Angeles-based Canned Heat, Albert was introduced to the rock-ballroom circuit in 1968 and moved to California. Canned Heat also helped him secure a deal with Imperial Records, and although the results were uneven, many of his tunes from that period still hold up today. After six years without a new record out, the guitarist was signed to Chicago's Alligator label on the strength of his 1978 tour of Scandinavia. He has since cut seven albums for the label, including *Showdown*, his collaboration with Cray and Johnny Copeland, which won a Grammy in 1986.

While he and his band, the Icebreakers, still tour the club circuit steadily, these days Albert is at the peak of his career. He has even made such unlikely inroads as TV commercials (for Seagram's Wine Coolers with *Moonlighting*'s Bruce Willis) and movies (his scene-stealing cameo in *Adventures In Babysitting*). For the album *Spillane*, avant-garde composer John Zorn conceived a sort of "Concerto For Albert Collins," titled "Two-Lane Highway," with the bluesman playing and telling a story. The PBS documentary *Ain't Nothin' But The Blues* used Albert as its focal point, showing him in action at Antone's. His idiosyncratic style is also the subject of a revealing instructional cassette available from Hot Licks.

Typically, the guitarist is humbly taking his newfound visibility in stride. The blues is hard work, and few work harder than Albert Collins–as anyone who saw his performance at LiveAid with George Thorogood can attest. Collins is far from a purist; his brand of blues has always contained larger measures of rock and funk than most. But if the music alone doesn't win inductees over to his camp, there's always the 150' cord he uses for his entrance, and often he wades through the audience and out the front door, like a Teletoting politician stumping for supporters.

His Alligator albums show that not only has Collins gotten a lot of mileage out of his "Iceman" tag, but he has got-

ten a lot of mileage out of a Telecaster, a capo, and his bare hands.
"I was told when I started to play,"
he states in *Ain't Nothin' But The
Blues*, "that simple music is the
hardest music in the world to play.
And blues is simple music." In the
following interview Albert discusses both the inspiration and
the execution of his deceptively
simple craft.

*What kind of music did you
hear before you moved to Houston?*

I heard a lot of music, but it
was on radio. I wasn't into playing
music, but I was around my uncle,
Campbell Collins, who's a minister. He played guitar, and I used to
watch him. But during that particular time I wasn't really too interested in playing–I was so young. I
always liked that piano, though. I
used to go to church every Sunday
and see them playing piano. Guitar wasn't really of no interest to
me, but I used to hear it. When I
was 12 or 13, I got interested in
guitar. I got a chance to hear more
music when I got to the big city,
you know.

*Who were the first musicians
who really had an effect on you?*

Actually, Lightnin' Hopkins,
from a long time ago. He used to go and play at family
reunions–we called them "associations." He'd come to my
mother's house, and I used to sit on the porch and watch him
play. So I started liking guitar. I still had that thing–I wanted to play piano and organ. So I bought an organ, but it got
stolen from me.

You definitely play guitar a lot like an organ.

Yeah, I try to make my chord structures like a [Ham-
mond] B-3.

Was what you heard at that age mostly church organ?

Church organ, yeah. I didn't hear nothing about Jimmy
Smith and them until around '60 and '61. That's when I really got introduced to Brother Jack McDuff and Jimmy
McGriff. I really got into McGriff in 1966 because I met him
when I moved to Kansas City, Missouri, and I sat in with

"Lightnin' Hopkins was kin on my mother's side."

him. That's why I wanted him on *Cold Snap*. He's always
been my idol–him and Jimmy Smith. I've got two favorites,
but Jimmy McGriff played more the type of thing I wanted
to hear, when I met him in Kansas City. He played jazz, but
he'd make it sound so bluesy. I could fit and play with him.
That's around the time I met Wes Montgomery before he
died. I listened to him a lot, and George Benson.

Did you ever play in those types of organ trios?

Yeah, in Kansas City, with an organist named Lawrence
Wright. A bass player couldn't get a job there. That's what
was in my ear when I came to California.

*Besides being influenced by organists, did you pay much
attention to the guitarists who played in those kinds of
groups–people like Grant Green?*

Oh, yeah. I was around Grant Green there; that's where I

first met him too. He'd sit on a stool and play. I sure hated it when he died, because he was a real nice guy.

Who were your favorite guitarists back in Texas?

Who I was really around were T-Bone Walker, Lowell Fulson, Gatemouth Brown, Guitar Slim, and B.B. and Freddie King. The first time I met anybody from Chicago was when Jimmy Reed and Little Walter came to Texas to play. My band and I backed up Little Walter when I first met him, in the early '60s. He had a big hit then with "Juke." Then in 1966 I met up with Howlin' Wolf in Kansas City. It wasn't until the late '70s that I met Buddy Guy, Muddy Waters, and people like that. I'd heard them, but I'd never seen them. I was always into the Texas music–like horn players, instead of harps [harmonicas]. Not many harp players coming out of Texas. T-Bone Walker and Gatemouth Brown always had shows together, the Battle of the Guitars, and that really inspired me. Freddie was more like the guys out of Memphis. I think B.B. inspired him more than anybody else. You can tell by the licks he plays sometimes, and his singing.

What were the Battle of the Guitars shows like?

They were real exciting. I saw T-Bone and Gatemouth, and also T-Bone and Lowell Fulson. They had the big bands because, you know, in Texas at that time the bigger the band, the better. It wasn't just a rhythm section; that was for, like, a jazz group in a small club. The big blues bands always had 13 pieces or even 18 pieces. I had ten pieces at one time, and then nine–and I wasn't even playing that well then. I had music teachers with me in my band–like [alto saxophonist] Henry Hayes–and they taught me how to do arrangements for horns. That's why I like brass in my band.

What was Guitar Slim like as a person?

He was a real nice guy–he just drank too much. Died when he was 33 years old. He was a tall guy, and he played the guitar down around his knees. He'd wear pink suits, red shoes–he had a hell of a show. When I saw him, he was playing a [Fender] Broadcaster, I think.

Did you get the idea for the long guitar cord from him?

No–you'd be surprised. I thought of the idea myself, before I saw Guitar Slim do that. A sax player named Big Jay McNeely used to walk out in the audience. So I went down to the music store and said, "I want a 150' cord." The guy looked at me and said, "What do you want that much guitar cable for?" "I'm gonna start playing out in the audience." He started laughing at me. That was in 1953. Then when Guitar Slim came through, he probably had been doing it all the time, but that was the first time I saw him.

Have you tried any wireless transmitters?

Yeah, I tried those, and I was going to buy one. But Bruce Iglauer at Alligator said, "What you started out with is a tradition." I don't use no electronics.

Your style is so powerful and electric; obviously at some point you took a left turn from your early influences such as John Lee Hooker and Lightnin' Hopkins.

Well, they really inspired me when I went to guitar. I really wanted to do that, and I used to sit down and play all those guys' records. I met B.B. when I was 20 years old, and he told me, "Man, find your own identification. That'll help you through the world." I said, "Okay." That's what I did–I tried to find my own identification. I didn't want to play like B.B. or T-Bone Walker.

When you hear younger blues players, you must hear a lot of your influence coming out in their playing.

Oh, yeah, I have pretty good ears, and I can hear it. I hear when Stevie Ray Vaughan is playing like Albert King, a little B.B., then he goes into Jimi Hendrix or me. I appreciate a musician being versatile, but I look at them and think, "Well, can he get his own identification?" I wonder about that a lot. There's so much music around, and you get one particular music in your ear, and then you start playing like this other person. I don't listen to that.

The type of power and tone you got on, say, "Frosty" in 1962 was unlike any guitarist who'd come before. Did you listen more to horn players to develop your sound and style?

Most of mine was horn players and organ players. Because the guitar players, I didn't want to sound like them. What I did was sit down with my band–I had eight pieces–and arrange the horn parts. We didn't name it "Frosty" then. We played that tune for about a year, and people started liking it. "What do you call this tune, man?" I was doing a lot of instrumentals in them days, because they were selling good. I called that tune "Diddley Dah"–because of that horn riff at the start. But that sounded so corny, so when I did the 45 for Bill Hall and Jack Clement in Beaumont, Texas, I called it "Frosty"–because my first 45 had been "The Freeze." Janis Joplin was 15 when I cut that; she used to hang around the studio all the time, and Johnny Winter. She knew Hall and Clement, because Beaumont and Port Arthur, where she was from, were right there together. Me and Johnny have some stuff that's never been released–us playing together back then. I think Hall and Clement have it in Nashville.

When did you first start using reverb?

I started using reverb in 1965. "Frosty" was just a plain, dry amp.

If you'd given your songs titles like "The Scorcher," people would be referring to the hot *sound of Albert Collins.*

Well, I tried to make a little identification for my own, you know. We played in Corpus Christi one night, and on our way back to Houston, it was raining real bad and the windshield was fogged up. The bass player said, "Albert, why don't you turn your defrost on?" I thought, "Damn, 'De-frost'!" Finally I cut an album with a group of girls called the Dolls, and they had some time left over in the studio–like an hour and 40 minutes–so Henry Hayes said, "Why don't you do that tune, 'The Freeze'?" So we cut a 45 on *their* time. Sold about 150,000 copies in three weeks' time. That's what started getting my name halfway out there. But when my name really started to spread was when I cut "Frosty." I didn't follow it up until then because I had a good day job. I was playing at night and driving a truck in the daytime. And I mixed paint for automobiles for six years.

When you went to Duke/ Pea-cock Records…

[Producer] Don Robey said I played too much like T-Bone.

Did you?

I didn't think I did, but he told me to come back in a couple of months, if I had something going. My feelings was kind of hurt, so when I cut "The Freeze," he went and got Fenton Robinson from Chicago and cut an instrumental called "Double Freeze." But I put mine out first; they had a dance called the freeze. Robey had my records stopped on the radio by paying them to play "Double Freeze." Then he tried to get me to sign with him, but I said, "When I offered it to you before, you said no. I'm with Hall and Clement now."

"I got the idea for the capo from Gatemouth Brown."

You were one of the first blues players to experiment with funk-type rhythms.

Right. That's from the organ players. Also, at that time, around '59 or '60, I could have been playing with James Brown, but I couldn't read. That's the reason I didn't get the job. Everyone in my band could read, though, and that's how we played gigs like the Holiday Inn and all the white clubs. I had to lay the blues aside; I'd just comp. We got over, though, and I learned a lot from that. "Begin The Beguine," "Canadi-

an Sunset"–my band could play all that [*plays the bass line to "Canadian Sunset"*]. They'd take care of the rest of it [*laughs*]. If I had just played blues, I'd be back on the chitlin' circuit. I was trying to keep bread on the table, you know.

When you play funkier stuff, are you pretty much using the same blues licks, except with different phrasing and rhythm?

Just the rhythm is changed, that's all. It's just like playing a blues [*plays a one-chord funk pattern and then solos over the rhythm using exclusively blues licks*].

"B.B. told me, 'Man, find your own identification. That'll help you through the world.'"

Before you cut records on your own, did you have much experience playing as a sideman?

No, I never played sideman. Always had my own group. See, I had one of the best bands in the Southwest, as far as blues bands. We could play jazz, blues, pop-like "Body And Soul," "Tennessee Waltz." Gatemouth Brown plays a lot of jazz too.

Is it hard for you to learn a tune by watching another guitarist do it?

I have to go home and play it. I have to listen to it because my positions are different.

How did you come to use a minor tuning?

My cousin, Willow Young, played like that, but he played in his lap like he was playing a steel guitar. I just got that tuning from him.

Why did you take up guitar without using a pick?

It just came naturally because I was taking piano lessons once a week for about four months. When I did pick up a guitar, Willow didn't play with a pick, so that's how I learned. The first tune I played on a guitar was "Boogie Chillun." Took me two weeks to learn it. John Lee Hooker kind of inspired me-him and Lightnin' Hopkins. I tried to play with a pick, man, but I couldn't do it.

That's one of the secrets to your tone.

It's like a muffled sound, yeah. I used to play with all my fingers, and now I play like I'm playing a bass [with the thumb, index, and middle fingers].

When you get that really stinging sound, are you yanking up on the strings?

Just picking like this [*demonstrates his string-grabbing technique, pulling up on the strings*]. Freddie King used fingerpicks and a thumbpick. You know, Johnny Guitar Watson [another bare-fingers player] used to play with me, but he played piano; that's his major instrument. He's rough on piano, man-and organ.

When did you start playing Fenders?

I went to a Fender in 1952. But it wasn't a Telecaster; it was an Esquire. I got introduced to that through Gatemouth Brown. I wanted a Telecaster, but I couldn't afford it, so I went down to Parker Music Company in Houston and had them put a Telecaster neck on my Esquire body. I cut "The Freeze" and "Frosty" and all that stuff on it. Before that, I had an Alamo guitar, a hollow box, where you put a pickup on it, and I played Epiphones in 1950 and '51. I got the idea for the capo from Gatemouth too. I started without one, but I looked at Gatemouth and said, "Man, you're using that choker." We used to call it a choker. I said, "You get a lot out of that guitar." I hung around him for a while, and his brother played with me, too-Widemouth Brown-and he used a choker too. Now I can't play without one.

Essentially, then, you play as if you're in first position and just move the capo up to whatever key you're in.

Well, see, I know where my *Bb*, my *C*, and my *D* are, but my positions are different from the way you'd play because you play in standard tuning. Mine is *D* minor. [*Spelled F, C, F, Ab, C, F, low to high, it's an F minor triad, or a Dm7b5 without the root.*]

So if the band is playing in C, where would you put your capo?

At the seventh fret. *D* is at the ninth fret, and *Bb* is at the fifth fret. Up at the twelfth fret is my *F*.

Do you actually capo it that high?

Yeah [*demonstrates, playing in a five-fret range with the capo at the twelfth fret*].

Was it a dramatic change, switching from an Epiphone to a Fender Esquire?

It really changed because the Epiphone was like a Gibson, and I'd always feed back in front of the amp. In '65 I finally got a Telecaster.

So on "Frosty" and the records prior to '65 you were using the Esquire with only the rear pickup.

Yeah, with a Telecaster neck on it. When I came to California, I had a 1959 Tele. The first job I played in L.A., at the Hollywood Palladium, it got stolen. I was doing this Teenage Fair thing, and they had Gibson, Standell, and other companies, and Fender gave me another guitar. It was a Telecaster but with a hollow body, and I didn't like it, so I took it to Ace Music in Santa Monica and traded it for the one I've got now, a 1961. Been playing on it ever since. When I bought it, it had the humbucking pickup already on it.

Do you use that pickup very much?

I use both of them. I play in the middle position.

That's an unusual Tele because it's blonde with white binding on front and back.

I had that done. See, I had it refinished about nine or ten years ago, and they put the border around it. I had two guitars done like that, and one of them I gave to the Hard Rock Cafe in Chicago. I'm fixing to get mine refinished again. I tell them, "Don't mess with nothing inside. Just leave the pickups. Just finish it."

If you had to use a different type of guitar, could you still get your tone?

Almost. I like Gibsons. I tried to buy a Gibson one time, but the neck is different–it's squarer and wider. I got so used to Telecasters, and they have a better bite than a Gibson. The only person I've seen really get down to playing on a Gibson is B.B. I've got big frets on my Telecaster, and that makes a difference too. I get most of my sound from the amp that I use, and I always like to use my own amp. Sometimes I use an old Twin, and I can almost get the sound. My amp is a [100-watt] Quad Reverb. I've been using it since 1972.

Those are pretty loud amps.

Oh, yeah [*laughs*]. They're loud! I've got two of them. I only use one of them onstage, though.

Is your volume always set at 10?

I always play my amps that way–ever since I've been playing. I change tubes about every six months. I put the treble all the way on 10, the middle on 10, and I don't use bass, intensity, or none of that. Reverb I set at 4.

Do you record with the Quad?

Right. Before they came out with the Quad in '72, I used a [Fender] Bandmaster piggyback model. I cut a lot of records with it. I've still got the bottom, with two 12s, but I lost the top. I'd sure like to find me one.

Most Tele players take the bridge plate off. Why did you leave it on?

That's just what I started out with. So now I rest my hand on it and mute with my left hand. I tried the Strat, but it felt different because I'm so used to that plate. I wound up resting my hand on the strings. And the Strat sounds different from a Tele; the Strat is for rock and roll, actually.

What's that on the cover plate?

In 1979 I was doing a TV show in Rotterdam, in Holland, and they had some lighting effects. So they got this piece of [reflective] tape and said, "This would be nice to go on your guitar." I've been using it ever since. You can buy it in stores.

Why do you play with the guitar strap over your right shoulder?

I started out with the strap across my body, but I felt too strapped in, like I couldn't move.

When you're comping, you usually play through the 12-bar changes without moving your hand on the neck. [Author's note: Remember, Albert tunes to an *Fm* chord. Positioning the capo at the second fret, for example, yields a *Gm*. The first diagram's fingering–illustrating Albert's I chord–would be *G6*. Next, Albert refers to the IV chord. In the key of *G*, the IV chord is *C*; however, the IV can be *implied* by merely lowering the 3rd of the I chord, which is what Albert does in his second example.]

Yeah, this is how I make my "I" chord:

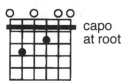

And this is how I make my "IV" chord:

And I mute with my ring and little fingers. I play octaves just like this:

Do you always move the capo to whatever key you're in, or do you play in more than one key in the same capo position?

I move it to the key I'm in. Only problem I ever had playing with another guitarist onstage was with Albert King–

because he's left-handed, and I can't look at it when he's playing. I first met Albert in Kansas City in 1965. He tunes to a chord. I picked his guitar up one time and said, "Man, he plays weird too [_laughs_]!" The way he plays, it sounds like a slide to me–the way he bends.

You both bend some pretty big intervals.

Like this? [_With the capo at the ninth fret, in_ D, _Albert bends the second string up a whole-step, from_ F _(at his twelfth fret) to_ G. _He then drops down a fret and bends the_ E _at the eleventh fret up a minor third to_ G.]

Doesn't having the capo there, with less string length, make it harder to bend?

It used to, but I guess my fingers got toughened up. Because it used to hurt my hands. They used to call this [the capo] a handicap, but that's what I've always used.

Do you fret with your little finger very often?

Not very much. You could cut that one off, it wouldn't matter.

Did you concentrate for a long time on your intonation? When you bend, it's always right on pitch–in contrast to Buddy Guy, for instance, who often bends up to notes that don't necessarily have anything to do with the key of the song.

Well, see, Buddy's been introduced to Jimi Hendrix. That's the reason why he plays like that. Buddy really don't like to play blues no more. He's into the Jimi Hendrix thing. I'm not sure, but I hope he knows what he's doing, because, like, if I wanted to play like Jimi Hendrix–I'm noted as a blues player. People say, "Hey, man, what you doin'?" _Ain't_ no more Jimi Hendrix. I _try_ for my intonation to be true.

Your tone and phrasing are very vocal-like, and in fact you seem to sing along with almost all of your guitar licks.

I do. That's why I used to get hoarse on the road. When I play, I'm grunting with it; it's just a habit I have. I've been doing that for years, long before I ever heard George Benson doing it–back when Ray Charles used to do it. I used to sit in high school, humming with my mouth, and then I'd go home and see if I could play it with my hands.

Your vibrato sound is quite a bit different from, say, B.B. King's or Otis Rush's.

It's in my wrist [_shakes a note with his ring finger pushing the string side to side_]. I always use my ring finger; I can't do that thing B.B. does [referring to King's fluttering index-finger vibrato technique].

How did you hook up with Canned Heat in the '60s?

Canned Heat were the ones who really got my albums out. They played at the Music Hall in Houston in 1968, and Lightnin' Hopkins was on the show with them. So they said, "Man, we're lookin' for Albert Collins." And Lightnin' said, "Well, I know where he's playing at." I was playing at a place

called the Ponderosa, and they came in and asked me if I wanted to come to California. They were on Imperial Records, and they wanted to get me on the label. So I left Houston in July and went to Kansas City, where my wife's from, and then she went out to Palo Alto, California, while I played some jobs. So I came out to California in November. My first job was the Fillmore West, with Fleetwood Mac and Creedence Clearwater Revival. I met a lot of them rock groups, man, in '68 and '69–the Doors, Grand Funk, Buddy Miles, a group called the Flock with that violin player [Jerry Goodman]. We had a lot of fun together. Then I did _Love Can Be Found Anywhere_, and [Canned Heat's] Bob Hite wrote the liner notes. The Imperial records didn't get off too good, you know, so after they folded I got with this label in Denver, Colorado, called Tumbleweed and did _There's Gotta Be A Change_.

Some of your phrasing on that album sounds a little like Albert King.

You think so? It probably was, at that time, in 1972. Then Tumbleweed went out of business, and I didn't cut another record until 1979. I worked all up and down the West Coast and back in Texas. I kept working, but the money wasn't real good.

Didn't you quit for a year or so?

Yeah, I quit for about a year, around 1971. I worked with my landlord, doing construction on Neil Diamond's house. After a while he said, "Man, this is not for you. You gotta start playing." I had gotten disgusted with it because I wasn't making no money. I started to get me a truck-driving job, but my wife said, "No, you better go back to music." You just get to the point, you know, where it looks like everybody's making it but you.

Your style seems a lot closer to rock than a lot of blues players. Is that because you listen to a variety of music?

Yeah, I even listen to rap music. But I was listening to a lot of psychedelic music then, starting in 1969, when I really got introduced to it. And I was around Jimi for a minute, when he was 17. I took his place with Little Richard, when he left to play with a group called the Drifters. I worked like 15 dates with Little Richard. Me and Little Richard have been friends for years. By doing that, I got introduced to that kind of rock and roll, instead of just playing blues. I was raised up mostly around jazz musicians–horn players like Arnett Cobb, when he was real popular, and Illinois Jacquet, whose father used to play alto with me.

What was it like recording the John Zorn album? How much of that was improvised?

That was an experience for me. He just told me what was going to be happening, and I just played my stuff around their feel. But he had two drummers [Ronald Shannon Jackson and Bobby Previte]; it went into different moods. They were really good. [*Hums a jungle tom-tom rhythm and plays his patented bends over the top.*] It's a story that I check into a motel, and I go into a room and find a dead man in there. Weird. I enjoyed it, though. It was something different, but I was still playing the same thing. The organ player [Big John Patton] comes from Texas too, so I could communicate with him real well. He knew where I was coming from.

What was it like working with Robert Cray on the Showdown *album?*

Oh, it was beautiful because Robert and I played together for three years. I played for his high-school graduation party in 1971–that's when I first met him. The class had to pick between me and Frank Zappa [*laughs*]. I played up in the Pacific Northwest a lot, so I started using Robert and Richard Cousins, his bass player.

You're at the peak of your success right now–Grammys, movies, TV commercials. After so many years, did it hit you by surprise?

Yes. I didn't think it was ever gonna happen. I was thinking about going back home at one time, and my wife said, "Why do you want to go back? There's nothing there. Keep on playing–somebody'll see you." One time I played at the Whisky Au-Go-Go in Hollywood, in '69–which was the last time I saw Janis Joplin. She came to my show, and the last words she said when she walked out the door were, "You're gonna make it. Keep on." That was the last time I seen her. I watched her grow, from a kid. She always wanted to sing; I was glad to see her get on with it, man.

What was the turning point that got you across to a bigger audience?

Europe really did it. I did a tour of Scandinavia in 1978, before I cut with Alligator. A lot of people over there thought I was dead. I went over there, came back, and cut an album with Bruce Iglauer in '79, and then went back again–to other countries, like England, France, and Germany. Then people back home started noticing what was happening.

What was it like playing at Live Aid?

I was excited, man [*laughs*]. That's when I really got stage fright–about the first time in my life. I looked out and saw all those people, and George Thorogood said, "Hey, man, you scared?" I said, "Yeah!" He said, "Me too. Let's go get 'em!"

From the beginning, were you always so animated onstage?

Oh, yeah. Once I see some people out there smiling, and it looks like they're in my corner, then it's time for me to go to work.

July 1993

Five years after Dan Forte's Albert Collins cover story, Jas Obrecht interviewed the Iceman in San Francisco for the cover of *Guitar Player*'s Gods of the Telecaster issue. Albert picked up his guitar during the interview, turning that old blonde plank into a nagging wife, a screaming desire, a sucker punch, Gatling gun, squawking chicken, or graveyard howl.

Why would you recommend the Telecaster for playing blues?

Because a Tele is a little bit softer sound than a Strat. A Strat is mostly, like, for rock and roll. And a lot of country players use Teles. It's a more mellow-sounding guitar.

But you're not known for having a mellow sound.

No, not really. [*Laughs*.]

Can you get your sound on a Les Paul or a 335?

I haven't tried it yet.

You've never played those guitars?

No. One of these days I'm gonna try me a Les Paul, I guess. But it's just so heavy, I never wanted to play one. See, I play off my right shoulder, you know.

Not many players wear a guitar like that.

Yeah, I don't like seat belts, but I put 'em on! [*Laughs*.] I feel like I'm penned in, man.

You're also one of the few players who've left the stock cover plate over the Tele's bridge.

That's another reason why I never played a Strat, 'cause I rest my hand there when I play. Fender was gonna make me a Strat with a cover plate, and I told them no.

Are Teles tough?

Oh, yeah. They can take a lot of road trips. I've dropped mine a lot of times, man, and it ain't hurt nothin'. Just put scratches on it.

Was your Tele originally routed for a stock pickup and then redone for the humbucker?

Yeah, that's right. When I got that guitar in 1969, that was already in it. I think it's a Gibson humbucking, like a Les Paul or something on that order. I have a regular switch on the Tele, but I can use both pickups, though. I had a 1959 Telecaster–got it stole from me while we were playing. I got this one I have now from Ace Music Company in Santa Monica, California. I got a fret job on it a few weeks ago, and it's alright. The edge of it kind of got a little sharp, but it's working out alright. We used big frets.

How did you get binding on a '61 Tele?

That's not stock. I had that put in there in 1982 in L.A. I had two guitars, and they did both. One of them is at Hard

Rock [Cafe] in Chicago. I'm gonna get that binding redone again–hopefully real soon.

With all of the string yanking and snapping you do, you must have strong hands.

Yeah. I have those grips to keep my hands strong, and it helps a lot for me, because I don't play with a pick. Never.

Do you break more strings during tuning or playing?

Playing. And all of them break, man–the big *E*, the *D*. I just break 'em because of the tension. You know, I was thinking about tuning lower a long time ago. I wouldn't break no strings then. Stevie Ray did that too. I'm gonna try it.

Turning everything up to 10, do you ever have problems with your hearing?

I don't have any problems. Actually, I don't stand in front of the amplifier. I can't play in front of my amplifier. I turn my amp on an angle. It's a Fender Quad Reverb. Remember when Nixon got shot? Was that Nixon? That guy that used to be the governor of Alabama?

George Wallace?

I got that amp the same day he got shot. Out of New York.

Do you carry spare amps?

Got a Twin I take with me. But I got two Quads.

They're hard to find.

I know it. Soon as I find them old JBL speakers, I'm gonna play with both of 'em.

Why do you like that particular amp?

Because it gave me the power that I wanted. That amp was given to me from a music store out of New York, through Tumbleweed Records. The man said, "This is the amp for you, man." That was the first time I ever seen one that said "Fender Quad." And that amp was loud!

Do you carry a spare guitar on the road?

Yeah. That's one of the Fender Albert Collins models. But the one they gave me is too heavy. They gonna correct it for me. What happened is they made it out of the wrong wood. I gave them my guitar and let them weigh it, because that guitar is light. The one they sent is too heavy.

What does having a Fender endorsement deal mean to you?

It means a lot to me because I've been playing their products since 1952. I feel good that they let me be an endorsement on that stuff, because I've been playing their equipment so long, you know.

Do you still use a 100-foot cord?

Yep. I'm trying to stay away from the wireless. Wireless changes your sound. I have one, but I don't use it.

You've got an unusual capo.

Uh huh. I got 'em out of Texas. Can't find this kind nowhere. They're tryin' to find some more. I had a bunch of

them that got stole from me.

Where did you get into using capos?

Gatemouth Brown. His brothers used to play with me. One played drums–named Bobby Brown–and one played guitar. What happened was I went to go see Gatemouth and T-Bone Walker play at the Civic Auditorium, and all of a sudden he put this capo on, and I said, "Wow, what is that he's usin' on that guitar?" So I asked him about it, and he said, "Man, you need to use this. It'll make your style. Make yourself sound good." I said, "Well, what does it do, man?" 'Cause I was trying to play, and I was playing in one key only. And he said, "Well, this changes. You can play different keys, like *Bb*." I usually be at *C*, *Bb*, so I capo up quite a bit. And my chord stretches are different.

See, I started out trying to play piano. So I found what key I could play in by playing the notes on the piano, and I'd learn all the key changes on the board of my guitar. I took piano lessons when I was a kid, but I didn't take 'em long. It was during the winter, man. I was stayin' in Normangee, Texas, and the lady lived in Bryant, Texas, which is 35 miles away. And it wasn't paved roads then. Every Friday she would come to give piano lessons. And in the wintertime she couldn't come, and that's when my cousin would leave me his guitar. He was trying to teach me to play, and he'd leave me his guitar every weekend. He'd go out and have his fun, and when he come back on Sunday, I'd give him his guitar back.

Why did you become a guitarist instead of an organ player?

I always wanted to be an organ player. I think when I try to comp my chords when I play guitar, it's like playing an organ, because I been around organ players. Jimmy McGriff was really my favorite organ player. I bought me an organ, had a guy was gonna teach me, and I got my organ stole from us on the highway, so I just got away from it through the years. My wife bought me another one, so I got one at home now, so I'll let my organ player now teach me again.

What was your first solidbody?

Fender Esquire. The first time I seen one of them was with Gatemouth.

Why were you attracted to a solidbody?

I was playing a Epiphone hollowbox. And the minute I seen Gatemouth with that Esquire, he said, "Here. See if you like this." He said, "I might give it to you!" [*Laughs.*] I played it, and I said, "Whoo. I sure like the neck on this, man." He said, "They sell them down at Parker Music Company." I was still in Houston, so I went down and put me a down payment on one. Yeah, that's when I departed from the Epiphone.

Have you recorded with an acoustic guitar?

Never cut nothin' with acoustic, no. I wanted to play electric guitar, man. When I got away from acoustic, man, I started listening to T-Bone Walker, Gatemouth, B.B. This is way before I was knowing about Albert King. I got into the big band sound, you know. I wanted the horn section.

Why did Texas blues guitarists tend to play with horns and big bands, while guys in Mississippi and Chicago favored small combos?

You know, a lot of people ask me what's the difference between Chicago blues and Texas blues. We didn't have harp players and slide guitar players out of Texas, so most of the blues guitars had a horn section. That was the difference. A long time ago Aretha Franklin came to Texas, and she was working with a trio. And she didn't sell too good when she came to Texas with the trio. So when she put out this tune about the "Dr. Feelgood" and came back to Texas with a big horn section, people were three deep around the corner. The bigger the band is, the better they like it in Texas. It's hard to go down through there with just a rhythm section and get good response.

When you were a child, you reportedly put rattlesnake rattles inside your guitar.

Mm hmm. Some other people used to take pennies and put them in their hollow box. It gets a good sound. The rattlesnake rattles–you dry 'em out and put 'em in. Lightnin' Hopkins taught me that trick.

Would you shake the guitar while you're playing?

Nah. You just put 'em in. People down in Texas used to go rattlesnake hunting. You take about four or five of those rattlers, dry 'em out, and put them inside your hollowbox guitar. I used to take pennies and put them inside of mine. Like tin pennies, copper pennies.

What's the theory behind this?

I don't know. A lot of people did it around before my time, and I started doing it too. I couldn't really tell the difference, but you can tell the difference with the rattlesnake rattlers, though. I guess it's because the rattlers inside makes a weird sound.

Do you still have that guitar?

Well, I hope it's still there, but I doubt it's there. The place got burned, and I had it up in the loft. Stayed there for years and years, man, and after my aunt died, I took over the property. And those people had kids, and they set the place on fire. So I had it remodeled.

Is this the guitar someone made for you out of an oak tree?

Yeah. That guy used to play with Ernest Tubbs–he was a country and western singer. This guy used to have a walnut farm, and I used to drive a truck for him. He said, "I'm gonna make you a guitar." I said okay, and it was so big I couldn't hardly get my hand around it. [*Laughs.*] Yeah.

But you made your first guitar out of a…

Cigar box. People back in them days couldn't afford no guitar, man. I took a hay-baling wire, and it was rough, man! You couldn't do nothing with it, so I just be banging it! [*Laughs.*]

How did you know Lightnin' Hopkins?

See, the Hopkins was kin on my mother's side, and my mother was around the Hopkins when I was little. You know, Lightnin' was much older, but he watched me grow.

Did people have a lot of respect for him?

Oh, yeah. Ever since I been knowin' Lightnin', I never knowed him to have a job! He always played guitar. We'd have family reunions–they called them "associations" in those days–and he used to play out on the grounds. So many crowd of people be around to hear him, man. The oldest guy I met from the old acoustic players was Li'l Son Jackson. I met him when I was real young, and him and Lightnin' used to run together. I saw him one time–I think he used to live somewhere in Dallas, Texas. But them other people, like Blind Lemon and all, I never got to see them.

Blind Lemon was dead by 1929.

That's before I was born! But when I was a kid, Li'l Son Jackson used to come around to a little town called Marquez, Texas.

Those associations must have been fun.

It was a lot of fun, yeah. In those days, you didn't find people fighting each other, shooting and all this kind of stuff. Everybody was glad. Some people come around, and you haven't seen 'em in ten years. Man, they glad to see each other. That's why they were family reunions, man. They were on church grounds, and they had stands, like barbecue stands, and tents set up.

Did any of those musicians ask you to sit in?

No, I didn't sit in with nobody when I first started, because actually I didn't start playing till I got into Houston, Texas, after that. I learned in a little town called Normangee, Texas. That's about 125 miles from Houston. I worked on a ranch there for four years. I used to love doing that ranch work, you know. Then I went into truck driving. Drove a truck for like 12 years. This is the same time I was in the Rhythm Rockers. I wasn't doing no long-distance [hauling]. The only long-distance I had was when I started working for a company called Maddox Furniture. We'd go, like, Louisiana, Dallas/Fort Worth. I quit that. I didn't want to go on the road.

When you were starting out, B.B. King reportedly gave you some good advice.

Yeah, I met B.B. when I was 21 years old. He had some relatives live right across the street from a club I was playing at, called the Jockey Club. That was in Houston. He came to sit in with me. That's when he had "Three O'Clock In The Morning"–that was a big hit then. He said, "Man, find your own identification. That'll help you through the world."

You did it. Even on your earliest records, you don't sound like anybody else.

[*Laughs.*] Oh, no, man, I don't.

There are only a few of you–B.B., Albert King, John Lee Hooker...

John Lee was my idol, man. That was my beginning–him and Lightnin' Hopkins. First tune I learned how to play on guitar was "Boogie Chillun." And I learned how to play it in two weeks. [*Picks up Tele and plays "Boogie Chillun."*] That old man, he can be rough, man. He's still rough! He kills me. I love watchin' him.

Do you play "Boogie Chillun" onstage?

No. Only time I mess with that is when I'm with John Lee.

So you started out tuning your guitar to an open chord.

Right, sure did. At 17, I tried to play standard tuning. I had a guy brung some beginners books, you know, and I couldn't play that standard tuning. So I went back to the way I learned how to play. That's the reason I wanted to get my own style from that "Vastapool" [open-*D* tuning] they called it, cross-tuning. I learned that from Willow Young. He played with the guitar on his lap, like he was playing lap steel. He could play with a knife. He was a good player. He never played professionally, though. He just passed away last year. He was my cousin.

What were your favorite blues records back then?

I used to listen to Jimmie Lunceford, Tommy Dorsey, Jimmy Dorsey. I was into the big band sound then. That's what I would listen to. When I first got my horn section, I had nine pieces–wouldn't get paid much! [*Laughs.*] I had two music teachers played tenor and alto. I had two trumpets, trombone. Now I'm using two trumpets and a tenor–that's all I've used for like ten years. That's the sound I always did like–first trumpet, second trumpet.

How long have you been playing with horns?

Well, I had my horn section before I met Piney Brown. He was a singer. He lives in Dayton, Ohio. I was, like, about 26 when I went with him. That was the first time I ever went on the road playin' music. I wanted to go, but the problem I had was one of the guys and Piney Brown's manager, they got to fighting in the car, man. Me bein' young, I ain't never been around all this, so I took all my stuff out of the car, took my little amplifier and guitar, and started sitting by the side of the highway. So the state troopers picked me up and asked me where I was goin'. I said, "I'm trying to get back to Houston, Texas." They asked me, "Well, why you sittin' out here on the highway?" I said, "Well, I was in this car and people got to fightin' and I got out. I want to go home, and I haven't got

paid." So I told them what kind of car they was ridin' in, so they called ahead and had 'em stopped. Man, they made them send me home! [*Laughs.*] That was in Louisiana, and they don't play that, man. They took them all to the police station, and they said, "Now, you want to file charges on these people?" I said, "No. I just want my money."

What are your rules of the road?

I look down on drugs. I never had drugs in my life with nobody. And I was right here in San Francisco in 1969, during the free love days.

That must have seemed strange to you.

It was a challenge for me because it looked like I was in another world. But I always tell them kids, "Man, you don't have to do that to play no music. To function, you don't need them drugs." I don't like drugs, man. I won't be around no drugs. People ask, "What you be on to have all this energy?" I say, "I'm high on energy. I'm high on nature."

You've co-written several songs with your wife Gwendolyn.

Yeah. We did "Conversation With Collins," "Master Charge"–that was one of the biggest ones she wrote for me. She write 'em down, and on some of the verses I add on.

Did she write the music?

No! My wife never did listen to no blues when I first met her. [*Laughs.*] Know what my wife listened to? Country and western. That's all she got in our car–Patsy Cline, Boots Randolph. See, my wife came from Kansas City, Missouri. She was a nurse there when I first met her. She wasn't raised up in the country. And in them days, she would listen to the Shirelles and those kind of people, Elvis Presley. It was strange when I met her: She said, "I don't listen to no blues."

Do you have a collection of blues records?

Very few. He's gone, but I've always liked Albert King's stuff. I played a lot of Lightnin' Hopkins stuff too. Albert King's tuning is a little bit different than my tuning. I picked his guitar up one time, and it's almost to a chord. It's like you playin' a slide–I think that's the way he's got that guitar tuned. He heard me and said, "Put my guitar down, man!" [*From low to high, Albert King tuned Lucy C, F, C, F, A, D.*]

Like B.B. King, you now make your home in Las Vegas.

Yeah. Where I live is very quiet–it ain't like L.A.! I used to live on Pico Street in the Wilshire district–very busy. It used to be real nice when I moved out there, and it got worser and worser. Got to the point where I was scared to go outdoors after 9:00 at night. I said, "I can't live like this!" A war zone, man.

Describe the recording projects you're working on.

I got almost two albums in the can. I'm doing some reissue stuff, and then I'm doing new stuff on my new album. The reissues I'm recutting are "Don't Lose Your Cool,"

"Frosty," "Tired Man." There's quite a few–about 19 of them. Some of them have got new arrangements, because I didn't want to go just directly the same. B.B. King will be playing on one of them, and I did some playing on his new album too. I'm also gonna have Elvin Bishop and Eric Clapton on it, and Gary Moore is on it already. Gary and I did a song about "If Trouble Was Money," and it was nice. Gary is easy to work with, man. I did a tour with him in 1990. The new songs have a little bit of an R&B feel, and I did both records with Jim Gaines in Memphis.

Over the past 35 years, you've cut blues for Liberty, Imperial, Tumbleweed, Blue Thumb, Alligator, Charisma, and other labels. What are your best guitar tracks?

"Iceman" and "Put The Shoe On The Other Foot" on *Iceman*, "Honey, Hush" [*Ice Pickin'*], "If You Love Me Like You Say" [*Frostbite*], "Frosty" on *Frozen Alive* , "Don't Lose Your Cool" [*Don't Lose Your Cool*], "Too Many Dirty Dishes" on *Cold Snap*, and "The Things I Used To Do" from *The Complete Imperial Recordings*. I like these new records I'm doing now too.

A SELECTED ALBERT COLLINS DISCOGRAPHY

Solo albums: *Frosty* ('62-'63), Brylen; *Ice Cold Blues* (Liberty and Imperial, late '60s), Charly; *Live At Fillmore East* ('69), Red Lightnin'; *Truckin' With Albert Collins* ('69), MCA; *The Cool Sound Of Albert Collins* (Imperial cuts from *Love Can Be Found Anywhere* and *Trash Talkin'*), Crosscut; *The Complete Albert Collins*, Imperial; *The Complete Imperial Recordings* ('69-'70), EMI; *Iceman*, Atlantic; *There's Gotta Be A Change* ('71), Tumbleweed; *Molten Ice* (live, '73), Red Lightnin'; *Albert Collins With The Barrelhouse Live* (Holland, '78), Munich; *Ice Pickin'* ('78), Alligator; *Frostbite* ('80), Alligator; *Alive & Cool*, Red Lightnin'; *Frozen Alive!* ('81), Alligator; *Flash Frozen* (live in Japan, '82), Yupiteru; *Don't Lose Your Cool* ('83), Alligator; *Cold Snap*, Alligator; *Iceman* ('91), Pointblank/Charisma.

With others: Robert Cray and Johnny Copeland, *Showdown!*, Alligator; Dave Alexander, *Oakland Blues* (Albert is credited as "Houston Twister"), World Pacific; John Zorn, *Spillane*, Elektra/Nonesuch; Etta James and Joe Walsh, *Jump The Blues Away*, Verve; Gary Moore, *Still Got The Blues* ('90), Charisma; John Lee Hooker, *Mr. Lucky* ('91), Pointblank/Charisma; John Lee Hooker, *Boom Boom* ('92), Pointblank/Charisma; John Mayall, *Wake Up Call* ('93), Silvertone; B.B. King, *Blues Summit* ('93), MCA; Debbie Davies, *Picture This* ('93), Blind Pig.

Anthologies: *Smackin' That Wax: The Kangaroo Records Story 1959-1964*, Collectables; *Down Home Blues* (includes an early 45 with Big Walter Price), Rattlesnake; *Guitar In My Hands, Vol. 1* and *Vol. 2*, Moonshine; *Tenth Anniversary Anthology, Vol. 1–Live From Antone's*, Antone's; *Antone's Anniversary Anthology, Vol. 2*, Antone's; *Genuine Houserockin' Music*, Alligator; *Blues Masters, Volume 3: Texas Blues*, Rhino; *Blues Masters, Volume 9: Postmodern Blues*, Rhino; *The Alligator Records 20th Anniversary Collection*, Alligator; *Legends Of Guitar–Electric Blues, Vol. 2*, Rhino.

Soundtracks: *Feds*.

On film: *San Francisco Blues Festival* ('83); *Ain't Nothin' But The Blues* (live at Antone's, PBS); *Adventures In Babysitting* ('87); *An Evening Of Blues With Gary Moore* ('90), Charisma.

Michael Bloomfield

April 1979

BY TOM WHEELER

ICHAEL BLOOMFIELD'S LEGEND won't go away. Though he is passionately committed to discovering, dusting off, and reinterpreting the dozens of musics in virtually every corner of America's post-Civil War folk heritage, his audiences are often unaware of that fact, or are more interested in hearing him recreate the sounds of the records that made him one of the world's preeminent blues-rock guitar superstars in the late '60s, albums such as *Super Session* (with Al Kooper and Stephen Stills), and LPs recorded by Bloomfield's various groups, including the Paul Butterfield Blues Band and the Electric Flag.

"It's a real problem, a *big* one," he explains. "The records I have recorded in the last few years are very poorly distributed, or if they are well distributed there are no print ads, or the company doesn't have enough money to promote them the way I'd like them to." These records include *Analine, Count Talent And The Originals, Michael Bloomfield,* and an album produced by *Guitar Player* magazine and nominated for a Grammy in 1977, *If You Love These Blues, Play 'Em As You Please.*

"On a recent Canadian tour," Mike continues, "I talked to hundreds of people, and only *two* had heard of those records. This is the bane of my existence, because a lot of times people come to see something from ten years ago–*12* years ago–they're coming to see *Super Session,* the Flag, I don't know what. They're coming to see Butterfield or whatever. It's because they aren't aware of the more recent stuff. I always make a disclaimer. I say, now listen, you're not going to hear what you heard ten years ago, although you might hear bits and fragments of it. If I could recreate it, I would. I wouldn't mind it. But I hope that you will take it for what it is. Try to remove your prejudgment, and take it for what it is. If you like it, great; if you don't…"

In the eyes of the late-'60s record-buying public, Mike Bloomfield was tall in the saddle. After all, he was an onstage accomplice The Day Dylan Went Electric at the 1965 Newport Folk Festival, and after several albums and tours with various bands he turned on thousands of guitar players and countless other fans to Chicago-style electric blues.

Unlike the music of Jimi Hendrix and Eric Clapton, whose blues roots were one step removed and sometimes obscured by the smoke and sparks of the acid-rock milieu, Bloomfield's blues were unadorned, accessible, assimilable. His guitar technique churned with such soulfulness that he broke a color line of sorts, demonstrating a blues sensibility

uncommon among white instrumentalists and earning respect from the sacred heroes of his youth. "Without a guitar," he once said, "I'm a poet with no hands."

For the most part Bloomfield shunned the conspicuous hallmarks of hot-licks, '60s-style electric guitar–distortion, feedback, and special effects–and instead, like the purist that he is, chose a bare-knuckles, plug-in-and-blow approach that continued a tradition discovered and embraced in the blues clubs of Chicago's seamy South Side. His consummate skill as a string bender (plus a fascination for the microtonal capabilities provided by bending) allowed him to extract the blue nuances of pitch. His dynamic pick attack, natural sustain, lyrical tone, and savory vibrato combined to infuse his art with a street eloquence, and his spontaneous but purposefully directed solos were charged with plenty of tension/release and call-and-response, comparing favorably with the best of the high-drama blues heavyweights like Albert King. In other words, as Michael himself might say of a favorite guitarist, he played his ass off. In recent years he has devoted more time to acoustic music, and his popularity among guitar players remains high.

Michael's personal quirks reveal contrasts, though not inconsistencies. For example, when it comes to worshipping Ray Charles, B.B. King, or his other blues heroes, he is an idolator to the core (or, as he puts it, to the tits). And yet during the 1960s he never related to being the star that he was, and in fact–as he discusses in the following interview–he considers popular hero worship to be potentially detrimental, perhaps even vaguely immoral. He is much more interested in current work than past glories. He played guitar on Dylan's "Like A Rolling Stone" and on *Highway 61 Revisited* –both seminal recordings monumentalized by pop historians–and he's referred to the latter as "that album *Highway 61* or whatever it's called."

Michael's roomy, single-level house is jammed with the tools and accoutrements of a hardworking performer and a music lover–dusty guitars with grime-caked strings, a Fender Twin in the hall, another in the kitchen, stacks of jacketless albums, photos of musicians and other friends, tacked-up clippings, an inexpensive stereo that sometimes works–but there are no rock-star trappings, no pretenses.

Bloomfield's musical credentials are the real thing. He has taught musicology at Stanford University. He is a blues historian, a curator of sorts. He loves music for its own sake. And yet he has participated in commercial ventures which he describes below as "amazing scams, filthy lucre," one of which was the historic *Super Session*. Another contrast: Even though Mike's choices of instruments helped ignite popular rages the world over–for Telecasters (during his Butterfield days) and especially for Les Pauls, both gold-tops and sun-

bursts–he is not equipment-oriented at all in the materialist sense. His guitars are there to be played–and played *hard* (abused, some would charge)–not to be ogled, coveted, bragged about, or traded like so many baseball cards.

Mike, 35, lives atop a steep hill in Mill Valley, just across the Golden Gate Bridge from San Francisco, and he seldom leaves; the less he tours, the better he likes it. He never made much money on the road with previous bands, and although he'd like to reach people all over the country who want to see him, he cannot tour very profitably without a hit single. Even if he could, he wouldn't hit the road very often anyway. Away from home he is an almost hopeless insomniac, a self-described displaced person. He once checked into Stanford's sleep clinic, where optimistic doctors promised to help. They wired him up to machines and hunkered down, waiting for him to fall asleep. He didn't. He stayed awake almost all of the time, occasionally lapsing into what's known as a hypnogogic state but never experiencing real sleep. After 14 days the doctors, now defeated and depressed, threw up their hands, advised him never to travel, and gave him a lifetime prescription for unlimited downers. When he's home in Mill Valley, though, he's okay. Sleeps great.

Over the past few years one of Mike's primary interests and sources of income has been the scoring of films, including *The Trip*, *Medium Cool* (photographed by his cousin, Oscar-winner Haskell Wexler), *Steelyard Blues*, Andy Warhol's *Bad*, and a wad of porno movies including *Sodom And Gomorrah* and the Mitchell brothers' *Ultra-Core* series. Michael plays northern California clubs, and income from these dates, movie scores, records, and songwriting supports him comfortably, though not luxuriously.

Mike Bloomfield is an especially animate interviewee. He'll talk at length to almost anyone who cares about music, and his conversations bulge with vivid anecdotes about hundreds of figures from musical Americana. He is both colorful and quotable ("Heroin gave me pimples"). He is a well-read, thoughtful, and serious student, and yet his eye still has the gleam, his mouth the grin, of a kid who would not only dare to show his young fat white face in a South Side club, but who would also have the gall to practically force himself into an onstage jam alongside the baddest guitarslinger in town.

Are your audiences sometimes surprised to see Michael Bloomfield the fingerpicker, the acoustic guitarist, the solo performer?

Yes, sometimes they are. There are certain places where they know me and they come to hear me play the solo thing, but at most gigs I'll get someone out there who screams, "*Super Session!*" When someone yells that I really can't

Michael at home in Mill Valley, California, 1979.

the audience has orgasms, and they have to carry out the big fat women over the heads of the crowd. That's all well and good, but I am just not a compulsive junkie for mass ego glut. Bob Marley explained to me that he found it emasculating and demeaning to play in front of people sometimes. He didn't mean that it was feminine or anything, just that it was depersonalizing. It takes away some of your personal store of self, because the audience doesn't know who you are, and you're exhibiting some of your innards in front of strange people. Playing in front of strangers leads to idolatry, and idolatry is dangerous because the audience has a preconception of you even though you cannot get a conception of them, really. You have to look upon them as a herd. Every time I get together with anyone, I try to break it down quickly, this herd situation.

So that the other person does not look at you as a fixed image, an inflexible symbol?

Yes, exactly, so that they are not experiencing just a face on a record cover that maybe they smoked their first dope to. Instead, they're talking to me, a person, doing what I do now. People resent it sometimes when we move on and we don't fit their preconceptions. I'm the same way, really I am. I'm an idolator to the tits, man. When I go to see somebody, I want to see them onstage the way I see them in my mind. I want to see B.B. with a processed hairdo.

But you didn't relate to being a rock star yourself?

No, I didn't, not at all, even when it was happening. I couldn't even conceive of myself as a rock star. I had no idea it was happening. I was into researching old forms of music and belonging to folklore societies and meeting old players and going to folk festivals. I'd been playing bluegrass and country blues for years, and I just never pictured myself as a big electric guitar hero. I would buy someone else's record and picture them as a rock star, but I could never see it in myself.

You didn't see yourself as the American Eric Clapton?

No, never. Clapton, I thought, now *here's* a guy, here's a *rock star.* Boy, did he play. I thought, if I could only do what

imagine what's going on in his mind. I mean, here's a guy who's sitting up there onstage alone, fingerpicking–how's he going to do it? Where's the organ going to come from? The horns? What are you supposed to do, man [*laughs*], play the *changes* or something? Play the solo?

That's what they know; that's "Michael Bloomfield."

I know, I understand it. I swear, I remember when I was at a certain age I'd just want to hear the solo or something myself.

During the '60s, were you stimulated by all the attention?

Well, I don't need ego fixes. I'm sort of embarrassed by adulation. As much as anyone else, I enjoy energy transference. Like in its highest form I guess you would see it in a church, where you have a good preacher who goes nuts, and he could do. I thought that he had taken the blues just absolutely as far as it could go. And when Hendrix came along I just wanted to burn the guitar. I'm sure Eric felt the same way. So I didn't relate to being a rock star at all. I read a lot of stuff about all that, but it wasn't real for me. All of those social implications and ramifications of a rock star trip–I was never into it.

Tell us about the record you made for Guitar Player *magazine,* If You Love These Blues, Play 'Em As You Please.

Everywhere I go, man, everywhere, someone asks me where they can get that record. It's crazy. I'm not that big a seller, but that album would be my biggest of all time, no doubt about it, if it were better distributed. I know it's my best record, me at my hottest.

Are there particular cuts that you think are especially good?

Yes, the playing is just so hot on some of the songs. Not only just for me, but also for blues playing in general. There's one called "City Girl," and one called "WDIA." It's just great blues playing, that's all I can say.

It also contains authentic reproductions of old-time recorded sounds.

That's right. I was striving to get the sounds of various old records, and that came through. I was trying to look at not just different guitar styles, but also the whole setting, the feel, the persona, the ambience of certain musics–sort of a musicological period movie. I mean, I wasn't just copying licks. And now I really like to hear it. The other records that I did–I hear them now, and I hear clunkers here and there. But the *Guitar Player* record I really like to hear over and over again.

Do you have any special recording techniques?

Well, no, except I like to put that little Kay amp in the bathroom at the studio. It sounds wonderful, especially if the bathroom has a shower stall. That gives it a wonderful tone and echo.

Do you use fingerpicks?

No, usually I don't. I use the thumbnail, or bare meat. With lap guitars, though, I do use a plastic thumbpick and metal fingerpicks. But on a regular guitar, I can't get agile enough if I'm wearing those things. For flatpicks, I like the really hard kind, a Fender hard. Actually, I hardly use a flatpick when I'm playing electric. I used to use one, but lately I've just been putting it in my mouth, and I leave it there. I find that I get a much funkier blues sound with my thumb or my nail. The strings I use are the Fender Rock And Roll set.

Do you lose speed by forgoing a flatpick?

Yes, I'll never be as fast with my fingers as I am with a pick, but the tone is worth it.

How do you bend so far without the other strings getting in the way?

You bend underneath the other strings. That's the way I do it.

Was Analine *your first predominantly acoustic album?*

For sure. And I play a bunch of guitars, a banjo, bass, drums, piano, organ, ukulele, tiple–all sorts of things.

One cut on Analine, *"Peepin' An' A Moanin' Blues," is about voyeurism. Where did that song come from? What was your influence?*

One of the very biggest gospel publishers is a guy named Thomas Dorsey. He's in his seventies now, lives in Chicago, a rich old black man. He wrote "Precious Lord Take My Hand," "Peace In The Valley"–he's one of the truly great gospel writers. In his youth, though, he wrote obscene songs. He recorded as Georgia Tom. It was Tampa Red and Georgia Tom; Tampa Red played guitar, Tom played piano, and they recorded a lot of filthy songs. There was a whole school of double-entendre tunes, like "I've Got A Hot Dog For Your Roll" and "Long John The Dentist." Oh man, there was "Copulatin' Blues"–all sorts of stuff. That was my influence for "Peepin.'"

One of the song titles on Analine *is "Mr. Johnson And Mr. Dunn."*

That was named for Lonnie Johnson and Eddie Lang. Lang changed his name to Dunn. They made a bunch of race records for black audiences. Everything was real segregated, and Lang didn't want to mess up Lonnie Johnson's trip–they were both real successful jazz guys–so he changed his name to Blind Willie Dunn, and the two of them made some fabulous records under those names. Lonnie Johnson played a very unusual 9-string guitar on a lot of those tunes.

The Michael Bloomfield *album has a particularly sleazy quality.*

Yeah, that worked out. It was exactly planned that way by Norman Dayron–who's my producer–and me. It was to be as raw and as sleazy as possible. Two of the cuts were recorded live in a club, and I think those are the best tracks: "Sloppy Drunk" and "Women Loving Each Other."

You're not going to hear "Women Loving Each Other" on Top-40 AM radio.

Why not? If I am ever on *Johnny Carson* or something, that's definitely one tune I'd like to do. That's an old song, man, from the '30s, I think. It was written by a guy who's still alive. I told the record company to give him credit on the liner for the song, but something happened–there was some reason why he wasn't credited. His name is William Borem.

But could you get away with performing that tune on the air, on TV?

Maybe I couldn't get away with it. Maybe it is offensive,

I don't know. But it's one of the tunes about lesbianism that I really like. There's a ton of them, and there's old songs about transvestites, about transsexuality, about hermaphrodites–actual songs *by* hermaphrodites, blues about them. There's a guy named Guilford "Peachtree" Payne who had breasts and a penis and made records about that–"Switch-Hit Loving" and all this really strange stuff. As a matter of fact, on the song "Peach Tree Man" [*Count Talent*]–that's where I got the title.

There's another song on Michael Bloomfield *called "See That My Grave Is Kept Clean."*

That's an A.P. Carter song, but I sure didn't know it was by him until I looked it up.

Where does the song come from? What's the genre?

Are you kidding? It was a hit by Blind Lemon Jefferson, one of his two or three biggest hits. He was a star–chauffeured around in a limo–a real star. He died in the most ridiculous circumstances. In 1929 he froze to death in the gutter trying to get from one part of Chicago to another. His chauffeur had split. One story has it that his guitar froze right to his hand. Very odd. He was a freaky guy, blew his money like mad. Being blind, I think he was gypped a lot. Who knew–was it a five, a ten, a hundred? But his records really sold. Anyway, I didn't know A.P. Carter wrote "See That My Grave Is Kept Clean." I learned it from Blind Lemon Jefferson a long, long time ago. It seems like I've known it all my life. It's strange. Blind Lemon's grave is *not* kept clean. I've been there. You should see it. Boy, his plea was not at all answered. His grave is a mess, weeds all over.

He was one of your early influences?

Yes, when I was a kid. You ever seen a picture of him? He was so fat that he had to play a small ladies' guitar on top of his sumo wrestler's belly. And he was really a great player, very fast, very strange. Blind Lemon didn't play with a beat–you couldn't dance to his music. I don't know how he got so popular. He also had a very high, emotional, whiny voice–really a blind man's voice.

How long have you been playing this kind of music?

Much longer than I've been famous for playing rock and roll. These people played this music for dances. One guy with his guitar would play for a whole roomful of people to dance to in the '20s and '30s, and I started discovering these old blues records when I was 13 or 14, and I've been playing it that long, though not on record. Audiences don't always know. They think, I don't know–maybe they think I just saw Leon Redbone on *Saturday Night Live* and just got into it or something [*laughs*].

Who was your first rock and roll influence?

Scotty Moore, Elvis' guitar player. Also Cliff Gallup, who played with Gene Vincent's Blue Caps. See, when I was

around 15, I couldn't really differentiate between rockabilly and blues. It all sort of sounded the same to me. I lived in the suburbs of Chicago, and all I knew was that it all had a lot of energy. I still do some of that rock and roll stuff in my gigs, like "Fool" by Sandford Clark. I've often wondered what happened to that guy. I do "Endless Sleep," too, by Jody Reynolds. It's in *F.* I don't know what happened to him, either.

But a lot of the blues and rock sounded alike for a time?

Yeah, it all had this sort of outlaw quality to it that I was *dying* to get into any way I could. There was an outlaw group of kids in the suburbs–greaser sort of hoodlum kids–and I used to look at them and I wanted to be sort of like that, a Presleyesque, greasy guy. I couldn't really tell which I wanted to be more–a Presleyesque, greasy hillbilly or a jivey blues singer.

Where did you first encounter the blues?

On the radio. As I searched the dial at nights when I was a little kid I found that Chicago had seven or eight black stations, and about three of them catered to Southern blacks and played nothing but blues. *Then* I heard the difference. The rockabilly was fabulous, and I loved it, but then I started hearing nothing but endless B.B. King records, endless Magic Sam and Muddy Waters and Howlin' Wolf and so on, and I was thinking, oh my *God,* this is... this is another world, another realm, the jungle, the city. And when I found out that these guys all lived right there in my town, and that all I had to do was to take a subway and I could go hear them–I could actually go *see* them–that just killed me.

Were you also going to see the rock and roll shows?

Yes, but they were different. They were sort of depersonalizing, which is the way I wanted it, because they were like idols, you know. They had records, and they were up on the stage, removed, with the bright lights and all that. That's how it should be. But man, when I went to blues clubs it was a whole different story. There they were, the guys I would hear on the radio, about an inch from my face. The clubs were open until 4:00 in the morning, and they'd be there for seven sets a night, 40 minutes a set, working their buns off. And they were in their prime, a lot of them.

How many white people in the audience?

One. Or sometimes I'd go along with a pal. Gradually I discovered others, like Nick Gravenites and Paul Butterfield, with whom I eventually played in various groups.

Did you sit in much with these players?

I sure did. I never thought much about it–I knew I was a guitar player; I knew I was fast and hot. I'd started playing in rock and roll bands when I was 15, and I was good then, and I was about 16 or 17 when I started going to blues clubs. I knew that at the time I couldn't play blues, but I could play something similar to it–bluesy guitar–and I was dying to sit in. I came in with my guitar, and there wasn't anybody who was going to stop me. I would walk onstage, literally from out of nowhere, uninvited [*laughs*], and just say, "Hey, *mind if I sit in?*" while I was going ahead and plugging in my guitar. Many times it would be like a freak show to the audience. They'd like it–this fat little Jewish child plugging his guitar in and doing whatever he did. And I didn't get the notes out correctly, as blues, but it was near enough.

Who did you jam with?

There was no one I *didn't* jam with. I played with every living musician who played electric blues. The only guys I didn't play with were the ones who stayed in their regions. If someone never left Louisiana or Texas, then I wouldn't get to jam with him. Everyone else, though.

Muddy Waters?

Muddy, Magic Sam, [Howlin'] Wolf, Otis Rush, B.B. King, Albert King, Freddie King, Little Milton, Junior Wells, Little Walter, Chuck Berry–I played with most of these guys dozens of times–plus a lot of more obscure guys like Eddie King, a guy named [Eddie] Clearwater, a guy named Brewer Phillips, Mighty Joe Young, Otis Spann, Lee Jackson. Then I started getting scholarly about it and began to study it, and I found out that there were guys who had made records in the '40s who still lived in Chicago, guys who were big stars in their day. Like there was Washboard Sam; his real name's Robert Brown–he wrote "I'm Going To Move To The Outskirts Of Town," "Mama Don't Allow No Guitar Pickin' Around Here," and other things. I would find out where these guys lived and check *them* all out, too. I'd visit with them, learn from them. Everyone I could think of, I looked them up. There was Jazz Gillum–he wrote "Key To The Highway." There was Tommy McClennan, who wrote "Guitar King," which is on my album [*Michael Bloomfield*]. Endless guys.

Aside from history and folklore, how do all of the many musical forms you play come together? Is there a common thread, some basis for artistic integration?

I know what you're talking about; yes, there's a way in which I relate to all of these blues and folk forms. There's sort of a macrocosmic integration, a general artistic influence on me. I like simple sonorities. I have no present interest in spaced-out electric stuff; I admire it, but it doesn't tug at my heart. I like simpler things. I am a musicologist by bent. I am rooted in American music of all sorts–Cajun, Mexican, all the jazz players up to Django Reinhardt, like Teddy Bunn and Eddie Lang, plus all the blues and folk forms, music you play on all the fretted instruments.

And they all influence what you are trying to do now?

Yes. I began to realize some time ago that if all of these

many hybrids could flow through me, then that would be what I was looking for. I wanted to innovate, rather than imitate, and yet I was doing old material. To innovate, you have to bring enough of yourself to the reinterpretive process, so that imitation becomes innovation. As Elvis tried to sound like the Ink Spots or Big Boy Crudup or various blues singers, he ended up sounding like Presley.

Do you see yourself as a musical caretaker of sorts?

Well, a lot of these songs are dying. I don't know many people our age–even black people–who play blues or care about blues. Where are the young bluesmen? Freddie King's dead. Magic Sam's dead. I have some black friends who are music teachers and folklorists, and *I'm* teaching *them*. Culturally it's so weird, a Jew teaching a black about blues. I would like to help keep those forms alive, so that people will know: This is how America played.

Was there ever a period when you were musically inactive?

There was a period when I didn't play guitar at all, around '70 or '71. I was really down and out, and I lived in this little dive. The Flag had just broken up. I had cut *Super Session*, and then I got really into shooting junk.

What were the effects of heroin?

Heroin gave me pimples. And I put the guitar down, didn't touch it. See, a junkie's life is totally, chronically fucked. You either eat and move and be productive, or else you're a junkie. There's no choice. Or at least there wasn't for me.

What were you doing besides shooting junk?

Well, shooting junk is very full-time. You've got to get out there and get that dope, hustle–sell televisions or whatever. If you're into being passive and nonproductive, that's one thing, but I knew that it'd hurt me. Shooting junk made everything else unimportant, null and void, *nolo contendere*. My playing fell apart.

Were you able to work with other musicians?

Not at all. Being on junk can immediately disintegrate a good band. Like I knew one guy, a great musician, really a sweet guy, and everyone loved him, a soulful little guy. But he was the worst junkie I'd ever seen in my life. If he was one millimeter away from death by overdose, he was content. He'd be at a recording session and go into the bathroom for 20 minutes and come back almost purple, different shades of blue, various shades of loss of oxygen. That's where he wanted to be, and he would *play* like this. His hands would still move, but they would move... *slow*. It was very strange watching him play. Just from a practical standpoint, a musician like that who was heavily into dope was not a very good guy to have in a band–someone you knew might die at any minute. I mean, we'd have a rehearsal and he'd hit coma.

So you couldn't play when you were on junk?

Oh *God*, no. Some people can do something behind it–they can play, they can go to the gig, they can control their motor functions. I'd just lay there and watch TV and smoke cigarettes and nod off or whatever. I couldn't keep my act together, couldn't function. Actually, there was no prolonged period like this–it was more of an on-and-off type of thing.

What made you decide to quit?

It was a very moving experience; it affected me deeply. I'll tell you about it. Some of the best San Francisco Bay Area guitar players came to see me–Terry Haggerty from the Sons Of Champlin and Carlos Santana and others. And they said to me, man, you ought to be ashamed of yourself to charge admission at the door to see you, because you're a fucking joke, you're a laughingstock. We used to *learn* from you. When Butterfield came to town we all came to see you. We *loved* you, we loved what you did. How can you be who you are? How can you put your name on a marquee and charge money to see this ludicrous exhibition of what

Michael Bloomfield used to be? You're a fraud. You can't even *hold* a guitar anymore.

How did you respond?

Well, I just said, hey, I'm not into that anymore. I'm into watching the *Tonight Show* and shooting dope. I'm into stoned leisure.

And did they leave?

No, they stayed. They wouldn't let up. They sat down, and they said, now listen to us play, man. And they *played*. Hag started playing, and, oh my God, he was better than I ever was. It was unbelievable. From then on I vowed: never again. If you're going to get up there in front of people, God *knows* you better be good. That those guys would do that, to come over, to come down on me so hard, to get the balls to do that… it so moved me that these people wanted to see me playing again, it affected my heart tremendously. What nice guys, what gentlemen. That got me back into guitar.

[Mike Bloomfield died of a drug overdose in February 1981.]

A SELECTED MICHAEL BLOOMFIELD DISCOGRAPHY

Solo albums: *Bloomfield: A Retrospective* (two-record set including "Born In Chicago" from Newport '65), Columbia; *Super Session* ('68), Columbia; *Live Adventures Of Mike Bloomfield And Al Kooper* ('69), Columbia; *It's Not Killing Me* ('69), Columbia; *Junko Partner* (live, late '60s), Intermedia; *Triumvirate* (with John Hammond and Dr. John, '73), Columbia; *Mill Valley Session* ('76), Polydor; *If You Love These Blues, Play 'Em As You Please* ('77), Guitar Player Records; *Analine* ('77), Takoma; *Count Talent And The Originals* ('78), Clouds; *Michael Bloomfield* ('77), Takoma; *I'm With You Always* (live, '77), Demon; *Between The Hard Place And The Ground* ('80), Takoma; *Living In The Fast Lane* ('80), Waterhouse; *Michael Bloomfield & Woody Harris* (instrumental gospel), Kicking Mule; *Cruisin' For A Bruisin'* (last recordings, '81), Takoma; *Best Of Mike Bloomfield*, Takoma; *A True Soul Brother* (reissue of material from *Michael Bloomfield & Woody Harris* and *If You Love These Blues, Play 'Em As You Please*), Sky Ranch.

With the Paul Butterfield Blues Band: *Paul Butterfield Blues Band*, Elektra; *East-West*, Elektra; *Golden Butter*, Elektra. Anthologies: *Blues Masters, Volume 4: Harmonica Classics*, Rhino; *Blues Masters, Volume 7: Blues Revival*, Rhino.

With the Electric Flag: *Long Time Coming*, Columbia; *Best Of The Electric Flag*, Columbia; *Best Of The Electric Flag*, Back-Trac; *La Grande Storia Del Rock*, Curcio (Italy); *The Monterey International Pop Festival*, Rhino.

With Bob Dylan: *Highway 61 Revisited*, Columbia; *Biograph*, Columbia; *The Bootleg Series Volumes 1-3*, Columbia.

With others: Janis Joplin, *I Got Dem Ol' Kosmic Blues Again, Mama!* ("One Good Man"), Columbia; Muddy Waters and others, *Fathers And Sons*, Chess; John Hammond (Michael plays piano), *So Many Roads*, Vanguard; James Cotton, *Two Sides Of The Blues*, Intermedia.

Anthologies: *Live At Bill Graham's Fillmore West*, Columbia.

Soundtracks: *The Trip* ('67); *Medium Cool* ('69); *Festival* (with Bob Dylan at Newport); *Steelyard Blues* ('73); *Andy Warhol's Bad* ('77); *Sodom And Gomorrah* ('77).

BACK WHEN BANDS LIKE CREAM and Led Zeppelin were vying for blues-rock supremacy, an unknown Texan was praised in *Rolling Stone* for playing some of "the gutsiest fluid blues guitar you've ever heard." The hype worked: Johnny Winter signed a huge deal with Columbia, stayed close to his roots, and emerged a bona fide American blues-rock guitar hero. Half a lifetime later, Winter remains true to his original vision.

Johnny cut over a dozen albums under his own name between 1968 and '80, covering everything from acoustic blues and electrified slide to standards by Dylan and the Rolling Stones. Late in the '70s he dedicated himself to resurrecting Muddy Waters' career, producing and playing on the legend's *Hard Again, I'm Ready, Muddy "Mississippi" Waters Live*, and *King Bee*. Winter signed with Alligator Records in 1984 and spattered white-hot blues on *Guitar Slinger, Serious Business*, and *Third Degree*. He jumped to MCA/Voyager for *The Winter Of '88*, but found the experience less satisfying than his Alligator stint.

Let Me In, Johnny's new release on Pointblank/Charisma, is as flamboyant and blues-approved as his best major-label material. His driving romp through "Illustrated Man" delivers tongue-in-cheek commentary on his elaborate tattoos, while "Life Is Hard" showcases his strongest suit, slow blues. Johnny conjures voodoo slide on "Medicine Man" and "If You've Got A Good Woman" and journeys downhome on dobro for the acoustic title track, recalling Robert Johnson, Son House, and early Muddy Waters.

He was in the mood to talk blues when we met in his hotel room one winter's eve. A few hours later, Johnny had a capacity crowd at San Francisco's Fox Warfield rocking in the aisles to his shouted vocals, blazing solos, and mysterioso slide.

Why have you dedicated your career to playing blues?

Just because it makes me feel the best. I really like a lot of other kinds of music, but blues just does something to my insides. I don't get tired of it or bored with it at all. I've learned more and I'm playing better now than I ever have. I really enjoy country music, especially now that it's more like what I grew up thinking was rock and roll. Rock music now doesn't really have too much to do with the '50s rock and roll. Some of the songs you see on the Nashville Network might have a steel guitar or a fiddle in there someplace, but lot of them are just straight R&B and rock and roll.

You've revived a lot of '50s music.

Johnny Winter

August 1992

BY JAS OBRECHT

Oh, yeah. Probably because I'm not much of a songwriter and have a hard time coming up with enough songs myself. I'm always looking for good new writers so I won't have to do that. But it's what I grew up listening to, and that's why I still feel so strongly about it. The music from the mid to the late '50s just sounds so good, the way that everything just came together perfect. It's so *hard*–rock and roll and blues really had a great sound in those days.

You seem to know an endless variety of turnarounds.

It's just listening to all those records, because I probably listened to literally every blues record I could find. I don't know any more where those turnarounds come from. I guess I mix them up, and they kind of come out my own way. But if I'm really trying, I can sit down and say that this is so-and-so's lick or that's something that such and such a guy would have played.

Some of the slide on Let Me In–*especially "If You've Got A Good Woman"–has the Muddy Waters feel.*

Yeah. After *Let Me In* was over, my producer Dick Shurman said, "You seem to play more Elmore than you did Muddy." I said, "I don't know, there's still plenty of Muddy in there." But I could kind of see what he meant–I did more in the *E* tuning than in *A*. Actually, during the last few years of his life I don't think I ever heard Muddy play in the *A*. He would tune his guitar to an *E* chord and just put his capo wherever it needed to go. Though on a lot of his early records he played in the *A* tuning too.

The songs he made on Stovall's plantation back in '41…

Yeah, that was great stuff.

Pretty close to Robert Johnson.

Sure was. On "I Be's Troubled," he did that really nice rhythmic thing that you never heard him do on electric guitar. He really did have an excellent feel for sound for that stuff.

The version of "Rollin' And Tumblin', Part 1" that he cut in '50 with Baby Face Leroy Foster sounds like it could have come from the Delta during the 1920s.

Yep. It's just electrified. That was it, the only difference. When I heard slide for the first time, on an album called *The Best Of Muddy Waters*, I couldn't believe it. It was so unique, so original-sounding. At first I thought it was a steel guitar, and then I heard one cut that I was sure was just one guy playing guitar. Muddy would fret the guitar sometimes, and other times he would use a slide. He almost always went for single lines. He wore such a short slide on his little finger that he couldn't get but about two strings with it at the very most.

Didn't he use a socket wrench?

Yeah. At first it feels natural to play with the slide on your ring finger, but if you wear it on your little finger, you can do a lot of fretwork with the other three fingers. The advantage of using open tunings is that when you barre, you have a chord to work with. You can have that chord ringing down in the bass notes while you play the top strings with your fingers or slide. I always use a thumbpick and the first two fingers of my right hand, so I keep the bass strings going with my thumb and play leads with my fingers, especially if I'm by myself. Muddy used a thumbpick too. I'm using my fingers more than I used to. I really like the sound of snapping the strings a little bit. I still use the thumbpick at the same time: I play a note down with my thumbpick and then pick up with my fingers.

Have you experimented with different types of slides?

Yeah. You know, they called slide "bottleneck" in the old days, because most of the guys broke the necks off bottles, and that's what they played with. I tried playing with the crystal on my wristwatch. I've used lipstick holders, Coricidin bottles, every kind of bottle. Some things were too light, and nothing seemed to fit my finger right. All the slides I ever tried in music stores were too big. Man, it was really hard at first, and I was using my ring finger. And there was one guy that did more for my playing than anybody. It was a guy who worked with the Denver Folklore Society. He told me that I really should be using my little finger, even though it didn't feel right. He explained that it would be a lot better in the long run because I could fret and play chords too. He took me down to a plumbing supply place, stuck my finger into all these different conduit pipes, and found one that fit. I never saw the guy again after that, but I still got the same slide that he helped me get in '67. I've lost it and refound it a million times. This guy really did so much for me, and I never have seen him to say thanks.

What's the difference in tone between glass and metal?

Glass definitely has a real nice sound. I love Ry Cooder's playing and his sound, and he seems to always use glass. For a while I was using a test tube that was cut off, and it wasn't quite right. It wasn't quite thick enough to get a good sustain. Metal, of course, sounds more metallic, and most of the time I like that better. The glass sound is a little bit mellower and different. I wish that I had a glass slide the right size because for some things it would be better. But I like that harsh metal sound–that's why I like National guitars. The more metal, the better.

Besides Muddy, who are your blues guitar heroes?

Oh, definitely Robert Johnson. I'd like to have seen him in a good Mississippi juke joint or barrelhouse. Son House, of course. T-Bone Walker was always one of my favorites. If anybody invented the electric blues style, it was T-Bone. I learned probably more from listening to his stuff than any other guitar player. He just had a great way of turning the meter around, and some of that early jazzy stuff is just amazing. He could do things right along with the horn sec-

The man and his Firebird, early '70s.

favorite new slide players. He knocks me out. Otis Rush still is great if you get him on a good night. He seems to have good and bad nights, but he's an excellent player. There's so many good guys out there.

What songs would you nominate for a blues guitar hall of fame?

Wow, there's so many! One of the leads that always really impressed me was Matt Murphy with Memphis Slim: "This Time I'm Through" was the name of it, and it was a really good lead. I've never forgotten it. In fact, at the time that I heard it, I thought that this guy's got to be the fastest guitar player in the world. It doesn't sound quite as fast to me now as it did when it was new, but it's still a great record. And some of Otis Rush's stuff was just unbelievable. He had two or three great minor things. Just about any of Otis Rush's Cobra stuff really knocks me out, like "Checking On My Baby" and "Three Times A Fool."

Are kids growing up with compact discs missing anything?

Yeah. I still don't have a CD player myself, but I think that eventually CDs will get to where they get some of that brittleness out. I'm old-fashioned about a lot of things. I like tube amps. I'm sure transistors will get as warm a sound, but right now the brittleness of a lot of CDs and transistorized amps bothers me.

Have there been any constants in your equipment setup over the years?

I've pretty much changed equipment a lot. I've been using a Music Man amp that I had when I was working with Muddy. I've really liked that, but it's pretty much a copy of the old Bassman amp, just four 10s. I've still got a Bassman at home in Texas–that's probably my all-time favorite amp. I got one of the new ones, and it just didn't sound exactly like I remember them. Maybe it's just because the used ones were broke in better. I used that Bassman for years and then switched to a Concert or a Super Reverb, and that's just

tion, just unbelievable stuff. It was more big band jazz with a blues flavor than a straight blues thing. And I always thought Lightnin' Hopkins was a real cool guy, because he could do big shows and then go out and play on the corner or on a bus or in a little juke joint. It didn't seem to bother him a bit. He could go from acoustic guitar to electric guitar or from playing by himself to playing with a band. Lightnin' was a real blues guy.

Who are the impressive modern players?

I always liked the way that Albert Collins plays. He sounds real different, I guess because he uses a different tuning, and I'm not even sure what it is.

An Fm.

Wow! That's strange. He definitely doesn't sound like anybody else; I like his stuff a lot. Roy Rogers is one of my about the same thing with a little more power. The four 10s work better than any other configuration. I've used all kinds of different guitars, and they still keep making improvements. Some of the stuff I reject, but some of it's real good.

What's the best of the new technology?

That's hard to say. I'm not a big technology fan, like a lot of guys.

But you were using a headless guitar years ago.

Yeah, I still use that Lazer, but I couldn't care which end the pegs are on. I just really like the way that it feels, and it has a real nice sound. I definitely used the Lazer the most on the new record. I used my Gibson Firebird for the slide stuff, and a couple of Nationals for the acoustic. The action on the Firebird is real high. In fact, I've got to do something about it. The neck's been broken so many times, and it's real old. Right up by the headstock, the strings almost touch, and it's way, way off up by the pickups. It's corroded, and the finish is gone. I'm either going to have to have it fixed again or retire it. I've got a lot of old Firebirds, so when I completely use that one up, I can go to another one. This is the same one I used to play in the '60s.

How do you set your controls for slide?

I always have my amps set the same way: treble all the way on, no bass, no middle, and usually the volume's on seven-and-a-half or eight. But if I really want a super-distorted sound, I'll go ahead and turn it all the way up. The guitar is usually pretty much all the way up with all the treble on.

Do you solo during basic tracks?

Yeah. If there's a couple of guitar tracks on a song, I usually do the one that has most of the leads first. If there needs to be a little rhythm or something else, I'll do that later. As far as solos go, man, I don't know what I'm gonna do until I'm playing it. Usually I don't even know how many solos I'm gonna take. "Life Is Hard" didn't have any overdubs at all, except for the vocal. We did the four pieces together. I remember Mac [Rebennack, a.k.a. Dr. John] saying that it reminded him of a lot of the early Duke Records stuff. Well, I learned a lot of guitar from Bobby Bland, because he had great guitar players. My favorites are "Farther On Up The Road," "I Smell Trouble," and "I Don't Want No Woman"–I don't know exactly which guys play on those, but those records are amazing. I really learned a lot from them. [*Author's note: Bland recorded these songs in 1957 with Clarence Hollimon on guitar.*]

What's the story on your steel-bodied Nationals?

My real old one's got a great, great slide sound, but the neck is so bowed that you almost can't fret it at all. And then I got a new one in about '70 that looks exactly the same way, but it actually says Dobro on it. It's really got a great sound, and instead of the joining of the body at the twelfth fret like

most of the old ones, it's joined at the fourteenth. The strings are too close to play slide on, so I usually use both of those guitars–the one for slide and the other for fretting. I don't have one that's set up exactly right where I can do both on the same guitar. I've got a lot of old Nationals, and all of them sound completely different.

What's the best way to record Nationals?

Boy, it's always hard to get a good sound on that. This time we recorded it in the bathroom, with the mike right over my head. On *Third Degree* we had a little trouble. I was unhappy with the way that worked–it just didn't have the same nice echo. This time I was hearing things real nice.

Did you cut the vocals at the same time?

No, I never do the vocals and the guitar at the same time.

The National on "Let Me In" sounds propulsive, like Son House.

Yeah, I learned a lot of my old original slide stuff from Son. There were two albums that came out on Columbia that really helped a lot: Son House and Robert Johnson. Son House didn't play as much–it was more primitive–so when I was trying to figure out how the guitar was tuned and all that, Son House was actually an easier one because he didn't do as much. After I learned Son House stuff, it was a lot easier to graduate to the Robert Johnson. But those two albums and the Muddy Waters stuff is really where I learned most of my slide.

Did Muddy Waters ever give you advice about guitar playing?

Not really. I always was watching what he was doing, and I'd learned pretty much everything from just listening to the records for all those years. But it definitely was still cool to be able to work with the guy. Bob Margolin said that Muddy would work on stuff with him. But I had studied and loved Muddy's records for so long that I pretty much had gotten everything down before we started working together. Muddy was always real supportive of me. I remember him telling me a couple of times that people talk about white people not being able to play the blues. He said, "Man, you can play as good a blues as anybody I ever heard–just that good old lonesome sound." That really made me feel good. Sometimes you could read interviews where some people were trying so hard to get him to say bad stuff about me, and he just wouldn't do it. I loved him, man, and it was real mutual. I wish he was still around.

Did you and Muddy share a common admiration for any older blues musicians?

Muddy didn't talk that much about older guys. I remember asking about Robert Johnson in particular. He said that he had heard about Robert in Mississippi and went out to a club where he was playing. He said that Robert sounded so good, he just listened for a while and left, just amazed. He really did like Son House a lot; he seemed to think of Son kind of like a father figure. He learned a lot from him, and he always referred to Son House as the old man. Muddy was real modest about his own guitar playing. He didn't feel like he was that great. I remember him saying, "Well, even an old man probably can outplay me, but I got something now that works." He knew what he did was cool, but it wasn't about technique. He just had a way of putting it all together.

Have the CD reissues of your earliest recordings been done with your approval?

Not really. Most of the stuff is being put out by an asshole who doesn't have any rights to put it out. I never see any money from that stuff at all, and that doesn't make me happy. When they leave the music alone, it's okay. But in some cases they'll overdub other people to try to update the stuff, and I hate that. There was one album–*The Johnny Winter Story*, I think–where they overdubbed a guy who couldn't play much slide at all, and they said, "This is Johnny Winter playing his early slide style." It just made me crazy when I'd hear it. It's horrible stuff. I never played as bad as this guy, even when I first started. It's just total bullshit, and that really bothers me. On one cut they overdubbed a drummer who was all out of time. Ugh!

Winter rocks the San Francisco Blues Festival, September 1989.

What are the best Johnny Winter guitar performances?

I always kind of liked "Boot Hill" [on *Guitar Slinger*]. The slow blues "Third Degree" was one of the prettier songs. "Be Careful With A Fool" [*Johnny Winter*] was interesting. Man, it's so hard just to pick one song, and it's been so long since I've heard a lot of this stuff. It's easier to pick albums: I like the first Columbia record. I like *The Progressive Blues Experiment* for what it was. My favorite rock and roll record was

Still Alive And Well. I don't know if it's just because this record is new, but I seem to really enjoy listening to *Let Me In* as much as any of the records that I've made.

Do any songs move you so much that you'll only play them on special occasions?

Usually the more powerful a song is, the better that I like it, unless it's just something so emotional that I couldn't do it. Like going to Muddy's funeral, I just didn't see how Pops Staples did a song. Man, I couldn't play at the funeral of somebody that I love. That real strange Robert Johnson song that reminds me of Skip James' "Devil Got My Woman" is one of the most emotional songs I know of.

"Hell Hound On My Trail"?

Yeah. There's something about both of those tunes that really knocks me out. Nobody sounds like Skip James. He's among the most emotional singers and guitar players–you can just feel it. I've heard that he didn't want other people to learn how he was doing things. Some guys are that way. Earl Hooker once said, "When you're playing on somebody's record, you don't want people to learn your stuff, so just play dummy guitar!"–you know, the standard old stuff. To me that seemed crazy! If you're making a record, that's where everybody hears you, but some guys are that paranoid.

What can you tell guitarists who get stuck playing the same patterns?

That happens to everybody. Sports guys go into slumps, and I'll go through a period where I feel like I've played all this stuff before. And then for some reason–I don't know what it is–I'll get to a period of playing music that sounds real fresh. Or I might just hear an old record or somebody new, and all of a sudden it'll just open a bunch of doors and I'll just start playing better. There's so many different ways of putting it together that it never really is old. If you're tired of it sometimes, just put the guitar down for a week or so and listen to a few records. The main thing is just hearing a lot of music and putting it together the way that you want to. Just keep on playing and ride it out.

"Blues music makes me feel the best."

A SELECTED JOHNNY WINTER DISCOGRAPHY

Solo albums: *Early Winter* (KR and Frolic singles, late '50s-early '60s), President; *Living In The Blues* ('59-'68), Thunderbolt; *Birds Can't Row Boats* ('59-'67), Relix; *The Johnny Winter Story*, P-Vine; *Early Heat* (includes material from *Early Winter* and *The Johnny Winter Story*), Special Music; *Raw To The Bone* ('67), Thunderbolt; *Scorchin' Blues* ('68-'79), Epic; *The Progressive Blues Experiment* ('69), Imperial; *Johnny Winter* ('69), Columbia; *Second Winter* ('70), Columbia; *Live Johnny Winter And* ('71), Columbia; *Still Alive And Well* ('73), Columbia; *Saints And Sinners* ('74), Columbia; *John Dawson Winter III* ('74), Blue Sky; *Together* (with brother Edgar Winter, '76), Blue Sky; *Nothin' But The Blues* ('77), Blue Sky; *White, Hot & Blue* ('78), Blue Sky; *Back In Beaumont* ('81), Thunderbolt; *Guitar Slinger* ('84), Alligator; *Serious Business* ('85), Alligator; *Third Degree* ('86), Alligator; *The Winter Of '88*, Voyager/MCA; *Let Me In* ('91), Pointblank/Charisma; *Hey, Where's Your Brother?* ('92), Pointblank/Charisma.

With Muddy Waters (on Columbia/Blue Sky): *Hard Again; I'm Ready; Muddy "Mississippi" Waters Live; King Bee.* Legacy's *Blues Sky* reissues some of these tracks.

With others: Jimmy Reed, *Live At Liberty Hall, Houston, TX, 1972*, Fan Club; Sonny Terry, *I Think I Got The Blues* ('81), Mad Albino; John Lee Hooker, *Mr. Lucky*, Charisma/Pointblank.

Anthologies: *Blues Masters, Volume 9: Postmodern Blues*, Rhino; *The Alligator Records 20th Anniversary Collection*, Alligator; *Legends Of Guitar–Electric Blues, Vol. 1*, Rhino; *Genuine Houserockin' Music*, Alligator; *Texas Guitar Greats*, Home Cooking.

On film: *Live* (45-minute performance at Toronto's Massey Hall, '83, released by Media); *I Was There When The Blues Was Red Hot* ('93).

Also available from Miller Freeman Books

Acoustic Guitars and Other Fretted Instruments
A Photographic History
George Gruhn and Walter Carter
A lavishly illustrated book telling the story of American fretted instruments from the 1830s to the present. Features hundreds of unique color photographs of acoustic guitars, mandolins, and banjos. "A bonanza for fret-burners everwhere." –*Billboard*
ISBN 0-87930-240-2 $39.95

All Music Guide: The Best CDs, Albums & Tapes
Edited by Michael Erlewine and Scott Bultman
Reviews the best recordings in twenty-six musical categories including classical, rock, gospel, country, rap, and jazz, with a total of 23,000 listings. This is the guide for everyone who's walked into a music store and felt overwhelmed by "what to choose?"
ISBN 0-87930-264-X $24.95

The Musician's Guide to Reading & Writing Music
Dave Stewart
For the brand new rocker, the seasoned player, and the pro who could use new problem-solving methods, a clear and practical guide to learning written music notation.
ISBN 0-87930-273-9 $7.95

Bass Heroes
Styles, Stories & Secrets of 30 Great Bass Players
Edited by Tom Mulhern
Thirty of the world's greatest bass players in rock, jazz, studio/pop, and blues & funk share their musical influences, playing techniques, and opinions. Includes Monk Montgomery, Jack Bruce, James Jamerson, Stanley Clarke, Paul McCartney, and many more. From the pages of *Guitar Player* magazine.
ISBN 0-87930-274-7 $17.95

The Musician's Home Recording Handbook
Practical Techniques for Recording Great Music at Home
Ted Greenwald
This book gives the basics for musicians who want to produce high quality home recordings using the equipment at hand. Musicianship, not equipment, is the essential ingredient in a great recording; the author shows how anyone with creativity and a can-do attitude can produce great recordings.
ISBN 0-87930-237-2 $19.95

Secrets from the Masters: 40 Great Guitar Players
Edited by Don Menn
Featuring the most influential guitarists of the past 25 years: Chuck Berry, Joe Satriani, Eddie Van Halen, John Scofield, Pete Townshend and many more. Combines personal biography, career history, and playing techniques. From the pages of *Guitar Player* magazine.
ISBN 0-87930-260-7 $19.95

The Fender Book
A Complete History of Fender Electric Guitars
Tony Bacon and Paul Day
Tells the complete story of these hugely popular, versatile, and fascinating guitars, from the classic 1950s Telecaster and Stratocaster to current models. Illustrated with unique color photographs of outstanding and unusual Fender models.
ISBN 0-87930-259-3 $19.95

Gruhn's Guide to Vintage Guitars
An Identification Guide for
American Fretted Instruments
George Gruhn and Walter Carter
This portable reference for identifying American guitars, mandolins, and basses contains comprehensive dating information and model specifications for nearly 2,000 instruments by all major U.S. manufacturers.
ISBN 0-87930-195-3 $22.95

Guitar Player Repair Guide: How to Set Up, Maintain, and Repair Electrics and Acoustics
Expanded and Updated Second Edition
Dan Erlewine
Whether you're a player, collector, or repairperson, this hands-on guide provides all the essential information on caring for guitars and electric basses. Includes 264 photos and drawings.
ISBN 0-87930-291-7 $22.95

The Gibson Super 400: Art of the Fine Guitar
Thomas A. Van Hoose
This book traces the evolution of the Gibson 400 including production details and tables, historical anecdotes, step-by-step restoration techniques, and pricing information. Numerous color and black and white photographs make this volume complete.
ISBN 0-87930-230-5 $49.95

Vintage Synthesizers
Groundbreaking Instruments and Pioneering Designers
of Electronic Music Synthesizers
Mark Vail
Focuses on the modern history (1962-1992) of the
electronic synthesizer, including in-depth interviews with
pioneering synth designers and users, performance
techniques, buying tips, and production and pricing
information.
ISBN 0-87930-275-5 $19.95

CyberArts: Exploring Art & Technology
Edited by Linda Jacobson
A rich anthology of essays and commentaries from over
50 leading multimedia visionaries on the topics of music,
graphics, animation, 3D sound, virtual reality, video and
film, toys, and games.
ISBN 0-87930-253-4 $22.95

THE BEST IN MUSIC BOOKS

Available at book stores and music stores everywhere

For more information, contact:
Miller Freeman Books, 600 Harrison St., San Francisco, CA 94107
Phone 415 905-2200 • Fax 415 905-2239